THE RECONSTRUCTION DIARY OF
FRANCES ANNE ROLLIN

THE JOHN HOPE FRANKLIN SERIES IN
AFRICAN AMERICAN HISTORY AND CULTURE

Waldo E. Martin Jr. and Patricia Sullivan, editors

The best scholarship in African American history and culture compels us to expand our sense of who we are as a nation and forces us to engage seriously the experiences of all Americans who have shaped the development of this country. By publishing pathbreaking books informed by several disciplines, the John Hope Franklin Series in African American History and Culture seeks to illuminate America's multicultural past and the ways in which it has informed the nation's democratic experiment.

A complete list of books published in the John Hope Franklin Series in African American History and Culture is available at https://uncpress .org/series/john-hope-franklin-series-african-american-history-culture.

THE

Reconstruction Diary

— OF —

Frances Anne Rollin

A CRITICAL EDITION

Edited by Jennifer Putzi

THE UNIVERSITY OF NORTH CAROLINA PRESS

CHAPEL HILL

Manufactured in the United States of America

Designed by April Leidig
Set in Garamond by Copperline Book Services, Inc.

Cover art: Portrait of Frances Anne Rollin from Leigh Rollin Whipper
Photograph Collection, Photographs and Prints Division, Schomburg Center for
Research in Black Culture, New York Public Library Digital Collections.
Closed diary and diary title page, gifts of the Carole Ione Lewis Family Collection,
National Museum of African American History and Culture.

Library of Congress Cataloging-in-Publication Data
Names: Rollin, Frances Anne, 1845–1901 author | Putzi, Jennifer editor
Title: The Reconstruction diary of Frances Anne Rollin :
a critical edition / edited by Jennifer Putzi.
Other titles: John Hope Franklin series in African American history and culture
Description: Chapel Hill : The University of North Carolina Press, [2025] |
Series: John Hope Franklin series in African American history and culture |
Includes bibliographical references and index.
Identifiers: LCCN 2025013890 | ISBN 9781469690018 cloth |
ISBN 9781469690025 paperback | ISBN 9781469690032 epub |
ISBN 9781469692388 pdf
Subjects: LCSH: Rollin, Frances Anne, 1845–1901—Diaries | African American
women political activists—Diaries | Political activists—United States—Diaries | African
American women authors—Diaries | Authors, American—Diaries | Reconstruction
(US history, 1865–1877) | BISAC: SOCIAL SCIENCE / Ethnic Studies / American / African
American & Black Studies | LITERARY COLLECTIONS / Diaries & Journals |
LCGFT: Autobiographies | Diaries
Classification: LCC E185.97.R69 A3 2025 | DDC 973.8092 $a B—dc23/eng/20250408
LC record available at https://lccn.loc.gov/2025013890

For product safety concerns under the European Union's General Product
Safety Regulation (EU GPSR), please contact gpsr@mare-nostrum.co.uk or write
to the University of North Carolina Press and Mare Nostrum Group B.V.,
Mauritskade 21D, 1091 GC Amsterdam, The Netherlands.

For Ione

CONTENTS

ILLUSTRATIONS

A Diary of Reconstruction

FRANCES ANNE ROLLIN'S 1868 DIARY has taken on a life of its own. No longer surrounded by tissue paper and cardboard, tucked away among scented hankies in dresser drawers, it is bringing its messages freely to the world.

I believe that feelings as well as thoughts are capable of continuing on through time. They travel as memories, as handed-down stories, as well as in the potent content of letters and diaries. There is particular power at play within diaries, those intimate writings that were most often originally intended to be private. And of course, there is an additional element to take into consideration when the reader is a family member, a descendant of the diarist.

When Jennifer Putzi contacted me via email regarding my great-grandmother's diary, I felt a sensation similar to what I felt that evening in 1973 when I first turned the delicate pages of the little leather book and glimpsed a faint, elegant handwriting that would soon become as familiar to me as my own.

Some years after that first moment, writing in my book *Pride of Family: Four Generations of American Women of Color* (1991), I would describe this feeling as being like a depth charge going off amid my life of writing and mothering. This time it was a gentler sensation, but clear. I felt that "Frank," as her family and friends affectionately called her, was surfacing again. I knew that it was time for an annotated edition of Rollin's diary to make its appearance in the world.

There are many rewards in these pages for those interested in the often daunting and changeable field of Reconstruction studies (1865–77). Rollin's story also opens windows that will expand our general knowledge about the nineteenth-century lives of both free and enslaved peoples of color in this country as well as adding to our understanding of women's lives during this period.

For me, there are personal rewards that continue a process begun more than five decades ago. When I reflect upon that time, I feel for my own ignorance of the history that was surrounding me then like a heavy cape. I am grateful for the clear emergence of that history here in *The Reconstruction Diary of Frances Anne Rollin*.

It seems fitting that the emergence of the diary took place at what might be considered the height of the potent second wave of feminism in the United States (the 1960s to the 1990s).

I was as yet unaware of having a great-grandmother whose passion for women's rights preceded mine. In addition to raising three small boys, I was contributing to my young family's income by working in New York as a freelance writer.

I was part of an intrepid group of gifted women writers who met periodically at each other's lofts and apartments in New York City. Affectionately, we called these energy-charged gatherings the Ladies Literary Luncheons. It was an exciting time, and we were bent on shaking up the status quo for women. We aspired to make ourselves known in magazines, television, theater, film, and all the arts—even comedy. Women could do anything, we were certain of this. Women could even be funny: the early *Saturday Night Live* was a playground for some.

The budding *Ms.* Magazine was making waves with a focus on women never seen before. I suggested to the editors that I write about the women in my family. Those who had raised me were reticent about their own lives, and I had already noticed that the men in the family had been afforded more public acclaim than they. I wanted to change that.

There was my mother, Leighla Frances Whipper, a glamorous songwriter, journalist, and mystery writer, and my grandmother, Virginia Eva Wheeler, who had been a performer in Black vaudeville troupes and a dancer in the Black chorus lines of the 1920s and 1930s. Then there was my great aunt, Dr. Ionia Rollin Whipper, a physician and social reformer, who graduated medical school in 1903. To add to this stellar group, I had recently learned that my mother had in her dresser drawer an old diary written by her grandmother, who she described as a terrific woman, an "ancestor."

My mother had loaned the diary to historian Dorothy Sterling, who was conducting research for her future book, *We Are Your Sisters: Black Women in the Nineteenth Century* (1984); it was Sterling who sent it on to me. I did not know it yet, but in the years to come, she would become a friend and ally in my urgent quest for information about Frances Anne Rollin.

The package with the diary arrived amid my life of balancing mothering, writing, and marriage. I unfolded a simple covering of cardboard and tissue that revealed the book, with its thin and worn brown leather cover. There were delicate pages within, and a fine script, already fading, emerged as my eyes adjusted to it. I then took in a melancholy first entry:

January 1, 1868

I sent a letter to Mother today which I wrote last night the latest hour
nearly of the old year. The year renews its birth today with all of its hopes
and sorrows. Uncertainty and doubt are in its wake. For me and mine I
know not, but may God enable us whatever may be my lot. To murmur
not, but patiently bear, and wait and labor.

My response was visceral. As I listened to the breathing of my children—all under
four years old at that time—in the next room, I felt Frances Anne Rollin so close,
so alive, that I could almost hear her breathing as well. Here was an ancestor who
would share with me and with the world what seemed missing from the women
in my family, who, wonderful as they were, had kept their stories to themselves.
I knew that I would need to rise to the challenge of my great-grandmother's very
existence.

There were big questions: Why had no one told me of her until now? Why
was she not a family legend? And primary among them, who was Frances Anne
Rollin Whipper?

MY RESEARCH BEGAN at a time when scholars were just starting to look more
deeply into the details of the Reconstruction era, and opinions were shifting
about what had actually occurred then and its meaning for people of color and
the country as a whole.

Growing up during a time before African American studies were common, I
knew very little about it all. Nonetheless, I dove in, entering this complex arena
some years before the digital revolution changed the world. Gradually, I began to
see my great-grandmother and her world more clearly, but there would be many
more years of seeking answers. I have been enthralled by my own quest, both the
genealogical and the historical aspects of it.

Now, I salute the oh-so-satisfying research in these pages by Jennifer Putzi as I
reflect on some of my early journey of discoveries.

I found Frank first as a twenty-two-year-old woman—highly educated, well
read, and intellectually inclined. She was living with family friends in a small
room on Blossom Street in Boston, earnestly writing in her diary. Boston at the
time was a gathering place for many of the great writers, thinkers, abolitionists,
philosophers, and artists of the day, and my great-grandmother's time among
them was a precious moment like no other in her life. I shared the excitement

preserved on the pages as she expresses her joy at attending presentations by Charles Dickens and Ralph Waldo Emerson. Noted abolitionists Wendell Phillips and William Lloyd Garrison were among those who gave her encouragement and listened to her read the pages of her then-developing biography of Martin R. Delany. These were to be the most extraordinary moments of her life.

Even so, I sensed that Frank was feeling the weight of her own ambitions. She confided to her diary her desire to make her mark in literature. But major political forces of history were taking place in the country. Her home state of South Carolina was particularly galvanized in the wake of the passage of the Reconstruction Acts. Formerly enslaved men had the right to vote, discrimination by color was forbidden, and an inclusive state constitutional convention was gathering.

Frank was acutely aware that she was not considered a part of the body politic. The Fourteenth Amendment would be ratified later that year, on 9 July 1868, granting citizenship to all persons "born or naturalized in the United States," including formerly enslaved people, as well as "equal protection under the laws." Yet there would be no law allowing women's suffrage in her lifetime. The Nineteenth Amendment would be ratified on 18 August 1920, giving women the constitutional right to vote.

MY GREAT-GRANDMOTHER was born into a free family of color living in Charleston, South Carolina. The family arrived with a wave of immigrants fleeing the revolutionary uprising of enslaved peoples against the brutal colonial regime in Saint Domingue (now Haiti). Her mother, Margaret, would be a mystery to me for some time to come. William Rollin owned a combined lumberyard and brickyard and traveled the coast on business, often with his oldest daughter. The family, like so many others of their status in Charleston who were also relatives of the white population, skirted the existing laws against educating peoples of color, enslaved or free.

In the writing she was doing in Boston, Frank described the position of her family thus: "They were an intermediate class in all the slave states, standing between the whites and the bondmen, known as the free colored; debarred from enjoying the privileges of the one, but superior in condition to the other, more, however, by sufferance than by actual law."[1] Some were owners of enslaved people as well. When I learned that Frank's father's name appears on tax forms for four slaves, I began a quest, still underway, to understand more and possibly to clear

---

1. Rollin, *Life and Public Services of Martin R. Delany*, 30.

his name. The "ownership" of enslaved people might have been used by William Rollin as a cover for personal politics as well as underground activities. Prior to the Civil War, he was able to travel North almost at will on his lumber and brick business. It is entirely possible that he and the tightknit community of free African Americans along the East Coast used many ruses to accomplish their goals of transporting thousands of enslaved people to freedom.

I also take into consideration the intensely secretive activities of the Underground Railroad, and the family's close connections to known "conductors," including abolitionist and businessman William Whipper. Whipper was a resident of Columbia, Pennsylvania, and Philadelphia, where Frank attended the Quaker Institute for Colored Youth. He owned railroad cars that he, along with his partners, used to shepherd hundreds of enslaved people to freedom in Canada. He was also the uncle of William James Whipper, who would become Frances Rollin's husband. If no actual proof of William Rollin's involvement in resistance against the institution of slavery exists, his status will remain that of a beloved father, albeit without reprieve from guilt.

Frank seemed to have the support of her parents as she immersed herself in writing the biography of elder Black statesman and activist Major Martin R. Delany, a man who was a champion of Blackness and later became known as the Father of Black Nationalism. In Rollin's writing, she would describe the historic 1865 meeting with President Abraham Lincoln in which Delany argued for an all-Black US Army corps led by Black officers.

Lincoln appreciated Delany's value and influence and paved the way for his commission as a major, giving him the status as the first Black field officer in the US Army. While describing his preparations to enlist Black soldiers with "experience and knowledge gained in the military campaigns" in the wake of his appointment, Rollin hints at her own knowledge of the extraordinary hidden pathways to freedom: "Certain leading spirits of the '*Underground Railroad*' were invoked. Scouts *incog.* were already 'on to Richmond,' and the services of the famous Harriet Tubman, having been secured to serve in the South, had received her transportation for Charleston, S.C."[2]

The bitter cold of Boston that winter exacerbated Frank's already delicate health. Although her funds were short, she would nonetheless persevere, completing her book and seeing to the last details of Lee & Shepard's publication of *Life and Public Services of Martin R. Delany*, using the penname Frank A. Rollin.

William James Whipper is only briefly mentioned in my great-grandmother's

2. Rollin, *Life and Public Services of Martin R. Delany*, 182.

diary, but he was fated to play a major role in her life. On her return to South Carolina, with her new book in her bags, Frank was immediately caught up in the political excitement. Whipper was awaiting her in Columbia, and she paused there to follow up on discussions already begun by letter.

My great-grandfather had recently delivered an impassioned speech at the constitutional convention espousing women's suffrage. I imagine that he had Frances, the eldest of the five Rollin sisters, in mind. This would have had great appeal to my great-grandmother, who would have learned of it by mail while still in Boston.

Whipper's proposal for women's rights in 1868 was not adopted, but many groundbreaking laws were put in place: Race was eliminated as a restriction on male suffrage. The Black Codes that had flourished under the constitution of 1865 were overturned. There was no provision against interracial marriage, and the public schools were open to all races.

An enterprising lawyer from Pennsylvania, Whipper had recently opened Whipper, Elliott, and Allen in Charleston—the first Black-owned law office in the United States. Frank went to work there within days of her return to South Carolina, and it was not long before he proposed. Frank was clearly drawn to the concept of working alongside a partner with whom she could participate in the brave new vision of the equality of the races. A brand new democratic government was in the offing, and they would both be a part of it.

Even at the beginning, Whipper was controversial to some. An acquaintance (who may have been a former suitor) decried Rollin's returning to South Carolina under Whipper's auspices.

Frank had hoped to assuage any family resistance to the proposed wedding by showing off her book. But there were apparently several hours of back and forth with William Rollin before he relented, giving his permission for the wedding to take place. There were plenty of reasons for a father to object. It was all quite sudden. Frank had been away for months, and now she would be leaving home for good. He had envisioned a continued education for his daughter in France, but she had declined, wishing to stay closer to home. Moreover, the tenor in Charleston regarding newcomers from the North (pejoratively known as carpetbaggers) was often one of suspicion and resentment.

William Rollin, caught in the in-between chaos of postwar South Carolina, had little of the old-world connections to support him. He had been shot and wounded during the Civil War, humiliated by Union troops while protecting his vegetable garden. Whipper was an older man with a background completely foreign from that Rollin had provided for his eldest daughter. Whipper was eleven years Frank's senior, and a recent widower who also had a child being cared for by a housekeeper. But the momentum was strong, circumstances were extreme, and Rollin could not stand in his oldest daughter's way.

The marriage took place on 17 September of that momentous year, despite all misgivings. Rollin Whipper continued to devote herself to the betterment of her race, supporting her husband and the overarching cause they shared throughout her life. She brought her fine intelligence and her organizational and writing skills to their union, even when the couple worked together over a distance.

A few passages in the 1868 diary illuminate the short-lived excitement and glitter of the times. Frank mentions festive dinner parties and balls. Governor Robert Kingston Scott was an ally. It was a time of promise for my great-grandparents, including, at the onset, an unprecedented mixing of races socially and politically.

But just a few days after Frank's marriage to Whipper, in a terrible harbinger of events to come, a friend and colleague who had been a member of their wedding party was assassinated by members of the Ku Klux Klan. This is recorded in one of the last entries in her diary.

Brutally racist factions in South Carolina and Washington, DC, united to bring the Reconstruction era to a shuddering halt by 1877. Tactics aimed at disenfranchising and brutalizing African Americans included campaigns of misinformation, vilification of Black legislators, gerrymandering of districts, gun violence encouraged by "Rifle Clubs," and the steady rise of the Ku Klux Klan.

The political atmosphere for Whipper and other peoples of color in office steadily worsened, also putting strains on the couple's marriage. In addition, Frank had born five babies, two of whom had not survived infancy. Eventually, they decided that Frank would take the three children to a safer environment in Washington, DC, where there were old friends and acquaintances ready to assist. For a time, she worked for the government as a copyist. She also worked for an old acquaintance, Frederick Douglass.

Word has come down through associates and descendants of her friends that Frank "had a kind of literary salon" at her Sixth Street apartment and that she occasionally wrote stories for magazines and newspapers; she had a penname that is yet to be discovered. We may one day find other writings and surely even more details of her life and work will surface with time. I know that Frank worked hard, scraped and saved, but was often forced to borrow money. Even so, she managed to see my great-aunts and my grandfather (Ionia, Winifred, and Leigh) through school. Ionia graduated medical school in 1903, two years after Frank's death in 1901 at fifty-six years of age. I feel blessed to have spent time with both my great-aunt Ionia and my grandfather Leigh through to my early womanhood.

My grandfather told me that his mother never fully recovered from the chills she contracted while out campaigning door to door for the Republican candidate for president, James C. Blaine, in 1884. (The party of Lincoln was the more liberal party in those times.)

Toward the end of her life, as the century was drawing to a close, Frank returned to Beaufort, South Carolina, and to Whipper, now among those most vilified in the political arena, who had fought exhausting battles attempting to hold his own against white racist forces. As a final blow, he had been denied a legally won judgeship in Beaufort.

After a renewed search for information about Frank's final resting place, I have placed a plaque with both of my great-grandparents' names on the grounds of the historic Wesley United Methodist Church in Beaufort.

Frank, who wanted to "make her mark in literature," might gain some satisfaction from the fact that the Biographers International Organization has established the Frances "Frank" Rollin Fellowship, which "aims to foster the development of biographical works that encourage deeper insight into the complexity of race relations at the bedrock of American history."[3] The fellowship offers stipends to support work on biographical accounts of any African American figure whose story provides a significant contribution to our understanding of the Black experience.

In addition, the biography of Major Delaney on which Frank worked so hard that winter of 1868 became a primary source of material for later biographers and in the twenty-first century is widely available online and in print. My own book, *Pride of Family: Four Generations of American Women of Color*, is currently a Penguin Random House ebook and a Recorded Books audiobook.

As I write, I am steeped in nineteenth- and early twentieth-century considerations. Yet increasingly disturbing news from the twenty-first century comes in on a daily basis. The very tactics that brought down my great-grandparents' revolution have surfaced in our times with new vigor. Hateful attitudes and acts, even blatant attempts to disenfranchise African Americans have reemerged in full force in our country. An old family saying comes to mind: "It feels like we've climbed a big mountain, only to find ourselves down at the bottom again."

I am not alone in feeling the pain moving down through time. Many of us grieve anew for what happened to the dreams of our ancestors. (Reconstruction

3. Eric K. Washington, with Sarah Kilborne, Anne Boyd Rioux, and Sonja Williams, "BIO Announces New Fellowship in Support of African American Lives," Bio: Biographers International Organization, 8 October 2020, https://biographersinternational.org/topic/frances-frank-rollin-fellowship/page/2/.

has been called "America's Unfinished Revolution" by historian Eric Foner.) The cause of civil rights in our country is being challenged as never before. Sometimes I imagine Frances Anne Rollin Whipper with us as we witness the current state of racial divisions in the United States. I have seen her proud and fighting despite the bitter disappointments of her time. I see us that way too. She would recognize the vicious attacks, the struggles, and the dangers we are experiencing today. I believe she would set to work again to continue the fight for equality and justice. Strange as it seems, and as difficult as it is, we must *climb the mountain again*.

The publication of Jennifer Putzi's *The Reconstruction Diary of Frances Anne Rollin*, with its full portrayal of my great-grandmother's life and times, offers us the additional fuel needed to shore up our courage for the climb.

IONE
Kingston, New York

ACKNOWLEDGMENTS

THIS EDITION of Frances Anne Rollin's diary would never have come into being without her great-granddaughter, Carole Ione. Ione's research and writing on her entire family, but especially Frances Rollin, has served as both source and inspiration. *Pride of Family: Four Generations of American Women of Color* is a stunningly beautiful and incredibly well-researched book. Ione's willingness to donate Rollin's diary to the National Museum of African American History and Culture also enabled my access to it online at the Smithsonian Transcription Center during the COVID-19 lockdown. When I emailed her from out of the blue in August 2021 to relate my desire to publish an edition of Rollin's diary, Ione responded twenty minutes later with warmth and enthusiasm. We had our first Zoom meeting five days later. Her encouragement for this project has never faltered in the years we have known each other. She facilitated my access to the material diary at the Pennsy Collections and Support Center in Maryland in the spring of 2022 and provided guidance when I was finally able to make a research trip to South Carolina when libraries opened again. Ione also read and critiqued the manuscript for me, correcting my mistakes and offering new readings of sources. Finally, I am incredibly grateful for her beautiful foreword to the book. For all these reasons and more, *The Reconstruction Diary of Frances Anne Rollin* is dedicated to her.

There are many others to thank here, and I can only hope to remember everyone. I will begin with my intellectual and institutional homes here at William & Mary: the Department of English; the Gender, Sexuality, and Women's Studies program; and the Earl Gregg Swem Library. Arthur Knight, Liz Losh, and Claire Pamment have been wonderfully supportive chairs and program directors and have helped me get the funding required to focus on researching and writing. As the Swem Library Faculty Scholar, I have been given the gift of time—time away from teaching, time spent thinking and writing, and time with librarians who have amazing research skills. Thank you to Dean of University Libraries Carrie Cooper and to all the staff at Swem Library.

Frances Rollin Whipper's personal papers are limited, so I had to consult a wide range of archival materials to reconstruct her life and times. Candace Oubre and Michèle Morsei Gates of the National Museum of African American History and Culture kindly provided access to Rollin's material diary at the Pennsy Collections and Support Center in Maryland. Charice Thompson facilitated appointments at the Moorland-Spingarn Research Center at Howard University, where I was able to view the Leigh Whipper Papers as well as the diaries of other African American women such as Charlotte Forten and Laura Hamilton Murray. For the chance to view, photograph, and transcribe additional diaries, I am grateful to the Hallie Q. Brown Library at Central State University, the Historical Society of Pennsylvania, Special Collections at the Louisiana State University Library, and the New York State Library. I also want to thank the South Carolina Historical Society and the South Caroliniana Library at the University of South Carolina for access to their collections. Folks at the Charleston County Public Library were especially helpful. Archive librarian Sarah Hisnanick-Murphy not only answered questions during my visit but also responded to multiple emails after my return home. And while I never met her in person, Melissa Mabry, associate archivist at the Office of Archives and Records Management for the Roman Catholic Diocese of Charleston, provided essential assistance.

My research and writing projects would not go anywhere without plenty of people to talk and write with. Portions of this project were presented at the American Literature Association Conference, the Martin R. Delany Symposium, and the Society for the Study of American Women Writers Conference (all in 2018 and 2021). In December 2023 Valinda Littlefield and Rhonda Carey of the Institute for the Study of the Reconstruction Era at the University of South Carolina Beaufort invited me to give a talk at the Wesley United Methodist Church, in whose cemetery Frances Rollin Whipper and William Whipper are buried. The folks at Wesley United were especially welcoming and helped me understand what kind of community the Whippers found in Beaufort. Being in South Carolina helped me imagine the lives of my subjects, and I was pleased to be part of the NEH Summer Institute's project "Reconstructing the Black Archive: South Carolina as Case Study, 1739–1895," led by Susanna Ashton, Gregg Hecimovich, Kaniqua Robinson, and Rhondda Thomas, in 2023. The community of scholars at the institute was both inspiring and challenging, and this publication is better for the experiencing of traveling and learning with them.

Writing groups provide both community and feedback, without which I could not produce anything worthwhile. I have been meeting to talk about writing, research, teaching, and life in general with Faith Barrett, Desirée Henderson, Alex Socarides, and Theresa Strouth-Gaul since 2011. This long-standing relationship means that they sometimes understand my writing better than I do *and* that they are allowed to be absolutely brutal if they need to be. They are also kind, generous, and loving, and I do not know what I would do without their friendship. More recently, I have benefited immensely from the feedback and fellowship of a second group, consisting of Susanna Ashton, Mollie Barnes, Gregg Hecimovich, and Barbara McCaskill. I am continually awed by the expertise of these people and am grateful for their insights into my work on this project and others. My gratitude also extends to Mollie Barnes for facilitating my introduction to this group as well as for providing encouragement, intellectual engagement, and shelter during research visits to South Carolina. Jennifer Tuttle also read a complete draft of the introduction to Rollin's diary and provided invaluable feedback. Her research and editing skills are beyond compare.

One person mentioned in the previous paragraph deserves special thanks. Desirée Henderson's work on diaries, particularly in *How to Read a Diary: Critical Contexts and Interpretive Strategies for 21*st*-Century Readers* (Routledge, 2019), revived my interest in the genre and pushed me to think more critically about the relationship between material form and content in the manuscript diary. Desirée has also been one of my most important interlocutors and supporters for this project and for others in the works.

My deepest thanks go to historian and cartographer Rick Britton for creating the beautiful hand-drawn map of Frances Rollin's Boston for this edition of her diary. Rick's attention to detail is impressive. He is also a kind, caring person whose frequent emails—just to check in on me and the project—kept me motivated.

In the three years it took to produce this edition, many other people helped me with knotty research questions. Kimberly Blockett, Eric Gardner, Suzanne Krebsbach, Mary Maillard, Joe Orfant, Claudia Stokes, and Michael Winship kindly responded to emails containing queries about everything from religious eclecticism and Black Roman Catholicism to census documents and subscription publication. I am also grateful to the many people on Facebook who responded to my requests for transcription assistance. The list is too long for me to name everyone, but you know who you are.

Simon Joyce is more than just a *partner* partner, as we often have to say to distinguish our relationship from that of business partners. He has facilitated the production of this book in so many ways: holding down the fort when I travel, helping me decipher handwriting, reading my introduction, and listening to me talk endlessly about the many discoveries I made while researching Rollin's life. While I love traveling, researching, and writing, Simon, Sam, and Charley are still the center of it all. They put up with my absences and my distractions and love me anyway, as do Onyx, Archie, and even Jet.

A NOTE ON EDITORIAL METHODS

FRANCES ANNE ROLLIN'S DIARY is held by the National Museum of African American History and Culture (NMAAHC) in Washington, DC. A scan of the diary is available on the Smithsonian Digital Volunteers: Transcription Center (https://transcription.si.edu/), where I first encountered it in the fall of 2020. The diary remained in Frances Rollin Whipper's family after her death and was donated to the NMAAHC by her great-granddaughter Carole Ione.

The following transcription of Rollin's diary was prepared using the digital scan at the Transcription Center and proofread against the original at the NMAAHC's Pennsy Facility in Landover, Maryland.

As much of the original manuscript as possible appears transcribed in this book. I have not altered Rollin's spelling or punctuation except for minor changes such as transcribing "to day" as "today" and "to night" as "tonight." For sums in the front and back of the diary, I have also occasionally added a decimal point to indicate how a list of numbers should be read. Rollin wrote much of her diary in pencil, which has faded over the years. Thus, I have made my best guess as to the punctuation used in her entries, but I have not attempted to place commas, periods, or other marks where they are not indicated in the manuscript.

I have made the following changes, however, to facilitate the reading experience. Each page of the preprinted diary intended for daily writing is headed with the year, the day of the week, and the date, none of which were written in by Rollin herself. Except for the first entry, I have not retained the preprinted year in these headings. Dates appear here flush with the left margin, rather than centered as in the preprinted diary. I have not reproduced line breaks unless they occur at the end of a paragraph. Rollin occasionally ended a sentence in the middle of a line and began what I interpret as a new paragraph on the next line, flush with the left margin. I have retained this format rather than indenting paragraphs where I do not see an indentation in the original.

When unable to figure out a word, I have placed either my best guess or the word "illegible" in brackets. Insertions Rollin made above the line are indicated by carets (^) before and after the word or phrase, which itself is placed wherever I think she wanted the word or phrase to appear. When Rollin wrote words in either the left or right margin of a page, or above the first line of a page (between the date and the first line), I have mentioned this in a footnote. Strikethroughs in the transcription indicate words crossed out by Rollin; if I was unable to figure out what she had crossed out, I have placed the word "strikethrough" in brackets. No doubt I have made mistakes in my transcription, but I have made my best effort at precision with my understanding of Rollin's life and my familiarity with her handwriting.

Rollin maintained her diary between 1 January and 19 October 1868. She occasionally missed a day, which I have indicated by inserting below the date "No entry." in brackets. When she missed multiple days in a row, I have presented the affected dates in a time span and inserted below "No entries." in brackets.

Annotations throughout the diary identify people, places, and events and provide background information that will help readers understand Rollin's life and the cultures and communities in which she lived. For every person I was able to identify, I provided either an entry in the biographical notes or an annotation in the diary. Biographical notes provide detailed information on people, either individually or as families, mentioned multiple times by Rollin. If more than ten diary entries have passed between mentions of an individual and the person's identity is not clear from the surrounding context, I have identified them again in a footnote with a cross-reference to either the biographical notes entry or a more detailed note. Sometimes, despite my best efforts, I have been unable to identify a reference; rather than noting my failure, I have left such items unmarked.

TIMELINE

1791–1804	Haitian Revolution.
1816	AME Church in Charleston (Mother Emanuel) founded.
1822	Denmark Vesey is convicted for planning a slave insurrection in Charleston.
19 November 1845	Birth of Frances Anne Rollin (Whipper) (FR/FRW).
1857	FR visits Philadelphia with her father, William Rollin (first of several trips).
1859	FR moves to Philadelphia, where she boards with the family of Susan and Morris Brown Jr. She enrolls at the Institute for Colored Youth and attends St. Thomas's African Episcopal Church.
16–18 October 1859	John Brown leads raid on Harpers Ferry, Virginia.
20 December 1860	South Carolina secedes from the Union.
12 April 1861	Confederate attack on Fort Sumter.
1 January 1863	Emancipation Proclamation issued by President Abraham Lincoln.
July 1863	Siege of Charleston begins.
February 1865	Martin Delany commissioned a major in the Union army.
18 February 1865	Charleston surrenders to the Union army.
9 April 1865	Robert E. Lee surrenders to Ulysses S. Grant.
15 April 1865	Assassination of President Lincoln.
April 1865	FR returns to Charleston.

1 May 1865	FR begins a contract with the American Missionary Association to teach in Charleston. By the end of the year, she is teaching at the Zion School for the Presbyterian Commission of Missions for Freedmen.
November 1865	South Carolina Colored People's Convention held in Charleston at Zion Presbyterian Church.
March 1867	Passage of the Reconstruction Acts.
July 1867	FR is refused first-class passage on the *Pilot-Boy*, a steamer from Charleston to Beaufort. With the help of the Freedmen's Bureau, she brings a case against the pilot, Captain W. T. McNelty. He is found guilty and fined $250.
21 October 1867	FR leaves Charleston for Boston, where she boards with the family of John and Ann Bailey.
14 January–17 March 1868	South Carolina Constitutional Convention in Charleston.
24 July 1868	Military cedes control of South Carolina to civil authorities: South Carolina is officially reconstructed.
28 July 1868	FR leaves Boston for South Carolina.
17 September 1868	FR marries William J. Whipper (WJW).
Fall 1868	Publication of *Life and Public Services of Martin R. Delany*.
1869	Birth and death of daughter Alicia Whipper.
1870	Birth of daughter Winifred Rollin Whipper.
1871–72	FRW edits the *Beaufort County Times*.
1872	Birth of daughter Ionia Rollin Whipper.
1874	Birth of daughter Mary Elizabeth Whipper. WJW elected circuit court judge, but Governor Daniel H. Chamberlain refuses to sign commission.

1875	Death of Mary Elizabeth Whipper.
1876	Birth of son Leigh Rollin Whipper. Election of Rutherford B. Hayes as president with the "Great Compromise," bringing the end of Reconstruction.
4 March 1876	Katherine Rollin (sister) dies.
25 February 1880	William Rollin (father) dies. FRW's mother and sisters move to Brooklyn, New York.
1882	The Whippers leave South Carolina and move to Washington, DC.
March 1882	FRW is appointed to a clerical position in the Land Office in DC.
1883	Republication of *Life and Public Services of Martin R. Delany*.
1885	WJW returns to South Carolina and is elected county probate judge.
30 June 1885	FRW loses her position upon the rise of Democrats to power with the election of Grover Cleveland. FRW obtains position with Frederick Douglass, Recorder of Deeds in DC.
1888	WJW begins a thirteen-month prison sentence after refusing to relinquish his probate records after losing his judgeship.
1893	FRW loses her position with the appointment of C. H. J. Taylor as Recorder of Deeds during President Cleveland's second term in office.
1895	South Carolina Constitutional Convention.
1899	FRW leaves Washington, DC, and returns to Beaufort, South Carolina.
27 October 1901	FRW dies in Beaufort.
29 July 1907	WJW dies in Beaufort.

THE RECONSTRUCTION DIARY OF
FRANCES ANNE ROLLIN

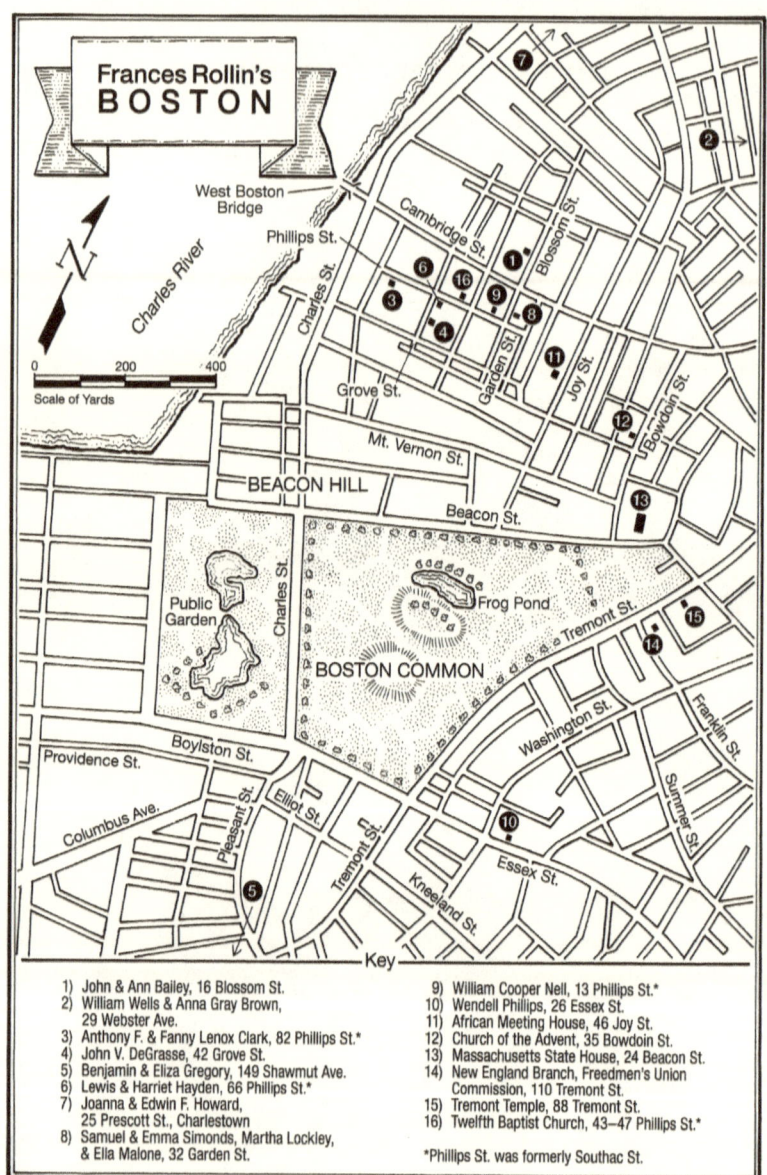

Frances Rollin's BOSTON

West Boston Bridge
Phillips St.
Charles River
Cambridge St.
Blossom St.
Charles St.
Grove St.
Garden St.
Joy St.
Bowdoin St.
Mt. Vernon St.

BEACON HILL
Beacon St.

0   200   400
Scale of Yards

Public Garden
Charles St.
Frog Pond
BOSTON COMMON
Tremont St.
Franklin St.

Boylston St.
Providence St.
Washington St.
Summer St.

Columbus Ave.
Pleasant St.
Elliot St.
Tremont St.
Kneeland St.
Essex St.

Key

1) John & Ann Bailey, 16 Blossom St.
2) William Wells & Anna Gray Brown, 29 Webster Ave.
3) Anthony F. & Fanny Lenox Clark, 82 Phillips St.*
4) John V. DeGrasse, 42 Grove St.
5) Benjamin & Eliza Gregory, 149 Shawmut Ave.
6) Lewis & Harriet Hayden, 66 Phillips St.*
7) Joanna & Edwin F. Howard, 25 Prescott St., Charlestown
8) Samuel & Emma Simonds, Martha Lockley, & Ella Malone, 32 Garden St.

9) William Cooper Nell, 13 Phillips St.*
10) Wendell Phillips, 26 Essex St.
11) African Meeting House, 46 Joy St.
12) Church of the Advent, 35 Bowdoin St.
13) Massachusetts State House, 24 Beacon St.
14) New England Branch, Freedmen's Union Commission, 110 Tremont St.
15) Tremont Temple, 88 Tremont St.
16) Twelfth Baptist Church, 43–47 Phillips St.*

*Phillips St. was formerly Southac St.

Introduction

ON 22 FEBRUARY 1868, twenty-two-year-old Frances Anne Rollin notes "Washington's Birth Day" on the top line of the page allotted in her leather-bound, pre-printed pocket diary. "But if things continue as they are," she goes on, "there will be but little Country left to celebrate it. For myself I am no enthusiast over Patriotic Celebrations as I am counted out of the body Politic."[1] The American Civil War, the nation's second revolution, had been over for almost three years, but despite living in Boston, the birthplace of the Revolutionary War, Rollin was reluctant to embrace the nation's history as her own. Nearly a year after the passage of the Reconstruction Acts of 1867, which reorganized the Southern states into military districts and required new state constitutions to ensure universal male suffrage, and just weeks after the constitutional convention in her home state of South Carolina, Rollin remained uncertain about the future of the United States and about her own place in "the body Politic." How far would Reconstruction go? Like many other African Americans in the years following the Civil War, Rollin was concerned about more than just suffrage for Black men. Would land be granted to the freedmen who had cultivated it when they were enslaved? Would former Confederates—still "Secesh" to her mind[2]—be restored to power, or would the promise of the Reconstruction Acts be fulfilled? As impossible as it seemed, might women, both Black and white, be given the vote? And how was Rollin—nearly a thousand miles and a four-day journey from home—to play a part in the future of Reconstruction in South Carolina?

1. Throughout this introduction and the notes for it and the diary, I refer to Frances Anne Rollin Whipper as "Rollin" prior to her marriage on 17 September 1868 and "Rollin Whipper" after that date.

2. Frances Anne Rollin Diary, 1 Aug. 1868, Carole Ione Lewis Family Collection, National Museum of African American History and Culture, gift of the Carole Ione Lewis Family Collection (hereafter cited as Rollin diary).

Frances Anne Rollin diary, 1868. Gift of the Carole Ione Lewis Family
Collection, National Museum of African American History and Culture.

As a teacher in post–Civil War Charleston from 1865 to 1867, Rollin had already contributed to the recovery of her state from the poison of slavery and the
destruction of war. When she arrived in Charleston after the Civil War, with connections in the local community and an excellent education from Philadelphia's
Institute for Colored Youth (ICY), which she began attending at age fourteen,
Rollin was well equipped to make an impression. While in South Carolina, she

encountered Martin R. Delany, the activist, physician, and adventurer who was one of the highest-ranking African American officers in the Union army when he was reassigned to the Freedmen's Bureau and stationed in Hilton Head, South Carolina, after the war.[3] Leaving behind his efforts to organize African Americans to emigrate to Africa, Delany wanted to reframe his past to position himself for further activism and perhaps even political office in the United States. He invited the ambitious Frances Rollin to write his biography, and she eagerly accepted, likely as much for the financial support he offered as for the opportunity for publication. Rollin's father was a Charleston businessman of mixed French and African descent whose fortunes had declined during the war. Frances and several of her younger sisters attempted through teaching to support themselves and their family, but although well trained as a teacher, she saw writing as her calling. Educating recently enslaved children, with fifty or more in a class, was fulfilling but likely exhausting work, leaving her little time to read and write. She was clearly anxious to publish her work in periodicals and to gain an entrée into book publishing—even though (or perhaps because) so few African American women had published books before her.[4] Frances achieved this goal when she published *Life and Public Services of Martin R. Delany*, under the name "Frank A. Rollin," in the fall of 1868.

3. There is some debate about who actually was the highest-ranking African American officer in the Union army. Delany often gets credit for this accomplishment, but both William N. Reed (1825–64) and Alexander Thomas Augusta (1825–90) were promoted to lieutenant colonel before the end of the war. Reed was second in command of the Thirty-Fifth US Colored Troops and died from wounds he received at the Battle of Olustee (20 February 1864). Augusta served as regimental surgeon of the Seventh US Colored Troops. He survived the war. I am grateful to Christopher Allen of Beaufort, South Carolina, for drawing my attention to Reed's life and career.

4. It is difficult to estimate how many books by African American women had been published prior to 1868, especially as some were "as told to" narratives published under the auspices of white editors (as in the case of Sojourner Truth, for example). As Meredith McGill has shown, other texts long assumed to be "books" are actually more ephemeral publications "indexed to oral performance" and "seek[ing] to contribute to the advancement of knowledge just outside of sanctioned institutions" (McGill, "Frances Ellen Watkins Harper," 60). By pointing out Rollin's desire to publish a book, I do not mean to minimize the importance of periodical publication; as the work of Benjamin Fagan, Frances Smith Foster, Eric Gardner, and others has shown, periodicals were central to the development of African American literature, even prior to the founding of the first Black newspaper, *Freedom's Journal*, in 1827. See especially Fagan, *Black Newspapers*; Foster, "Narrative of the Interesting Origins"; Foster and Haywood, "Christian Recordings"; and Gardner, *Black Print Unbound*.

LIFE

AND

PUBLIC SERVICES

OF

MARTIN R. DELANY,

SUB-ASSISTANT COMMISSIONER BUREAU RELIEF OF REFUGEES,
FREEDMEN, AND OF ABANDONED LANDS, AND LATE
MAJOR 104TH U. S. COLORED TROOPS.

BY

FRANK A. ROLLIN.

—— *" et niger arma Memnonis."*

BOSTON:
LEE AND SHEPARD.
1868.

Title page, Frank A. Rollin, *Life and Public Services of Martin R. Delany* (Boston: Lee & Shepard, 1868).

While very little scholarly attention has been paid to Rollin, she is generally acknowledged as an early contributor to the genre of African American biography, an example of what Lois Brown claims as "the early and formative influence of women" in the genre.[5] While many Black women, including Hallie Quinn Brown and Pauline Hopkins, published biographical literature later in the nineteenth century, Rollin may have only known of one other woman who had done so previously: Josephine Brown, whose biography of her father, William Wells Brown, was published in 1856.[6] Although Rollin was friends with Josephine's father, she did not know her personally, as Brown and his daughter seem to have become estranged soon after the publication of the biography.[7] As her diary reveals, Rollin learned her craft through reading and conversation with other Black biographers and historians, like Brown himself and William Cooper Nell, both of whom had published histories of Black military engagement in the United States. She likely imagined that the success of her book would lead to additional publications, perhaps even making a name for herself as an author. Rollin must also have hoped that the biography would place her at the center of political action in South Carolina. It would demonstrate her grasp of African American activism, Civil War history, and the politics of Reconstruction. While it was difficult to imagine what sort of role an African American woman could occupy in this man's world, it was surely just as impossible to imagine a Black man as a major in the Union army—and here she was, writing that man's biography.

Indeed, Rollin's diary, maintained in the same year that she wrote and published her book, demonstrates that she was thinking carefully about her own prospects even as she contributed to Delany's future career. It provides us with an intimate view of Rollin's commitment to what Kabria Baumgartner calls "purposeful womanhood." As Baumgartner notes, the idea of living for purpose is not singular to nineteenth-century African American women, but it had a different meaning for them: "African American women talked about leading a purposeful

5. Brown, introduction to *Memoir of James Jackson*, 3.

6. As Lois Brown points out, the first known biography by an African American author is Susan Paul's *Memoir of James Jackson*, published in 1835 (introduction to *Memoir of James Jackson*, 2–3). See also Brown, "Reclaiming Black Biography." It is important to note, however, that in this article Brown bases her 1883 dating of Rollin's Delany biography on the Reclaim Her Name edition (2020) produced by (corporate sponsor) Baileys and the Woman's Prize for Fiction: This was the year that Lee & Shepard reissued *Life and Public Services*, not the date of the book's original publication (1868).

7. Greenspan, *William Wells Brown*, 343–45.

life ... to motivate more women to value themselves and to do something of value in a world that failed to recognize them as valuable."[8] Rollin used her diary to create and sustain this sense of self-value: to reflect on and shape her days, document her self-improvement, and motivate herself to persevere. She tracks her reading and her writing as well as the sewing and copying she did to make money when Delany failed to remunerate her adequately for her work. She also records her social and political activities in her diary: visits to others as well as visits received; attendance at church meetings, fairs, and public readings; shopping with female friends; and other things. She writes with deep affection and appreciation about post–Civil War Black Boston and the community that took her in: among them were John and Ann Bailey, with whom she boarded; William Wells Brown and his wife, Annie, who "always treat me so hospitably that I can't help liking them";[9] and Lewis and Harriet Hayden, whose home provided a refuge for so many African American visitors to Boston. She also records her letters and visits to publishers in her efforts to place the biography. While she was not shy about discussing her "prospects in the literary world" with friends and mentors, the diary provided her a space to express her doubts and her self-encouragement.[10]

This introduction to the diary builds on the work of Carole Ione, Rollin's great-granddaughter and author of *Pride of Family: Four Generations of American Women of Color* (1991), to present the most extensive biographical treatment of Frances Rollin's life to date. Biography is, of course, essential to readers approaching the diary for the first time; while diaries can be read without documentation of the life behind them, readers benefit enormously from knowing who a diarist is and what they do outside of the diary itself. This discussion of Rollin's life extends beyond the end of the diary, the publication of her biography of Delany, and her marriage to William J. Whipper in part because so little work has been done on her life (or those of women like her) and in part because, while she did not continue to document her daily life in the diary, it continued to be of use to her. Diaries are not discarded after they are supposedly completed; instead, they are usually preserved, read, and occasionally written in yet again.

---

8. Baumgartner, *In Pursuit of Knowledge*, 4. Baumgartner's notion of "purposeful womanhood" relies upon historians' work on "respectability and racial uplift" but emphasizes the importance of "another idea shaping African American women's actions—not just the well-documented demand for respectability but also the related yet distinct call for *purpose*" (4 [*emphasis original*]).

9. Rollin diary, 10 Mar. 1868.

10. Rollin diary, 25 Mar. 1868.

In addition to facilitating the reading of the diary, Rollin's biography is a necessary scholarly endeavor for what it can tell us about nineteenth-century African American life and literature. Her life confounds so much of what we think
we know about Black women writers' lives in mid-nineteenth-century America.
While she writes and publishes in the urban Northeast, her upbringing among
the mixed-race elite in Charleston and education at the ICY set her apart from
other such authors of the period such as Harriet Wilson, Eliza Potter, Harriet
Jacobs, and Frances Ellen Watkins Harper. The daughter of a wealthy, mixed-race
businessman who employed Irish laborers and enslaved several African Americans himself, Rollin may seem to be an unlikely candidate for association with
the abolitionist and civil rights activists of antebellum Philadelphia and postwar
Boston as well as for biographer of Martin Delany. As it did for nearly all African
Americans, however, the Civil War changed the trajectory of Frances Rollin's life:
The growing sectional and racial tensions in Charleston likely caused her parents
to send her to Philadelphia in 1859 and kept her away from her family for the du-
ration of the war; its end and the emancipation of the enslaved prompted her return to South Carolina and her work as a teacher; and her association with Black
soldiers and Freedmen's Bureau officials brought about her authorship of Delany's
biography as well as her marriage and subsequent involvement in Reconstruction
politics. Her mobility to and from as well as between these and other geographical spaces also challenges our thinking about place-based African American
identities immediately following the Civil War. Eric Gardner notes that "black
struggles for identity formation were carried out in specific locations," but these
"locations" were tied together by Black mobility, rendering African American
writers "deeply tied to the rest of the black nation, as well as to the deeply contested multiracial nation."[11] This insight provides a useful framework for thinking about Frances Rollin's post–Civil War identity and commitment to African
American civil rights.

Other than the diary and the biography of Martin Delany, only two letters by
Frances Rollin Whipper—both likely incomplete and both written to the African American historian and bibliographer Daniel Murray—are extant.[12] While
this lack of primary texts complicates the reconstruction of her life, her proximity
to figures whose lives are fairly well documented allows me to make educated
guesses about her activities, her understanding of events, and even her opinions. I

11. Gardner, *Unexpected Places*, 13, 20.
12. Murray, "Sketch of Frances Rollin Whipper," n.d., Daniel Murray Papers, micro 577, Wisconsin Historical Society, reel 8. See appendix F.

also make use of extant documentation and research about institutions or groups with which she was involved: among others, the ICY in Philadelphia; various schools at which she taught in Charleston; the prosuffrage campaign led by her sister, Charlotte Rollin; post–Civil War Republican Party politics in South Carolina; and St. Luke's Protestant Episcopal Church in Washington, DC. I employ the reverse approach as well, considering what Rollin Whipper's life can help us learn about larger Black communities and networks.[13] Reading the archival evidence in this way, I am influenced by Black feminist scholars like Saidiya Hartman, Tiya Miles, and Marisa J. Fuentes yet also aware that, as a white scholar, my ability—my *right*—to treat archives as they do is legitimately contested.[14] I point interested readers to the work of Carole Ione, whose familial connection to Rollin and talents as a creative writer have facilitated a beautifully imaginative, but also deeply researched, engagement with the diary and the diarist. Throughout this introduction, I restrain my imagination, hoping that others who follow my work on Rollin Whipper and her diary will put such methodologies to good use.

Rollin's diary demonstrates a deep commitment on her part to life writing— not just to the documentation of the lives of heroic men like Delany, but the day-to-day accounting of her own life in the pages of her pocket-sized diary. As Joycelyn K. Moody notes, by the early nineteenth century, "self-authored and self-*authorized* documentation of Black lived experience, both individual and collective, had already become African Americans' oldest and most generative mode."[15] African American print culture abounded with life stories: content as varied as slave narratives, eulogies, sermons, and convention minutes, published in pamphlets, periodicals, and books demonstrated the personal and political uses of life writing. But as Rollin's diary shows, African Americans also engaged in life writing in manuscript genres like the diary, the letter, and the scrapbook, texts that offer us a different way of thinking about the matter of Black lives. For while, as John Ernest writes, "biographies offer a kind of closure, a sense of resolution, of

---

13. In this, I am inspired by John Ernest's "Life Beyond Biography: Black Lives and Biographical Research," in which he cautions against focusing on individual Black lives at the expense of communities: "Rather than use the tools available to us to place newly imposing monuments on an otherwise scarcely populated historical landscape, we could use the lives we know best as entrance into the lives and the worlds that remain unknown to any but the most determined archival researchers among us."

14. See especially Hartman, "Venus in Two Acts" and *Wayward Lives*; Miles, *All That She Carried*; and Fuentes, *Dispossessed Lives*.

15. Moody, "Crafting a Credible Black Self," 5.

completeness" that often belies the messy complexity of nineteenth-century Black life, diaries are, by their very nature, "measured, daily, and open."[16]

Approximately a dozen diaries by nineteenth-century African American women are in the public record.[17] These invaluable manuscripts provide scholars with a sense of how and why Black women wrote in their diaries, but they are clearly not representative of the number of diaries actually maintained by African American wives, mothers, and daughters; domestic laborers, dressmakers, and bookkeepers; students, teachers, and activists. For example, the young women in Rollin's social circles in Charleston, Philadelphia, and Boston probably kept diaries—it seems very likely that Rollin herself kept diaries in the years prior to 1868 and perhaps after—but if these have survived, they have not made their way into libraries and museums. African American families may be reluctant to relinquish such precious heirlooms to the hands of museum curators and librarians. When in 1970 writer and historian Dorothy Sterling encouraged Leighla Whipper, Frances Rollin's granddaughter, to donate her grandmother's diary to the Moorland-Spingarn Library "to have it available to scholars," Whipper said she was hesitant to "let Howard University have so personal a document."[18] Whipper generously loaned the diary to Sterling, however, who excerpted it in *We Are Your Sisters: Black Women in the Nineteenth Century* (1984), a collection of primary documents by and about African American women that placed special emphasis on the historical and literary importance of the diary as a genre. Whipper's daughter, Carole Ione, then became aware of the Rollin diary and attempted heroically to bring it to the public eye, first in "Discovering My Foremothers," published in *Ms.* in September 1977,[19] then in a screenplay titled "Diary of a Cultured Colored Woman," which was scheduled for the 1984 season of PBS's American Playhouse series but was never produced.[20] In 1991 Ione published *Pride of Family*, which

---

16. Ernest, "Life Beyond Biography"; Sinor, *Extraordinary Work of Ordinary Writing*, 16.

17. By this I mean that these diaries are preserved and catalogued in libraries or museums and are available to view and study. Other diaries likely exist in such collections but are uncatalogued or unrecognized as being written by Black diarists, while still others are likely held in private family collections.

18. Sterling to Lila Whipper, 30 April 1970; and Lila Whipper to Sterling, 11 May 1970, both Dorothy Sterling Papers, University of Oregon Libraries, Special Collections and University Archives, Eugene.

19. "Discovering My Foremothers" was published under the name Carole Bovoso, Ione's married name at the time.

20. See Bovoso to Sterling, 26 June 1982, Dorothy Sterling Papers.

was at the time the most complete documentation of Rollin Whipper's life. Convinced of its value to African American history and literature, Ione generously donated the diary to the National Museum of African American History and Culture in 2018 but never gave up on making it more widely available to readers. Other extant diaries by African American women have benefited similarly from the love and care bestowed upon them by family and friends. That of educator and elocutionist Hallie Quinn Brown, for example, was donated to Central State University by Brown's niece, Frances Hughes. Charlotte Forten Grimké's diaries were entrusted by her husband, Francis J. Grimké, to her dear friend Anna Julia Cooper, who, in turn, donated them to Howard University.[21]

Even when they are extant and available to scholars, diaries by African American women have historically been regarded as ordinary and unimportant in comparison to published texts: novels, collections of poetry, histories, and biographies like *Life and Public Services of Martin R. Delany*. Historians have generally paid more attention to diaries than have literary scholars, resulting in diaries being mined for useful information rather than appreciated as examples of a literary genre with its own conventions. Grimké's diary has received more critical attention, from both historians and literary scholars, than any other, in part because of her connections to important historical figures and events and in part because of its careful preservation by the Moorland-Spingarn Research Center at Howard University. Since 1953, the diary has appeared in two editions, with the latter one, by historian Barbara Stevenson, widely accepted as complete and definitive.[22] Yet more work needs to be done to place Grimké's diary in conversation with others that have already been recovered and edited (the Civil War diary of Emilie Davis, for example) as well as those that have received little or no critical attention. This work requires a thorough understanding of the diary as a literary genre as well as the varied literary, historical, and cultural contexts in which each was written. *The Reconstruction Diary of Frances Anne Rollin* is part of that effort.

A reading of Rollin's diary thus necessitates an introduction to the history of diary keeping in the nineteenth-century United States as well as the conventions

---

21. Two of Charlotte's five diaries had mistakenly been given to Howard University along with the papers of her husband. Cooper initially wanted all five volumes to be donated to the Library of Congress but was convinced by Ray Billington, their first editor, and Dorothy B. Porter, supervisor of the Negro Collection at Howard, to give them to Howard. See Porter to Billington, 21 June 1944; Billington to Cooper, 2 July 1944; Billington to Logan, 20 Aug. 1951; and Porter to Cooper, 8 Oct. 1951, all in Moody-Turner, *Portable Anna Julia Cooper*, 443–44, 445–46, and 447–48, respectively.

22. See Billington, *Journal of Charlotte L. Forten*, and Stevenson, *Journals of Charlotte Forten Grimké*.

of the diary genre. Diaries are often thought to be unsophisticated, uncomplicated, and unliterary. But as Philippe Lejeune notes, they cannot be judged according to "value systems that are fundamentally at odds with the diary's value systems."[23] Desirée Henderson explains: "Diaries deserve to be read in ways that acknowledge and grapple with the defining features of the genre. While it remains important to contextualize diaries historically, in terms of their material form and publication histories, within the biography of the diarist, and within larger debates in literary and autobiographical studies, readers also need to be able to understand the genre's specific forms and devices."[24] The material form of the diary is also crucial; while it is difficult to remember while reading an edited version, diaries are material objects with their own limitations and affordances. The materiality of the diary shapes how a diarist engages with it. Such an approach allows the reader to understand Rollin's agency as a writer, meeting her and her diary on their own terms.

Despite stereotypes about diaries as baring the heart and soul of the writer, most nineteenth-century diaries are prosaic; they conceal as much as they reveal according to a logic that is often difficult for a reader to determine. In a typical entry, this one dated Friday, 15 May 1868, Rollin writes: "At home watching the weather was to go to Lowell today but could not on account of the rain went to Lee & Shep. was told of the Major sending the money to them. Mr Lee being sick nothing could be done as yet. At the State House writing. Rain poured when coming home." It is easy to figure out who "Lee & Shep" are and why Rollin visits them. We also know why "the Major" sends them money. Lee & Shepard were the publishers of Rollin's Delany biography, and as often happened in the nineteenth century, Delany himself was subsidizing the production of the book. While waiting for it to be published, Rollin became a clerk or a copyist at the Massachusetts State House; while she often mentions "writing" in her diary, the writing she does varies widely: copying documents at the capitol building, working on the biography in the parlor, composing letters to friends and family, or recording the day's events in her diary. Using other entries, we can even surmise why she wanted to go to Lowell: a few days earlier, Rollin had written that she was "feeling allright went to Dr. Birmingham will not go out until Friday to his house."[25] First mentioned in the diary in late April, Dr. Samuel Birmingham was a Black physician who lived in Lowell, Massachusetts, but saw patients in an office on Cambridge Street in the

23. Lejeune, "Diary on Trial," 153.

24. Henderson, *How to Read a Diary*, 64.

25. Rollin diary, 11 May 1868.

West End of Boston.[26] He seems to have been treating Rollin for her ill health but may also have hired her to do some writing or editing work for him.

Even with all of this information to facilitate our reading of this entry, questions remain. Was Rollin disappointed in her inability to make the journey to Lowell? How did she feel about the fact that "nothing could be done as yet" with her book manuscript? Beyond that, what else happened on this day that Rollin chose not to write about? What did she do in the morning while watching the rain fall? What did she do after she came home that evening? Were these events less or more important than what does appear in the entry? While some of these questions might be answered with archival research—cross-checking of newspapers, for example, or the surfacing of primary documents written by those close to Rollin—others will remain unanswerable.

Rather than seeing this as some failure of the diary, however, it is our responsibility as readers to think carefully about how a typical entry like this works and what it did for Rollin. There are fascinating stories in Rollin's diary—friendship and romance, scandal and death, successes and failures—but to focus on these at the expense of what scholar Jennifer Sinor calls the "ordinary" is to miss the point of the diary completely.[27] While the entry for 15 May hints at larger stories, it also allows us to note Rollin's adherence to conventions of diary keeping: the observance of the weather, the winnowing of one's day into two or three activities, and the ordering of events into a manageable package. It also reminds us that while people may have read this diary, this diary was not written for others.

According to Philippe Lejeune: "A diary is a dark room that you enter from a brightly lit exterior. It is so dark in there you can't see a thing, but if you stay there for half an hour, you begin to see outlines, silhouettes begin to emerge from the shadows, you begin to make things out."[28] Diaries throw the reader into the midst of events without invitations, introductions, or explanations and without any point of reference except the dated entries. While the goal of this introduction is to familiarize readers with Frances Rollin's life and times as well as the genre and conventions of the diary, to be too familiar—to assume that we, as readers of a diary, somehow know Frances Rollin, perhaps even better than she knows herself—would be to presume too much, to attempt to make that room

---

26. See Joe Orfant, "The Sad, Curious Death of Mary Ann Birmingham," *Curious Mysteries* (blog), 21 March 2023, https://curiousmysteries.wordpress.com/2023/03/01/the-sad-curious-death-of-mary-ann-birmingham/.

27. See Sinor, *Extraordinary Work of Ordinary Writing.*

28. Lejeune, "Continuous and Discontinuous," 181.

our home. Indeed, Sinor cautions against becoming too comfortable with diaries, even if they are edited and put in print for ease of access: "A diary—by its form and content—demands that the reader never feel at home. A reader must always recognize her outsiderness, not only feel it but actively cultivate it. . . . The reader stands outside the action, the people and events that move through the diary, and outside a form of writing that is often illegible, out of order, coded and crossed out. We are not being invited in."[29] Diligent research might tempt us into thinking that we know what a diarist thinks or feels, but intimate acquaintance with the diary genre will help us understand that we are always "outside." But this makes diaries more, rather than less, interesting in that it reveals the agency of diarists and the affordances of the genre.

From Haiti to Charleston: The Rollin Family

Frances Anne Rollin was born in Charleston, South Carolina, on 19 November 1845, the eldest child of William and Margaret Rollin. While the exact details are unknown, William's father was likely Jean Baptiste de Caradeuc Jr., the white son of a wealthy aristocratic planter whose family left Saint Domingue in the early days of the Haitian Revolution.[30] While descendants remembered him as "a defender of king and France," the elder de Caradeuc was in favor of independence from France and, as commander of the National Guard of the West Province in Saint Domingue, commanded a "fully multiracial" troop of men.[31] Yet he was far from a true believer in racial equality: as enslaved people continued to rebel and the rights of free people of color were upheld by France, de Caradeuc decided to escape both Saint Domingue and his French creditors.[32] Due to his departure in 1792, prior to the burning of Cap-Français (modern Cap-Haïtien) in June 1793

29. Sinor, *Extraordinary Work of Ordinary Writing*, 87.

30. In *Pride of Family* (134–35), Ione describes finding an obituary for James Achille de Caradeuc glued into a scrapbook that belonged to her great-grandmother and then her grandfather, the actor Leigh Whipper. According to Ione, Frances Rollin Whipper had written "Charleston, January 14, '95" above the headline and "Nephew of Wm. A. Rollin" below. For her investigation into the de Caradeux family and their connections with the Rollins, see Ione, *Pride of Family*, 142–48. In the second edition of *Pride of Family*, published in 2004, Ione includes the de Caradeucs in the family tree preceding the preface. According to her, DNA testing has confirmed the familial relationship (Ione, pers. comm., 27 July 2021). All citations to *Pride of Family* refer to the 1991 edition unless otherwise indicated.

31. Geggus, "Caradeux and Colonial Memory," 238.

32. Geggus, "Caradeux and Colonial Memory," 239.

and the abolition of slavery in August 1793, de Caradeuc retained much of his fortune and many of the people he enslaved; he and his family established themselves comfortably on the outskirts of Charleston, South Carolina. His son and namesake, known as "Hercule," had two children by his legal white wife: Jean Baptiste (or John B.) de Caradeuc, born in 1814, and James Achille de Caradeuc, born in 1816. Sometime between the births of his two white sons, Hercule had a sexual relationship with William Rollin's mother, a free mixed-race woman, about whom very little is known.[33] Their son was born in 1815. It is not clear where the name "Rollin" originates. In Saint Domingue the mixed-race children of white men rarely bore their fathers' names; Hercule de Caradeuc seems to have carried on this tradition even though other mixed-race families in Charleston bore the names of their white progenitors.[34] William Rollin likely maintained a relationship with the de Caradeucs and the larger French émigré community, both Black and white. For most of Frances Rollin's childhood, her father ran a successful lumberyard that was likely tied in some way to a similar business conducted by the de Caradeuc family.[35] Moreover, baptismal records suggest that the Rollins worshipped at the Cathedral of St. John and St. Finbar, established in 1822 on Broad Street, along with other Black families with roots in Saint Domingue.[36] Suzanne Krebsbach notes: "The Catholic community in Charleston was inclusive, blacks and whites of every status worshiped together in the same edifice, possibly in the same pews. . . . Blacks were deeply immersed in the fabric of the church. That large numbers of black sponsors witnessed and sponsored the baptisms and confirmations of other blacks clearly demonstrates a lively Catholic culture among that community."[37]

While she likely attended the cathedral with her son, perhaps even had him baptized there, the identity of William Rollin's mother is unknown. Frances Rollin's maternal lineage is similarly unknown, but her mother, Margaret, may also have been descended from Haitian refugees. In 1880, after the death of her

33. In *Pride of Family*, Ione speculates about the exact relationship of William Rollin to the de Caradeucs. The scenario presented here seems most likely. See also Geggus, "Caradeux and Colonial Memory," 235–36.

34. For the late eighteenth-century controversy over naming practices in Saint Domingue, see Garrigus, *Before Haiti*, 165–67. For a discussion of the Noisette family, who did not adhere to these conventions, see Wikramanayake, *World in Shadow*, 15.

35. For the involvement of the white de Caradeuc family in the lumber business, see Geggus, "Caradeuc and Colonial Memory," 231; and Robertson, prologue to *A Confederate Lady Comes of Age*, 6.

36. Suzanne Krebsbach, pers. comm., 12 Apr. 2023.

37. Krebsbach, "Black Catholics," 153.

husband, Margaret claimed to have been born in Cuba, but her tombstone records her place of birth as "Granada, Spain."[38] Both of these claims may contain
a grain of truth, as the Spanish controlled the territory east of Saint Domingue
(what would become the Dominican Republic) prior to the Haitian Revolution.
Margaret's parents—perhaps born in Spain—may have been one of a group of refugees who went to southeastern Cuba during Napoleon's effort to recapture Saint
Domingue from the Black rebel army led by Toussaint-Louverture and eventually
Jean-Jacques Dessalines. After Napolean invaded Spain in 1808, all French citizens were expelled from the country; while most escaped to New Orleans, a small
number went to Charleston.[39] It is unclear why Margaret's family would have
accompanied these immigrants if they identified as Spanish rather than French.
Despite the best efforts of Rollin's descendants, it has proven impossible thus far
to trace Margaret or determine her parentage. While she is mentioned frequently
in Rollin's 1868 diary, no details are given that might lead to a fuller picture of
her family background or her personality. It seems certain, however, that she, like
her husband, was born and raised in "landscapes contoured by the slave power"
despite her own free status.[40]

A scene in the diary may point to the identity of at least one female relative.
On 1 March 1868, Rollin writes about participating in what she calls "a sitting
for spiritual purposes" with one of her suitors, William E. "Leedie" Matthews,
and the members of the family with whom she was boarding: "The table was
clearly lifted and twisted about and the spirit answered to C.L. I felt as though
it meant Grandma." The allusion to her grandmother here is interesting. Is this
her maternal grandmother, the mother of Margaret, or her father's mother? Both
are equally shadowy figures, indistinguishable from one another and likely unre-
coverable. "C.L." might point to the name "Charlotte," making one of Frances's
sisters this grandmother's namesake. The amorphousness of Rollin's mixed-race
family is particularly striking given the careful documentation of the white de
Caradeucs and their visibility in multiple archives. Letters, diaries, and wills document their relationships to one another—but not to the mixed-race relatives
they seem to have claimed publicly but kept at arm's length.

38. For Margaret Rollin's claim of Cuban birth, see Margaret Rollen entry, Kings County,
NY, Enumeration District 159, p. 552, Ancestry.com. For the claim of Granada as her birthplace, see Margaret Irving Rollin, Holy Cross Cemetery, Brooklyn, NY, Find a Grave, www
.findagrave.com/memorial/229790139/margaret-rollin.

39. Gillikin, *Saint Dominguan Refugees*, 73.

40. Johnson, "From Saint-Domingue," 427–28.

William Rollin and Charleston's
Free Black Elite Community

In a letter written just prior to her death in 1901, Rollin Whipper says of the time of her birth: "I could not have chosen a more auspicious time had the choice devolved upon me, for it was in the days when the free colored people were at the zenith of their prosperity. They possessed the trades with few exceptions and colored workmen were generally preferred."[41] While this recollection is likely tinged with nostalgia for the days of her youth, her sense of the privileges of free birth and light skin color in the 1840s reflects both the Rollins' status within Charleston society during the antebellum period and the difficulties of post-Reconstruction life in the South.

Whatever their origins or connections to extended white family, the Rollins found community within the free Black elite of Charleston: the Westons, the McKinlays, the Holloways, the Dereefs, and others whose family background, wealth, education, profession, and skin color contributed to their high social status within the larger free Black community. William Rollin may have been a member of the Brown Fellowship Society, an elite mutual-aid society that primarily accepted men with light-colored skin.[42] These families socialized together, attending dinners, receptions, and weddings as well as participating in voluntary organizations. As Marina Wikramanayake notes, "Their choice of partners in marriage, of sponsors for the baptisms of their children and of executors for their wills was invariably made from the small group of free black first families."[43] The fact that the Rollin family did not intermarry with these families seems more a result of the age of their five daughters—Frances, the eldest, was just sixteen when the Civil War began, and the youngest was born in 1858—than an indication of a lack of participation in the social activities of the elite. Their Catholicism and French culture may have created some distance between them and other Black families in Charleston. But references in Rollin's diary indicate that she and her family had long-lasting relationships with these families that shaped their prewar and postwar lives.

41. Quoted in Murray, "Sketch of Frances Rollin Whipper."

42. William Rollin's name is not on the 1844 roster for the Brown Fellowship Society, but his profession, position in society, and skin color make it likely that he was a member or was at least eligible to become one (Powers, *Black Charlestonians*, 180). Moreover, his grandson, Leigh Whipper, told Ione that he was a member (Ione, *Pride of Family*, 163). For a discussion of the members listed on the roster, see Harris, "Charleston's Free Afro-American Elite."

43. Wikramanayake, *World in Shadow*, 81.

Elite African American men in Charleston worked for a living. Historians Michael P. Johnson and James L. Roark describe them as "an aristocracy with calluses. Their wealth was only a fraction of that of Charleston's white aristocrats, and, unlike the white aristocracy, it did not consist of lush tidewater plantations or gangs of slaves. Instead, it was largely in the form of urban real estate, an outgrowth of their quest for economic security."[44] Many of them were tailors, barbers, carpenters, and butchers. Jehu Jones operated a luxury hotel, catering to the white South Carolina elite and other white travelers for seventeen years until his death in 1833. Like William Rollin, Richard Dereef and Robert Howard were wood merchants; in *The Condition, Elevation, Emigration and Destiny of the Colored People of the United States*, published in 1852, long before he gained the acquaintance of Frances Rollin, Martin R. Delany notes that Dereef and Howard kept "a large number of men employed, a regular Clerk and Book-Keeper, supplying the citizens, steamers, vessels, and factories of Charleston with fuel. In this business a very heavy capital is invested: besides which, they are the owners and proprietors of several vessels trading on the coast. They are men of great business habits and command a great deal of respect and influence in the city of Charleston."[45] While Rollin was not mentioned by Delany, his business clearly resembled those of Dereef and Howard in size and profitability. His success gave him access to power likely not afforded many Black men in antebellum Charleston. "My father was by birth, tradition and choice a staunch adherent of the church of Rome," Rollin Whipper writes in 1901, "and having a wood and lumber yard, and city contracts for material, with Sloops plying between the outlying plantations and the city, he gave employment to his church friends, all Irish, and had in consequence a large Irish following whom he was able to influence during election days. And though denied the right to vote himself he was much sought after by the candidates who wanted that Irish vote and in return for my father's influence toward securing it, looked carefully after his interest."[46]

Frances Rollin took pride in the achievements of her father and the free Black community: "Their lives and material prosperity," she notes in her biography

44. Johnson and Roark, introduction to *No Chariot Let Down*, 6.

45. Delany, *Condition, Elevation, Emigration, and Destiny*, 108–9.

46. Quoted in Murray, "Sketch of Frances Rollin Whipper." For evidence of William Rollin's ownership of a boat that he used in his lumber business, see Bill of Sale, 24 Sept. 1860, for "the Sloop Boat formerly named the 'Three Sisters' now the 'Water Wave' supposed to carry ten cords of wood," Records of the Secretary of State, Recorded Instruments, 247, South Carolina Department of Archives and History, Columbia, accessed via "South Carolina, Charleston District, Bill of Sales of Negro Slaves, 1774–1872," database, Family Search, www.familysearch.org.

of Delany, stood "in direct contrast to the repeated assertions of the advocates and apologists of slavery, that [African Americans] would, if free, relapse into barbarism, or would burden the states in which they were found for support."[47] According to historian Bernard E. Powers Jr., however, "the character of free black communities and their quality of life were dictated by the region's commitment to slavery."[48] After the enslaved insurrection organized by Denmark Vesey was foiled by Charleston authorities in 1822, legislation was passed that limited the ability of enslavers to manumit enslaved people and prohibited free Blacks from migrating to South Carolina. Those already there were closely monitored, with laws prohibiting their free movement and requiring them to acquire white "guardians" and to pay an annual capitation tax of two dollars, whose payment allowed the state to maintain documentation of all free Blacks in South Carolina. In 1850, five years after Frances's birth, the free Black community in Charleston had grown to 3,441 persons, or 8 percent of the city's total population, up from 3.6 percent in 1790.[49] The existence of each of these people depended on the largesse of white Charlestonians, who would certainly be quick to rein in their attendance at school, acquisition of property, and other freedoms if their behavior was found offensive or dangerous.

The names of William and Margaret Rollin appear regularly in the city capitation-tax books from the late 1840s through the 1850s. While this tax did not represent a financial burden for Rollin, the annual payment was a regular reminder of his lack of full citizenship despite his wealth and influence. His ability to pay it, however, was indicative of his elite status and his difference from the vast majority of African American men in Charleston. As mixed-race and relatively wealthy free Black residents, the Rollins were able to evade some of the restrictions placed on their community. As an adult, Frances remembered her father traveling to "all the principal cities" in the North—"Boston, Philadelphia, Providence, Newport, Portland and New York"—despite laws that prevented African Americans from reentering South Carolina if they left.[50] These records also reveal that, for most of Frances Rollin's childhood in Charleston, the family lived on the Charleston Neck in Wraggsborough on the corner of Washington and Chapel Streets. "The Neck," as it was called, was a combination of "industrial and residential sites" and had a diverse population, housing a mixture of "wealthy

47. Rollin, *Life and Public Services*, 31–32.
48. Powers, *Black Charlestonians*, 36.
49. Powers, *Black Charlestonians*, 36.
50. Quoted in Murray, "Sketch of Frances Anne Rollin."

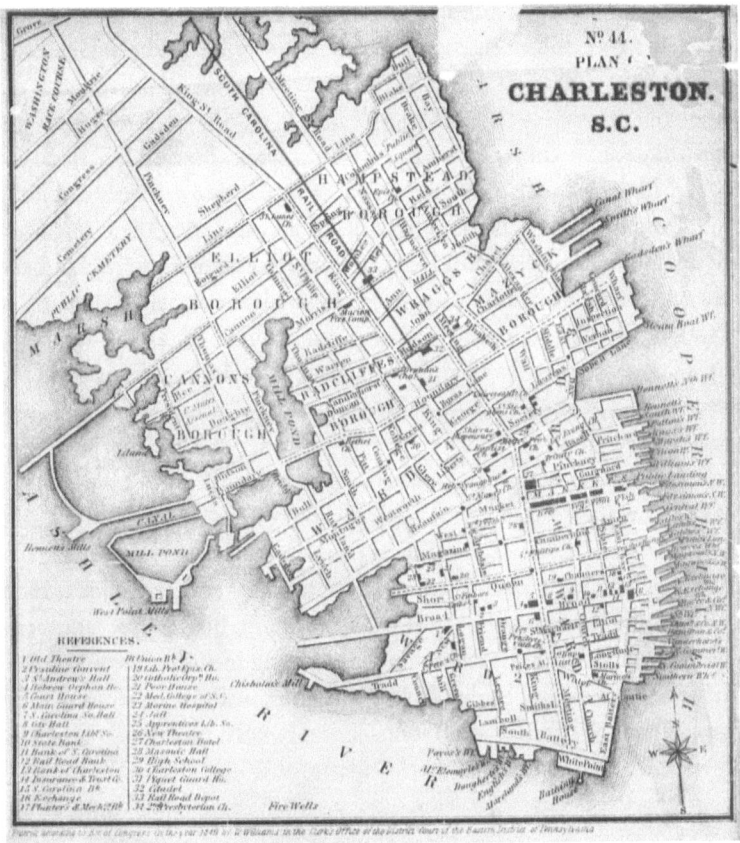

Wellington Williams, *Plan of Charleston, S.C.* (Philadelphia, 1849). University of
Alabama Libraries Special Collections.

planters, free blacks, immigrants, and slaves." Fifteen percent of the city's free
African American population lived there, "the largest percentage of free blacks in
any ward."[51] The Rollins lived just steps away from William Rollin's lumberyard
and close to the wharfs from which he would conduct business and travel north,
coming and going with a confidence denied free Blacks without his familial and
economic connections.

Supplying plantations with lumber or purchasing wood from them, Rollin
clearly benefited from the labor of the enslaved, whose birth and likely skin color

51. Joyce, "Charleston Landscape," 176.

placed them well beneath him in the careful social balance of South Carolina society. He also became an enslaver himself: in 1860 and 1861 he paid tax on one enslaved person, and in 1862 he paid taxes on three.[52] While there is no documentation of him owning enslaved people prior to 1860, it is entirely possible that he did. In 1850 approximately 266 free Black enslavers lived in Charleston, and Rollin may have been one of them.[53] Being of mixed race certainly did not prevent him from exploiting the labor of enslaved people during the Civil War, but records do not indicate why he did so. Did he require laborers for his lumberyard after the enlistment of Irish soldiers in the Confederate army? In the early years of the war, he began farming, even as he continued to maintain his lumberyard, moving it farther south to Williams' Wharf due to a railyard expansion in 1859.[54] He is also listed in the *Charleston Courier* as one of many South Carolinians engaged in "the manufacture of salt, one of the great necessities of the time." On Williams' Wharf he and a partner averaged four bushels of salt per day in service of the Confederate army, which used it to preserve food and cure leather.[55] Frances's father may have used enslaved people in any one of these operations. Like his white counterparts, he may also have regarded enslaved labor as the best and most profitable arrangement for his lumberyard, his "sloops," and perhaps even his home. He may also have believed that being an enslaver would convince Southerners of his loyalty to the Confederacy even as his daughter studied in a Northern school. What Michael P. Johnson and James L. Roark say of the mixed-race slaveowner William Ellison was likely true of William Rollin:

52. For 1860, see *List of the Tax Payers of the City of Charleston for 1860* (Evans & Cogswell, 1860), Charleston County Public Library. For 1861 and 1862, see Tax Book: Charleston Free Persons of Color, 1862, Charleston County Public Library, microfilm.

53. Koger, *Black Slaveowners*, 20.

54. In 1859 the *Charleston Mercury* featured a notice from William Rollin announcing that he was being forced to remove his lumberyard from the corner of Washington and Chapel to Union Wharf ("late Williams' Wharf"), "in consequence of the extension of the Northeastern Railroad yard" ("Removal," *Charleston (SC) Mercury*, 10 Sept. 1859, 3). The Northeastern Railroad was chartered in 1851 and completed in 1856. The Rollin family also moved at the same time; for the next few years, tax records list William and his family living at several different addresses throughout the Charleston Neck. The name of this wharf seems to have reverted to "Williams" during wartime, perhaps to avoid the association with the Confederacy's opponents. See "Salt Business Produced by the War," *Charleston (SC) Courier*, 16 Dec. 1862, 4.

55. "Salt Business."

Owning slaves . . . provided him with a kind of insurance. As a master, he effectively demonstrated to skeptical whites that race did not define his loyalties. Whites could never entirely overcome their suspicion that free Negroes were unsound on the issue of slavery. . . . By owning slaves, Ellison broadcast his orthodoxy on fundamental matters and confirmed that he was motivated by safe, mundane, and thoroughly acceptable acquisitive instincts. Whites could see that William Ellison's primary loyalty was not to the black masses with whom he shared racial ancestry but, like themselves (with whom he also happened to share racial ancestry), to self-advancement within the existing social order.[56]

Frances Rollin does not record her opinion of slavery prior to the Civil War. While it seems safe to assume that she became an abolitionist during her time in Philadelphia—it would have been difficult to avoid doing so at the ICY—she may have regarded the institution as natural prior to moving north in 1859 at the age of fourteen. She and the rest of her family may also have harbored abolitionist beliefs—may even, perhaps, have acted on these beliefs—but the necessity of secrecy makes this history difficult to recover.

It is impossible to know what William and Margaret taught Frances about the institution of slavery. She and her sisters would have grown up seeing enslaved men and women on the streets of Charleston, likely darker in skin tone than themselves and speaking the Gullah dialect. She likely witnessed brutality and suffering in private and public spaces throughout the city, despite her parents' efforts to shelter her. She must have also observed the deeply intertwined nature of Black and white life there, with free Black families related to enslaved Black people as well as to white people like the de Caradeucs. Perhaps enslaved women helped Margaret Rollin care for her daughters, especially as the family grew bigger. Did a young Frances question why she was free and they were not? Did she see herself as different in kind or degree?

While he could not protect his children entirely from witnessing the institution of slavery, William Rollin was, for the most part, able to keep his family safe from the prying eyes of the white public, claiming for his household the kind of privacy usually only afforded to white families. As Michael P. Johnson and James L. Roark note, however, "Privacy for every free Afro-American family depended on being above reproach in the eyes of whites, on never being suspected

56. Johnson and Roark, *Black Masters*, 66.

of aiding a runaway, of trading with slaves, or of meeting secretly with slaves for any purpose."[57] It also depended on constant accommodation to whites. Writing in her biography of Delany of free Black men like her father, Frances Rollin notes, "Business men found it in many instances impolitic to refuse requests for loans coming from influential white men, under whose protection they exercised their meagre privileges, and the payment of which it was equally impolitic to press, nor were they allowed to sue for debts."[58] Achille de Caradeuc, who was likely William Rollin's half-brother, suffered serious financial setbacks during the Civil War, leading to the sale of the family home; his own failure may have contributed to that of William, if he was forced to lend him money.[59] "How hard this is," Frances writes in reference to her father in her diary on 18 February 1868, that "the accumulations of years should in his most needed time be swept away! 'Ruin' is written in every homestead of South Carolina. But why should the unoffending suffer?" It is not clear why Rollin saw her father as "unoffending." Did she not know about his role as an enslaver? Or did she regard his enslavement of other African Americans as excusable or understandable in some way?

Frances Rollin's Charleston Childhood

Frances Anne Rollin was the eldest of five children, all daughters. Her sisters were Charlotte, or Lottie, born three years after her, in 1847; Katherine, or Katie, born in 1848; Louisa, born in 1855; and Florence, born in 1858, the year before Frances's departure for Philadelphia.[60] The gaps between the sisters' births—four years between Frances and Lottie, seven between Katie and Louisa—indicate that there may have been either other pregnancies that did not result in births or other children who did not survive infancy. Surely, William Rollin would have wanted

---

57. Johnson and Roark, *Black Masters*, 50.

58. Rollin, *Life and Public Services*, 31.

59. Robertson, prologue to *A Confederate Lady Comes of Age*, 10–11. Pauline de Caradeuc, the daughter of James Achille de Caradeuc, William Rollin's half brother, was Frances Rollin's first cousin. Born in Charleston in 1843, a year or two before Frances, Pauline grew up in Aiken, South Carolina, more than 100 miles away. There is no evidence that they knew one another personally.

60. As is the case with many nineteenth-century figures, birth dates are imprecise. My estimates are based on census records for 1850 and 1860, rather than on later census records and gravestone markers, which often reflect a fudging of details. These dates differ slightly from those of Ione, who records Charlotte's birth as 1849, Katherine's as 1851, Louisa's as 1858, and Florence's as 1861 (*Pride of Family*, 2).

a son to carry on his name and his business. Indeed, a death record from 27 June 1854 for a four-month-old male infant—"mulatto" and free—named "W. Rollins" indicates that a son might have been born earlier that year.[61] The loss of this only son would have been immense for the family, with nine-year-old Frances old enough to comprehend and share her parents' grief.[62] Frances's nickname, "Frank," and her father's treatment of his eldest daughter may hint at her status as a substitute for the son he never had. As an adult, Frank remembered traveling with her father, "who annually went North to buy goods."[63] The emphasis placed on her education was typical of mixed-race families in Charleston, but it points as well to a commitment to provide for this favored daughter, who was clearly headstrong and ambitious.

Black Charlestonians, enslaved or free, who sought education for their children understood that unobtrusiveness, secrecy even, was the key to obtaining the skills and services of any teacher, whatever their qualifications. Since the first legislation outlawing the teaching of enslaved people to write in 1740, African Americans in South Carolina found ways to access literacy skills, often "meeting before dawn and late into the night."[64] The presence of schools for enslaved people is, of course, difficult to document, yet as Heather Andrea Williams points out, the existence of laws preventing the teaching of reading and writing to enslaved people in schools indicates that "sporadic teaching" and "established schools" existed both before and during the Civil War.[65] The disrupted Vesey insurrection in 1822 prompted harsher restrictions against educating both enslaved and free Black children in South Carolina and the closing of schools like that taught by Daniel A. Payne, future bishop of the African Methodist Episcopal (AME) Church. In Charleston, however, schools for free children were eventually tolerated if strictly supervised. For example, Mary Weston, a member of the

61. W. Rollin entry, "South Carolina, U.S., Death Records, 1821–1971," database, Ancestry .com.

62. If this infant was indeed the child of William and Margaret, his name was likely William, like his father. The child is listed as having been buried in the cemetery of the Second Baptist Church, otherwise known as the Wentworth Street Baptist Church, instead of a Roman Catholic cemetery in accordance with William and Margaret's faith. It is possible that the infant was not baptized and was therefore not allowed burial in a Catholic cemetery. It is also possible that this child was born to someone in William's family, who then named him after Frances's father. Without more information, it is impossible to know.

63. Quoted in Murray, "Sketch of Frances Anne Rollin."

64. Williams, *Self-Taught*, 13.

65. Williams, *Self-Taught*, 16.

prominent Weston family who would eventually teach alongside Rollin in the postwar period, was arrested during the war for teaching free Black children. Upon the intervention of supportive whites, she was allowed to maintain her school "provided that no slaves were taught and that a white person was present at all times."[66]

As a very young child, Frances Rollin said that she attended a parish school in Charleston, "taught by an old French family. I was too young to go unattended. French was taught and I was lisping French long before I could clearly speak English."[67] It is unclear what school this might have been; while there were several schools for white girls taught by white refugees from Saint Domingue, none of these would have admitted free Blacks no matter their relations or the lighter color of their skin.[68] Rollin may also have attended another private school for the education of "the free colored people." After explaining her attendance at the "parish school" in her 1901 letter to Daniel Murray, she describes two schools

taught by white men, known as the Wilbour and Wood schools. They were of a very high grade, very exclusive and quite expensive.

Wilbour was the son of a slave broker, and very devoted to his pupils. His folks had means and why he taught a school kept for colored children was a mystery never made clear to us as children. He kept his school open each day, including Saturdays apparently anxious to avoid the loss of a day. Suddenly he gave up teaching and shortly after his mind was impaired, which necessitated his incarceration in an asylum of which he [is] an inmate to-day. My father designing to have me go abroad to enter a French boarding school at Paris employed private teachers to prepare me.

It is not clear whether Rollin tells Wilbour's story because it is interesting or because it represents a period in her own education, preceded by the parish school and followed by the private tutors. Was the "mystery" of this son of a slave broker educating Black pupils "never made clear to us as children" by her parents, observing this school from the outside, or was it never made clear only to the children attending classes, including Rollin herself?[69] Regardless, the school itself

66. Powers, *Black Charlestonians*, 150.

67. Quoted in Murray, "Sketch of Frances Rollin Whipper."

68. For information on one school run by white immigrants from Saint Domingue, see Leigh Fought, "Talvande, Madame Rose and Madame Ann Marsan (Mason) Talvande," *South Carolina Encyclopedia*, 28 June 2016, https://www.scencyclopedia.org/sce/entries/talvande-madame-rose-and-madame-ann-marsan-mason-talvande/.

69. "Wilbour" was likely the son of the prominent slave broker William Ward Wilbur, whose firm Wilbur & Son operated on State and Chalmers Streets in Charleston. In 1927, on the basis

and Rollin's awareness of it as a child (she groups herself with the "children" who do not understand why Wilbour maintains his school) indicates the complicated racial dynamics of the city in which she grew up.

Despite such circumstances and her own French heritage, a teenaged Frances Rollin seems to have resisted her father's desire to send her to Paris for further education, at least in part because it was "so far from home." As she explains in her letter to Murray, "it was finally settled I should attend school in Philadelphia, particularly since I had made many friends in that city while visiting in 1857 in company with my father."[70] While Rollin later regretted not taking advantage of the opportunity to be educated in a "French boarding school," her spirit and tenacity are evident in the resistance of this fourteen-year-old to her father's plans. It is also possible to read this as a rejection of her father's insistence on a French identity, perhaps in favor of one as "colored" or even "American." Remaining in Charleston, or even in the South, did not seem to be an option.

The decision to send Frances to attend the ICY in Philadelphia could not have been an easy one for William and Margaret to make.[71] While William Rollin traveled relatively freely from North to South during the antebellum period, contrary to laws restricting the movements of free Blacks, white Southerners became

---

of "research into family records and papers" and "correspondence and conversation with the few survivors of those days," C. W. Birnie claims that "one of the largest and best-known" of the antebellum schools for free Black residents was "conducted by W. W. Wilburn, a white man, on Coming Street, opposite Bull Street." Birnie continues, "He was paid a regular salary, not having to depend at all on tuition. The financial affairs of this school were managed by a Board of Trustees elected by the patrons. The earliest of these trustees of whom we have record were Benj. Huger, Joseph Sasportas, and William McKinlay" ("Education of the Negro in Charleston," 19). Huger, Sasportas, and McKinlay were all African American men of high social status like William Rollin.

70. Quoted in Murray, "Sketch of Frances Rollin Whipper."

71. The letters of the Ellison family provide some idea of both the urgency and the peril of the Rollins' decision. On 31 October 1860, two weeks after John Brown's raid on Harpers Ferry, William Ellison Jr. sent at least two of his children to Philadelphia. In a letter to his brother, Ellison explains that he had put his children on a steamer heading for New York. He had originally wanted to send them directly to Philadelphia, but the agents for the steamer *Keystone State* would not allow the children passage "unless [they] are cleared out of the custom house by some white person as [their] slaves" (William Ellison to Henry Ellison, 31 October 1860, in Johnson and Roark, *No Chariot Let Down*, 128.) As Michael P. Johnson and James L. Roark explain, "If they allowed a free colored person to leave [the state] who turned out in fact to be a slave, then they, the agents, were guilty of having aided a slave to run away, an offense punishable by death without benefit of clergy" (*Black Masters*, 129). The Ellison children were likely sent either to the ICY or the Lombard Street Primary School.

increasingly uneasy about and suspicious of him and his peers as sectional tensions increased. In defense of the Negro Seaman's Act, which was resisted by some Northerners, the presence of free Blacks returning South was figured as a disease on the body politic similar to the yellow fever. "In South Carolina," a lawyer for the state declared, "we think the presence of a free negro, fresh from the lectures of an Abolition Society, equally dangerous."[72] In the fall of 1859, following the Harpers Ferry raid, South Carolina's legislature considered but failed to pass bills to enslave or expel free Blacks.[73] One letter, written to the *Charleston Mercury* by someone calling himself simply "A Slaveholder," epitomizes the fears and frustrations of white elites just a week after the raid:

> What explanations can our municipal authorities give for the crowds of black children who throng our streets every morning on their way to school, with satchel well filled with books? Of the crowds who congregate in nightly "sittings-up"? Of the negro visitors to northern cities and watering places, who go and come regularly under the *very eye* of the *law*, and who return, possibly, with the personal acquaintance of the black *Douglas* and the white GREELEY? . . . Of the throngs who flock to "Zion" decked off in silks, satins and feathers, in the face of, and in open violation of those laws which were enacted by the light of *bitter experience*?[74]

White southerners recognized that, as Thulani Davis notes, "Black movement was dangerous" because, for both enslaved and free African Americans, "movement led not only to freedom but also to knowledge—knowledge developed in meetings and gatherings, and knowledge put toward organizing."[75]

Rollin had already left the South by the time of John Brown's raid, but just as Harpers Ferry heralded the coming of an even more violent national schism over slavery, it also indicated the arrival of tighter restrictions on and harsher punishments for free Blacks in the Southern states. William and Margaret must have been glad that their intelligent and opinionated daughter was safely in Philadelphia, rather than carrying her "satchel well filled with books" through the streets of Charleston. Yet their association with the radical ICY, if widely known, would likely have cast doubt on their loyalty to South Carolina and the institution of slavery, despite their wealth, social status, and slave ownership. Sending her away meant removing her from the social circles that both sustained them and, they

72. Quoted in Biddle and Dubin, *Tasting Freedom*, 15.
73. Johnson and Roark, *Black Masters*, 159.
74. "Where Are We Drifting To?," *Charleston (SC) Mercury*, 25 Oct. 1859, 1.
75. Davis, *Emancipation Circuit*, 19.

likely imagined, would shape her future. The Rollins must have also feared that it meant that Frances could never return home.

From Charleston to Philadelphia and the Institute for Colored Youth

Having received as thorough an education as her father could provide her, Frances Rollin left for Philadelphia and the ICY in 1859. There she attempted to maintain her connections to her home and family and establish new relationships—not knowing that it would be years before she would return to Charleston. Just prior to her sister's departure, twelve-year-old Charlotte Rollin inscribed a poem in her sister's friendship album:

> To Frank,
> Frank, thy departure from me seem
> As if first awakened from a dream
> Alas I find that thou art gone
> And I am left here all alone.
> I'll think by day and night of thee,
> Can'st thou but do the same for me,
> While sailing o'er the surging sea
> Oh breathe one word of love for me[76]

Anticipating her grief at the upcoming absence of her sister, Lottie pledges to think of her "day and night." A year younger than Charlotte, eleven-year-old Katie is clearly no substitute for the big sister Lottie adores; she dramatically but earnestly pronounces herself "all alone" without "Frank." Frances no doubt did not need a reminder to think of her family and to miss their daily presence. The Rollins and their daughters likely wrote frequently to their "Frank" and received letters in return. Filling the "Album of the Heart" that was gifted to her before her departure from Charleston with the signatures of her friends and acquaintances at the ICY, Frances also worked to create a community that bridged geographical distance and, as the Civil War commenced, national and political difference. These relationships would sustain her throughout the war and beyond.

Rollin was certainly not on her own during her time in Philadelphia; indeed,

---

76. This poem is reproduced in Ione, *Pride of Family*, 123–24. Ione recalls viewing the album, titled "An Album of the Heart," while visiting Howard University. Librarians at Howard have been unable to locate the volume in their collections, so my discussion of it is based on Ione's account of her research.

she was likely comforted by the presence of other free Black residents with ties to Charleston. She boarded with the family of Morris Brown Jr., a shoe- and boot-maker who was born in Charleston around 1812, and Susan Venning Brown, born in Charleston around 1815. The couple had five children, ages five to twenty, all born in Philadelphia. Brown was the son of Morris Brown Sr., founder of the AME church in Charleston in 1816, one year after the birth of William Rollin. As Bernard Powers notes, "The formation of the African Church in Charleston was a rebellious act of revolutionary proportions."[77] In the first year of its existence, the church was harassed by white Charlestonians, who arrested 140 members, including Brown Sr., who, along with four other ministers, was threatened with a month-long imprisonment if he did not leave the state. Brown chose imprisonment. In 1822, after Vesey's planned slave insurrection was discovered, Brown and his church were targeted again because Vesey and several other co-conspirators were worshippers there. Although he had played no part in the plan, Brown was forced to leave the city, and the church was destroyed. Arriving in Philadelphia with his wife and two young sons, Brown became assistant pastor to the Reverend Richard Allen at the AME church at Sixth and Lombard Streets. He died ten years prior to Rollin's arrival in the city, but his family continued as active members of the church and would no doubt have fostered her attendance there. Although it is not clear whether Frances lived with the Brown family during the entirety of her stay in Philadelphia, they must have provided a welcome refuge for the young girl upon her arrival.

The Browns lived at 913 South Street on the edge of the Seventh Ward, which had the largest population of African Americans in the city but was still racially mixed. Their home was just blocks away from the ICY. At age fourteen and possessing a solid education, Rollin likely would have entered the high school, which required the ability to read, write, and spell; do arithmetic as far as simple division; and understand the geography of the United States. (Students without this background attended the preparatory school until they were ready.) Applicants for admission to the institute were also required to "be of good moral character and orderly habits," with preference given to those who desired to train "as teachers and instructors of youth."[78] Whether Rollin pronounced herself interested in becoming a teacher is unclear. Given the limited options available to educated women and the examples provided by her teachers at the ICY, she likely envisioned herself in such a role as she walked to and from school, studied her lessons,

---

77. Powers, *Black Charlestonians*, 21.
78. *Institute for Colored Youth By-Laws . . . and Rules*, 12.

and wrote compositions for her classes. By the time Rollin arrived in Philadelphia in 1859, the school at Lombard Street had been open for seven years and offered a rigorous curriculum, which included composition, classical languages (both Greek and Latin), sciences, mathematics (including algebra, geometry, and trigonometry), geography, and philosophy.

The principal teacher of the Female Department upon Rollin's arrival in Philadelphia was Grace A. Mapps, a well-respected and ambitious teacher who came to have an enormous influence on many Black women of Rollin's generation. Likely the first African American woman to graduate with a four-year college degree, Mapps became a member of the faculty in 1852; she was joined in 1853 by her cousin, Sarah Mapps Douglass, who became a teacher in the Girls' Department. During a brief visit to Philadelphia in 1868, Rollin laments her inability to see Mapps, calling her one of her "idols." Visiting with Douglass during that same trip, Rollin reflects, "I drew years of comfort from seeing her once more."[79] In a letter written just before her death in 1901, she calls Mapps and Douglass "two of the noblest, purest and best women that ever graced the earth," adding, "the beautiful lives of these pioneers of higher culture for women are a benediction and inspiration for the women of our time."[80] Clearly, the cousins provided emotional support and sustenance as well as intellectual guidance and mentorship to the young women in their charge.

Rollin's intelligence, taste, manners, and southern origins seem to have made her popular with other students at the ICY. A poem by a male classmate preserved in Rollin's album praises the virtues of the "Ladies Sewing Circle," paying particular attention to the charms of Rollin and calling her "a gem of far off Southern clime":

> A lady of superior mind, aye talent too and grace
> Of very keen perception and a highly polished taste
> Her gay and social qualities are sung by every mouth
> Miss Rollin is the "Pretty" brilliant Star of sunny South.[81]

Rollin mentions in her diary several friends who might have joined her in the Sewing Circle: Caroline LeCount, Lizzie Kennedy, and Sarah Iredell, all of whom

79. Rollin diary, 30 July 1868.
80. Quoted in Murray, "Sketch of Frances Anne Rollin."
81. This poem is reproduced in Ione, *Pride of Family*, 130. While the line breaks are indicated, it is not printed as a stanza. I have taken the liberty here to imagine what the poem might have looked like in the manuscript, as the original cannot be located.

Frances Anne Rollin. Leigh Rollin Whipper
Photograph Collection, Photographs and Prints
Division, Schomburg Center for Research in
Black Culture, New York Public Library Digital
Collections.

became teachers after they left the ICY. She was also clearly friendly with Octavius V. Catto, a graduate who became a teacher of English and mathematics at the
ICY from 1859 to 1866. Catto was born in Charleston in 1840, and his mother
was a member of the influential Dereef family, who owned a lumberyard near
that of the Rollins. The Cattos moved north to Philadelphia in 1848, but Octavius and Frances likely had many acquaintances in common. In Rollin's letter to
Daniel Murray, she also mentions studying with John Wesley Cromwell, who
later became a journalist, lawyer, and educator; James Baxter, educator and US
minister to Liberia; and Harriet C. Johnson, an educator who was the only female
delegate to attend the National Convention of the Colored Men of America in
Washington, DC, in January 1869.[82] With her hunger for intellectual engagement

82. Cromwell, Baxter, and Johnson are all mentioned in *Objects of the Institute for Colored
Youth*. Rollin is not listed, which indicates that she might have graduated already or had left
school without graduating. It is clear that she remained part of the ICY community, but she
may have been forced by her father's economic hardships to teach or perform some other type
of labor prior to returning to Charleston in 1865.

and political action, Rollin would have fit right in with this group of ambitious young people.

ICY students engaged enthusiastically in the intellectual, political, and social activities of the school. Frances surely took full advantage of the library, which was open to students as well as their families and began with thirteen hundred volumes, expanding to two thousand in ten years. It included a wide variety of texts, "from *Rural Chemistry* and *Civil Engineering* to biographies of Julius Caesar, Marie Antoinette, Hannibal, Isaac Newton, William Penn, Cortez, and Patrick Henry. Also, lives of religious greats: Martin Luther, Mohammed, the Quakers George Fox; [and] histories of Egypt, Rome, Macedonia, Persia, New York City, and . . . Africa."[83] The ICY no doubt maintained a subscription to the *Christian Recorder*, among other newspapers and periodicals. According to the "Rules for the Government of the Library and Reading Room," however, "Books of an immoral tendency, plays, novels, and romances shall be excluded, and care shall be taken to furnish such only as are likely to give useful information and improve the minds of the readers."[84] Rollin's interest in reading and writing history can be traced to the influence of the ICY's collection. Given her passion for reading and the frequent borrowing of books recorded in her diary in 1868, she probably took advantage of the opportunity to check out one carefully selected volume at a time, returning it, as required, without turning down the leaves or "in any way mutilat[ing] the books or periodicals."[85] She may have been inspired to send her own work to newspapers and magazines, as Fanny Jackson Coppin, who arrived at the ICY in 1865, remembered Rollin as "a bright scholar" who "contributed to the publications just at the close and after the Civil War."[86] It is unclear whether these contributions were prose or poetry, fiction or nonfiction; they were likely published anonymously or under a pseudonym and have not yet been located.

Rollin also no doubt attended the ICY's annual lecture series, which featured prominent African American intellectuals and activists. During her time at the school, featured guests included ICY teachers Sarah Mapps Douglass and Robert Campbell, physician and lawyer John S. Rock, minister Jonathan C. Gibbs, and activist and author Frederick Douglass. She likely also went to antislavery concerts, fairs, and speeches and celebrated the implementation of the Emancipation Proclamation on 1 January 1863. She surely attended the annual examination and

83. Biddle and Dubin, *Tasting Freedom*, 166.
84. *Institute for Colored Youth By-Laws . . . and Rules*, 17.
85. *Institute for Colored Youth By-Laws . . . and Rules*, 18–19.
86. Coppin, *Reminiscences of School Life*, 107.

graduation of students every spring. Here she watched her friends and classmates recite their lessons and receive awards for "diligence and good conduct," "regularity of attendance," and "general good scholarship."[87] Both lecturers and graduates no doubt provided Rollin with models of African American intellectual and political engagement.

Rollin may have had a suitor or at least a romantic crush during her time in Philadelphia. In her diary she alludes to memories of a man she calls "P," for whom she clearly cared deeply. Whether these feelings were reciprocated is unclear. On July 5, for example, she "retired about eleven oclock to dream of P." He may have been a minister or a minister-in-training: on April 6 she paraphrases Isaiah 63:1 ("Who is it who comes from Edom with dyed garments from Bozra!") and remembers having "heard P read that lesson the Monday night after the surrender of Lee. Memory cherished as fondly as ever." Less than two weeks later, Rollin left for Charleston, perhaps cutting short a relationship that may have led to marriage if not for the possibility of returning home.[88]

While students at the ICY had always been encouraged to see themselves as being "fit . . . for spheres of usefulness," the Civil War opened up new opportunities, energizing the young scholars.[89] In June 1863, as elements of General

---

87. "The Examination of the Pupils of the Philadelphia Institute for Colored Youth," *Christian Recorder*, 11 May 1861, 69.

88. One intriguing clue indicates that "P." may have been white. Rollin writes in her diary entry for 8 February 1868: "M brought me his Report to the African Conference there I saw the subscription list and the name among them that stirs a thousand memories. Is as but a shadow or hope, or is a tangible reality for me?" She likely refers here to William E. Matthews's report to the Executive Board of the AME church on his fundraising activities. The 1868 report is not extant, but the 1869 report includes a short list of individual subscribers from Philadelphia. Of the twelve subscribers, eleven are named; the twelfth is listed simply as "Friend" ("Report of Mr. William E. Matthews," *Missionary Reporter*, 1 Jan. 1869, 15). Of these eleven, I can identify seven, all of whom are white. Only one is a minister, and only one has a name that begins with "P": the Reverend Phillips Brooks (1835–93). This possibility is more intriguing given that Rollins refers to her mystery man as "Phil" on July 9, when she writes, "dreamed of seeing Phil last night. I wonder if he is here!" And on July 30, when she stopped in Philadelphia on her way home to South Carolina, she laments not seeing "Phillips nor Grace Mapps my idols." Brooks was ten years Rollin's senior and an Episcopal priest, first at Church of the Advent and then at Church of the Holy Trinity, both in Philadelphia. He was an active supporter of the antislavery movement and the Union effort in the Civil War. After Henry Ward Beecher, Brooks was likely the most popular preacher in nineteenth-century America, and his progressive social beliefs and intellectual approach to religious doctrine would have appealed to Rollin. Without the 1868 report, however, it is impossible to say whether he is the mysterious "P."

89. *Objects of the Institute for Colored Youth*, 13.

Robert E. Lee's Confederate army approached Pennsylvania, Catto and Principal Ebenezer Bassett joined a group of African American leaders who called for
Black men to join Philadelphia's defenses as soldiers and eventually to defend
Harrisburg, the state capital. Catto's company of ninety men included a number of ICY students. On June 15 Philadelphian Emilie Davis writes in her diary,
"i saw a company of colerd recruits they looked quite war like," and upon the
group's departure for Harrisonburg, she announced, "to day has bin the most
exsiting i ever witness."[90] The potential soldiers and the larger Black community
were disappointed, however, when the Union commander in charge of the defense of Pennsylvania refused the assistance of Catto's company because US law
did not allow Black enlistment. Despite this rejection, the ICY faculty continued
to support the enlistment of African American soldiers: a broadside written by
Bassett and signed by dozens of African American leaders, including Frederick
Douglass, calls for "Men of Color, Brothers and Fathers!" to "stop at no subter-
fuge, listen to nothing that shall deter you from rallying for the Army.... Strike
now! And you are henceforth and forever Freemen!"[91]

Douglass also actively encouraged ICY students to think about other ways
they could contribute to the war effort and improve the condition of the formerly
enslaved in the South. After a visit to the school in 1862, he reported favorably
on his "interviews" with both students and faculty in *Douglass's Monthly*: "We
say to our dear young friends, both teachers and pupils, go on in the pursuit of
knowledge. The vocation of the colored scholar on this continent is soon to be
enlarged. You will not only be wanted at Fortress Monroe [Virginia], at Beaufort
[South Carolina], and other points along the slave coast of our country, but all

90. Emilie Davis diary, 15–16, 17–18 June 1863, vol. 1, Emilie Davis Diaries, Digital Collections, Penn State University Libraries, https://libraries.psu.edu/about/collections/emilie-davis
-diaries. Davis used a preprinted diary, with three pages per day, but in writing about a day, she
often used the space provided for the next day as well. Thus, it is difficult at times to provide a
precise date for an entry. Davis's use of nonstandard English also provides challenges to a tran-
scriber and editor. There are two published editions of Davis's diary, neither of which I quote
from here. While the edition by Judith Ann Giesberg retains Davis's spelling and punctuation,
the transcription is not entirely accurate. Karsonya Wise Whitehead's transcription is more
accurate in her edition, but she adds spelling corrections in brackets and inserts punctuation
marks. I have transcribed from the original diary using the cited digital scan provided by Penn
State University Library's Digital Collections.

91. "Men of Color" Recruitment Broadside, 1863, object 2012.133, Collection of the Smithsonian National Museum of African American History and Culture, Washington DC, https://
nmaahc.si.edu/object/nmaahc_2012.133.

"Men of Color" recruitment broadside, 1863. National Museum of African American History and Culture.

over the South."[92] Rollin may not have read Douglass's letter on his Philadelphia visit, but she surely attended the May 10 graduation of the class of 1864, at which Catto gave an inspiring speech about the responsibilities of the students in the world opening up before them:

> Those millions of human beings now scattered through the Southern country must eventually come forth into the sunlight of Freedom; and what a field will there then be opened for the benevolence of the wealthy, and the labors of the educated colored man! . . .
>
> Those people will need among them Christian missionaries, intelligent teachers and laborers, to direct them to that course of life and in those modes of industry which have always in the world's history contributed so much for peoples similarly situated. It is for the purpose of promoting, as far as possible, the preparation of the colored man for the assumption of the new relations with intelligence and with the knowledge which promises success that the Institute feels called upon at this time to act with more energy and on [a] broader scale than has heretofore been required. . . . It is the duty of every man, to the extent of his interests and means, to provide for the immediate improvement of the four or five millions of ignorant and previously dependent laborers who will be thrown upon society in the reorganization of the Union.[93]

The first to answer such a call was not a "colored man," but a woman. Enumerating the achievements of ICY graduates, Catto noted especially "the pioneer from our ranks," Sallie Daffin, who was "engaged in the commendable task of instructing the Freed children at Norfolk in Virginia."[94] Daffin, who was seven years older than Rollin, had entered the institute just a year before her, in 1858, having attended school previously until the age of eleven and then worked as a dressmaker. She graduated in 1860 and, as Eric Gardner notes, likely published her "first widely distributed text—an obituary of A.M.E. stalwart Jabez P. and Mary A. Campbell's son Gerrit Smith Campbell that appeared in the October

92. Frederick Douglass, "A Recent Visit to Philadelphia," *Douglass's Monthly*, Feb. 1862, 593–94.

93. Octavius Catto, "Our Alma Mater: An Address," 10 May 1864, A Great Thing for Our People: Institute for Colored Youth in the Civil War Era, online exhibit, Falvey Library, Villanova University, https://exhibits.library.villanova.edu/institute-colored-youth/their-own-words/our-alma-mater-address, accessed 6 June 2025.

94. Catto, "Our Alma Mater."

1859 issue of the *Repository of Religion*—while still a student at the institute."[95] Daffin's early publication may have inspired Rollin to send her own work out for consideration. As Catto intended, Daffin's service as a teacher almost certainly influenced Rollin to consider returning home to Charleston to teach the South Carolina freemen. She was among the first of the approximately sixty-five ICY students to teach in freedmen's schools throughout the South.[96]

The Work of Reconstruction in Charleston

For Frances Rollin, the South was not, as it was initially for Sallie Daffin, "a conceptual space, a missionary field, rather than a concrete location."[97] Instead, the South was home. In Philadelphia in July 1863, Rollin must have watched with mixed excitement and fear as the Union army began the siege of Charleston, blockading the harbor as well. Her father, mother, and sisters remained in the city, as did the mixed-race community among whom she had lived as a child. In her biography of Martin Delany, Rollin writes about the harrowing experiences of Black families under siege, vulnerable to the bombardment no matter where their loyalties lay. She describes "one case of sad interest" in which a twelve-year-old boy named Weston McKinlay was killed when a shell hit his grandfather's home.[98] The fate of this child, the grandson of Anthony Weston, one of the wealthiest of Charleston's Black elite, would likely have been known to Rollin because of her acquaintance with the family.

Returning to Charleston, Rollin would have found her beloved hometown nearly unrecognizable. A fire in December 1861 had burned 164 acres of the city, including the Cathedral of St. John and St. Finbar, damage that, with the war raging, had remained unrepaired. The Union naval bombardment of Charleston destroyed much of what had escaped the fire. White Northern journalists seemed stunned by the destruction. Whitelaw Reid called Charleston the "City of Desolation" in his 1866 account, and that same year Sidney Andrews similarly describes "a city of ruins, of desolation, of vacant houses, of widowed women, of rotting wharves, of deserted warehouses, of weed-wild gardens, of miles of grass-grown streets, of acres of pitiful and voiceful barrenness."[99] Both Reid and Andrews lament the destruction of Charleston but seem ambivalent about the scenes

---

95. Gardner, *Unexpected Places*, 142.

96. Butchart, *Schooling the Freed People*, 26. See also Butchart et al., "Freedmen's Teacher Project."

97. Gardner, *Unexpected Places*, 144–45.

98. Rollin, *Life and Public Services*, 191.

99. Reid, *After the War*, 57; Andrews, *South since the War*, 1.

View of ruined buildings through porch of the Circular Church (150 Meeting Street), attributed to George N. Barnard. Civil War Photographs, 1861–65, Prints and Photographs Division, Library of Congress.

they encounter. For example, Reid compares the "mad era" of secession in 1861 with the subdued and depressing streets of the postwar city: "There are crowds of armed men in the streets, but they move under the strictest discipline and their color is black. No battle blood mantles the faces of the haggard and listless Charlestonians one meets—it is rather blood born of low diet and water gruel. For the flush of victory we have utter despondency."[100] In the *Christian Recorder*, on the other hand, a Black correspondent who identifies himself as having been born in the city recounts returning home in August 1866 to see "unmistakable traces" of fire and siege: "hundreds of tall chimneys are still standing in spite of storm and lightning, as monuments of the terrible retribution of the Almighty upon a sinful and stiff-necked people." He adds, "It appears from these facts that the Almighty intends to have Charleston to remain as a warning to those who

100. Reid, *After the War*, 66.

wished to erect a government in the cornerstone of which was to have rested the abominable system of human slavery for all persons of African descent, who might happen to be within their domain."[101] This correspondent considered the price of emancipation worth the destruction.

Rollin likely agreed, even though the war had significantly altered the fortunes of her family. According to Carole Ione, the young woman returned to Charleston to find her father's lumber business ruined by the war. He and the family now relied on the sale of vegetables to Confederate troops to survive.[102] Moreover, when Union soldiers had encroached on his land at the end of the war, the livestock there were appropriated to feed the army and William Rollin was shot.[103] While his wounds were not serious, he must have wondered whether the liberation of Charleston was as good for free people of color like him as it was for the enslaved.

Ironically, it is entirely possible that the soldier who shot Rollin was African American. On 18 February 1865, the Twenty-First US Colored Infantry, made up at least in part of formerly enslaved men from Hilton Head, South Carolina, was among the first Union soldiers to enter Charleston, and their commanding officer ordered the regiment to assist the local freedmen in putting out the fires set by departing Confederate soldiers and random troublemakers.[104] On the twenty-first, another Black regiment, the Fifty-Fifth Massachusetts Infantry, entered the city. In her Delany biography, Rollin describes the "solider, mounted on a mule," who "dashed up Meeting Street, at the head of the advancing column, bearing in his hand, as he rode, a white flag which was inscribed, in large black letters, LIBERTY! and loudly proclaiming it as he went."[105] The Fifty-Fifth set up camp on the Charleston Neck, where Rollin had lived as a child and her family likely still resided.[106] A little more than a week later, the Fifty-Fourth Massachusetts Infantry, famous for their doomed assault on Fort Wagner less than two years earlier,

101. A Charlestonian, "Impressions of Charleston.—No. 1," *Christian Recorder*, 18 Aug. 1866, 129.

102. Ione, *Pride of Family*, 131.

103. Lila [Leighla] Whipper to Dorothy Sterling, 7 Feb. 1969, Sterling Papers; Ione, *Pride of Family*, 131.

104. Egerton, *Thunder at the Gates*, 270.

105. Rollin, *Life and Public Services*, 198–99.

106. Egerton, *Thunder at the Gates*, 270. It is not clear where the Rollin family lived after the war. Tax books for the City of Charleston have William Rollin at Henrietta Street in 1862 and King Street Road in 1863, both of which are located in the Charleston Neck. See Tax Book: Charleston Free Persons of Color, 1862; and Tax Book: Charleston Free Persons of Color, 1863, Charleston County Public Library, microfilm.

marched up King and Meeting Streets.[107] For the next six months, troops from these regiments occupied Charleston and its surroundings, maintaining order as angry whites resisted the loss of their city and, a few months later, the end of the war. With his light-colored skin, William Rollin may have initially been mistaken for one of the resistant Confederates—he may in fact have felt ambivalent about the arrival of Union troops in Charleston.

Sensitive to the loss of their authority over African Americans, both free and enslaved, white Southerners resisted Black independence and success. One likely representative white Charleston woman complained, "the city is guarded entirely by negro troops, [and] one cannot go out without being jostled by flaunting mulattos with *their* soldier beaux (white sometimes), or having favorite songs shouted in your face such as 'Down with the rebel' 'Hang Jeff Davis on the sour apple tree' 'I'll never be a slave.'"[108] During the fall of 1865, South Carolina's government passed the Black Codes, which effectively forced recently emancipated African Americans into unequal relationships with Southern employers. These laws demanded that Black "servants" address their employers as "master" and required laborers to work from dawn to dusk. They also imposed curfews, limited the right of laborers to marry, and generally attempted to restrict the upward mobility of African Americans. While many of these codes would not have directly affected the Rollin family, their passage conveyed white Southerners' resistance to change and hostility to all African Americans, regardless of skin color or status prior to the Civil War.

Recently returned from the North, Frances Rollin would have known some of the soldiers in the Fifty-Fourth and Fifty-Fifth Massachusetts, and she rapidly became acquainted with those she did not know. Like them, she had attended school in the North, traveling South to serve her country and her people when called. She did not fight on the battlefield, but the soldiers likely recognized a fellow traveler on what Thulani Davis calls "the Emancipation Circuit." While in Boston in 1868, Rollin received a visit from William H. Dupree and James Monroe Trotter, both Black soldiers who served in the Fifty-Fifth and spent the remainder of the war after the fall of Charleston occupying that city and nearby Orangeburg.[109] Rollin also visited with the white officer Joshua B. Treadwell, assistant surgeon for the Fifty-Fourth, both gossiping about his fellow surgeon Charles E. Briggs's flirtation with Charleston widow and author Susan Petigru King.[110] These visits are likely indications of a much larger acquaintance with the

107. Egerton, *Thunder at the Gates*, 271.
108. Quoted in Powers, *Black Charlestonians*, 78.
109. Rollin diary, 24 May 1868.
110. Rollin diary, 3 July 1868.

soldiers of the Fifty-Fourth and Fifty-Fifth in the months following the city's capture. For example, Rollin likely knew Stephen A. Swails, one of the few Black soldiers who, along with Trotter, was promoted to second lieutenant, during the early occupation of Charleston. Swails remained in the city after the war, marrying Susan Aspinall, a young mixed-race woman approximately Rollin's age, whose family seems to have been intimate with hers. Frances and Susan may have been childhood friends prior to Frances's departure for Philadelphia. In 1868 Stephen Swails became a state senator and was friendly with Rollin's future husband, William J. Whipper, visiting the couple two days after their wedding.[111] Just prior to her wedding, Rollin (soon to be Rollin Whipper) reported visits from the Aspinalls, likely Susan's parents, as well as several other local families.[112]

Rollin's most intimate acquaintance from the Massachusetts regiments was probably Charles Lenox, a barber from Watertown, Massachusetts, who was twenty years her senior. Lenox was the cousin of Charles Lenox Remond and Sarah Parker Remond, the Black abolitionist activists and lecturers from Salem, Massachusetts. Serving in the Fifty-Fourth, he survived the brutal assault against Fort Wagner, during which he held the regimental standard. In 1868 Lenox visited Rollin frequently in Boston, sometimes accompanying her on outings, and the two exchanged letters when he could not visit. Despite the pleasure they obviously took in one another's company, she seems never to have taken him seriously as a suitor. He may have indicated a disinterest in marriage due to ill health; in an entry from early May, Rollin first calls him a "hypochondriac" but then reinterprets his condition as "diplomacy," concluding: "A noble self sacrifice he has made through life for his father's sake. God will reward him someday."[113] Indeed, Lenox never married and lived with his father until John Lenox's death in 1887.

Whatever her own father's loyalties, Rollin must have been overjoyed to see her family for the first time in nearly six years. Despite some researchers' claims that Charlotte, Louisa, and Kate had followed their older sister north to be educated in Boston and Philadelphia, there is little evidence to prove that they ever left Charleston during the war.[114] They likely continued their education throughout

---

111. Rollin diary, 19 Sept. 1868.

112. Rollin diary, 29 Aug. 1868.

113. Rollin diary, 3 May 1868.

114. Carole Ione writes that Frances Rollin's "sisters Charlotte, Louisa, and Kate followed Frank to Philadelphia." She adds, "Charlotte and Kate also spent some time in Boston, enrolled at Dr. Dio Lewis's Family School for Young Ladies" (*Pride of Family*, 129). These claims are repeated in Dakers, *SC Suffragists*, and other sources. Dakers adds that Louisa attended a convent school in Philadelphia and explains that all the sisters remained in the North during the Civil

the war in Charleston private schools like those attended by Frances prior to her departure for Philadelphia. But given white concerns about Black literacy and the strain that war put upon relationships between free Blacks and their white neighbors, the Rollins would likely have kept relatively quiet about any educational or professional ambitions they might have had for their girls. Whatever education they received was apparently sufficient to qualify both Charlotte and Katherine (Kate) to teach in schools for Black children following the war.

The three Rollin sisters were among the thousands of men and women who taught in freedmen's schools opened in Southern states, first as the Union army occupied territory from Norfolk, Virginia, and Port Royal, South Carolina, to New Orleans, Louisiana, and then as the war ended in April 1865. While Southern teachers like the Rollins responded to the need in their own communities, Northern teachers were sponsored by organizations like the American Missionary Association (AMA), the National Freedmen's Relief Association, and the New England Freedmen's Aid Society. The first Northern Black educator to go South as a teacher was Charlotte Forten (later Grimké). She first approached the Port Royal Commission in Boston for assistance, but when they disappointed her—"They were not sending women at present"—she obtained the assistance of the Philadelphia Port Royal Relief Association.[115] In a letter to the AMA on January 18, 1864, New York native Edmonia G. Highgate likely expressed the feelings

---

War, unable to return home. The root of this misunderstanding may be the reliance on two articles published in New York newspapers in 1871: A. P., "The Queens of the South," *Sun* (New York), 29 Mar. 1871, 2; and "South Carolina," *New York Herald*, 13 June 1871, 15–16. The author of "Queens" claims that all of the Rollin sisters "were educated in Boston," while the author of "South Carolina" represents either Charlotte or Katherine telling a reporter: "Two of the girls have been educated at Dr. Dio Lewis' school, No. 29 Essex Street, Boston, and though Wendell Phillips sends his niece and the best families send their children there, we never found any one to sneer at us in that school. Louisa was educated at a convent school, in Philadelphia." The 1860 US census lists William and Margaret Rollin in Charleston with all of their daughters except for Frances, who was living in Philadelphia with the Browns. At the time Charlotte was thirteen years old, Kitty (or Kate) twelve, Louisa five, and Florence two. It would have been difficult for any of the girls to travel north during the war, especially after 1863, when Union forces began an active military campaign against Charleston harbor. Moreover, Dio Lewis's school for girls did not open until 1864 and was located in Lexington, Massachusetts. While Lewis did operate a business on Essex Street during the war, it was a gymnasium that offered physical education classes for men, women, and children as well as advanced training for "teachers of physical education" (Leonard, *Guide to the History of Physical Education*, 352). There is no evidence that either the gymnasium or the Lexington school accepted African American students.

115. Grimké, *Journals*, 14 Sept. 1862.

of many African American teachers when she writes of her desire to go "South or Southwest as [a] missionary. I have been engaged as teacher for two years and a half among my own people. . . . I know just what selfdenial, selfdiscipline and domestic qualifications are needed for the work and modestly trust that with God's help I could labor advantageously in the field for my newly freed brethren."[116] In March 1864 Highgate arrived in Norfolk, Virginia, where she taught a class of fifty second-grade students.[117]

Rollin does not seem to have contracted with any association before setting out on her journey from Philadelphia to Charleston. Just before her death, she remembered leaving Philadelphia "the very day Pres. Lincoln's remains passed through that city."[118] Lincoln's funeral train arrived in Philadelphia on 22 April 1865, which means that Rollin likely arrived home a few days later. She had surely heard from family and friends in the two months since Charleston fell to the Union army and either felt confident that she would find a teaching position or was simply too eager to get home to her family to care. Following the city's capture, white journalist and abolitionist James Redpath was named South Carolina superintendent of education, and on 4 March 1865, the Morris Street School became the first public school in the city open to Black children. When the students proved too numerous, six other schools were opened in the city, with more than 3,000 students in attendance. "Eighty-three teachers are employed," Redpath reported in the *New York Times*: "Seventy-four of them residents of Charleston before the evacuation by the insurgents. . . . No tests but loyalty and efficiency have been applied to applicants for positions as teachers. Necessity has compelled me to overlook the latter qualification in some instances, but this inconvenience will quickly be remedied. The best teachers will soon be in charge of all the schools."[119] In early summer of 1865, Reuben Tomlinson replaced Redpath of superintendent of education. By January 1866, Tomlinson reported the establishment of thirty-six schools in the state and noted, "scattered throughout the State, primarily in country places, a number of small schools [existed], taught by colored men and women, who have succeeded in mastering the arts of reading and writing." Such schools, he observed, "indicate an universal desire on the part of the freedmen for the means of education, and are a promise that they will not be slow to avail themselves of such means whenever they are placed within their

116. Highgate to Whipple, 18 Jan. 1864, in Sterling, *We Are Your Sisters*, 194–95.
117. Highgate to Whipple, 1 June 1864, in Sterling, *We Are Your Sisters*, 295–96.
118. Quoted in Murray, "Sketch of Frances Rollin Whipper."
119. "The Public Schools in Charleston," *New York Times*, 16 Apr. 1865, 3.

reach."[120] Many early teachers were replaced by better qualified applicants, but even in this atmosphere, Rollin had no difficulty finding employment.

Miss Frances Rollin, "Charleston Teacher"

By 1 May 1865, Rollin was working for Thomas W. Cardozo at Charleston's Saxton School, named after Union General and Freedmen's Bureau Assistant Commissioner Rufus B. Saxton, and being paid by the AMA. Thomas Cardozo and his brother, Francis L. Cardozo, were native Charlestonians born to a white Jewish father and a free African American mother named Lydia Weston. Like Rollin, the brothers had left Charleston in the late 1850s to continue their schooling, Thomas in New York City and Francis in Scotland. Returning with his family to Charleston in April 1865, Thomas supervised the educational activities of the AMA, hiring six African American "Charleston teachers," some of whom he reported as having been his "schoolmates."[121] These teachers were Henry S. Spencer, William O. Weston, Mary F. Weston, Margaret Sasportas, Amelia Shrewsbury, and "Miss Frances Rollin." In a letter to Reverend M. E. Strieby of the AMA, Cardozo reported that Rollin was "22 yrs of age, was educated at the Institute for Colored Youth in Philadelphia, is a member of the Prot. Episcopal Church, and presented a satisfactory letter from Rev. William J. Alston of Phil."[122] This "satisfactory letter" indicates Rollin's positive reputation as a student at the ICY as well as her movement away from the Roman Catholicism of her youth. Her Protestant conversion also seems to have facilitated her work as a teacher. In an earlier letter about the hiring of white teachers, Cardozo had reassured Strieby, "None of them are Catholic." This was apparently as important as their promise "to instruct the col. Children to the best of [their] ability and be as diligent with them as [they] would with white children."[123]

According to a report from early November 1865, Rollin taught reading, arithmetic, geography, and writing to a class of fifty "Intermediate" boys at the Saxton school.[124] These pupils may not have been the same children from week to week, at least initially. In a letter written to the *National Freedmen* and published in June

120. "From Reuben Tomlinson," *National Freedmen*, 15 Feb. 1866, 55.

121. Thomas Cardozo to M. E. Strieby, 16 June 1865, Black Abolitionist Papers.

122. Cardodo to Strieby, 16 June 1865.

123. Thomas Cardozo to M. E. Strieby, 10 May 1865, Edmund Lee Drago Collection, Avery Research Center, transcription.

124. Francis L. Cardozo to Samuel Hunt, 7 November 1865, Black Abolitionist Papers.

1865, James Redpath explained that many children "passed through our schools on their way from the interior to the islands . . . remaining just long enough with us to be taught three or four patriotic songs, to keep quiet, and to be decently clad, and then going off to give place to others, who will receive the same instruction and discipline and be shipped off." While Redpath did not "regret this movement," believing "it is full of promise for the future of the emancipated race," it must have been difficult for teachers like Rollin, already managing the demands of a large class of children with different gifts and experiences, many of whom had until recently been enslaved.[125] Instruction time lasted approximately three or four hours a day, beginning at 9:00 a.m. The job likely required large amounts of time and energy from teachers, many of whom were, like Rollin, relatively new to the profession. White physician and teacher Esther Hill Hawks writes in her diary on 26 July 1865 about visiting Thomas Cardozo's school: "Mr. Cardozo has several teachers and himself in the Normal Building, but everyone looked tired and worn, and the teachers especially were looking with great eagerness to its close."[126] Whether Rollin was one of the teachers Hawks encountered, she likely shared their exhaustion. The work did not conclude with the end of the school day either; teachers often conducted evening classes for adults and visited families to encourage school attendance and to see to the other needs of students. They also had to tolerate the hostility of white Charlestonians: Francis Cardozo told an AMA official that one Southern woman, "very finely dressed, and apparently quite lady like, stopped at the door the other day, while the children were singing, and said, 'Oh, I wish, I could put a torch to that building!'"[127]

Thomas Cardozo was dismissed from his appointment after a scandal involving a sexual affair with a student in Flushing, New York, where he had taught prior to coming South. His brother Francis soon took over the Charleston schools. In October Francis wrote to Reverend Samuel Hunt at the AMA complaining that there were no teachers waiting for him upon his arrival and the opening of the school. While he wanted "Northern teachers" for the school—"It would be better for the schools to have all, or nearly all the Teachers from the North"—he decided, "perhaps it is best to encourage the native Teachers." He took it upon himself to "hire four of the best of those that my brother employed last Spring": William Weston, Mary Weston, Shrewsbury, and Rollin.[128] Interestingly, these "native Teachers" knew their worth and demanded much higher salaries than they

125. James Redpath, "Charleston," *National Freedmen*, 1 June 1865, 150.
126. Hawks, *Woman Doctor's Civil War*, 168.
127. Francis L. Cardozo to George Whipple, 27 Jan. 1866, Drago Collection, transcription.
128. Francis L. Cardozo to Samuel Hunt, 10 Oct. 1865, Black Abolitionist Papers.

had received just months earlier: William Weston, who had been paid twenty-five dollars a month in June, asked for fifty dollars a month; Mary Weston and Frances Rollin each demanded forty dollars, rather than the fifteen dollars they had received in the summer. "These Teachers all wanted an immediate definite answer from me *before* engaging with me," Cardozo explained, "as they wanted to compare the salary of our Assn with that given by the Boston society, and accept the largest."[129] Hunt did not take Cardozo's advice, however, and paid Rollin only twenty-five dollars for her work at the end of November.[130] Presumably, the AMA thought they could pay Charleston teachers less because they often lived at home with their families. But combined with the conscious or unconscious underestimation of the skills and background of Black teachers, this treatment would have left Rollin open to considering other professional opportunities.[131]

Sometime in 1865, Rollin began to work for the Presbyterian Commission of Missions for Freedmen, teaching at the Zion School in Charleston under its principal, Mahlon Van Horne, a minister originally from New Jersey. In December 1865 *Harper's Weekly* published an engraving of a scene from a classroom at the Zion School, noting: "It is a peculiarity of this school that it is entirely under the superintendence of colored teachers. . . . It was the last of the colored schools established on the close of the rebellion by the Northern philanthropists—at whose expense they are maintained—and it had to provide for a harder set among its pupils, in some cases the refuse of other schools. This delayed its progress for some time; but when your artist visited it in July last, it was exhibiting a steady improvement under its principal, Mr. VAN HORN, of New Jersey."[132] While the accompanying image depicts a male teacher at the front of the class, three female teachers look on: two at the back of the room and one sitting in a chair at the front, seemingly with a book in her hand. It is tempting to imagine that one of these figures is Frances Rollin.

It is unclear how long Rollin taught at the Zion School. She is not listed as a teacher there in the May 1867 report from the Committee on Freedmen. Yet she remained in the Charleston area throughout most of 1867 and may have considered joining her sisters in their effort to open a Catholic day school for African American boys and girls on Line Street, despite her seeming departure from the

129. Cardozo to Hunt, 10 Oct. 1865.

130. Francis L. Cardozo to William E. Whiting, 22 Nov. 1865, Black Abolitionist Papers.

131. Mary Weston continued to hold out for a higher salary, threatening to leave the school and teach elsewhere. She eventually received a salary of thirty-five dollars a month (Francis L. Cardozo to Samuel Hunt, 9 Dec. 1865, Black Abolitionist Papers; Francis L. Cardozo to William E. Whiting, 30 Dec. 1865, Black Abolitionist Papers).

132. A. R. W., "Zion School, Charleston, S.C.," *Harper's Weekly*, 15 Dec. 1865, 790.

"'Zion' School for Colored Children, Charleston, South Carolina." From *Harper's Weekly*, 15 December 1866.

Roman Catholic Church. Both Charlotte and Kate had begun teaching in the freedmen's schools in 1865 under the auspices of the New England Freedmen's Aid Society.[133] By January 1867, they had apparently decided to strike out on their own. An advertisement for the school announced that, in addition to "Biblical Exercises," "Rhetorical Exercises," and "Plain and Ornamental Needle Work" (presumably for their female students), "the course of instruction will embrace the primary and more advanced branches of a liberal English education, such as the Alphabet, Spelling, Reading, Writing, Arithmetic, Grammar and Geography, . . . English Composition, History, Natural Philosophy, and Cutter's Anatomy."[134] The sisters worked to remind Bishop Patrick Neeson Lynch of his obligations

133. See Butchart et al., "Freedmen's Teacher Project." The source also lists a "Marie Louise Rollin" as having taught in Charleston in 1866–67 for the Presbyterian Committee of Missions for Freedmen, but this seems unlikely to have been Louisa Rollin, as she was only nine years old in 1867. For confirmation of Charlotte and Katie's employment, see "List of Teachers Now in Service," *Freedmen's Record*, Dec. 1865, 203.

134. "Day School for Colored Girls and Boys," reverse of letter from Charlotte and Catherine Rollin to Bishop Patrick Neeson Lynch, 29 Nov. 1867, Item 41S1, Pre-Diocesan and Episcopal Papers, Archives and Record Management Office, Roman Catholic Diocese of Charleston.

to them and their school, writing to ask for money for rent and supplies and reminding him that "the church should meet the question fairly and squarely of educating its black members, and act on it with courage and candor, it is right they should *be educated* and *let the church so declare it.*"[135] This commitment, they insisted, had to be accompanied by compensation for the sisters' work, as they "can't subsist on air." They continued: "We have been teaching earnestly & as we hope faithfully since January all now without compensation and our *modus operandi* for the present (if you will sanction it,) is that one of us will take care of the school and the other proceed to NY, Philada & Boston with letters from you to the Roman Catholic Bishops there and lay the status of the school before them and our purpose in forming it. Being identified with the blacks by blood and complexion doubtless our efforts to obtain assistance will be signally crowned with success."[136]

Whether Bishop Lynch provided the Rollin sisters with letters to Northern bishops, at least one of the sisters did travel north to seek support for the school. On 30 November 1867, a letter from "W." appeared in the *National Anti-Slavery Standard* reporting on a meeting of Quakers pledged to "'the aid and elevation of the freedmen.'" In addition to Frances Ellen Watkins Harper, who "was present by invitation" to talk about "her journey through several of the Southern states," guests included "a colored woman named Mrs. Higate" (likely Hannah Francis Highgate, mother of teacher Edmonia G. Highgate), who had taught the freedmen in Mississippi, and "a young colored woman who hails from Charleston, South Carolina. Her name is Rollins."

Upwards of two years this young woman and her sister have been teaching in their native city. Their school has numbered as many as one hundred and thirteen children. These comprise the poorest of the poor, the lowliest of the lowly, the very outcasts of a miserable and neglected class. With singular benevolence of spirit, these two sisters have applied themselves to the work of gathering these wretched little ones together, and giving them instruction. Thus have they been engaged over two years without receiving or soliciting compensation from any source, presenting a rare example of

135. Charlotte and Catherine Rollin to Bishop Patrick Neeson Lynch, 21 Feb. 1867, Item 39E7; Charlotte and Catherine Rollin to Lynch, 3 Nov. 1867, Item 41M7, both in Pre-Diocesan and Episcopal Papers, Archives and Record Management Office, Roman Catholic Diocese of Charleston.

136. Charlotte and Catherine Rollin to Lynch, 3 Nov. 1867.

active philanthropy and personal devotion in a forlorn field of labor. May they have a sure reward!

The present mission of Miss Rollins is to secure funds to aid in the erection of a suitable school building, as well as to ask for some tangible encouragement for herself and sister in the prosecution of their labor of charity and love.[137]

Despite their interest in the presentation, "W." lamented the inability of the organization to grant any funds to "Miss Rollins." Likely because of this and other failures, there is no evidence that the Rollin school survived past the summer of 1868.[138]

Frances Rollin and the *Pilot Boy*

After teaching at the Zion School, Frances is next found in the historical record on 22 July 1867 being refused a first-class ticket on the ferry *Pilot Boy* going from Charleston to Beaufort, South Carolina, a town on Port Royal Island, one of the largest of the Sea Islands. Occupied by the Union army early in the war and largely abandoned by the white planters who had established it as a summer retreat, Beaufort was central to the work of the Freedmen's Bureau. Rollin sued the white captain of the *Pilot Boy*, W. T. McNelty, under a military order that required equal access to all races on streetcars and steamboats throughout the state. Her actions were likely precipitated by the streetcar protests in cities like Richmond, New Orleans, Savannah, and Philadelphia earlier that year. After the governor of Pennsylvania signed a law prohibiting discrimination on streetcars on 22 March 1867, Rollin's friend Carrie LeCount was refused access to a streetcar. She took a copy of the law to a police officer who then arrested the conductor and fined him $100.[139] Protests in Charleston in March and April resulted in the ejection of an African American woman named Mary P. Bowers from a streetcar on 17 April. Bowers filed a complaint with the Freedmen's Bureau, which resulted in the Charleston City Railway Company decision on 3 May 1867 to open streetcar service to "all

137. W., "Philadelphia Correspondence," *National Anti-Slavery Standard*, 30 November 1867, 2.

138. Charlotte and Kate seem to have gone north once again in the early 1870s to solicit funding, perhaps for another school. For a discussion of Lucretia Mott's account of their visit, see Ione, *Pride of Family*, 175–76.

139. See "Caroline LeCount (1846–1923)," A Great Thing for Our People: Institute for Colored Youth in the Civil War Era, online exhibit, Falvey Library, Villanova University, https://exhibits.library.villanova.edu/institute-colored-youth/graduates/caroline-lecount-bio, accessed 6 June 2025; and Biddle and Dubin, *Tasting Freedom*, 352.

persons." Assistant Commissioner Robert Kingston Scott wrote to the president of the company, "Allow me to congratulate you that a spirit of liberality has prevailed in your counsels, and I feel confident that the colored people of this city will appreciate your acquiescence in a demand which is sanctioned by the spirit of the age."[140] McNelty apparently felt no such "spirit of liberality" and resisted efforts by the Freedmen's Bureau to force him to open first-class passage to African Americans.

On 30 July 1867, the case was tried at the Citadel, the former military academy that US troops had occupied since the end of the war, and the Rollin sisters' sworn testimony provides a clear account of the confrontation with McNelty. It also offers a glimpse of the bond between these bright young women, all of whom seem to share a sardonic wit and a strong sense of their own worth. According to Frances's testimony, on 22 July the sisters and their father went to Accommodation Wharf, opposite 176 East Bay Street, so that Frances could take the steamer to Beaufort. Frances told her interviewer that she had "business of great importance" to tend to there but, disappointingly, does not specify its nature. Departing from their house at 224 Meeting Street, less than a mile away from their former home at the corner of Washington and Chapel, the Rollins may have proceeded along North Market Avenue, crossing through the bustling City Market, likely already busy in the early morning hours. Frances and her father boarded the boat to buy a ticket and encountered the stewardess. The clerk recorded Frances's narrative of the events as follows:

> He [William Rollin] said . . . , I wish you would take care of my daughter, she came some answer that she cant come here she will have to go aft, this is $8, he said he expected to pay that price he asked the reason, she said she had nothing to do with it & he would have to see the Purser, my sister went off with my father & returned & said they refuse to sell a first class ticket & you cant go. While about leaving Mr. Ferguson asked what was the matter, my father said my daughter has been refused a 1st class passage on the boat, & did not see what the objection was that I was as good as any lady in the land, Mr Ferguson then asked how many were going I told him there was but one going and that one had as much right as any one else.[141]

140. "The City Car Difficulty," *Charleston (SC) Daily News*, 6 May 1867, 1.

141. Frances Rollin Testimony, Captain W. T. McNelty Court-Martial, 30 July 1867, case file OO-2437, Entry 15AA, Court-Martial Case Files 1894–1917, Record Group 153, Records of the Office of the Judge Advocate General, National Archives and Records Administration, Washington, DC.

Frances and her father asserted her right to first-class passage on economic and class terms: she had the money to pay for passage and was "as good as any lady in the land." Race, they implied, should have nothing to do with it.

Ferguson, the co-owner of Accommodation Wharf, went in search of Captain McNelty, who was directed to explain the situation to the Rollins. Interestingly, Frances's sisters proceed to berate McNelty for his prejudice, not waiting for their father to take the lead; in this scene one gets a sense of their confidence and self-assertion as well as William Rollin's approval of and pride in their resistance. Katie testified: "I asked Capt. McNelty if he refused to sell a first-class ticket to persons on account of complexion. . . . Capt. McNelty shrugged his shoulders and answered indifferently, 'Yes,' and afterwards said his Boat was too small," meaning, presumably, that he did not have room to adequately separate white and Black passengers.[142] Charlotte later continued, "I told him Francis was not such a very large person, that it was not necessary to charter an extra size boat to convey her." The sisters' next comments indicate that the encounter may have been a planned protest, like those involving Black women on streetcars: "Katie told him she had supposed that Gen Sickles G.[eneral] O.[rder] removed such obstacles, assuming a contemptuous curl of the lip he [McNulty] said it did not hold good to his boat. I told him that I believed though his boat insignificant, the order held good to it, & he [would] find out if he didn't believe it."[143] On August 17 the court found McNelty guilty and fined him $250.[144] The notice of the decision was reprinted throughout the state and beyond, demonstrating the commitment of the Freedmen's Bureau to protecting the civil rights of Black South Carolinians.

Whether the protest was planned or not, Rollin's bravery in pursuing this suit is evident from the hostility with which McNelty's defeat was noted by newspapers both near and far. In Georgia the *Savannah Republican* denounced the hypocrisy of Northerners imposing a fine on McNelty, "an honest, law-abiding, tax-paying citizen of South Carolina," because "it is not the same as he would receive under similar circumstances in Massachusetts or any other Northern state."[145] From Indiana, the *Vincennes Weekly Western* criticized "Uncle Dan" Sickles, commander for military districts in the South, for "converting negro wenches into '*first class* passengers,'" insisting that the general and his like "glory

142. Kate [Katherine] Rollin Testimony, Captain W. T. McNelty Court-Martial, 30 July 1867.

143. Charlotte Rollin Testimony, Captain W. T. McNelty Court-Martial, 30 July 1867.

144. "The Rights of Common Carriers," *Charleston (SC) Daily News*, 21 Aug. 1867, 3.

145. Quoted in "Consistency, Thou Art a Jewel," *Daily Phoenix* (Columbia, SC), 3 Sept. 1867, 2.

in seeing all the prejudices and traditions of the people of the South trampled under foot by such an exercise of power and brute force!"[146] In the post–Civil War environment, the privileges that Rollin enjoyed as one of the mixed-race elite could be easily ignored, leaving her vulnerable to ejection from a steamboat and insult in the pages of the newspaper. The *Argus*, published in Albany, New York, similarly condemned General Sickles's judgment in the case and highlights Rollin's vulnerability by going on to provide details about a case that followed hers in the Post Court on 30 July. "A little later," according to the *Argus*, "some half-dozen respectable white men were ordered to be imprisoned for one, two, and three months, and fined in various penal sums, for an offense no higher than an assault and battery upon a negro girl under circumstances of extraordinary provocation, even as shown before a drum-head court martial, where the judgements [*sic*] were rendered, upon the testimony of the girl herself."[147] This refers to the conviction of a justice of the peace and six other white men for inflicting 140 lashes on a Black girl, taken "from the schoolhouse to the woods," "because she resisted being whipped by a daughter of one of the parties, the negro girl successfully whipping the white girl" instead.[148] Self-defense in this case is seen as "extraordinary provocation" on the part of the African American girl, resulting in a brutal assault. Equally provoking, no doubt, was the bravery of these young women to testify as to their experiences of discrimination and violence. Women like Rollin and this unnamed "negro girl" persisted in attempting to claim the justice and equality promised them by the federal government, but in the process they made themselves vulnerable to retribution and attack.

Rollin either had no alternative to McNelty's steamboat or, just as likely, refused to be intimidated: on 14 October 1867, just months after the court-martial was decided, the *Charleston Daily New* lists her as one of twelve passengers taking the *Pilot Boy* from Savannah, Georgia, "via Beaufort, Hilton Head," to Charleston.[149] The case against McNelty and the *Pilot Boy* made the next stage of her life possible in two important ways. First, it facilitated her travel to and from Hilton Head, where she likely met with Martin R. Delany. Second, it no doubt provided her with further evidence of her ability to achieve great things in a society that did not generally expect greatness from young Black women.

---

146. "'Gagging' the Press," *Vincennes (IN) Weekly Western*, 27 Sept. 1867.
147. "Sickles a Candidate for Martyrdom," *The Argus* (Albany, NY), Aug. 26, 1867.
148. "From Washington," *Boston Daily Advertiser*, 21 Aug. 1867, 1.
149. "Passengers," *Charleston (SC) Daily News*, 14 Oct. 1867, 4.

Major Martin R. Delany and the Promise of Authorship

During the McNulty case, Rollin apparently first met Martin R. Delany, who served as assistant subassistant commissioner of the Freedmen's Bureau at Hilton Head from August 1865 to August 1868.[150] But she could not have escaped knowing *about* Delany prior to this encounter: his name was likely mentioned in the same breath as that of Charles Lenox Remond and Frederick Douglass during her sojourn in Philadelphia. It is even possible that she knew him personally prior to the *Pilot Boy* case: her "business of great importance" leading to that case could have been interviewing Delany or obtaining documents for the biography. There is no contemporary documentation of their first encounter: all we know is that their meeting proved fateful for the ambitious young woman.

Born free in Charles Town, Virginia, in 1812, six years prior to William Rollin's birth, Martin Delany was the son of a seamstress and an enslaved laborer. His mother was forced to move with her children to Pennsylvania after she was threatened with imprisonment for teaching them to read and write. There he was educated and, as a young man, became active in the colored-conventions movement and the transportation of refugees from slavery. Having apprenticed as a doctor, Delany attended Harvard Medical School for a few months but was dismissed in 1851 due to the objections of racist white students. He soon committed himself to the cause of Black emigration, organizing a national conference in 1854 "to consider our claims to the West Indies, Central and South America, and the Canadas."[151] Delany was known for his "pride of race," or what Rollin called his "most defiant blackness": "It is frequently said by those best acquainted with his character, that in order to excite envy in him would be for an individual to possess less adulterated blackness, as his great boast is, that there lives none blacker than himself."[152] As Tunde Adeleke notes, "for many early-nineteenth-century

---

150. In 1971 both Victor Ullman and Dorothy Sterling claimed that Rollin and Delany met when, as Sterling puts it, "he helped her file a complaint against the captain of the *Pilot Boy*" (*Making of an Afro-American*, 279). Ullman is bit more vague but adds other unconfirmable details, writing: "How much Delany had to do with the case [against McNelty], we do not know, but throughout the summer and fall of 1867, he was working with Miss Rollin on his biography. . . . They conferred often, at Hilton Head, Beaufort, and Charleston" (*Martin R. Delany*, 410). In a 1969 letter to Frances Rollin's granddaughter, Sterling explains that she is sharing information with two other people researching Delany's life (Sterling to Lila [Leighla] Whipper, 13 January 1969, Sterling Papers). Likely, one of them suggested this possibility to the other, as no primary source that I have located indicates that this was, in fact, how Rollin and Delany met.

151. Delany, "Call for a National Emigration Convention," 240.

152. Rollin, *Life and Public Services*, 22.

black Americans, Delany had come to represent the quintessence of blackness, to exemplify black capabilities at the very best."[153]

After touring the Niger Valley in 1859 with Jamaican-born Robert Campbell, a science teacher at the ICY, Delany published the *Official Report of the Niger Valley Exploring Party* (1861) and made plans for a settlement of Black Americans in Abeokuta, Nigeria. But the beginning of the Civil War gave him new hope for the future of African Americans in the United States. In his earlier book, *The Condition, Elevation, Emigration, and Destiny of the Colored People of the United States* (1852), Delany had concluded, "We love our country, dearly love her, but she don't love us—she despises us, and bids us begone, driving us from her embraces; but . . . whatever love we have for her, we shall love the country none the less that receives us as her adopted children."[154] As he became convinced that a Union victory in the war would lead to freedom and political equality for African Americans, however, Delany joined wholeheartedly in the effort to persuade President Lincoln to emancipate the enslaved and to allow Black enlistment. Once Lincoln agreed, Delany worked to recruit Black soldiers and in 1865 received a commission into the Union army as a combat major. After the war ended, he was appointed to the Freedmen's Bureau and stationed at Hilton Head, where he oversaw government-owned plantations and the formerly enslaved laborers who worked there. He advocated passionately for what he called a "Triple Alliance" between Southern white landowners, Black laborers, and Northern capitalists in which all would benefit by the development of the Southern economy.

Given her father's wealth prior to the war and his subsequent losses, Delany's "Triple Alliance" may have appealed to Rollin. His past activism in the abolitionist movement would certainly have interested the ICY graduate, whose vision of racial justice was formed by his peers. Why exactly Delany chose Rollin to write his biography, however, is just as mysterious as the nature of their initial meeting. He must have been impressed with her education and her social connections, both North and South. But how did she prove her skill as a writer? Did she hand over carefully preserved poems clipped from Northern newspapers or essays written in response to prompts provided by her teachers at the ICY? Did she tell Delany about her dream of becoming an author, a public figure like him, perhaps even like Frances Ellen Watkins Harper, whose letters, speeches, poems, and short fiction she must have read in the *Christian Recorder*, *The Liberator*, and the *Anglo-African Magazine*, among other publications?

---

153. Adeleke, *Without Regard to Race*, xix.
154. Delany, *Condition, Elevation, Emigration, and Destiny*, 213.

Martin R. Delany. Courtesy National Park Service,
Gettysburg National Military Park, Museum
Collection, GETT #38209.

By the fall of 1867, Frances Rollin had a commission to write Major Delany's biography and a promise of financial support. On 21 October 1867, the *Charleston Daily News* noted her departure from town on the steamship *Manhattan*, bound for New York City.[155] Five days later—two months before the diary opens—the *Christian Recorder* announced Rollin's arrival at a boardinghouse in Brooklyn run by an African American woman named Nancy Hankerson.[156] Nancy's

155. "Passengers," *Charleston (SC) Daily News*, 21 Oct. 1867, 4.
156. "Arrivals at Mrs. Hasikerson's [*sic*] Boarding House," *Christian Recorder*, 26 Oct. 1867, 171. In the 1867 New York City directory, Benjamin Hankerson is listed as a porter living at 21 Greene, the same street at which "Mrs. Hasikerson" is said to live in the *Recorder* notice (*Trow's New York City Directory*, 1867). In an 1869 advertisement from the California newspaper the

husband, Benjamin, was a porter, perhaps on a steamship like the *Manhattan*, and would have been perfectly positioned to direct respectable African American travelers to his home, where his wife would provide them with food, lodging, and sociability in an unfamiliar city.[157] While an 1869 advertisement indicates that "Mrs. Hankerson" did occasionally publicize her business in print—"Good accommodation for families and single gentleman"—she likely relied on word of mouth and a good reputation.[158] Like Rollin, some of the other residents listed in the *Recorder* notice would have stayed only briefly, traveling through New York City on their way elsewhere. Others might have been longer-term residents. Together, though, they provide a snapshot of post–Civil War Black society, achievement, and mobility, giving a sense of the society in which Rollin moved just prior to her year in Boston.

Rollin likely met some of the residents for the first time upon her arrival in Brooklyn. Anderson Ruffin Abbott, for example, was the first Canadian-born Black physician who served in the Union army. He was also part of the medical team who tended to President Lincoln after he was shot in Ford's Theater in April 1865. Rollin may have been reluctant to ask Dr. Abbott about his experiences that fateful evening but no doubt respected him for his part in what she would later call "The National Calamity."[159] Elizabeth Taylor Greenfield, a singer known as the Black Swan, went on a thirty-city tour in the 1850s; during a European tour, she became the first African American artist to sing before British royalty. By 1868, Greenfield was still touring, but she also taught music in her home in Philadelphia.[160] Elizabeth Keckley, former dressmaker to Mary Todd Lincoln,

---

Elevator, "Mrs. Hankerson" offers "Good accommodations for families and single gentleman" at 193 Prince Street ("New York Boarding House," *Elevator* [San Francisco], 16 July 1869, in Where Did They Eat? Where Did They Stay: Black Boarding Houses and the Colored Conventions Movement, online exhibit, Colored Conventions Project, https://coloredconventions .org/boardinghouses/where-did-they-stay/). By 1869, Benjamin Hankerson is listed at 193 Prince Street (*Trow's New York City Directory*, 1869). The 1870 US Census lists Nancy Hankerson, age fifty-four, as the wife of Ben Hankerson, porter (Nancy Hankerson entry, Ward 8, Enumeration District 10, New York, US Census, 1870, database, Ancestry.com). Several boarders are noted as living with them at the time of the census, including most notably the "Sculptress" Edmonia Lewis, who was visiting New York after several years in Rome.

157. Williams-Forson, "Where Did They Eat?," 91, 95.

158. "New York Boarding House."

159. "The National Calamity" is the title of chapter 29 in the Delany biography, in which Rollin recounts the major's response to the assassination. See *Life and Public Services*, 203–8.

160. Gardner, "Elizabeth Taylor Greenfield."

was enslaved until her late thirties, when she purchased her freedom and eventually opened a thriving dressmaking business. After the president's death, she published *Behind the Scenes; or, Thirty Years a Slave, and Four Years in the White House* (1868). Rollin may have been in awe of these well-known African Americans and was likely eager to make their acquaintance.

Rollin was already acquainted with other residents of the boardinghouse. Ennals J. Adams was a Presbyterian minister born in Maryland who had been sent to Sierra Leone by the AMA during the Civil War. He traveled south under the aegis of the AMA after the war to minister to the recently enslaved at, among other places, the Shaw Presbyterian Church and the Glebe Street Presbyterian Church, both in Charleston. His appeal to these audiences evidently made him less attractive to some who, like Thomas Cardozo, did not like that "he preaches for the class with whom I cannot worship for want of intelligence."[161] A notice in the *Charleston Daily Courier* demonstrates that Adams opened his congregation to soldiers of the Fifty-Fourth Massachusetts as well.[162] He and Rollin exchanged letters during her time in Boston, and he would play an important role in her life after she returned to the South in August 1868. Also at the boardinghouse was Joseph H. Rainey, who was born in Georgetown, South Carolina, but lived in Charleston as a child. He worked as a barber prior to the Civil War, but after being drafted to work on the Confederate fortifications, he escaped to Bermuda, where he waited out the war. Rainey returned in 1865 and became involved in politics, attending—along with Delany and Adams—the South Carolina State Convention of Colored People in 1865.[163] He departed Charleston on the *Manhattan* along with Rollin and may have escorted her through the streets of Brooklyn to their boardinghouse after their arrival.[164]

The most intriguing name on Hankerson's list of residents is William E. Matthews (referred to as "Leedie" in Rollin's diary). Born to free parents in Baltimore, Maryland, he worked for the city's Galbraith Lyceum during the Civil War, promoting African American education. In February 1866 Matthews was

---

161. Quoted in Drago, *Initiative, Paternalism, and Race Relations*, 68.

162. "Preaching on the Sabbath at the Glebe-Street Presbyterian Church, for the benefit of the 54th Massachusetts Volunteers, Freedmen and Others," *Charleston (SC) Daily Courier*, 29 July 1865, 2.

163. Foner, *Freedom's Lawmakers*, 174–75.

164. "Passengers," *Charleston (SC) Daily News*, 21 Oct. 1867, 4.

included—along with abolitionist and orator Frederick Douglass, the New York caterer George T. Downing, and Pennsylvania businessman William Whipper (the uncle of Rollin's future husband)—in a delegation of Black men to the White House to demand that President Andrew Johnson support the equality of African Americans and the enfranchisement of Black men. While Douglass and Downing spoke for the delegation, Matthews was earning a reputation as "Maryland's young, but eloquent and popular orator."[165] In 1867 he became an agent for Bishop Daniel Payne and the AME Church, raising money for the establishment of new churches throughout the South.[166] Matthews may have met Rollin while traveling to Charleston, Payne's birthplace and the home of Mother Emanuel, the oldest AME church in the South. It is also possible that the two only met at the boardinghouse, introduced perhaps by Adams or by Keckley, who knew Matthews from their work for the freedmen immediately following the war.[167] In any case, Rollin's diary reveals this relationship to be far more important than this brief notice in the newspaper makes it out to be.

It is difficult to know how long Rollin stayed in New York City. She disappears from view after the announcement of arrivals at the boardinghouse but reemerges in Boston at the end of the year, spending fifty cents to purchase an "Illuminated Diary" from Taggard and Thompson's Booksellers' and Newsdealer's Agency on Cornhill Street, about a fifteen-minute walk from where she boarded with the Bailey family on Blossom Street. Covered in black leather, the diary is the size of a woman's hand and closes with a small flap that fits into a strap on the cover of the volume. While the flap would not ensure privacy, it would keep the pages safe from the other contents of one's drawer or pocket. In an ornate hand, Rollin inscribed her name and current address in the inside front cover: "F. Rollin / 16 Blossom St. / Boston / Mass."

165. Hannible, "A Letter from Hannible," *Christian Recorder*, 15 Dec. 1866, 198.

166. This campaign was incredibly successful. Thulani Davis notes that AME membership in the South "grew from tens of thousands in the Civil War years to hundreds of thousands in the 1870s and 1880s" (*Emancipation Circuit*, 61).

167. Matthews and Keckley seem to have known one another prior to this encounter. An 1863 newspaper item reported on an "Emancipation Jubilee" at the Fifteenth Street Presbyterian Church in Washington, DC, organized by Keckley in her role as president of the Ladies' Contraband Relief Association. Matthews was a featured speaker at the event. "The Emancipation Jubilee Last Night," *Evening Star* (Washington, DC), 17 Apr. 1863, 3.

Inside front cover and title page of Frances Ann Rollin diary, 1868. Gift of the Carole Ione Lewis Family Collection, National Museum of African American History and Culture.

Materiality, Form, and Convention in the Nineteenth-Century Diary

In purchasing a diary and inscribing her name inside, Frances Rollin was no different from thousands of other young women in post–Civil War America. The origins of the diary as a genre go back to the sixteenth century, with the gradual introduction of the concept of individualism and the individual self as distinct from, but certainly intertwined with, the family, church, or national identity. Coinciding with rising literacy rates, increasing leisure time, and access to writing materials, the notion that the individual *mattered* led to the documenting of one's own life. Almanacs, account books, and commonplace books were early forms of this sort of writing, and the diary as a genre often developed in the margins and the unused pages of these texts. As the practice of diary writing took hold, diarists reserved bound books for the practice. Other factors may also have contributed to its increasing popularity. Stuart Sherman, Phillippe Lejeune, and others argue that the rise of the diary was influenced by clock and watch technology and a greater concern with the usage of time. Lejeune notes: "Once it was measurable, the time of everyday life became precious and irreversible. Writing would allow us to make better use of it, and to keep track of it."[168] Some scholars point to the feminine nature of the diary form, with Felicity Nussbaum suggesting, "it is possible that women invented such a form, that they began the idea of private, and later, public articulation of quotidian organization of internal experience."[169]

Our understanding of the history of diary keeping is indelibly shaped by what has been left behind, retained, and preserved by family members and institutions. Diaries maintained by important white men—politicians, businessmen, military commanders, and soldiers—are simply more likely to be preserved and archived than are the diaries of women, people of color, and working-class people. It seems clear, however, that diary keeping required some amount of leisure time and financial capital. This is not to say that non-white, non-elite Americans did not keep diaries. But they were less likely to do so, less likely to preserve them or to have them preserved by descendants, and far less likely to have them valued by archivists, historians, and literary scholars.

If they had the materials and the time to keep a diary, nineteenth-century African American women, like others, were often prompted to begin one by their sense of living through an important personal or historical moment. In March 1881, for example, thirty-year-old Wilberforce University graduate and elocutionist Hallie Quinn Brown began a Southern tour, accompanying AME Bishop Payne "through his diocese reading at some of the principal cities." She purchased a blank book with red marbling on the cover and wrote on the first page:

A Journal.
   In which will be found the odds and ends of a traveling career, begun March 16th in the year of our Lord 1881, by a girl who has an idea that she is not a cipher nor a figurehead; and who here will write the humble name of
   Hallie Q. Brown, of Wilberforce, O—Green Co.[170]

As a devout Christian, Brown clearly worried that keeping a diary meant that she thought too much of herself—a "figurehead" for the Methodist Church or for Wilberforce University or a "cipher" with secrets to record. She minimizes her diary, claiming that it consists merely of "odds and ends," but the fact that she began it prior to her tour indicates that she thought her travels would be important, at the very least, to her. After the 1881 tour with Payne, Brown began

168. Lejeune, "Counting and Managing," 59. See also Sherman, *Telling Time*.
169. Nussbaum, "Toward Conceptualizing Diary," 134.
170. Hallie Quinn Brown diary, 1881, box 45, Hallie Quinn Brown Papers, Hallie Q. Brown Memorial Library, Central State University, Wilberforce, OH.

performing with the Wilberforce Concert Company to earn money for the support of the university; although she allowed her diary to languish in between tours, she wrote every day of her "traveling career" for several years and maintained a sporadic diary habit throughout the rest of her life.

African American diarist Emilie Davis began her diary on 1 January 1863, the day that the Emancipation Proclamation became official, freeing all enslaved people in Confederate-held territory and permitting the enlistment of Black men in the Union army. There is no indication of whether Davis kept a diary prior to 1863. The Historical Society of Pennsylvania, which holds her three volumes of diaries, has no other papers written by or about Davis. It seems likely, however, that the significance of the day inspired her to begin writing. "To day has bin a memorable day," she writes, "and I thank god I have bin spard to see it the day was religously observed all the churches were open we had quite a Jubilee in the eveni I went to Joness to a Party had a very plesent time."[171] While the beginning of the Civil War inspired many to begin documenting their lives, for Davis, the end of slavery in Union-occupied territory prompted her own efforts at recordkeeping and self-improvement. As Karsonya Wise Whitehead notes, "It was a historic time, and perhaps Emilie felt that her voice and her experiences were significant enough to be recorded in the annals of history."[172] In her exuberance, Davis's cramped and sometimes illegible handwriting fills the page, largely disregarding the divisions between days provided by the preprinted volume.

Rollin seems to have begun her own diary, purchased upon her arrival in Boston, out of a desire to mark the personal and historical importance of 1867. As the state of South Carolina instituted a new constitution and a new government, she moved to a new city and embarked on a project that she hoped would fulfill her dreams of authorship. She was not naïve, however, and acknowledged that the future was uncertain. Writing, like Davis, on the first of the year, she notes: "The year renews its births today with all of its hopes and sorrows. Uncertainty and doubt are in its wake. For me and mine I know not, but may God enable us whatever may be my lot. To murmur not, but patiently bear, and wait and labor."[173]

Others did not clearly identify the impetus for their diaries but may have begun writing simply because they had received diaries as gifts. While Laura Hamilton

---

171. Emilie Davis diary, 1863, vol. 1, Emilie Davis Diaries, Digital Collections, Penn State University Libraries, https://libraries.psu.edu/about/collections/emilie-davis-diaries.

172. Whitehead, introduction to *Notes from a Colored Girl*, 8.

173. Rollin diary, 1 Jan. 1868.

Murray never stated why she began her diary on 17 February 1885, an entry in her husband's diary a few days earlier reads, "Bot this book 10c & another for L."[174] Freeman H. M. Murray's own diary begins on the day of their wedding on 26 December 1883: "This day finds me after a courtship with various vicissitudes lasting about six years a married man. Getting a wife pretty and petite, handsome and handy, loving but not lazy, and a disposition that meets mine exactly, affectionate."[175] Having kept a diary consistently throughout their marriage, Freeman may have thought that Laura would also find the experience rewarding. As she was approximately six months pregnant at the time, he may also have wanted the two of them to document their growing family together. Her first entry is far more prosaic than his, however, noting only visits to friends, shopping, and attendance at church.[176] Emma Waite, a diarist who worked as a domestic servant and hotel cook in Saratoga and New York City, similarly began writing because she had received a diary as a gift: the inside front cover of her preprinted, three-days-per-page diary reads, "Presented by M. E. Hunter To Emma Waite Saratoga Springs With A 'Happy New Year.'" Waite documents the gift of the diary on 6 January 1870—"received this diary this evening as a present from Mrs. Hunter"—but her writing on the spaces provided for all the days prior indicates her having written these entries after the fact, likely on the evening of the sixth.[177] Her commitment to the diary—at least to the experiment of it—is clear, despite having not purchased the volume herself.

Although not every writer used a preprinted pocket diary like Davis, Waite, and Rollin, the manufacture of such volumes in the mid-nineteenth century indicates the popularity of diary keeping at the time. These diaries were affordable and portable, allowing travelers to carry them wherever they went—or to tuck them into a drawer to be written in just before going to bed at night. This may have been why Rollin selected the "Illuminated Diary for 1868," with a small drawing on the title page of a ship at sail, a lone seagull flying just above the intervening waves. Below this image is the publisher's name: "Taggard & Thompson, No. 29 Cornhill, Boston." Its purchase points to Rollin's location in Boston in

174. Freeman Murray diary, 14 Feb. 1885, vol. 3, folder 42, box 3, Freeman Henry Morris Murray Papers, Coll. 074, Ser. G, Moorland-Spingarn Research Center, Howard University.

175. Freeman Murray diary, 26 Dec. 1883, vol. 1, folder 42, box 3, Murray Papers.

176. Laura Murray diary, 17 Feb. 1885, folder 53, box 4, Murray Papers. According to the finding aid for the Murray Papers, this diary is in folder 52, box 4; it is actually in folder 53.

177. Emma Waite diary, 6 Jan. 1870, New York State Library.

1868 as well as her geographical transience, moving between Northern and Southern states with relative ease and confidence. While she likely wrote in her diary
at night, she kept it handy while traveling, first on a trip to Portland, Maine, in
mid-March and then on a journey home to South Carolina in late July and early
August.

These preprinted diaries were easy to navigate, their format dividing the days
into neat, even spaces—sometimes three days per page, sometimes just one—
waiting to be filled. As Molly McCarthy notes, "The page-a-day format kept the
days moving forward and never stopped asking for, or expecting, an entry each
and every day no matter how mundane."[178] The preprinted diary encouraged dailiness, prompting an acknowledgement of each day, what Jennifer Sinor calls "the
diurnal contract."[179] For example, Waite inscribes an entry in her diary every day,
clearly committed to its maintenance no matter what her circumstances. For long
stretches at a time in March 1872, however, she notes only the weather:

> March 4: Cloudy but very cold again
> March 5: Cloudy and cold as blazes. it seems to me that we are never
>   agoing to have warm weather again.
> March 6: quite mild and pleasant.
> March 7: Snowing.
> March 8: Cleared off quite pleasant.
> March 9: A nice bright day but very windy
> March 10: It has clouded up and has grown colder.
> March 11: Cold and cloudy.

It goes on like this for several days until 17 March, when she recounts a day out,
spent with her friends Ida and Anna. "Saw Maria," she adds, "but she did not
speak as usual." This outing, along with the ongoing drama of her conflict with
Maria, adds occasion to the otherwise measured diary.

While Rollin did not write every day, she clearly recognized the imperative to
do so in brief entries like that for 14 January 1868: "Writing quietly today nothing
of importance." Even when ill, she notes her inability to write more extensively
in the diary: "Sick in bed still fever and chill."[180] It is these entries that often get
left out of edited volumes, such as the earliest edition of the diaries of Charlotte
Forten (Grimké), published in 1953. Ray Billington, the editor, notes the dele-
tion of "large sections in the period between 1854 to 1862." He explains, "These

178. McCarthy, *Accidental Diarist*, 7.
179. Sinor, *Extraordinary Work of Ordinary Writing*, 26.
180. Rollin diary, 9 June 1868.

describe the weather, family affairs, the landscape, and other matters of purely local interest."[181] But Jennifer Sinor encourages us not to dismiss such "ordinary writing," noting that these are "the very qualities that mark the diary as a distinct kind of writing, rather than simply distant kin of the literary."[182] Remaining aware of the dailiness of the diary, rather than constantly searching for its literary qualities, allows us to think about how people are using their diaries.

Preprinted diaries especially were created for use. The reference matter included in the "Illuminated Diary" prior to the dated pages intended for daily entries point toward the uses to which its manufacturers imagined the volume might be put. For example, a table labeled "Difference of Time" allowed users to determine "the Difference of Time between that of Boston and the places therein named." Time was not regulated in the United States until 1883, when the railroad industry began using a standard time system with four zones. While this system did not become official until 1918, most of the country quickly adopted it. As Rebecca Solnit explains, "Before the railroads, each city and region kept its own time by the sun: noon was when the sun was highest overhead."[183] By consulting the table, Rollin would have known that noon in Charleston was thirty-five minutes and twenty-eight seconds after noon in Boston. She may also have consulted the list of "Rates of Postage," which usefully related how much it cost to send a letter, newspapers, or "seeds, cuttings, roots &c" anywhere in the United States. The list of the moon's phases and the tides in Boston and New York would have reminded her that, however interested Northerners might have been in the political goings-on of the former Confederate states, she was in their world now.

In a broader sense, Rollin's diary allowed her to order her day, choosing what to include and what to leave out, but she did not make these decisions based on some foretold conclusion. She was not writing an essay or a novel and had not outlined the trajectory of the diary before writing it. There was, as Sinor says of all ordinary diaries, "No foreshadowing. No climax. No closure."[184] And despite the stereotype of the diary as confidant, Rollin, like others, did not reveal all to her diary or to its later readers. At times, this is because she did not need to elaborate: writing "in the middle of things," in the middle of her own life, she had no need to explain who people are and what they meant to her.[185] At times, however, she kept her secrets to herself: using initials or nicknames in place of names; referring to some

181. Billington, introduction to *Journal of Charlotte L. Forten*, 40.
182. Sinor, *Extraordinary Work of Ordinary Writing*, 15.
183. Solnit, *River of Shadows*, 59–60.
184. Sinor, *Extraordinary Work of Ordinary Writing*, 11.
185. Sinor, *Extraordinary Work of Ordinary Writing*, 14.

"thing" bothering her, rather than saying exactly what it is; or simply not writing, leaving the page provided for a day frustratingly blank.[186] These silences can frustrate the reader hoping to find out more about Rollin's life and relationships.

Rather than lamenting silences and absences, though, we can focus on what the diary does. It must have been painful for Rollin to leave South Carolina again, so soon after her return home at the end of the war. She would have been especially reluctant to depart with the passage of the Reconstruction Acts in early 1867, the formation of the Republican Party in South Carolina, and the vote, less than a month after her departure, in favor of a new constitutional convention and a new state government. Among the 124 delegates selected to attend, 70 were African American.[187] Among them were names that Rollin would have recognized: Francis Cardozo, for whom she worked in the freedmen's schools; Richard Cain, superintendent of AME missions and minister of Emmanuel Church on Calhoun Street; William E. Johnston, a minister, cabinetmaker, and former suitor; and Robert Carlos De Large, a member of the mixed-race elite and the Brown Fellowship Society. The opportunity to write and publish Delany's biography, however, was too good to pass up, and being in Boston would allow her to establish contacts with publishers. Given the tightly intertwined Black community in the northeastern states, her time at the ICY had no doubt provided her with connections to African American families, churches, and activist networks in the region. Recording in the diary her attendance at various churches, public lectures and readings, and political meetings; her many visits to and from both new and old friends; and her letters from family and friends in South Carolina and elsewhere surely made Rollin feel some continuity between past and present as well as comfort in her new surroundings. Her network had not changed, only expanded, providing her with new opportunities. As was typical of Frances Rollin, she embraced these opportunities eagerly, always hungry for more.

The 1868 diary also reveals her desire for self-improvement and her ambition as a writer. Indeed, it allows us to see Rollin as a writer focusing on her own life at the same time she is writing about Delany's. In other words, his life is not the only one worthy of documentation. Both of their lives, the diary demonstrates, are extraordinary stories of African American struggle and achievement. As Molly McCarthy claims, one of the most notable features of the daily diary—and the key to its success—is its "self-centeredness." While Rollin fashioned and maintained a sense of community within her diary, she also "created an identity that

186. For one example of such obfuscation, see Rollin diary, 12 Apr. 1868.
187. Holt, *Black over White*, 35.

was clearly [her] own."[188] But of course community and the self are not so easily separated, especially for African American diarists. Desirée Henderson notes that "the act of claiming selfhood through writing is laden with political and ideological significance."[189] Between the writing of her diary and the writing of the biography of Delany, Rollin is clearly creating a sense of self that is deeply engaged with and responsive to the social and political issues of her historical moment.

Frances Rollin and Black Boston

Although it is not clear how she was put in touch with them, Rollin was extremely fortunate in boarding with John Baptiste and Ann Eliza "Annie" Bailey. John Bailey was a sparring (boxing) instructor who owned his own gymnasium on Tremont Row. Born free in Baltimore in 1815, he began his career as a "skilled pugilist" who "traveled to Boston and Philadelphia for exhibitions."[190] Between 1835 and the end of the Civil War, he owned and operated businesses—gymnasiums and pistol galleries—in Boston, Baltimore, and San Francisco, not only catering to a white clientele but also training Black boxers.[191] By 1870, he owned $5,000 in real estate and was by all standards an incredibly successful businessman.[192] In 1868 seven of the Baileys' eight surviving children lived with the couple at 16 Blossom Street in the West End of Boston. Their eldest, Mary E. Hare, lived in her parents' home with her husband, William. Rollin documents the birth of the couple's son on 13 January 1868: "Mrs Hare's baby born." While John's business was very successful, the Baileys may have taken in boarders to earn some extra money. As was often the case with elite Black families, the Bailey children contributed to the family economy: in 1870, Emily, twenty-eight years old, was a dressmaker, while Henry, twenty-one, was a waiter and James, nineteen, was a printer.[193] But thanks to their parents' active participation in the movement for equal school rights, which succeeded in 1855, most of the children likely received a quality education.

The Bailey family provided Rollin with safety and security as well as a socially and politically active and supportive community. While she paid for her room

188. McCarthy, *Accidental Diarist*, 151.

189. Henderson, *How to Read a Diary*, 67.

190. Moore, "Fit for Citizenship," 455.

191. Moore, "African American Athlete," 437.

192. John B. Bailey entry, Boston Ward 3, Suffolk County, Boston, MA, US Census, 1870, database, Ancestry.com.

193. John B. Bailey entry, US Census, 1870.

John B. Bailey, Professor of Sparring and Gymnastics. Lithograph,
A. Trochsler, ca. 1870.

and board, this was more than just an economic arrangement. Perhaps most important for an aspiring author, Rollin was allowed a room of her own in which to read, write, and sleep, and the family seems to have respected her need for privacy. The fact that Annie was the aunt of the author, activist, and lecturer Frances Ellen Watkins Harper likely rendered their family sympathetic to the ambitious young writer in their midst; their familial relationship with the successful writer surely interested Rollin, who may have listened to the Bailey children read letters from their cousin in the parlor that they shared.[194] By opening up their home, the

194. Ann E. Bailey's parents were William and Frances Watkins of Baltimore, Maryland (Ann E. Bailey entry, "Massachusetts, U.S., Death Records, 1841–1915," database, Ancestry. com). While she was sixteen years younger than William Watkins, the uncle who raised Frances Ellen Watkins Harper, Ann seems to have been his sister, making her Harper's aunt. This

Baileys also furnished "protective socializing rituals" for "city-bound youth" like Rollin, ensuring her respectability as a young Black woman living apart from her own family.[195] They were perfectly located to facilitate her integration into the community. The West End neighborhood had the largest population of African Americans in Boston and was home to leaders in the Black community like writer and activist William Cooper Nell, caterer Joshua B. Smith, and minister Leonard Grimes. Nell's sister, Louisa, and her husband, Ira Smith Gray, also boarded with the Baileys in 1868, providing Rollin with additional ties to Black society.[196] She socialized often with the Bailey family and clearly enjoyed their company. She shared a love of Charles Dickens with John, who accompanied her to see the British author read from *A Christmas Carol* on 27 February 1868. In early April she accompanied Annie to Lynn, Massachusetts, to visit friends, and on Independence Day attended fireworks with John and his young son Peter.[197] Her closest relationship seems to have been with Emily, who was six years older than her. The two young women visited and sewed together, and when Frances was in bed with a fever and a chill in early June 1868, Emily, Rollin writes, "attended me very kindly."[198]

Rollin took note of many such visits and social activities, and the diary is invaluable for its documentation of Black community and social and political networks in post–Civil War Boston. At the center of these networks were families like the Haydens. As they had done for many other African American visitors to Boston, Lewis and Harriet Hayden welcomed Rollin to their home and furnished her with valuable personal and professional connections. Both were born into slavery in Kentucky, but they escaped after their marriage in 1842 to avoid separation. The couple settled in Boston, where Lewis opened a used-clothing store and worked as an agent for the American Anti-Slavery Society. He and Harriet housed refugees from slavery in their home on Southac Street (later renamed

---

is confirmed by an announcement of Harper's death in the home of her cousin, Mrs. E. C. Mundrucu. "Items of Race Interest," *Freeman* (Indianapolis), 11 March 1911, 2. Emily Bailey, John and Ann's daughter, was married to Theodore Mundrucu in 1887. Harper's will leaves a significant part of her money and property to the Bailey cousins; Emily Mundrucu served as her executor. Frances E. W. Harper, no. 487, Wills 471–97, 1911, "Pennsylvania, U.S., Wills and Probate Records, 1683–1993," database, Ancestry.com. See also Gardner, "African American Literary Reconstructions," 438.

195. Peel, "On the Margins," 814.
196. *Boston Directory*, 1867, 1868.
197. Rollin diary, 9 Apr., 4 July 1868.
198. Rollin diary, 7 June 1868.

Phillips Street). Lewis provided clothing, shelter, and transport to fugitives, while Harriet devoted her domestic and emotional labor to the cause of freedom.[199] During the Civil War, Lewis was a recruiter for the Fifty-Fourth Massachusetts Regiment and after the war was awarded a patronage position as a messenger in the secretary of state's office. Between January 1868 and the end of July, when Rollin returned to South Carolina, she recorded eleven visits to the Haydens at their home. Lewis returned visits to her at the Baileys' several times as well. The Baileys and the Haydens lived just five minutes apart, and there were likely far more visits exchanged than were documented. Lewis also facilitated Rollin's employment as a copyist at the Massachusetts State House in May. "God bless his kind heart," Rollin wrote in her diary, "for all he has done for me and others."[200]

She also developed intimate relationships with the Howard family. Edwin Frederick Howard was a caterer and hairdresser who lived with his wife, Joanna Turpin Howard, and their children in the South End of Boston. The Black population of the South End had increased after the end of the Civil War, as migrants from the Southern states moved north to find work. The Howards shared a home on Shawmut Avenue with Joanna's sister, Eliza, and her husband and young son. Rollin may have been drawn to them because of their family's South Carolina roots: Joanna and Eliza's father, Joseph Thomas Turpin, had been enslaved in Charleston but was emancipated as a young man and moved with his former enslaver, William Turpin, to New York City. When William died in 1835, Joseph was left a fortune in real estate, some of which he earmarked for his children's education.[201] As a teenager, Joanna attended the Young Ladies Domestic Seminary, "the first *racially integrated* female seminary in New York, if not in the entire North."[202] According to Kabria Baumgartner, the seminary was "a site where [both white and African American young women] could learn and participate in social reform practices."[203] Joanna Howard learned that lesson well, taking an active role alongside her husband in the equal school rights movement in Massachusetts. She also passed these values on to her children: her daughters, Jean Imogene and Adeline, became educators, and her son, Edwin Clarence, became a physician.

---

199. Stephen Kantrowitz notes that while most payments from Boston's Vigilance Committee were to men, women played a large role in the sheltering of fugitives from slavery. Of the Haydens, he writes, "the couple's labors were complementary and mutually necessary" (*More Than Freedom*, 189).

200. Rollin diary, 8 July 1868.

201. Baumgartner, *In Pursuit of Knowledge*, 62–63.

202. Baumgartner, *In Pursuit of Knowledge*, 47.

203. Baumgartner, *In Pursuit of Knowledge*, 71.

Harriet Hayden carte-de-visite, ca. 1864. Division of Political History, National Museum of American History, Smithsonian Institution.

Rollin was particularly close with Adeline "Addie" Howard, who was her age and may have shared her determination and sense of adventure. Addie was intimate friends with Edmonia Lewis, a young sculptor of mixed African American and Native American heritage who had boarded with the Howard family in 1865.[204] In the summer of 1865, Edmonia and Addie traveled to Richmond, Virginia, intending to teach freedmen. By August, their trunks were stolen from their boardinghouse, and Edmonia returned north, sailing for Europe in hopes of promoting her career as an artist.[205] Twice in her diary, Rollin reports Addie sharing photos of Lewis, including some "taken in her Studio dress."[206] Rollin and Addie visited one another often and occasionally went on outings, such as when they, William E. Matthews, and Harriet "Hattie" Lockley sat together at an "Exhibition" at the Tremont Temple, a Baptist church that was also used for public events. The girls clearly delighted in making fun of the entertainment. In her diary account Rollin announces herself "agreeably disappointed with the whole performance," adding "together we enjoyed ourselves."[207]

Part of the value of Rollin's diary lies in its detail about these sorts of leisure activities and social engagements enjoyed within the Black community, what Tara Bynum calls "the matter of Black living."[208] For Rollin and for others in her community, such pleasures do not diminish the reality of racism in the post–Civil War United States. As Imani Perry writes: "Joy is not found in the absence of pain and suffering. It exists through it." It is, she explains, "insistence."[209] Like the exhibition Frances attended with Leedie, Addie, and Hattie, some of these pleasurable activities took place in the presence of and in engagement with white people. Others occurred outside of the white gaze: Rollin recounts in her diary quiet evenings in the Baileys' parlor with just the family, visits to the homes of Black friends, and even a party with "lots of my gentleman friends," with singing, dancing, and "several games."[210] The pleasure she took in this community is apparent even in the brief notation of events in her diary.

204. In the 1865 Massachusetts census, Edmonia Lewis is listed as a "sculptress" boarding with the family of Alfred and Martha Howard. The couple shared a home with Alfred's brother, Edwin, and his wife, Joanna. Addie, also living there, was like Lewis twenty years old. See Howard Family in biographical notes.

205. Untitled, *The Liberator*, 25 Aug. 1865, 135.

206. Rollin diary, 9 May 1868.

207. Rollin diary, 30 Mar. 1868.

208. Bynum, *Reading Pleasures*, 1.

209. Imani Perry, "Racism Is Terrible. Blackness Is Not," *The Atlantic*, 15 June 2020, www .theatlantic.com/ideas/archive/2020/06/racism-terrible-blackness-not/613039/.

210. Rollin diary, 13 Apr. 1868.

Interestingly, given the number of Black churches in the West End and Beacon Hill, Rollin did not restrict her worship to any single place or denomination. She did not participate actively in any one church community. Nor did she oppose attending church or religious meetings with white people. Indeed, she seems to have found community with those who questioned organized religion and its trappings in post–Civil War Boston. Having left her Roman Catholic faith behind in her Charleston youth, she likely attended both St. Thomas's Episcopal Church in Philadelphia as well as Mother Bethel AME Church, down the street from the ICY. In the course of 1868, she records attending services at the African Meeting House and the Twelfth Baptist Church, both Black churches, as well as the West Unitarian Church, the Mount Vernon Congregational Church, and the Church of the Advent (Episcopal), all of which were white churches. She often attended services with friends but also went alone. Rollin was interested in spiritual reform, refusing to take a seat in a church that charged pew rent; participating in a "sitting for spiritual purposes," or a séance; and attending the first annual meeting of the Free Religious Association, a nonsectarian, freethinking organization founded in 1867 that promoted the belief in human perfectability and rationalism.[211] Rollin's eclecticism is fascinating because it indicates the acceptability or at least tolerance of religious pluralism in the African American community.

Rollin's record of her social activities is also compelling for what it reveals about the supportive network of Black South Carolinians spread across the Northeast. Desperate for news from home and comfort from others who likely felt displaced, Rollin "went both to Mrs Barreu's and Mrs Edwards to hear something" one February day.[212] The Barreaus and the Edwards, along with other families mentioned in the diary, were likely among the many free Black people who fled South Carolina just prior to secession, uneasy about the tightening restrictions on all African Americans, enslaved or free. Rollin's good friend Ella Mahone was another such refugee, having left Charleston with Black carpenter Samuel Simonds and his wife, who may have been relatives and seem to have served as foster parents for Ella. Rollin accompanied Ella to church and to the theater; their time together may have been filled with reminiscences of home and talk about the future. The example of the Barreas, the Edwards, the Simonds, and Ella may have made Rollin consider making a home for herself in the North as well.

Marriage to a Northerner would have likely necessitated a permanent move. At twenty-three years old, Rollin was of marriageable age with plenty of suitors, and she took romance seriously: indeed, she carefully notes in her diary the visits,

211. Rollin diary, 23 Feb., 1 Mar., 29 May 1868.
212. Rollin diary, 16 Feb. 1868.

gifts, and letters of her many admirers, dismissing those whose ambitions did not match her own. After dancing with one young man at Dancing School, for example, she reports, "He escorted me home and played the gallant to perfection." But she then adds wryly, "If I intended waltzing through life I might fancy him for a partner."[213] Waltzing was a delightful way to occupy one's time at Dancing School, but Rollin was not looking for ease or comfort. She wanted to work—for South Carolina, for her country, and for her own future as a writer.

Harvard undergraduate Richard Greener was a more suitable candidate. Born in Philadelphia and raised in Boston, Greener had attended Phillips Academy and Oberlin College prior to matriculating at Harvard. In 1870 he would become the first Black graduate of Harvard, but in 1868 Rollin found him a bit too full of himself. Having shared part of her manuscript with him, she observes to her diary: "He is cynical and apt to discourage instead of acting otherwise. He lives in a grand intellectual sphere and is accustomed to [win] only perfection."[214] Although he would spend several evenings "very pleasantly" with her throughout the end of May, nothing seems to have come of their friendship.[215]

Rollin's relationship with William E. "Leedie" Matthews, however, was serious enough that she likely considered a future with him. The two met (or were reunited) at Hankerson's boardinghouse in late October 1867, and Frances must have spent a significant amount of time with Leedie before writing in her diary: "He is ambitious . . . , but he does not . . . originate, or yet to search out for himself enough. He is malleable in an intellectual sense and in an atmosphere of the kind might expand. I think he will yet make his mark."[216] Leedie is mentioned on sixty-three occasions in Rollin's diary, more than three times as often as any other individual. He visited her at the Baileys and accompanied her on outings. When he went out of town on business, the two corresponded. When he returned, he reported to her on his successes and, on one occasion, his narrow escape from a house fire.[217] He brought her books, newspapers, and flowers. They also argued. In late April, for example, Rollin writes: "Leedie came about nine oclock. We quarreled about Dickens. He is so thoroughly selfish that it makes him rude in every thing."[218] He returned the next day to pick up where they left off. At

213. Rollin diary, 3 Apr. 1868.
214. Rollin diary, 3 Jan. 1868.
215. See, for example, Rollin diary, 29 May 1868.
216. Rollin diary, 6 Jan. 1868.
217. On the fire, see Rollin diary, 30 June 1868.
218. Rollin diary, 24 Apr. 1868.

W. E. MATHEWS.

William E. Matthews, ca. 1880s. From William J.
Simmons, *Men of Mark: Eminent, Progressive, and
Rising* (Cleveland: Geo. M. Rewell, 1887).

home reading, Rollin was interrupted by a visit in which "Leedie came told me
of my computed faults pedantic and soulless."[219] After an argument earlier in
the year, she had concluded, "I am not sure he understand[s] the highest female
character."[220]

Rollin clearly admired Leedie for his ambition but wondered if his relationship with her was strategic: "L[eedie] came and wanted to impress me with the
belief that he loves me," she notes in late February. "He might see that it would
be advantageous to have me near to direct him but further than that I do not
know. I read after he left. I wrote several letters."[221] The paratactic nature of the
diary, in which the most mundane activities follow what to contemporary readers
seem like important revelations, prevents us from seeing how Rollin took Leedie's
profession of love. As she read and wrote letters that night, did she imagine what a

219. Rollin diary, 25 Apr. 1868.
220. Rollin diary, 23 Feb. 1868.
221. Rollin diary, 28 Feb. 1868.

life with him might look like for her? She wanted to be more than "advantageous" to the man she married. But she clearly thought about marriage in a practical sense as well. Others apparently shared her sense of Matthews's ambition and his potential; in 1867 AME Bishop Benjamin Tanner wrote of him, "A young man is he of the sublimest talents—a brain that is fruitful as the clouds; a spirit as fretful as the Arab's steed, and a heart of singular fidelity."[222] It is not clear why their relationship went no further than it did, although there are hints in the diary. The last time Rollin mentions having seen Matthews is on 7 July, five days before she stops writing in the diary for two weeks and twenty days before she leaves Boston. "We differed as usual," she explains. She seems to have begun to write the word "quarreled" but changed her mind, perhaps preferring "differed" to explain her sense of their incompatibility. On 28 July, her last day in Boston, Matthews was not among the crowd of friends who came to say goodbye.

Literary Enjoyment in Boston

Later in life, Rollin wrote about her time in Boston: "Those months contained such a wealth of literary enjoyment that the memory of them remains with me still."[223] Chief among these enjoyments when the diary opens is the American tour of the British novelist Charles Dickens. Rollin seems to have heard Dickens read several times in the winter of 1867–68. She records taking delight in his performances of various characters, from Tiny Tim to Daniel Peggotty—"he knows his characters so thoroughly that he and they are inseparable when acting"—but she also thoroughly enjoys observing the audience of "Upper Tendom," "brilliant authors and handsome women."[224] Not even Ralph Waldo Emerson, who she frequently read and clearly admired, could live up to the British novelist, although she calls a lecture by the great Transcendentalist "a rare intellectual treat."[225]

Like Charlotte Forten (Grimké), whose diary includes lists of her reading from 1853 through 1857 and often records her impressions of those books, Rollin was a bibliophile who seems to have gauged her personal growth by the number and quality of books she read.[226] Her documentation of her reading demonstrates a

222. Quoted in Bragg, *Men of Maryland*, 100.

223. Quoted in Murray, "Sketch of Frances Rollin Whipper."

224. Rollin diary, 27 Feb. 1868.

225. Rollin diary, 30 Jan. 1868.

226. While Barbara Stevenson's 1988 edition of Forten's diary is more complete than earlier editions, it does not include these lists and nor even note their existence. See, for example,

passion for both history and biography: she mentions Alphonse de Lamartine's *History of the Girondists; or, Personal Memoirs of the Patriots of the French Revolution* (1847) five times, perhaps taking a particular interest in this book given her French heritage and her own work as a historian and a biographer. Thomas Babington Macaulay's *History of England* (1849) was another favorite, mentioned eight times over the course of the year. Rollin also read Emerson's essays; a biography of Josiah Quincy, mayor of Boston and president of Harvard; and Harriet Martineau's *The Hour and the Man*, a novel about the rise and fall of Haitian revolutionary Toussaint-Louverture.

Rollin's reading is also evident in her allusions to and quoting of texts throughout the diary. These quotes often function as a kind of personal shorthand, allowing her to reference emotions or beliefs without going into detail or perhaps without entirely confronting them. In an entry about the elusive "P.," for example, she quotes from Robert Burns and Emerson:

> Today my dream of P is stronger than ever upon me,
> my every effort has the same source like Burns.
> "E'en then a wish, I own its power
> A wish that to my latest hour
> Shall strongly heave my soul
> That I for poor auld Scotland's sake
> Some usefu' plan or beuk can I make
> Or sing a song at least."
> Perhaps it will all come right some day. "The Gods are
> to each other not unknown" and hearts gravitate to
> each other by the same divine necessity.[227]

Rollin's quotation of the Scottish poet's "Epistle to Mrs. Scott" implies that her own creative endeavors are in the service of her home, just as Burns's were to his. Placed in the context of her "dream of P.," however, the quote also suggests that the "useful plan" or book that she is writing "for pool auld" South Carolina's "sake" is somehow tied to her feelings for her Philadelphia suitor. Was he, perhaps, like her from South Carolina but attending school or working in Philadelphia?

Charlotte Forten, "List of Books Read from November 1853 to December 1854," Diary 1, 24 May 1854–31 Dec. 1856, folder 1814, box 40–45, Francis James Grimké Papers, Moorland-Spingarn Research Center, Howard University.

227. Rollin diary, 26 Mar. 1868.

Was he a writer as well? Perhaps he had supported her desire to write and publish something that would promote the cause of Reconstruction in South Carolina. Her quotation of Emerson's "Character," in which he proclaims that "divine necessity" brings about the meeting of those fated to "gravitate to each other," indicates her belief that she and P. will be reunited. Perhaps the ambition or sentiment in such expressions felt inappropriate to Rollin. Or perhaps they were so serious, so heartfelt, that she could only articulate them in the language of writers she loved.

Being in Boston gave Rollin access to more established writers who she had likely only encountered before in print; in person, they provided her with company, advice, and feedback on her work. For example, Rollin treasured her acquaintance with the white abolitionist and civil rights activist Wendell Phillips. She recounts her visit to his home in Chelsea in late March: "he greeted me so kindly, we conversed a long while about my prospects in the literary world and on leaving he gave me a copy of his Speeches which is as precious to me as the apple of my eyes God bless the great hearted kingly Phillips give him length of days and strength to continue steadfast to the end."[228] Elsewhere she calls him "a masterpiece of humanity" after Phillips loaned her Emerson's essays, invited her to an "Anti Slavery Festival," and offered to listen to her read from her manuscript.[229] She had a much closer relationship with African American writer and historian William Cooper Nell, who published *The Colored Patriots of the American Revolution* in 1855. His work would have been an inspiration to Rollin, who aspired to recount the service of African Americans in the Civil War just as Nell had done for the Revolutionary War. Moreover, he provided practical assistance in her writing and in securing a publisher for her biography of Delany. On 4 February, for example, he facilitated an introduction to the abolitionist and publisher of *The Liberator*, William Lloyd Garrison. Just a week later, Garrison wrote a letter of introduction for Rollin to the publisher and editor James T. Fields, senior partner at the prestigious publishing firm Ticknor and Fields, asking him "to confer with [her] in regard to publishing a biography of Major M. Delany, which she has written *con amore* and very creditably to herself."[230] In early March, Nell listened to Rollin read from her manuscript, likely providing valuable feedback as she prepared to send it to the publisher for review.

228. Rollin diary, 25 Mar. 1868.
229. Rollin diary, 20 Jan. 1868.
230. William Lloyd Garrison to James T. Fields, 11 Feb. 1868, box 23, James Thomas Fields Papers, mssFL, Huntington Library, San Marino, CA. See appendix A.

After Fields rejected her manuscript, African American author, activist, and lecturer William Wells Brown may have provided an introduction to Lee & Shepard, who would eventually publish the book. Brown published *The Negro in the American Rebellion* with the firm in 1867 and, after the success of their marketing campaign, published a fourth version of the novel first released in 1853 as *Clotel; or, The President's Daughter* (retitled *Clotelle; or, The Colored Heroine*). The first time Rollin mentions Brown is in early March, immediately following her initial visit to Lee & Shepard "about the Book." After returning to the Baileys' home, she writes, "He seems so honest in his kindly interest in me."[231] Throughout the rest of the year, she exchanged several visits with him and his wife, Annie; accompanied him to an entertainment given by the Freemasons; and attended his lecture "on the origin of the African Race."[232]

Rollin's most extensive engagement with another Black woman author was with Elizabeth Keckley, whose book *Behind the Scenes; or, Thirty Years a Slave, and Four Years in the White House* was published by G. W. Carleton and Company in 1868. After likely having become acquainted with her the previous October, Rollin was surprised to receive a letter from Matthews in April that "informed me of Miss Keckley's debut as a literary lady." She continues, "I am fast losing confidence in her mainly I fear there is too much sham every where."[233] To have lost confidence implies that Rollin once did have confidence in Keckley: what must these two ambitious women have talked about during their initial encounter at the boardinghouse? Did either of them reveal their literary aspirations to the other? The nature of the "sham" about which Rollin is concerned is revealed days later after she reads Keckley's book: "I finished reading it before five oclock," she writes. "It is well written but not by Mrs K that's clear." Rollin pronounces herself "more than astonished" a couple of days later when Leedie tells her, "Mrs Keckley is studying for a Reader."[234] She and the Baileys attended one of Keckley's public readings from her book in June. "I felt nervous all the while," Rollin writes. "It was poor to say the least of it. We went up and spoke to her at the conclusion of it. It is too late in the day for her to attempt it especially without a first class teacher."[235]

Jennifer Fleischner explains that Keckley had remained in New York City

231. Rollin diary, 10 Mar. 1868.
232. Rollin diary, 17 Mar., 10 May 1868.
233. Rollin diary, 11 Apr. 1868.
234. Rollin diary, 16, 18 Apr. 1868.
235. Rollin diary, 25 June 1868.

throughout the winter of 1868, working on her narrative with the assistance of James Redpath, who had, since his days as superintendent of education in Charleston, started the Boston Lyceum Bureau. She insists that Keckley "wrote in her room at night" and the day following "met with Redpath ... to go over the previous night's work."[236] Redpath is represented as responsible not only for obtaining a publisher for the volume but also for having letters from Mary Todd Lincoln to Keckley printed as an appendix to the narrative without Keckley's permission. The details of this working relationship are hazy, however, as Redpath seems never to have taken credit for his work with Keckley or, as Frances Smith Foster points out, come to her defense when reviewers attacked her for the book's representation of Mrs. Lincoln.[237] Doubts about Keckley's authorship of her book were introduced in early reviews of *Behind the Scenes* and persisted into the 1930s, when Francis J. Grimké wrote a letter to the *Journal of Negro History* responding to critics who doubted Keckley's existence or her ability to write such a book. Anna Nelson suggests that "Keckly threatened white-authored versions of American past," and that efforts to "connect Keckly's text to white authors represent a cultural desire to mediate this authoritative black presence in American history."[238] Scholars generally seem to have agreed that without evidence to the contrary, it is safe to assume that Keckley was the sole author of *Behind the Scenes*.

Frances Rollin's doubts about Keckley's authorship may be, as some assert, evidence of the snobbery of an elite Black woman who "sniffed" at the idea of this formerly enslaved woman writing a book.[239] Yet as Elizabeth Young and Barbara Ryan each note, Rollin's diary could point scholars toward a more nuanced consideration of authorship in *Behind the Scenes*.[240] An experienced teacher of children with limited educational experience, Rollin may have been qualified to

236. Fleischner, *Mrs. Lincoln and Mrs. Keckley*, 316.

237. McKivigan, *Forgotten Firebrand*, 116; Frances Smith Foster, "Historical Introduction," in Keckley, *Behind the Scenes*, lii. Fleischner (*Mrs. Lincoln and Mrs. Keckley*, 359n78) follows Foster, who asserts: "In the absence of proof to the contrary and given what we know about her personality and previous history, it seems foolish to assume that for such an important act, Madame Keckley would settle for an informant's role. Certainly she, like most published writers, worked with editors and consultants. And, as the dismay over the unedited letters reveals, some publishing decisions were made without her consent" ("Historical Introduction," l). Foster is responding to nineteenth-century reviewers who treated Mary Todd Lincoln as the subject of *Behind the Scenes* and refused to believe that Keckley could have written the book.

238. Nelson, *"Behind the Seams,"* 554.

239. Fleischner, *Mrs. Lincoln and Mrs. Keckley*, 359n78.

240. Young, *Disarming the Nation*, 125–26; Ryan, "Behind the Scenes," 49.

recognize the extent of Keckley's literacy skills. And her acquaintance with James Redpath—she visited him on the same day that she finished Keckley's book—might hint at a deeper understanding of the circumstances of the book's composition and publication.

Whatever the truth is behind the scenes of the authorship of *Behind the Scenes*, Rollin's comments on Keckley in her diary are of particular interest when read in the context of the publication of her own book. Having been rejected by Fields and with her manuscript under consideration at Lee & Shepard's, Rollin was no doubt envious of Keckley's success. Whether because of Matthews's letter or for some other reason entirely, she awoke the morning after hearing of Keckley's "debut" in a thoughtful mood. "Musing on evry thing," she writes on Easter Sunday, "the bitterness of past injustice arises up to me when I should leave vengeance to him who today breaks the bondage of the tomb and tramples sin under his feet and arise and go to him who said Come unto me all you that labor and are heavy laden and I will give you rest."[241] While it is not entirely clear what she is referring to here or in what way she has been treated unjustly, she clearly sees herself as hard done by. Rollin feels that her "labor" has not been rewarded—perhaps in the way that Keckley's has with the publication of her book. She writes at the bottom of her entry, "[best] not leave any room," filling up the empty space with these words and effectively preventing herself from going into detail about the "past injustice."

The Labor and Economics of Authorship

The daily demands of the diary allow readers to track Rollin's progress on her biography of Martin Delany. She likely left South Carolina with much of her collected material, having already interviewed her subject repeatedly. *Life and Public Services of Martin R. Delany* contains a number of speeches, letters, and military orders reproduced in part or in full; the only source for the majority of these documents would have been Delany himself.[242] While in Boston, Delany and Rollin corresponded regularly: according to the diary, she received eight letters from Delany between January and July and wrote at least three herself, although I suspect each of Delany's letters received an answer. There is no diary for 1867, so we cannot know how many letters they exchanged between her arrival in New York in late October and the end of 1867. Rollin likely used correspondence with

241. Rollin diary, 12 Apr. 1868.

242. Most of Delany's papers were destroyed in a fire at Wilberforce University in 1865. It is hard to imagine that he did not have this loss in mind when they discussed the insertion of such documents in *Life and Public Services*.

her subject to ask clarifying questions about details in the narrative. Some of the quoted sections in the biography may have come directly from the major's letters to her. Rollin likely also acquired information from Black Bostonians who knew and had worked with Delany.

The diary also serves as a record of payments received from Delany meant to support her during her writing of the biography. Three of his letters to Rollin contained a check: one for fifty dollars, one for forty dollars, and another for an unspecified amount. While the arrangement between them is not spelled out in the diary, Rollin seems to have been promised financial support during her time in Boston. Her disappointment in the sums sent by Delany is evident in the diary: in February, for example, she records the receipt of a letter and a check for fifty dollars, adding: "I am afraid that I can not afford to pursue the course marked out. To write one must be above want I should think."[243] In July, when taking on copying work at the Massachusetts State House provided insufficient money for her day-to-day needs, she writes, "Went out to sew today I thought when I begun literature that ended but I find it otherwise."[244] Around the same time, she reports being "tried beyond endurance" by Delany and laments, "To think Major Delany should prove so recreant to his many promises."[245] The value of the biography to scholars of Martin Delany's career might render us prone to dismiss Rollin's complaints, but it is worth noting that the ninety dollars we know he sent her would barely cover her room and board for three months: according to the sums recorded in the blank pages of the diary, her room and board was approximately thirty-four dollars per month. Even as she negotiated the publication of the biography with Lee & Shepard, then, Rollin was forced to undertake copying and sewing work from early May until her departure from Boston at the end of July. She also entertained the idea of going back to teaching. In early March she visited Charlotte Forten, clerk for the Teachers Committee of the New England Branch of the Freedmen's Commission, to discuss accepting a teaching position in Maryland.[246] A month later, however, perhaps encouraged by the progress on her book with Lee & Shepard, she had decided not to take the position. Rollin seemingly could not help recording the response in her diary: "Miss Forten informed me that the Association will not send any teacher as I cannot go."[247]

243. Rollin diary, 24 Feb. 1868.
244. Rollin diary, 1 July 1868.
245. Rollin diary, 6 June 1868.
246. Rollin diary, 6 Mar. 1868.
247. Rollin diary 4 Apr. 1868.

Rollin's accounting of her labor and her finances draws our attention yet again to the diary as a tool. Other African American women of the period used their diaries in similar ways: Emma Waite wrote occasionally about her paid labor in her daily entries but maintained a careful account of money received and paid in the back pages of her diary. Hallie Quinn Brown recorded the receipt of her pay during her Southern tour as well as the amounts paid during shopping trips for dresses, hats, and mittens. Editors of diaries generally leave out financial accounts, but they are often central to the events recorded on the pages and can provide us with a sense of how writers engaged with the physical diary. "Money, as much as time," Molly McCarthy notes, "was a strong impetus for ... diary keeping, but the connection between diary and money ... calls to mind the persistent metaphor of 'keeping account,' a phrase most associated with the Protestant tradition of diary keeping that called upon the faithful to keep a daily account that tracked their spiritual progress toward salvation."[248] Despite her regular church attendance, Rollin was not particularly concerned with her own "spiritual progress toward salvation"—at least she did not use the diary to record such concerns. Instead, her accounts are wholly practical. As a young woman effectively on her own, with her father's businesses having failed or failing and her sisters struggling to maintain their school in Charleston, Rollin did not have the luxury to worry about faith instead of finances.

Some preprinted diaries provided pages at the back for "Cash Accounts." Rollin seems to have begun her accounting here, first in January 1868 and then in earnest in February, invited—indeed instructed—by the diary to do so. But she soon began keeping lists of accounts in the front and back covers of her diary. Perhaps the sporadic nature of her income made it difficult to work out her monthly accounts. Perhaps she felt comfortable keeping track of her expenses (for paper, soap, shoes, braiding, and cotton cloth, among other items) in her head. Or perhaps she came to see the diary as more of a personal account and made her financial records in some other volume that has since disappeared. That some diarists made use of preprinted diaries primarily to keep accounts while maintaining a personal diary in another volume is indicated by the papers of Katharine Johnson, a young woman of color born free in Natchez, Mississippi, in 1842, who maintained a diary sporadically between 1864 and 1874 in a bound book. Beginning in 1872, Katharine began keeping her financial accounts in a preprinted diary, despite still having space in the bound book had she chosen to combine such

248. McCarthy, *Accidental Diarist*, 5.

records with her personal diary.[249] By contrast, Rollin seems not to have minded the intertwining of her two accounts, personal and financial, in a single volume.

Rollin's concern with her financial circumstances and her commitment to authorship rendered the publication of her Delany biography an absolute necessity, even as she came to understand that she had to leave Boston and return home to South Carolina for other reason. She worked to cultivate the relationship with Lee & Shepard, visiting their offices more than a dozen times from 10 March to 28 July, her last day in Boston, and developing enough of a friendship with William Lee that he gifted her copies of Henry David Thoreau's *A Yankee in Canada* (1866) and the memoirs of Juliette Recamier, the French socialite and salonniere, prior to her departure.[250] He had earlier loaned her Keckley's *Behind the Scenes* and a copy of the transcripts of Andrew Johnson's impeachment trial. In April Rollin argued for Delany's continued relevance to the radical conversation in South Carolina, while Lee worried about what he saw as Delany's increasing conservatism: she writes in her diary, Lee "thinks Major Delany a Conservative. I fear he is set against him in consequence of his refusal of the Senatorship of So[uth] Ca[rolina]."[251] Lee was reacting to Delany's refusal to consider a nomination by the Colored Members of the State Nominating Convention in Charleston in early 1868 that he run for Congress; responding to the committee, the major insisted that he was "entirely opposed at this period of political experience of the country, to any person identified with the black race entering any council of the nation as a member."[252] His views on Black political leadership shocked those who, even if they had not agreed with his stance on emigration, at least admired his resolve and radicalism. By 1868, however, it seemed clear that Delany had turned to reconciliation as the solution to local and national racial politics. Rollin does not indicate whether she agreed with Lee's opinion of Delany. What her diary does make clear is that she was well informed of and enthusiastic about

249. See Katherine Johnson notebook, Jan. 1872–July 1876, vol. 50, and Johnson diary, 1864–74, vol. 31, William T. Johnson and Family Papers, Free People of Color in Louisiana: Revealing an Unknown Past, Louisiana State University Libraries, Special Collections, Baton Rouge. For an edited version of Johnson's diary, see Gould, *Chained to the Rock of Adversity*, 67–91.

250. Thoreau's *A Yankee in Canada, with Anti-Slavery and Reform Papers* is a collection of essays edited by Sophia Thoreau, William Ellery Channing, and Ralph Waldo Emerson, originally published by Ticknor and Fields in 1866. *Memoirs and Correspondence of Madame Recamier*, translated and edited by Isaphene M. Luyster, was published by Roberts Brothers in 1868 just prior to Rollin's departure from Boston.

251. Rollin diary, 6 Apr. 1868.

252. Quoted in Adeleke, *Without Regard to Race*, 102.

the South Carolina Constitutional Convention in January 1868 and the subsequent election of the nation's first Black-majority state legislature.

The title page of *Life and Public Services of Martin R. Delany* identifies its author as "Frank A. Rollin," a name that was not quite a pseudonym, as family and friends had called Frances "Frank" since childhood.[253] Moreover, Rollin was well known at least within the Black community to be at work on the biography: on 21 December 1867, a correspondent from Washington, DC, reported to the *National Anti-Slavery Standard* that a "life of Maj. Martin R. Delaney is in preparation.... The author of the volume is Miss Frances Rollin, a finely educated and talented young colored lady of Charleston, S. C."[254] The announcement was reprinted in February in the San Francisco *Elevator*.[255] This is not to say that the use of a masculine-sounding name was not strategic. It is possible that Lee & Shepard assumed that Black readers would buy the book based on their interest in Delany as well as their pride in Black authorship. White readers, however, may have required a male name on the cover to see it as sufficiently authoritative, particularly as, like William Wells Brown's *The Negro in the American Rebellion*, Rollin's biography was sold by subscription, rather than stocked by bookstores.[256]

253. Many scholars have assumed that "Frank" is a pseudonym. See Murray's profile of Frances Anne Rollin Whipper in appendix F. See also Foster and Davis, "Early African American Women's Literature" 20.

254. R. J. H., "Notes from the Capital—Personal and Literary," *National Anti-Slavery Standard*, 21 Dec. 1867, 2.

255. "Biographies," *Elevator* (San Francisco), 21 Feb. 1868, 2.

256. For a discussion of the publication and marketing of *The Negro in the American Rebellion*, see Greenspan, *William Wells Brown*, 435–39. The title and copyright pages of *Life and Public Services* were deposited with the Library of Congress on 21 August 1868; it is not clear if or when the finished book followed. On the copyright page, someone has written "female" next to the name "Frank A. Rollin" (*Life and Public Services*, images 4133–34, Copyright Title Pages, Early Copyright Records Collection, 1790–1870, Library of Congress Rare Books and Special Collections Division, Washington DC, www.loc.gov/resource/rbccpmat .copy0043/?q=delany&sp=4133&st=image. Also deposited with the Library of Congress, a list of titles to be published by Lee & Shepard in the fall of 1868 includes *Life and Public Services* by "Miss Frank R. Rollin," which, unlike any other title on the list, is indicated to be sold by subscription. It is also the only book on the list that does not include the month of its release; all of the others include publishing dates between September and November 1868 ("To Be Issued This Fall by Lee & Shepard, ... Boston," image 3655, Copyright Title Pages, Early Copyright Records Collection, www.loc.gov/resource/rbccpmat.copy0043/?sp=3655&q=delany&r=-0.501,-0.018 ,2.003,1.196,0. A notice in the *Christian Recorder* upon the 1883 rerelease of the biography implies that the book was being sold by subscription at that time as well: "The sale of the first edition of Major Delany's book was suppressed at the South, because it discussed the vital question

Rollin seems to have brought copies of the proof pages with her when she left Boston. Having traveled from Columbia to Charleston to visit her family, she notes, "Carried my book home for Pa."[257] The book was likely not published until the fall, however, as an introduction to the biography is signed "Charleston, S. C., October 19th, 1868." Rollin may have written the introduction in response to an early review in the *National Anti-Slavery Standard* announcing its publication but immediately undermining Rollin's authorship: "Miss Rollins, a Charleston (colored) lady, has written a biography of Major Delaney. It is, in fact, an autobiography."[258] While the comment is a bit difficult to parse, the reviewer seems to be suggesting that Delany had written the "biography" with very little input or assistance from Rollin. As if in direct reply, Rollin's introduction assertively claims the military historian's voice, an expert not only on war but also on its aftermath:

> At the close of every revolution in a country, there is observed an effort for the gradual and general expulsion of all that is effete, or tends to regard progress; and as the nation comes forth from its purification with its existence renewed and invigorated, a better and higher civilization is promised. . . .
>
> As the sullen roar of battle ceases, as the war cloud fades out from our sky, we are enabled to look more soberly upon the stupendous revolution, its causes and teachings, and to consider the men and new measures developed through its agency, the material with which the country is to be reconstructed.[259]

Martin Delany, she insists, is one of these men, but she is author of his biography, the narrator and interpreter of his "life and public services."

On 7 November the *Christian Recorder* published its own review. The author, identified only as "Sometimes," insists that the biography had been eagerly anticipated, not only for its subject matter but also because they "were all anxious to know with what amount of strength and grace the authoress would wield the pen; for the book is the work of a woman, notwithstanding the very masculine Frank, which the writer seems to have preferred to the more gentle and certainly more

---

of Home Rule in the Southern States, striking hard blows at the ruling party and its corruptions. Major Delany having now acquired a large interest in the book will engage personally in its sale, both North and South." "Literature," *Christian Recorder*, 19 July 1883, 3.

257. Rollin diary, 29 Aug. 1868.

258. "Personal," *National Anti-Slavery Standard*, 26 Sept. 1868, 2.

259. Rollin, *Life and Public Services*, 7. See appendix B for the complete text of her introduction to the book.

feminine Frances." Before actually reviewing the book, however, he sketches Rollin's life story, including her recent marriage to William J. Whipper: "Since turning her attention to book-making, she has performed another very sensible act in taking herself a husband." The reviewer clearly approves more of her personal life than he does her writing, going on to call her writing style "strained" and her manner "labored," and struggles to say anything more positive than "judged by the average of books, the work is a success." However ambivalent the majority of the review, he is firm in his assertion that the biography, "as a book for *colored* people, . . . will serve a useful end." As far as its author's writing career, he concludes, "Miss Rollin has made a fair beginning; she will do better in the future; she exhibits the elements of a writer of no mean order."[260]

Perhaps because this review was decidedly tepid, the *Christian Recorder* reviewed *Life and Public Services* again in March 1869. That reviewer, identified only as "Rufus," commended the book as both "a *lively, strongly* written, *truthful*" biography and "a chronicle of the leading events connected with the colored race for the last 30 years in America." It "shows a capacity and knowledge of details in authorship, that will win laurels for Frank A. Rollin in future."[261]

Becoming Frances Rollin Whipper

It is not clear when or why Rollin decided to return to South Carolina. Her reasons for doing so were likely a combination of poor health, limited finances, homesickness, and a fierce desire to be amid political events in her home state. Uncharacteristically, she stopped writing in her diary between 13 July and 27 July. On the twenty-seventh she wrote simply, "Up early and went out." The next day she announced that it was her "last day in Boston dear dear Boston."[262] She then provides a detailed account of her journey, first by boat to New York, then to Philadelphia, where she met "old friends the affectionate greeting and the interest manifested I can never forget."[263] From there she took another boat to Portsmouth, Virginia, stopping briefly at Fortress Monroe, where she no doubt reflected on the sacrifices of African American troops in the Fifty-Fourth and

260. Sometimes, "Miss Rollin's Book of Major Delaney," *Christian Recorder*, 7 Nov. 1868, 1. See appendix D.

261. Rufus, "Life and Services of Maj. Martin R. Delaney," *Christian Recorder*, 20 Mar. 1869, 1. See appendix E.

262. Rollin diary, 27, 28 July 1868.

263. Rollin diary, 29 July 1868.

Fifty-Fifth Massachusetts Regiments. Ironically, given her struggle to be provided with first-class accommodations on the *Pilot Boy*, she was then forced to ride in the Jim Crow car ("a close dirty car") to Raleigh, North Carolina, where she stayed the night with African American activist and recently appointed member of the Raleigh Board of Commissioners James H. Harris and "his very amiable wife."[264] On the train to Charlotte, North Carolina, she found herself "much annoyed by the stares of the poor whites" who no doubt found the confident demeanor and fashionable attire of this young Black woman offensive. "Secesh women abounded therein," Rollin notes with disgust.[265] Reaching Columbia, South Carolina, around six o'clock in the morning, she was met at the depot by "Mr Whipper . . . with his buggie."[266]

Prior to her arrival at the depot, there is only one identifiable mention of William J. Whipper in Rollin's diary: on 7 July 1868, she records receiving a letter from a South Carolina friend, having the proofs for her book delivered, walking with friends "in the Bridge" (likely the footbridge crossing the lagoon in Boston Public Garden), and arguing with Leedie Matthews. She concludes her entry by noting that "Whipper was not chosen speaker [of the South Carolina House of Representatives] as I expected." But it is likely that there are other, earlier references to Whipper that are more difficult to identify. In an April entry, for example, Rollin writes, "Heard this morning from Mr Adams and WW. news of the murder of Ben Capers by Arthur Chisolm."[267] Ennals Adams, Charleston minister and fellow resident at Hankerson's boardinghouse in October 1867, was married to Amelia W. Purnell Adams, the daughter of Benjamin Whipper's sister and therefore William J. Whipper's cousin.[268] Given this familial connection, it seems likely that Rollin would have met Whipper prior to her stay in Boston and may have become friendly enough to maintain a correspondence during her time there.[269] She had definitely secured employment as a clerk to the Judiciary Committee of the state house of representatives, of which Whipper was chair, prior to leaving Boston. Arriving in Columbia on a Sunday morning, Rollin received guests at her boarding place and attended church. On Monday, she went "to the

264. Rollin diary, 31 July, 1 Aug. 1868.
265. Rollin diary, 1 Aug. 1868.
266. Rollin diary, 2 Aug. 1868.
267. Rollin diary, 20 Apr. 1868.
268. McCormick, "William Whipper," 44n82.
269. Willard B. Gatewood suggests that Rollin may have known Whipper or his extended family during her time in Philadelphia ("Rollin Sisters," 54).

Committee Room" and got right to work.[270] It is less clear exactly when she and Whipper became romantically involved. Did he court her by letter while she was still in Boston? Rollin twice notes in her diary of having written a "letter to Willie."[271] While she knew many men in Boston named William—Matthews, Nell, Brown, Lee, and Garrison—and several others in South Carolina, the only one she ever calls "Willie" in the diary is William J. Whipper.[272]

Born in 1834 in Glenville, Pennsylvania, Whipper was the son of a free Black man named Benjamin Whipper and his wife, Sophia King Whipper.[273] Benjamin, the child of a Black woman named Nance and a white man who may have enslaved her, was likely himself enslaved at birth. How he and his siblings obtained their freedom is unknown. But Benjamin's younger brother, William Whipper (for whom William J. was likely named), would come to be one of the wealthiest Black men in the United States. In an echo of William Rollin's success in South Carolina, William Whipper and partner Stephen Smith owned a lumberyard business in Columbia, Pennsylvania, that included holdings in real estate, railroad cars, and a steamship. He was also an activist and an agent on the Underground Railroad, facilitating the escape of hundreds of freedom seekers.[274] Many of these were directed to Chatham, Ontario, where Benjamin settled with his wife and younger son, Thomas, sometime in the late 1850s.[275] If the younger William ever lived in Chatham, there is no record of it. He seems to have been on his own at an early age; in the 1850 US census, he is living with and working as a laborer for a white Kennett County family in Chester, Pennsylvania. By 1855, at the age of twenty, he registered as a seaman, but in 1858 he was living in Charlestown, Ohio, where he became active in the colored conventions movement and antislavery movement.[276] In April 1859, as part of a statewide campaign organized by the Ohio State Anti-Slavery Society, Whipper attempted to vote in defiance of

270. Rollin diary, 3 Aug. 1868.

271. Rollin diary, 29 Apr., 25 May (quote) 1868.

272. See Rollin diary, 18, 21 Sept. 1868.

273. Sources differ as to where Whipper was born. I rely here on Ione, *Pride of Family*, 164. For Whipper's birthplace as Penningtonville (now Atglen), Pennsylvania, see William James Whipper entry, "U.S. Citizenship Affidavit of U.S.-Born Seaman at Select Ports, 1792–1869," database, Ancestry.com.

274. Locke, "William Whipper."

275. The 1861 Canadian Census lists Benjamin Whipper, a forty-nine-year-old farmer born in the United States, as living with his wife, Sophiah, and son, Thomas, in Kent County, Canada West. Canada Census of 1861.

276. William James Whipper entry, "U.S. Citizenship Affidavit of U.S.-born Seaman."

the striking down of a law granting suffrage to individuals with more than one-half white ancestry. In a letter to the *Anti-Slavery Bugle*, Whipper described the ensuing controversy, in which a white man who had supported his right to vote was forced to appear before the court.

> They next quietly informed me that I would have to keep quiet, or I would be the next victim. I am thankful for the information, but must inform them that their threats are not sufficiently alarming to induce me to obey, although they have Squire Selby, and the State of Ohio—a patriotic firm—with the army and navy, with bristling bayonets, great open-mouthed cannons, thousands of armed men, captains, majors, and generals. I guess they will conquer, but conquer who? not the Mexicans, nor the Brighamite Mormons. Well, then, who is it? A colored man in Charlestown, Portage County, Ohio, who stands armed with the statute of Ohio, and a determination to insist upon his rights, notwithstanding the established custom of past years. So come on with your forces, for being quiet is no part of my mission.[277]

In 1861 Whipper participated in the attempted rescue of Lucy Bagby, the last enslaved person to be returned South under the Fugitive Slave Act. Carrying an iron bar, his role was to board the train transporting Bagby and her guards and knock out the coupling pin, marooning the car so that armed men could abduct the woman and make their escape. He was discovered, however, and forced to leave the train.[278]

According to Whipper's Civil War service record, he was a lumberman, perhaps working for his uncle, when he joined the Thirty-First Colored Infantry, but he must have trained as a lawyer either while living in Charlestown, Ohio; York, Michigan (where he registered for the draft); or New Haven, Connecticut (where he enlisted in March 1864).[279] He may also have met his first wife, Mary

277. William J. Whipper to Benjamin S. Jones, 15 Apr. 1859, Black Abolitionist Papers.

278. Cheek and Cheek, *John Mercer Langston*, 374.

279. William J. Whipper entry, "U.S. Compiled Service Military Records of Volunteer Union Soldiers Who Served with the United States Colored Troops: Infantry Organizations 31st through 35th, 1861–1865," database, fold3 by Ancestry.com, www.fold3.com. Following Joel Williamson, scholars often claim that Whipper was "born in Michigan and . . . served as a clerk in the office of Detroit lawyer" (*After Slavery*, 330–31). But Williamson's source for this information is a Democratic South Carolina newspaper, the *Anderson Intelligencer*, which reported on Wright, Elliot, and Whipper being admitted to the state bar. This piece disparaged the reputations of the judges who admitted them and professed to summarize the background of the

Elizabeth, in one of those places.[280] The Thirty-First Infantry took part in the Battle of Cold Harbor in June 1864 and the subsequent siege of Petersburg and Richmond. They then fought at Appomattox in April 1865 and likely witnessed the surrender of Robert E. Lee and his army. Whipper had a checkered career as a solider: he was court-martialed twice and demoted from sergeant to private nine months after being promoted.[281] Yet his record should be regarded with an awareness of what Black soldiers experienced during the war: meagre pay (if any), enforced manual labor, racism from white soldiers and officers, and the constant threat of capture by Confederates who had declared that they would kill rather than imprison African Americans taken wearing a uniform. Like many Black soldiers, Whipper seems to have resisted such treatment by extending his furloughs without permission and risking the charge of desertion.

Mustered out of the army in November 1865, Whipper headed for South Carolina, settling in Charleston, where he quickly found a use for his legal knowledge. According to "A Charlestonian" writing in the *Christian Recorder* in September 1866, Whipper, "a colored lawyer from Ohio," was practicing law in the provost court in the city. These courts, authorized by the military, handled all violations of the law. "We hope he will soon get his pocket full of greenbacks," the correspondent added. "He often pleads against some of the best lawyers in the city."[282] Mary Elizabeth joined Whipper in Charleston in early 1866, when the couple had a baby they named Cyrenius and adopted a fifteen-year-old boy named Demps Powell, who had been enslaved in Louisville, Georgia. When Major General William Tecumseh Sherman's Union forces crossed that state during the March to

---

three lawyers based on "their own account." "W. J. Whipper," the author of the *Charleston News* piece quoted explains, "was before the war in a lawyer's office in Detroit, Michigan, but, whether as office boy, clerk, or student I do not recollect" ("Admitted to Practice," *Anderson Intelligencer*, 30 Sept. 1868, 2). This article seems unreliable, and only Whipper's draft registration places him in Michigan.

280. Very little is known about Whipper's first wife. Her maiden name may have been Byrd. In *Black Society*, Gerri Major notes her birthplace and that of her son as New Haven, Connecticut (177). The 1880 census lists Cyrenius (as "C. B. Whipper") as the child of parents born in Michigan. Cyrenius is listed as having been born in Michigan as well. It is possible that Mary Elizabeth gave birth to her son before joining her husband in South Carolina, but Cyrenius spent nearly all his childhood in that state.

281. William J. Whipper entry, "U.S. Compiled Service Military Records of Volunteer Union Soldiers."

282. A Charlestonian, "Impressions of Charleston. No. Four," *Christian Recorder*, 22 Sept. 1866, 149.

the Sea, Demps sought freedom along with thousands of other enslaved people and followed the army until the end of the war. Having met Demps in the streets of Charleston and discovered that he had no home or family, Whipper sent him to Mary Elizabeth with a note asking her to give the boy breakfast. That evening he asked Demps if he would like to join their family. Perhaps Whipper saw himself in the boy, left to fend for himself at a young age.[283] His kindness to Demps provides a glimpse into the character of the man Frances Rollin was to marry: generous, warm, and perhaps a bit too impulsive.

In 1868 Whipper, along with Robert Brown Elliot and Macon B. Allen, opened the nation's first African American law firm on Broad Street in Charleston. Even as he built his practice, however, Whipper was active in South Carolina politics and the reconstruction of the state along democratic lines. He participated in the South Carolina Constitutional Convention held in Charleston in early 1868. The *Charleston Daily News* described him as "a clear, sharp, forcible speaker" with "an abundance of common sense." But they noted, he "will give trouble to any man, white or black, in the convention who crosses foils with him in debate."[284] Nearly two weeks later, the paper reinforced this opinion, calling him "as smooth in his style and imperturbable in action as if he lived on a diet of sweet oil. Nothing ruffles him. He stands a cross-fire in debate like a porcupine, and returns dart-for-dart."[285] Whipper was one of many Black leaders who advocated some moderation to facilitate the success of the convention, voting to halt the confiscation of land and disfranchisement of former Confederates.[286] He was a fierce advocate of civil rights measures, however, and when white Republicans proved irresolute on a bill prohibiting discrimination in all public accommodations, he accused them of "lurking in committee rooms and around the outside of this hall for the purpose of avoiding the vote."[287] His motion to strike the word "male" from the suffrage clause in the constitution was voted down despite his passionate advocacy. "I acknowledge the superiority of woman," Whipper pronounced. "There are large numbers of the sex who have an intelligence more than equal to our own, and I ask, is it right or just to deprive these intelligent beings of the privileges which we

283. Demps Whipper Powell, "A Providential Revelation: Relationship with the Whipper Family," box 114-1, Ser. B, Leigh R. Whipper Papers, Moorland-Spingarn Research Center, Howard University, typescript, 2–3.

284. "The Convention," *Charleston (SC) Daily News*, 15 Jan. 1868), 1.

285. "The Convention," *Charleston (SC) Daily News*, 28 Jan. 1868, 1.

286. See Holt, *Black over White*, 125–27; and Williamson, *After Slavery*, 143–44.

287. Quoted in Holt, *Black over White*, 143.

Judge William J. Whipper, ca. 1882–92. Portrait Collection. Photograph and Prints Division, Schomburg Center
for Research in Black Culture, New York Public Library
Digital Collections.

enjoy? Sir, I look upon that disposition which denies them suffrage as essentially
contemptible and wrong."[288] It is easy to imagine Frances Rollin in John Bailey's
parlor reading the proceedings of the convention and nodding approvingly at this
man granting the "superiority of woman."

Rollin's diary is silent on the end of her relationship with Leedie Matthews.
A similar silence surrounds the death of Mary Elizabeth Whipper. In a memoir
written late in life, Whipper's adopted son Demps Powell says only that she died
in Beaufort in 1867. Afterward, he explains, "Mr. Whipper having been elected a
member to the State Legislature, [h]e then moved to Columbia, S. C., where he
could better function in the many important issues that would arise. I was left

288. *Proceedings of the Constitutional Convention of South Carolina*, 837.

with a neighbor, and to attend the local school of Beaufort. (Bud) Cyrenius and his nurse went with his father to Columbia."[289] Whatever the nature of their acquaintance prior to her return to South Carolina, Whipper's courtship of Frances Rollin began immediately, and despite resistance from some family and friends, the two were married approximately six weeks later.

On that momentous day Rollin writes in her diary: "Up by times this morning getting ready. Married by Mr Adams. Very nervous."[290] Soon afterward, the *Charleston Daily News* announced the wedding of the "*Hon.* W. J. WHIPPER, of Beaufort, S.C., to FRANK A., eldest daughter of WILLIAM ROLLIN, *Esq.*"[291] Rollin's account of the wedding in her diary is followed by a brief comment about their journey to Columbia: "Found it very annoying at Branchville impudent conductor." The rest of the entry is filled with names and details about the reception: "C. Elliott & Lee at the depot. A. O. Jones Capt Lottie & Kate Ella Tolland at the house. Quite an ovation. In the evening a grand reception all the State Officers nearly ditto for the members of both Houses."[292] The "impudent conductor" constitutes an interruption to an otherwise joyous and celebratory day, but it is unclear what was "annoying" about his conduct or what exactly he did to be judged "impudent." More than thirty years later, Rollin returned to this experience in her letter to Daniel Murray:

> On the 17th of [September],[293] 1868, I had a never-to-be-forgotten and almost tragical experience; a few days before my marriage. I was leaving Columbia for Charleston to attend as clerk to the Judiciary Committee of which Mr. Whipper my intended husband was chairman. He accompanied me to the cars though I was going alone. I attempted to enter the ladies car, the conductor holding the knob of the door abruptly said, "You can't go in there this is my private car." Mr. Whipper ordered the cars open, the conductor sullenly obeying, but in turn took the white ladies who had been seated there, into another car. I entered and rode the entire distance having the whole car to myself, the conductor not even venturing to collect my ticket. But he had his revenge a few days later. We were married

289. Powell, "Providential Revelation," 4.

290. Rollin diary, 17 Sept. 1868.

291. "Married," *Charleston (SC) Daily News*, 2 Oct. 1868, 3.

292. Rollin diary, 17 Sept. 1868.

293. The transcript of this letter, likely made by Daniel Murray, reads "November," rather than September. I've corrected this mistake here, as it is unlikely that Rollin would have forgotten the date of her own wedding.

in Charleston and started for our home in Columbia accompanied by the officiating clergyman, we had a fine car from Charleston to Branchville, 58 miles distant where three railroads met, and where a change was necessary to reach Columbia. As our party boarded a first-class car and were about to enter we were confronted by our antagonist, pistol in hand, who had changed with the regular conductor for the purpose, backed by an armed scowling mob, he shouted to us, "I am Master here and you go into that car you do it at the peril of your lives." Seeing remonstrance would have been futile, resistance death, since we were wholly unprepared for such a scene we were obliged to submit. I did not, however, faint or show how terror stricken I was, but the nervous chill came on when we were several miles away from the platform at Branchville.[294]

It is difficult to say why Rollin Whipper is so much more voluble about the conductor's behavior in 1901 than she was in 1868. Perhaps she did not want the confrontation to take up much space, either physically or mentally, for the day of her wedding. While diaries are often read as unfiltered, unedited memory, it is important to note that diarists make decisions about what to write; they also maintain silence about issues that they do not want to confront or waste time on. It is possible, of course, that Rollin Whipper overelaborates in the letter to Murray, creating an amalgamation of a lifetime of violent encounters on public transportation. Writing in 1901, a year in which more than one hundred African Americans were lynched in the United States, Rollin Whipper is aware that were such a confrontation to happen at the turn of the twentieth century, it would have led to "that bridal party . . . swinging to cypress branches, riddled with bullets and later their bodies . . . food for vultures."[295]

Soon after her wedding, Frances was confronted with the violence of Reconstruction South Carolina and perhaps looked back upon the "impudent conductor" encounter as a lucky escape. For a few days, she wrote about visits from African American politicians Alonzo Ransier, Robert Smalls, Stephen Swails, Robert C. De Large (Frances noted that "Bob & W were not speaking"), William E. Johnston (who to Frances's amusement "congratulated Willie"), and others as well as their wives.[296] She soon falls silent, however, no doubt busy with the whirl of social activities. On 18 October she returns to the diary to write, "At

294. Quoted in Murray, "Sketch of Frances Rollin Whipper."
295. Quoted in Murray, "Sketch of Frances Rollin Whipper."
296. Rollin diary, 18 Sept. 1868.

Church today heard of the brutal murder of poor Randolph at Cokesbury on Friday last." And the next day she notes simply, "Randolph buried this afternoon at Columbia."[297] An Oberlin graduate and a Methodist Episcopal minister, Benjamin Franklin Randolph represented Orangeburg County at the constitutional convention and was subsequently elected to the state senate. He was also made chair of the state central committee. While campaigning on behalf of the Republican Party, he was shot and killed as he stepped off a train in Cokesbury, nearly one hundred miles west of Columbia. Democratic newspapers defended the assassination, blaming Randolph for bringing it upon himself with his "flaming and incendiary speeches."[298] The African American *Charleston Advocate*, on the other hand, insisted: "His death adds another name to the long list of martyrs who have fallen in this great struggle for equal rights in Church and State. We are ready to ask, How long shall these outrages be continued in a land of boasted civilization and freedom?"[299]

Rollin Whipper's notation of Randolph's death is comparatively brief. It is also the last formal entry in her diary. Frances was not naïve or deluded about the violence of the Reconstruction South, but the murder of Randolph was likely a harsh reminder of the dangers of political engagement for Black South Carolinians. Her fear did not prevent her from becoming more deeply involved in local and national politics on behalf of her race, her gender, her state, and ultimately her nation.

Family, Politics, and the End of Reconstruction in South Carolina

After their wedding, Frances Rollin Whipper devoted much of her time to William Whipper's political career. She continued to serve as clerk to the Judiciary Committee of the South Carolina House of Representatives.[300] She also provided invaluable support to her husband when he was attacked and misrepresented by his Democratic political opponents and the press. Writing of their partnership, Daniel Murray noted in 1901: "Mr. Whipper possessed the necessary ability and

297. Rollin diary, 18, 19 Oct. 1868.

298. "Murder of B. F. Randolph, Negro Senator from Orangeburg," *Orangeburg (SC) News*, 24 Oct. 1868, 3.

299. "Assassination of the Rev. B. F. Randolph of the South Carolina M. E. Conference," *Charleston (SC) Advocate*, 24 Oct. 1868, 2.

300. Quoted in Murray, "Sketch of Frances Rollin Whipper."

courage to command any honor in the gift of his party, while his wife had all the ambition, zeal and bravery to urge him to the front. She was his trusted aid in his political battles and like the Duchess of Marlborough the last to acknowledge defeat, at times he chafed under her guardianship, to which she would reply, 'You may be a wiser and better politician, but I fancy my womanly intuition can read more accurately the signs of the coming storm than all your weather-wise experience.'"[301] Her social skills were also deployed in the service of William's career. In her professional and social life, Rollin Whipper told Murray that she "daily came into contact with the most prominent men of the State black and white of both political parties."[302] One of their most important relationships was with Governor Robert Kingston Scott, a transplant from Ohio who had served as an officer in the Union army and assistant commissioner of the Freedmen's Bureau in South Carolina. Rollin Whipper called Scott "one of the manliest specimens of the white officials" in Reconstruction South Carolina, explaining: "He and his equally whole-souled wife gave public receptions to which the member[s] of the Legislature and any distinguished strangers who might at the time be in the City, were invited. On these occasions, there were generally about as many white as colored present. . . . I have frequently been their guest both at private and public functions."[303] The Whippers surely also entertained guests in their own home in Columbia, where Frances's grace and intelligence no doubt proved an advantage to her husband.

Rollin Whipper also used her literary abilities to benefit his career. In the early 1870s, she edited the *Beaufort County Times*, a newspaper that Whipper published for his constituency. "It was customary among the prominent South Carolina politicians to get their views before the people through the medium of a personal organ," she explained in 1901. "My husband had his and as editor I acquired some little experience in newspaper work both as editor and contributor."[304] It is possible that Demps Whipper Powell, who had trained as a printer, assisted with the newspaper, perhaps while attending Claflin University, a school for Black students in Orangeburg, South Carolina.[305] Only one copy of the *Times*

301. Murray, "Sketch of Frances Rollin Whipper."

302. Quoted in Murray, "Sketch of Frances Rollin Whipper."

303. Quoted in Murray, "Sketch of Frances Rollin Whipper."

304. Quoted in Murray, "Sketch of Frances Rollin Whipper."

305. "Demps Whipper Powell: Civil War Veteran, Enumerator, Patriarch," US Census Bureau, US Department of Commerce, Economics, and Statistics Administration, www.census .gov/library/fact-sheets/1890/adcom/demps-powell.html. For Powell's training as a printer, see also Powell, "Providential Revelation."

is extant—a Christmas issue, dated 21 December 1872.[306] It is difficult to know exactly what Rollin Whipper contributed to this particular issue, as none of the items are signed. Given the unlikelihood that the Whippers employed any writers for the paper, however, it seems possible that all the original content was written by Frances, identified on the masthead as "Editress," and perhaps her husband. The content of the *Times* consisted largely of reprints from other newspapers (for example, "Girls Who Bet," from the *Woman's Journal*), summaries of stories from other newspapers (for example, "Progress of American Iron Industry," from the *New York Times*), and some local and political news. These last pieces, as well as the fiction and poetry that appeared, may have been written by Rollin Whipper. A short story on the first page of the extant issue, "The Hermit's Stocking: A Christmas Tale," is about a lonely hermit who is encouraged by a young boy to put up his Christmas stocking on a tree in the woods. In the morning he finds a baby there and, after some initial reluctance, decides to take the infant to the boy's house to find food for it. There he receives "one of the warmest welcomes that ever was seen." Delighted with his newfound popularity, the hermit decides to keep the baby. "So he took a frame house in the village, and had a cook-stove and things, and a good woman to take care of him and the child, and there he lived happy as a king."[307] While the story is clearly intended as entertainment rather than serious commentary and the characters are not identified by race, the story brings to mind Rollin Whipper's own adopted sons, Demps Powell and Cyrenius "Bud" Whipper. Such blended families were not uncommon following the Civil War, with children orphaned by slavery or battle finding—if they were lucky enough—new homes within the African American community.[308]

Less than a year after their wedding, on 7 July 1869, the Whippers' first child, Alicia, was born, but she died several months later. Winnifred was born in 1870 and Ionia in 1872, followed by another daughter, named Mary Elizabeth after William's first wife, who only lived for about a year. The Whippers' only son, Leigh, was born on 29 October 1876 shortly before Frances's thirty-second birthday. The family seems to have moved between Columbia, Charleston, and

306. This sole remaining issue of the *Beaufort County Times* is at the Patricia D. Klingenstein Library, The New-York Historical Society, New York City.

307. "The Hermit's Stocking: A Christmas Tale," *Beaufort County Times*, 21 Dec. 1871, 1.

308. W. J. Megginson observes: "Orphans were often found among African Americans. Slave inventories sometimes specifically mentioned them, Freedmen's Bureau agents dealt with orphans, and many children in the 1870 census seem to be orphaned" (*African American Life*, 142).

Beaufort in these early years. Later in life Leigh Whipper remembered living in Beaufort with his parents and his brother Bud, while his sisters, Winifred and Ionia, lived in Charleston with relatives, probably attending school.[309] His devotion to and pride in his mother is apparent in a letter he wrote: "Old Man Whipper was no Fool when he picked our Mother for his wife."[310]

If Frances kept a diary during this time of her life, it has not survived. Two recipes penciled into the 1868 diary on the pages provided for 17 and 18 November ("Spiced Beef" and "Macaroni Pie") point toward a far more domestic existence than she was accustomed to as a young, unmarried woman. These recipes also indicate the continued utility of the diary: its use had clearly changed, but it remained a resource for Rollin Whipper. On June 28, 1869, just before the birth of her first child, Frances made a list on one of the "Memoranda" pages found at the end of the preprinted diary. Beginning with "sheets" and "Pillowc," the list consists mostly of clothing items: "Shirts," "Chemises," and "Drawers," among other things. Was this a laundry list, perhaps, or a list of items to pack for her lying-in period or a visit to Charleston? It is not clear. What is clear is that the diary remained on hand for Frances's use long after she ceased documenting her daily existence. Its presence in the Whipper household for years to come is indicated by Winifred's scrawled signature on blank pages for November 9 and 10. Did the young girl see her mother rereading her diary, reminiscing about her time in Boston, and attempt to make her own mark in this important book? Perhaps Frances showed the diary to her young daughter in an attempt to inspire her to begin her own diary-writing practice.[311]

Despite the intensification of her domestic responsibilities in the years following her marriage, Rollin Whipper no doubt joined her sisters in their salon, hosted in their Columbia home on Senate and Sumter Streets. An 1871 article published in the *New York Sun* was racist and unreliable, like much of the

309. Leigh Whipper to Dr. Ionia Whipper, 8 Sept. 1930, in *Letters from Black America: Intimate Portraits of the African American Experience*, ed. Pamela Newkirk (Beacon, 2009), 28.

310. Leigh Whipper to Dr. Ionia Whipper, 8 Sept. 1930, 29.

311. There is no extant diary for Winifred Whipper. Carole Ione explains that Ionia Rollin Whipper "kept diaries when she could" during her work as a physician. "Two diaries have come down to me: a leather-bound book titled *Day by Day: A Perpetual Diary*, kept intermittently between 1920 and 1929; and a spiritual diary dating from the late 1930s" (*Pride of Family*, 17–18). Ione later donated the former to the National Museum of African American History and Culture. See "Diary of Dr. Ionia Rollin Whipper," 1923, Carole Ione Lewis Family Collection, Collection of the Smithsonian National Museum of African American History and Culture, https://nmaahc.si.edu/object/nmaahc_2018.101.2.

newspaper coverage of the Whippers and the Rollins, but it was likely accurate when it represented their salon as "a kind of a Republican headquarters."[312] Charlotte and Kate had, by 1869, begun work as clerks at the South Carolina State House. Charlotte's appointment to the Adjutant General's Office was considered newsworthy, with the *National Anti-Slavery Standard* printing an excerpt from a correspondent who found "Miss Rollin" "highly educated and accomplished."[313] In South Carolina, however, white editors and reporters represented the women's employment as an unwarranted political favor at best and a form of concubinage at worst. On 6 September 1870, the *Charleston Daily News* reported on the

> comely mulatto woman who draws one hundred dollars a month from the State militia fund. . . . The name of Governor Scott's pet may be Lucy, or Kate, or Sarah Jane, for all that we know or care. But we repeat that there is a light mulattress, or quadroon, in the bureau at Columbia, who was appointed to do nothing, and has done nothing, with exemplary fidelity, at an expense to the State of seventy-five and one hundred dollars a month. This girl goes by the name of Rollin, or Rawlins, and was appointed to her place by his Excellency Governor Scott, commander-in-chief of the army and navy in South Carolina, upon whose order her salary is regularly paid."[314]

This hostile response to the Rollin sisters was likely a result of their employment for the government, their intimacy with both Black and white politicians, and their fierce and vocal advocacy for woman suffrage.

Indeed, the Rollin sisters were among the first women suffragists in Reconstruction South Carolina. On 3 March 1869, Charlotte addressed the Judiciary Committee of the state house of representatives, protesting the denial of a woman's "right, as a citizen, to vote and hold office." She compared the granting of woman suffrage to "the enfranchisement of the black men of the South, which was demanded as an imperative political necessity."

> And yet, how nobly did the loyal women of the South bear their share of the toil, hardship and privation during that long and sanguinary struggle for the Union and the liberty of the *bondmen*. . . . Be it said to the eternal honor of the women of my own race, they *never* faltered nor fainted in their deeds of kindness towards the defenders of the republic. Who comprehended more quickly than they the meaning of the fierce contest between the South and

312. A. P., "Queens of the South,"2.
313. "Personal," *National Anti-Slavery Standard*, 31 July 1869, 2.
314. "The Fair Major of the Ring," *Charleston (SC) Daily News*, 6 Sept. 1870, 2.

the North, and whose prayers were more constantly rising to the Throne of our Common Father in behalf of those who were on the side of the Union, of justice, and the right? And shall such women be denied their natural and inalienable right to the ballot? If the franchise has been given the black man, not only as a political necessity, but as a reward for his loyalty and services in our now victorious cause, what excuse can be devised for withholding it from the equally loyal and serviceable women of the South? For these noble and heroic women I claim the right of citizenship and the privilege of the franchise.[315]

Charlotte's passionate argument is most striking for the way she claims the right of suffrage for all women based on the actions of Black women ("for the women of my own race") during the Civil War. With her sisters supporting her, Charlotte continued to take the organizational lead, forming the South Carolina chapter of the American Woman Suffrage Association in 1871, with meetings held at her home and that of the Whippers.[316] On 13 March 1872, Whipper and his allies attempted to pass an amendment to the state constitution to grant woman suffrage, but it was quickly rejected by the legislature.[317]

Despite their previous intimacy, Whipper accused Governor Scott of corruption in 1871 and led an unsuccessful effort to impeach him. He then joined a reform ticket within the Republican Party to challenge Robert Smalls for the state senate. Born enslaved in Beaufort, Smalls had stolen the Confederate steamship *Planter* and, after picking up his own family and those of the crew, delivered it to Union forces. He went on to command the *Planter* throughout the remainder of the war, earning enough in salary and prize money to purchase the Beaufort mansion of the man who had enslaved him. Like Whipper, Smalls served as a delegate to the South Carolina Constitutional Convention and was elected to the house of representatives. While the two had once worked together, opening a school for Black children in Beaufort in 1867 and founding the Beaufort Republican Club, the ugly election campaign initiated a rivalry between them that historian Edward A. Miller Jr. has called "fratricidal."[318] According to Eric Foner, at around the same time, Whipper operated a plantation on the Ashepoo

---

315. Charlotte "Lottie" Rollin, "To Exercise the Same Privileges," speech to the Judiciary Committee, House of Representatives of South Carolina, 3 Mar. 1869, Speaking While Female Speech Bank, https://speakingwhilefemale.co/womans-vote-rollin1/.

316. "Woman Suffrage in South Carolina," *Sumter (SC) Watchman*, 1 Feb. 1871, 2.

317. "Woman Suffrage in South Carolina."

318. Miller, *Gullah Statesman*, 44–45, 249.

River and was reported to Governor Scott for having inadequately compensated the people working for him.[319] This was just the tip of the iceberg, though, when it came to Whipper's controversial reputation. Frances's husband was known as an extravagant spender and a lover of leisure and luxury, including drinking, gambling, and horse racing. His great-granddaughter Carole Ione has recounted family stories about his brother lending him money to cover gambling debts; she also has located evidence revealing that Frances Rollin Whipper put property in her name to prevent its confiscation to cover such debts.[320] Given the racist coverage of Black politicians by many South Carolina newspapers, it is difficult to know the extent of his problems.

In 1874 the legislature elected Whipper a circuit court judge, but Governor Daniel Chamberlain refused to sign the commission, charging him with incompetence and moral inferiority. Chamberlain was a Republican but had been elected on a Fusion platform, and thus he was eager to court Democratic support. The fact that he had no authority to ignore or overturn the legislature's vote did not prevent him from doing so, angering Black legislators who had voted overwhelmingly for Whipper. Robert Brown Elliot, Whipper's friend and law partner who was now Speaker of the General Assembly, insisted that Chamberlain's resistance was the result of racism. As Peggy Lamson notes, "For an office of such significance and power to fall to a black [man] was insupportable" to Democrats and to Chamberlain if he wanted the approval and support of Democrats.[321] Bitterly disappointed, Whipper moved his family to Beaufort, where he practiced law.

Frances and William's disappointment was part and parcel of the larger failure of Reconstruction, which ended with the victory of Republican Rutherford B. Hayes in the 1876 presidential election. His opponent, Democrat Samuel J. Tilden, received approximately 260,000 more votes than Hayes but was short electoral votes due to disputed results in Florida, Louisiana, and South Carolina. In what is now called the Compromise of 1877, Hayes was pronounced the winner of the election in exchange for ceding control of the South to Democratic governments and pledging noninterference in what were seen as Southern affairs. On 10 March 1877, a delegation of Black South Carolinians met with President Hayes to appeal this decision but were told that "the use of the military forces in civil affairs was repugnant to the genius of American institutions, and should

---

319. Foner, *Freedom's Lawmakers*, 227.
320. Ione, *Pride of Family*, 137–38.
321. Lamson, *Glorious Failure*, 220.

be dispensed with, if possible."[322] On 3 April Hayes ordered the removal of US troops in South Carolina, opening the door for ex-Confederate extremists to take control of state government. As Robert B. Elliott noted several years later, the Republican Party dissolved "like a rope of sand."[323] For Frances Rollin Whipper, it was the end of an era. "From 1868 to 1876 I was prosperous and happy," she wrote in 1901. "In the latter year the treachery of Rutherford B. Hayes to the Republican governments of the South caused their overthrow and with it my personal and political aspirations in the Southland vanished as completely as the filmy realities of a dream."[324] Her sister Kate's death from tuberculosis in 1876 must have reinforced Frances's sense that this was the end of an era for her family.

Washington, DC, and Back Again: Like Horatius She Held the Bridge

The death of Frances's father in 1880 prompted another return to the diary: on the last dated page provided in the volume—2 January 1869—Frances turned the book on its side and wrote, "William Rollin died morning of the 24th Feb. 80 about two oclock ~~Feb~~ In the 65 years of his age."[325] The notation indicates that she was likely not keeping a diary at the time and treasured this record of the year of her marriage and the publication of her book. The documentation of her father's death in this location may also point to Frances's awareness that her father's love and support had enabled the achievement of her dream of authorship and the other adventures recorded in the diary.

A dispute with her mother over the right to administer her father's estate left Frances estranged from Margaret Rollin, who had moved with Charlotte, Louise, and Florence to Brooklyn after her husband's death.[326] It is not clear why they settled there. Almost a decade earlier, the *New York Sun* quoted one of the sisters telling a reporter that they would like to move to Brooklyn to attend Henry Ward Beecher's Plymouth Church: "We all love Mr. Beecher so much. I could put my

322. Quoted in Zuczek, *State of Rebellion*, 199.

323. Quoted in Holt, *Black over White*, 209.

324. Quoted in Murray, "Sketch of Frances Rollin Whipper."

325. According to William Rollin's death record, he died on 25 February 1880 and is buried at "St. John's Evangelical," likely the Cathedral of St. John the Baptist in Charleston. See William Rollin entry, "South Carolina, U.S., Death Records, 1821–1971," database, Ancestry.com.

326. See "Petition of Margaret Rollin," 31 Mar. 1880, case 262-0011, Charleston County Probate Court, South Carolina Room, Charleston County Public Library, microfilm.

arms around his neck and kiss him for the great service he has done us. Besides, we are just a little bit afraid of the Ku Klux Klan."[327] This representation of the undifferentiated Rollin sisters' desire to kiss Beecher, who would soon be exposed by Victoria Woodhull for his affair with a parishioner's wife, indicates the general unreliability of the *Sun* article. Yet it is possible that one or more of the Rollins sisters did mention their desire to move to Brooklyn as early as 1871. The article concludes, "But for their color they might move in the highest circles of Washington and New York society."[328]

Perhaps because they tired of being told what they might accomplish "but for their color," or perhaps because of their justifiable fear of racial violence, Margaret, Charlotte, Louise, and Florence seem to have passed as white in Brooklyn. Listed as "white" in the 1880 US census, Florence was a music teacher, while Charlotte taught in the public schools. Their place of birth is listed as Cuba. While this may have been true of Margaret, it certainly was not of her daughters, who were, like Frances, born in Charleston. It is not clear whether the Rollins passed only for practical purposes, otherwise associating with the African American community in Brooklyn, but it seems unlikely. Florence's marriage to James F. Kernan, the white son of Irish immigrants, in 1884 and the naming of their two children Manuela and Diego indicates that this was more than a simple mistake on the part of the census taker or an occasional performance to alleviate difficulties in particular circumstances.[329] Margaret died in 1889 and was buried in Holy Cross Cemetery in Brooklyn; the inscription on her headstone, written in Spanish, commemorates the death of "nuestre madre, Margarita Rollin, nacio en Granada Spain"—"our mother" who was "born in Granada, Spain."[330] In the 1900 census, Charlotte and Louisa (now "Mary") were said to have been born in Uruguay; they would claim South American birth in every census after this. In a pointed erasure of her experiences of the Civil War and Reconstruction, Charlotte declared that she had immigrated to the United States in 1877. It is not clear whether the sisters were ever in touch with Frances and her family after their move to New

327. A. P., "Queens of the South," 2.

328. A. P., "Queens of the South."

329. Florence Rollin and James F. Kernan entry, "New York, New York, Extracted Marriage Index, 1866–1937," database, Ancestry.com.

330. On her death certificate, Margaret is listed as "Margarita." She is said to have been born in Martinique in 1825, and her father and mother are said to have been born in England and Granada, respectively. See Margarita [Margaret] Rollin entry, "New York, New York, U.S., Index to Death Certificates, 1862–1948," database, Ancestry.com.

York City. Both Louisa and Charlotte lived to see the passage of the Nineteenth Amendment, giving women the right to vote, in 1920: Louisa died in late 1921, while Charlotte worked as a teacher until her death in 1929. Both sisters were buried with their mother in Holy Cross Cemetery, sharing a headstone.[331] Florence, who died in 1934, was buried in the same plot.[332]

Following her father's death and what must have felt like a betrayal on the part of her mother, Frances Rollin Whipper also left South Carolina, taking her children to Washington, DC, where she was employed as a clerk in the Land Office in March 1882. Difficulties with her husband may have contributed to the move, but he seems to have joined the family there for a few years, perhaps in an attempt to reconcile, perhaps to escape South Carolina politics. Married and with a growing family, Demps Whipper Powell remained behind in South Carolina, serving as postmaster of Coosaw, a town in Beaufort County, and then in 1890 began working at the Charleston Navy Yard for the US Navy. He also served as an enumerator for the US census in 1890 and 1900.[333] For whatever reason, Rollin Whipper seems not to have considered joining her sisters and mother in Brooklyn. Whether their relationship was irrevocably damaged by the dispute over her father's estate or the family were estranged by their crossing of the color line, Frances maintained her ties to her husband and her race, building a future for their children in the nation's capital. In this she was similar to many elite African Americans at the time who found social, political, occupational, and educational opportunity in Washington, DC.

Her education, marriage, employment with the government, and previous acquaintance with African American society in Philadelphia and Boston would have eased Rollin Whipper's adjustment to Washington. According to Carole Ione, Frances held a "veritable salon" in her DC home and continued her work for the Republican Party, campaigning for James G. Blaine in the 1884 presidential election.[334] Daniel Murray has noted that "Mrs. Whipper during her residence

331. Margaret Irving Rollin, Find a Grave, www.findagrave.com/memorial/229790139/margaret-rollin; Lottie [Charlotte] M. Rollin, Holy Cross Cemetery, Brooklyn, NY, Find a Grave, www.findagrave.com/memorial/229790268/lottie_m-rollin; Marie Rollin, Holy Cross Cemetery, Brooklyn, NY, Find a Grave, www.findagrave.com/memorial/229790599/marie-rollin.

332. Florence [Rollin] Kernan, Holy Cross Cemetery, Brooklyn, Kings County, NY, Find a Grave, www.findagrave.com/memorial/173344646/florence-kernan.

333. "Demps Whipper Powell," US Census Bureau.

334. Ione, *Pride of Family*, 192.

Frances Anne Rollin Whipper, ca. 1870–79.
Leigh Rollin Whipper Photograph Collection,
Photographs and Prints Division, Schomburg
Center for Research in Black Culture, New York
Public Library Digital Collections.

in Washington enjoyed the reputation of being a very fine conversationalist."[335]
While in DC, she likely renewed her acquaintance with Charlotte Forten, married since 1878 to Francis Grimké, minister to the Fifteenth Street Presbyterian
Church. Richard Greener had moved to the capital in 1879 to become dean of
the Howard University Law School and attended the Reverend Grimké's church.
Other families with South Carolina connections included the Cardozos, the
Purvises, and the McKinlays. (Whitefield McKinlay, who moved to the capital
around the same time as the Whippers, was the brother of Weston McKinlay,
whose death by Union artillery fire Frances had written about in *Life and Public
Services.*) Rollin Whipper was also no doubt in residence at the time of a scandal
that broke in early 1883, when William E. Matthews, now owner of a lucrative real
estate and brokerage firm, reputedly spent the night with a young schoolteacher in
his room at a boardinghouse on Fourteenth Street. Rollin Whipper would have

335. Quoted in Murray, "Sketch of Frances Rollin Whipper."

been interested not only because of her past relationship with Leedie but also because the woman was the younger sister of Dr. Benjamin A. Boseman, William J. Whipper's fellow legislator and the postmaster of Charleston from 1873 until his death in 1881.[336] The couple were married a few days later.[337] Whether Frances and Leedie resumed their friendship before his sudden and premature death in May 1894 is unclear.[338]

Rollin Whipper and the children joined the recently built St. Luke's Protestant Episcopal Church, "an architectural symbol of black bourgeois culture," where the activist intellectual Alexander Crummell served as pastor; Frances was confirmed there on 11 March 1883 along with eleven other candidates.[339] St. Luke's was attended by the capital city's Black elite, who saw themselves as representatives of all that African Americans had accomplished since the Civil War, as well as by local whites.[340] Rollin would no doubt have listened with interest to Crummell's Thanksgiving 1884 sermon on Psalms 105.1, "'Tell the people what things he hath done.'" One newspaper reported the sermon to be "highly interesting" and explained, "The preacher set forth in an impressive manner the wonderful changes of the last twenty years—emancipation, mental elevation, moral and spiritual improvement, and acquisition of many millions of property."[341]

Rollin Whipper may have attended one of the many literary societies active in Black society at the end of the nineteenth century. It is tempting to imagine her participation in the Bethel Literary and Historical Society, at which members "engage[d] ... in healthy and productive debate on the political matters that affected them most directly," such as Black education, leadership, business, and religion. Her friend from the ICY, John Wesley Cromwell, was one of the founders

336. Euretta Bozeman was not from Charleston, so Rollin Whipper would not have known her prior to moving to DC. The scandal was widely reported in local newspapers, and an investigative committee made up of Frederick Douglass, Alexander Crummell, and another man interviewed those involved in the affair. See Maillard, *Whispers of Cruel Wrongs*, 100.

337. "Matthews-Bozeman," *Evening Star* (Washington, DC), 4 Jan. 1883, 4.

338. Thomas H. Clarke, "Wm. E. Matthews Is Dead," *Washington (DC) Bee*, 4 May 1894, 3.

339. Moses, *Alexander Crummell*, 204. For Rollin Whipper's confirmation, see Frances Whipper, confirmation certificate, Diocese of Maryland, St. Luke's Church, Washington, DC, 11 Mar. 1883, box 114-1, Leigh R. Whipper Papers, Ser. B, Moorland-Spingarn Research Center, Howard University. According to one newspaper, Episcopal Bishop William Pinkney preached a sermon and "administered the rite of confirmation to 12 candidates," one of whom was Rollin Whipper ("Events in the Churches," *Evening Star* [Washington, DC], 12 Mar. 1883, 4).

340. Ralph, *Dixie*, 369; Chapin, *American Court Gossip*, 42.

341. "Thanksgiving Notes," *Evening Star* (Washington, DC), 28 Nov. 1884, 2.

(along with Daniel Payne) of the society, of which he published a detailed history in 1896.[342] She may also have resumed her writing career while in Washington, perhaps inspired by an 1883 reissuing of *Life and Public Services* from Lee & Shepard. A 1939 profile of Leigh Whipper, who became an actor, tantalizingly alludes to two other books supposedly written by his mother: *Western Romance*, "based on the love story of a trooper in the Ninth Cavalry," and *Curse of Cain*.[343] These titles may have been imagined by the author of the profile, but they may have been based on information provided the reporter by Rollin Whipper's son. Their existence cannot be confirmed based on the scant information provided. In 1901, two years after leaving the capital, Rollin Whipper told Daniel Murray, "I write now occasionally an article for the press under a nom de plume, sometimes for others." Publishing under a pseudonym or not signing her work at all seems to have been a habit for Frances, beginning with the pieces published while she was a student at the ICY. Although she likely wrote and published throughout her life, this practice makes it difficult, if not impossible, to reconstruct her body of work.

By 1885, William J. Whipper had returned to Beaufort, where he was elected county probate judge. His election prompted Frances's removal from the Land Office. The reason given for her dismissal was that, as a married woman, she had no need for a salary of her own, but the motivation was clearly political. "'Offensive partisanship' was the case assigned," she later wrote, "but in further explanation I was told, that my husband's holding an office (having been elected County Judge) made me ineligible."[344] In December 1885 the *Washington Bee* reprinted a piece from the *National Free Press* announcing her dismissal:

> Mrs. Whipper, of South Carolina, was discharged from her position in the general land office, as copyist with the salary of $900 per annum, for the reason that she was a married woman. She was industrious, capable, and efficient. There was nothing against her in any way.... This action on the part of the honorable secretary and commissioner of the general land office may be alright and proper, but there are open ground[s] for sharp criticisms for what they have done in the case of Mrs. Whipper, in connection with what they have done in many other cases.

The editor of the *Bee* followed the reprint with a note clarifying that, while they appreciated the *Free Press*'s criticism of the Land Office, there was more going on:

342. See Cromwell, *History of the Bethel Literary and Historical Association*.
343. Hope Bennett, "Hollywood Pictorial," *Chicago Defender*, 12 Aug. 1939, 20.
344. Quoted in Murray, "Sketch of Frances Rollin Whipper."

"The above is an extract from a democratic paper. It must be remembered that Mrs. Whipper is a colored lady and the unwritten law says that a Negro shall not have the same rights that are accorded to white people."[345] This "unwritten law" was made apparent in the coverage by the *Charleston News and Courier*, which reprinted a piece from the *New York Herald* announcing Frances's removal and claimed, "This colored woman was an offensive partisan, and gave almost all of her time to talking politics." The *News* added, "The South Carolina woman referred to is the wife of W. J. Whipper, the colored Probate Judge of Beaufort County and one of the meanest and the most vicious of all the Republican leaders in the State during 'the years of good stealing.'"[346]

After her dismissal, Frances was almost immediately hired by Frederick Douglass, who had been confirmed as recorder of deeds in 1881. She continued working at the office after President Grover Cleveland replaced Douglass with another African American appointment, lawyer James C. Matthews, in 1886 but was discharged again in 1895. On 26 October the *Washington Bee* reported, "Mrs. Francis Whipper, who was such a friend to the Recorder of Deeds has been discharged from the Recorder's office."[347] They provided a sense of her personality when another column in that issue announced, "Mrs. Whipper is talking about giving an entertainment to those who discharged her."[348] She may have found work again briefly, as she is listed in the city's 1898 directory as a "copyist."[349]

Frances remained loyal to Whipper throughout controversy, even during a thirteen-month prison sentence he served beginning in 1888 for refusing to relinquish his probate records after losing his judgeship in a rigged election.[350] After the narrow election of former Governor "Pitchfork" Ben Tillman to the state senate in 1894, he and his political allies determined to overhaul the 1868 constitution passed by Whipper and his colleagues and disenfranchise Black South Carolinians.[351] In 1895 Whipper was one of just six Black delegates to the convention (and the only six Republicans, as opposed to seventy-six in 1868), five of whom

345. "The Case of Mrs. Whipper," *Washington (DC) Bee*, 12 Dec. 1885, 2.

346. Quoted in Ione, *Pride of Family*, 192, 193.

347. "Mrs. Whipper Discharged," *Washington (DC) Bee*, 26 Oct. 1895, 8.

348. "Amusements," *Washington (DC) Bee*, 26 Oct. 1895, 8.

349. *Boyd's Directory of the District of Columbia* (1898).

350. Ione, *Pride of Family*, 193–94.

351. Clemson University's Special Collections and Archives holds most of the Benjamin Ryan Tillman Papers and the books from his library, including, oddly, an 1883 copy of Rollin, *Life and Public Services*. Tillman's signature is inside the front cover of the book.

represented Beaufort. The convention proposed a number of measures to prevent African Americans from voting, including the limitation of suffrage to men who owned at least $300 in property and those who were able to read and write from the state constitution. Voters also had to prove state and precinct residency and pay a poll tax. Addressing the delegates, Whipper said of the 1868 convention: "I am proud of the work done in that convention. The way it has stood the test has shown there was nothing dangerous in it." Of the new constitution, he asserted: "We are going to make this fight all along the line. I know that nothing I can say will change a single vote. I do say that sooner or later, God being always right, right will eventually prevail. We want you to understand that we do have rights, and they must sooner or later be recognized." After the final vote on the new constitution, Robert Smalls, on behalf of the Beaufort County representatives, abstained from signing it.[352]

Rollin Whipper told Daniel Murray that her husband had an "indomitable spirit" that "sustain[ed] him in refusing to surrender." "In the meantime," she added, "I supported the family in Washington. (Like Horatius she held the bridge.)"[353] Referencing Thomas Babington Macauley's poem about Horatius's successful effort to hold the gate to Rome against an Etruscan attack, Frances clearly conveys her sense that her family—and those of other African Americans during Reconstruction—was vulnerable to racist discrimination and violence from white Americans. Holding the bridge for her husband meant keeping her family safe and intact while he took on the political establishment in South Carolina.

Indeed, Frances's protection enabled Cyrenius, Winnifred, Ionia, and Leigh to succeed socially, academically, and professionally. An 1885 newspaper article reported that Bud Whipper, now likely known exclusively as Cyrenius, attended Howard University during the day and the Spencerian Business College at night.[354] He remained in Washington, DC, working as a printer until approximately 1890, when he moved to Savannah, Georgia.[355] Ionia, Winnifred, and Leigh attended DC public schools, and all three matriculated at Howard

---

352. *Journal of the Constitutional Convention*, 730.

353. Quoted in Murray, "Sketch of Frances Rollin Whipper."

354. "Locals," *Washington (DC) Bee*, 23 May 1885, 3.

355. See *Boyd's Directory of the District of Columbia* (1885, 1886, 1887, 1888 [which lists Cyrenius as a reporter]). Cyrenius is listed as a printer in *Sholes Directory of the City of Savannah* (1890, 1891, 1896, and 1900); as a laborer in *Sholes Directory* (1892); and as a porter in *Sholes Directory* (1898).

University.[356] The social activities of the Whipper daughters were frequently noted in the local newspaper, from Winnifred's participation in a "parlor sociable" in early 1886 to the sisters spearheading the formation of the Teachers Beneficial Association in 1898.[357] Upon graduation from Howard, Winnifred became a teacher in the DC schools. According to Carole Ione, she also "did clerical work . . . while she studied for a nursing certificate."[358] Tragically, Winnifred died of tuberculosis in 1907 at the age of thirty-seven. Ionia taught for ten years before entering Howard Medical School. She graduated in 1903, one of just four women in her class. She devoted her career to treating women patients, opening a maternity home in Washington for Black unwed teenagers in the early 1930s. After training as a lawyer, Leigh Whipper began acting in 1900, when in order to earn money to pay his landlady, he took a role in a stage performance of *Uncle Tom's Cabin*.[359] He eventually starred in multiple plays and films and in 1920 was the first African American actor to join Actors Equity, a labor union for workers in live theatrical performances. Leigh cofounded the Negro Actors Guild in 1937. While he took a different route from that of his siblings, he likewise fulfilled his parents' dreams of Black leadership and excellence.

Ill health forced Rollin Whipper to leave Washington in 1899 and return to Beaufort and her husband. It is unclear whether she intended to remain there: a notice in the *Washington Bee* claims that she was "visiting home in the South," adding, "We hope she will return much improved in health."[360] Very little evidence survives to show what her life in Beaufort was like. She clearly retained her grace and dignity: Demps Powell's daughter, born in 1894, retained a memory of Frances Rollin Whipper "beautifully dressed, stepping out of a buggy, carrying a parasol." She told Carole Bovoso (Ione) in the 1970s, "She was so dignified that the neighbors ran to their nearest windows when she walked out, just to see her move."[361] The 1900 US census does not list an occupation for Frances, but it is difficult to imagine her being idle.

356. Quoted in Murray, "Sketch of Frances Rollin Whipper." For Winnifred's attendance at Howard, see *Catalogue of the Officers and Students of Howard University*.

357. "Locals," *Washington (DC) Bee*, 27 Mar. 1886, 3; "The Week in Society," *Washington (DC) Bee*, 14 May 1898, 5.

358. Ione, *Pride of Family*, 194.

359. Ione, *Pride of Family*, 151.

360. "Observations of Themis," *Washington (DC) Bee*, 19 Aug. 1899, 5.

361. Quoted in Bovoso, "Discovering My Foremothers," 20.

In her 1901 letters to Daniel Murray, the only known extant pieces of her writing other than the diary and the biography of Martin Delany, Rollin Whipper seemed uncertain about her legacy: "I thank you sincerely that you deem me worthy to be inscribed among those who have contributed to the progress and uplifting of the race. I have always classed myself with those who never reached the mark they had in sight, though perhaps in some other sphere, 'the soul must win the goal that erst were possible.'" The quote is from "Has Been" by the white poet Ella Wheeler Wilcox:

> That melancholy phrase, "It might have been,"
>   However sad, doth in its heart enfold
>   A hidden germ of promise; for I hold
> *Whatever might have been shall be.* Though in
> Some other realm and life, the soul *must* win
>   The goal that erst was possible. But cold
>   And cruel as the sound of frozen mould
> Dropped on a coffin are the words "has been."
>   "She has been beautiful," "he has been great,"
> "Rome has been powerful," we sigh and say.
> It is the pitying crust we toss decay,
>   The dirge we breathe o'er some degenerate state,
> An epitaph for Fame's unburied dead.
> God pity those who live to hear it said![362]

One can interpret Wilcox's poem as being about Rollin Whipper's own individual regrets, her failure to achieve the goals she had set for herself as a young woman while writing in her diary in Boston, as well as a lament for the "degenerate state" of South Carolina and the failure of Reconstruction that brought it about. Yet Frances focuses on the first part of the poem, the "hidden germ of promise" that *Whatever might have been shall be.* While she feels that she had not "reached the mark [she] had in sight," it is possible, she grants, that she will be judged differently with the passage of time.

Frances Rollin Whipper died on 17 October 1901 at the age of fifty-six. Appropriately enough, given her eclectic religious beliefs, she was given an Episcopal funeral service in a Baptist church and was buried in the cemetery at the Wesley United Methodist Church in Beaufort. When her husband died five years later, he was buried there as well. Their resting place seems appropriate, as the church

362. Wilcox, "Has Been" was first published in *Lippincott's Monthly Magazine*, Feb. 1891.

on West Street was, like the Whippers, central to the history of the Civil War and Reconstruction in South Carolina. Built in the 1830s, United Methodist served a mixed-race congregation prior to being adopted as a school for freedmen during the war. On Sundays Black and white soldiers worshipped together, along with freedmen and their families. During Reconstruction, the church was used as headquarters for the expansion of both the Methodist Church and the Republican Party. Since the Civil War, it has served a primarily African American congregation.

Unfortunately, the graves of Frances and William Whipper have been lost to time (and the elements). Whatever markers once stood have disappeared as well. In 2022 Carole Ione placed a monument in the cemetery to note it as the resting place of her great-grandmother and grandfather. It commemorates "the memory of two distinguished Beaufort residents whose lives and actions continue to inspire through time." Though her husband's name is listed first, as it would have been in life, he is not allowed to overshadow his wife. William J. Whipper is a "Reconstruction Era Legislator, Activist and Proponent of Women's Suffrage, Trial Attorney, and Probate Judge," but Frances Rollin Whipper is a "Diarist, Biographer, Abolitionist, Educator, and Author."[363] She fulfilled so many more roles as well, some that we do not know about, and others that are difficult to articulate. But it begins and ends with writing, with language: "Diarist"; "Author." Like that marker, this edition of Frances "Frank" Anne Rollin's 1868 diary marks the "life and public services" of a remarkable woman who is no longer one of "Fame's unburied dead."

363. Judge William James Whipper, Wesley United Methodist Church Cemetery, Beaufort, SC, Find a Grave, www.findagrave.com/memorial/261480454/william-james-whipper; Frances Anne "Frank" Rollin Whipper, Wesley United Methodist Church Cemetery, Beaufort, SC, Find a Grave, www.findagrave.com/memorial/261480287/frances_anne-whipper.

Biographical Notes

THE FOLLOWING individuals and families are mentioned frequently throughout Frances Rollin's diary. I have not provided entries for people mentioned repeatedly within a short stretch of entries; for example, Dr. Samuel Till Birmingham is an important figure in the diary, but the six references to him are all within a three-week time period, which makes it easier for readers to remember him. Family descriptions here are for families with two or more people mentioned in the diary and who seem important to Rollin *as a family*. The names of individual family members who are mentioned even once in the diary are featured in boldface. Birth and death dates for individuals vary across sources; I have made my best guess at the correct dates rather than indicating a range.

Families

BAILEY FAMILY

Rollin boarded with the Bailey family at 16 Blossom Street during her time in Boston. **John Baptiste Bailey** (1817–86) was an African American boxing teacher who owned his own sparring academy that catered to a white clientele. He was born in Maryland and trained as a pugilist.[1] He married his wife, **Ann Eliza "Annie" Bailey** (1819–97), sometime in the late 1830s. Ann's maiden name was Watkins, and she was likely the sister of William Watkins Jr. of Baltimore, Maryland, thus the aunt of African American author and activist Frances Ellen Watkins Harper.[2] After running a successful gymnasium and pistol gallery in

1. Moore, "Fit for Citizenship," 455.
2. Ann E. Bailey entry, "Massachusetts, U.S., Death Records, 1841–1915," database, Ancestry .com; Fannie Gaskins entry, "Pennsylvania, U.S., Death Certificates, 1906–1970," Ancestry.com;

Baltimore, John and Ann moved their family to California in 1851, perhaps to avoid tightening legal restrictions on free Black residents in Maryland. They returned east in 1853 and relocated to Boston.[3] John assisted William Cooper Nell in his efforts to integrate Boston schools. The couple likely had nine children, seven of whom lived with them in 1868: **Mary E.** (Hare) (1838–?) **Emily C.** (Mundrucu) (1842–1919), **Frances Ann** (Gaskins) (1845–1920), Henry A. (1848–71), **James L.** (b. circa 1851–?), Parker Nell (1855–1912), and **Peter** (1860–?).[4] Another son, Garrison Bailey, died at four years old in 1862.[5] John and Ann's son John L. Bailey (1843–95) was not recorded as living with the family after 1850 but died in Boston in 1895.[6] Census information indicates that the Baileys often shared their home with African American lodgers like Rollin.[7] While living with them, Rollin seems to have been especially close to Emily, but she also spent time with Mr. and Mrs. Bailey and several of the other children. Emily worked as a dressmaker and married Theodore M. C. Mundrucu (1839–98) in 1887, just after her father's death.[8] Ann Bailey died in Boston ten years later.[9]

BROWN FAMILY

William Wells Brown (1818–84) escaped from slavery in Kentucky when he was nineteen years old. Settling first in Buffalo, New York, and then in Boston, he

---

"Items of Race Interest," *Freeman*, 11 Mar. 1911, 2; *Fortieth Anniversary Report of the Secretary of the Class of 1881 of Harvard College*; Francis Watkins entry (mother of Ann E. Bailey and William Watkins), Baltimore Ward 5, Baltimore, MD, US Census, 1850, database, Ancestry.com.

3. Moore, "Fit for Citizenship," 458.

4. Ann E. Bailey entry, "Massachusetts, U.S., Wills and Probate Records, 1635–1991," database, Ancestry.com; Ann E. Bailey entry, US Census, 1850; Anne E. Bailey entry, Boston Ward 5, Suffolk, MA, US Census, 1860, database, Ancestry.com; Annie E. Bailey entry, Boston Ward 3, Suffolk, MA, US Census, 1870, database, Ancestry.com; Ann E. Bailey entry, Enumeration District 725, Boston, Suffolk, MA, US Census, 1880, database, Ancestry.com.

5. Garrison Bailey entry, "Massachusetts, U.S., Death Records, 1841–1915," database, Ancestry.com.

6. John L. Bailey entry, "Massachusetts, U.S., Death Records, 1841–1915," database, Ancestry .com.

7. Lucinda Mitchil entry, Charlestown Ward 2, Middlesex, MA, Massachusetts State Census, 1855, database, Ancestry.com; Edward Brown entry, Boston Ward 5, Suffolk, MA, Massachusetts State Census, 1865, database, Ancestry.com; Mr. Talbot entry, Massachusetts State Census, 1865.

8. Emily C. Bailey and Theodore Mundrucu entry, "Massachusetts, U.S., Marriage Records, 1840–1915," database, Ancestry.com; John B. Bailey entry, "Massachusetts, U.S., Death Records."

9. Ann E. Bailey entry, "Massachusetts, U.S., Death Records."

became an activist, author, and lecturer. He also traveled widely in the United States and the United Kingdom to promote the cause of abolition and, after 1850, to avoid being returned to slavery under the Fugitive Slave Law. In 1847 he published *Narrative of William W. Brown, a Fugitive Slave, Written by Himself,* then went on to publish travel writing, plays, novels, and histories, including *The Negro in the American Rebellion* (1867), the first book about African American soldiers in the Revolutionary War. During the Civil War, he worked to recruit Black soldiers for the Union army. With his first wife, Brown had two daughters; in 1860 he married his second wife, **Anna Elizabeth Gray Brown** (1835–1902).[10] The couple had one child, a daughter named Clotelle, who died at the age of eight in 1870 shortly after the census was taken.[11] In the 1850s and 1860s, Brown likely read medicine with a physician, and by 1854, he opened up his own practice with an office in Boston. He was also active in the temperance movement. Rollin would no doubt have been familiar with Brown's work as an author and a lecturer as well as the biography of Brown published by his daughter Josephine Brown (1839–74) in 1856. After William's death in 1884, Anna moved in with her brother-in-law to care for the daughter of her deceased sister. She died in 1902.[12]

EZEKIEL FAMILY

Born in Beaufort, South Carolina, **Philip E. Ezekial** (1827–?) and his wife, **Georgianna (or Georgia) Wilson Ezekiel** (1833–?), had at least four children: John W. (1854–?); Arthur H. (1856–1926); Philip (1857–?); and **Ann A.** (1858–1936).[13] Prior to and likely during the Civil War, Philip worked as a tailor in Beaufort, and his wife was a milliner there; while he continued his occupation after the war, his wife was able to stay home as the family accumulated a comfortable if small fortune

10. Anne E. Gray and William Wells Brown entry, "Massachusetts, U.S., Town and Vital Records," database, Ancestry.com.

11. Clotelle Brown entry, "Massachusetts, U.S., Birth Records, 1840–1915," database, Ancestry .com; Clotilde Brown entry, "Massachusetts, U.S., Death Records, 1841–1915," database, Ancestry .com; Annie G. Brown entry, Cambridge Ward 2, Middlesex, MA, US Census, 1870; Clotilde Brown entry, "Massachusetts, U.S., Death Records." The names of Annie G. and Clotilde have been reversed in the census.

12. Information on the Brown family comes largely from Greenspan, *William Wells Brown.*

13. Arthur H. Ezekial entry, "Georgia, U.S., Death Index, 1919–1998," database, Ancestry .com; "Ezekiel, Philip E.," in Foner, *Freedom's Lawmakers,* 72; Philip E. Ezekial entry, South Helena, Beaufort, SC, US Census, 1860, database, Ancestry.com; P. E. Ezekial entry, Beaufort, Beaufort, SC, US Census, 1870, database, Ancestry.com.

in real estate.[14] Philip served in the South Carolina House of Representatives, representing Beaufort County alongside William J. Whipper from 1868 to 1870. In 1871 he was appointed postmaster of Beaufort, a position he held until at least 1885.[15] While in Boston, Frances received letters from Mr. and Mrs. Ezekiel and at least one from "little Ann Ezekial."[16] Ann married trial justice John A. Richmond in Charleston in 1883.[17] While John seems to have died prior to 1900, Ann became a nurse and moved to Chicago, where she died in 1934.[18] The dates of her parents' deaths are unknown.

HAYDEN FAMILY

Harriet Bell Hayden (1816–93) and **Lewis Hayden** (1811–89) were born enslaved in Kentucky and married in 1842. Lewis had been married before, but his first wife and child were sold by their enslaver, and he never saw them again. At the time of her marriage to Lewis, Harriet had a son named Joseph (1839–?). In September 1844 the three escaped slavery with the assistance of the white Methodist minister Calvin Fairbank, who later received a fifteen-year prison sentence for his involvement. Eventually settling in Boston, their home on Southac (later Phillips) Street served as a refuge for Black fugitives, emigrants, and visitors to the city. Harriet's day-to-day management of the couple's boardinghouse and home was essential to their active participation in the Underground Railroad. Lewis ran a clothing store and worked as an agent for the American Anti-Slavery Society. In addition to sheltering fugitives at his home, he was an active member of Boston's third Vigilance Committee. During the Civil War, he was a recruiter for the Fifty-Fourth Massachusetts Regiment of the US Colored Troops. Their son, Joseph, served in the Union navy but died of disease in camp at Mobile Bay, Alabama. A supporter of John A. Andrew, who became governor in 1861, Lewis was awarded a patronage position as a messenger in the secretary of state's office; he is believed to be the first African American employee of the State of Massachusetts. He used this position to find Frances Rollin work as a copyist. The couple also

---

14. US Census, 1860; US Census, 1870; Philip E. Ezekial entry, Beaufort, Beaufort, SC, Enumeration District 041, US Census, 1880, database, Ancestry.com.

15. Philip E. Ezekial entry, "U.S., Appointments of U.S. Postmasters, SC: Abbeville-Greenwood," database, Ancestry.com; "Ezekial, Philip E.," in Foner, *Freedom's Lawmakers*; Philip E. Ezekial entry, US Census, 1880.

16. Rollin diary, 24 Mar. 1868.

17. Annie A. Ezekial and John A. Richmond entry, "Charleston, South Carolina, U.S., Marriage Records, 1877–1887," database, Ancestry.com.

18. Ann C. Richmond entry, "Illinois, U.S., Deaths and Stillbirths Index," database, Ancestry.com.

provided sanctuary and community for Rollin, and she visited them often in their home. In 1872 Lewis was elected to the Massachusetts state legislature and served one term. He died in 1889. At her death in 1893, Harriet used the whole of the couple's estate to endow a scholarship for Black students at Harvard University Medical School.[19]

HOWARD FAMILY

Joanna Louise Turpin Howard (1826–72) was born in New York, the daughter of Adaline Leggett Turpin (?–1839), a free Black woman from New York, and Joseph Thomas Turpin (1795–1835), a formerly enslaved man from Charleston, South Carolina.[20] She attended the Young Ladies' Domestic Seminary in Clinton, New York, and in 1840 married barber and caterer Edwin F. Howard (1815–93).[21] The Howards were active in the antislavery movement and worked with William Cooper Nell to end segregation in Boston's public schools. Their daughter, **Joan Imogene Howard** (1848–1937), attended the Wells Grammar School in Boston and went on to the Girls Normal and High School. She and her sister, **Adeline Turpin "Addie" Howard** (1844–1922), both became teachers and school principals. In 1868 Imogene was a teacher in the Colored Grammar School No. 4 in Boston.[22] The Howards' son, Edwin Clarence Howard (1836–1912), studied medicine in Liberia from 1861 to 1865; he graduated from Harvard Medical School in 1869.[23] Rollin likely met the Howard family when she moved to Boston in 1867.

KENNEDY FAMILY

Rollin knew **Elizabeth "Lizzie" B. Kennedy** (1846–1922) from the years she had spent in Philadelphia just prior to and during the Civil War. Lizzie's father, Robert (1818–63), was a musician and her mother, **Sidney** (1820–70)—referred to as "Mama Sidney" in the diary—was a dressmaker or a mantua maker.[24] Robert and Sidney had four children: John (1844–90), Lizzie, Robert (1848–?), and

---

19. Information on the Hayden Family comes largely from Kantrowitz, *More Than Freedom*.

20. Baumgartner, *In Pursuit of Knowledge*, 62–63.

21. Baumgartner, *In Pursuit of Knowledge*, 47.

22. Scruggs, *Women of Distinction*, 157.

23. "Edwin Clarence Joseph Turpin Howard, MD, Class of 1869," Perspectives of Change: The Story of Civil Rights, Diversity, Inclusion, and Access to Education at HMS and HSDM, online exhibit, Harvard University, accessed 19 Feb. 2025, https://perspectivesofchange.hms .harvard.edu/node/15.

24. Robert Kennedy and Siddney Kennedy entries, Philadelphia Lombard Ward, Philadelphia, PA, US Census, 1850, database, Ancestry.com; Robert Kennedy and Sidney Kennedy entries, Philadelphia Ward 7, Philadelphia, PA, US Census 1860, database, Ancestry.com.

Isadora, or "Dora" (1861–98).[25] Lizzie attended the Institute for Colored Youth with Rollin and later is listed in the 1870 census as a schoolteacher.[26] By 1872, she was married to Peter J. Augustin (1828–92), a Black caterer eighteen years her senior; the couple had four sons together.[27] Dora married Charles Howard Van Vranken of Albany, New York, in 1883 and lived there with him and their four children until her death in 1898.[28] Lizzie continued to work for and perhaps even run her husband's catering business after his death.[29] Sometime after 1904, she moved to Albany, New York, to live with her brother-in-law, Charles, and her niece, Elizabeth K. Van Vranken, a twenty-five-year-old nurse.[30] Lizzie died in Albany in 1922.[31]

LOCKLEY FAMILY

The barber John Lockley (1815–64) and his wife, **Martha Ann Lockley** (1815–86), moved with their daughters **Harriet** (1845–87) and **Mary Louisa** (1847–1918) from Virginia to Boston in the 1840s. In census records, Harriet's birthplace is consistently listed as Virginia, while Mary is said to have been born in Massachusetts in 1847.[32] John's death in 1864 left Martha Ann fairly comfortable, as the 1870 census lists her with $5,000 in real estate. Boarders lived at the Lockley residence as well, including Ira N. Gray (the son of Ira Smith and Louisa Nell Gray),

25. Robert Kennedy, household, US Census, 1850; Robert Kennedy, household, US Census, 1860; John R. Kennedy, household, Philadelphia Ward 7, District 19, Philadelphia, PA, US Census, 1870, database, Ancestry.com.

26. "The Examination of the Pupils of the Philadelphia Institute for Colored Youth," *Christian Recorder*, 11 May 1861, 69; Elizabeth B. Kennedy entry, US Census 1870.

27. Peter J. Augustin, household, Enumeration District 146, Philadelphia, PA, US Census, 1880, database, Ancestry.com.

28. Isadora K. Van Vranken entry, "Menands, N.Y., U.S., Albany Rural Cemetery Burial Cards, 1791–2011," database, Ancestry.com; Isadora Van Vranken, Albany Rural Cemetery, Menands, NY, Find a Grave, www.findagrave.com/memorial/137060522/isadora-van_vranken.

29. Elizabeth B. Augustin, in *Gopsill's Philadelphia City Directory for 1899* and *Boyd's Co-Partnership and Residence Business Directory of Philadelphia*, 1904.

30. Elizabeth B. Augustin entry, District 0050, Albany Ward 11, Albany, NY, US Census, 1910, database, Ancestry.com.

31. Elizabeth B. Kennedy Augustin, Albany Rural Cemetery, Albany, NY, Find a Grave, www.findagrave.com/memorial/141107625/elizabeth-b-augustin.

32. Harriet E. Lockley entry, Boston Ward 6, Suffolk, MA, US Census, 1870, database, Ancestry.com; Mary L. Lockley entry, US Census, 1870 and 1880.

Ella Mahone, and the Simonds family.[33] Mary attended the Bowdoin School in Boston.[34] She was working as a bookkeeper in 1868, as she was in 1870 when the census was taken. During Rollin's year in Boston, she visited the Lockley home often and seemed to enjoy a friendship with both Harriet and Mary. In 1872 Mary married St. John Appo (1845–1928) from Hartford, Connecticut, in Boston.[35] They had four children and may have also passed as white later in life. While they are noted as "mulatto" in census records for 1880 and "Black" in 1900, in the 1910 census, St. John, Mary, and two of their children are documented as white; Mary's death certificate also notes her race as "white."[36] Harriet did not marry. She and her mother were living with Mary's family in Hartford at the time of the 1880 census, but Martha Ann died in Washington, DC, in 1886.[37] Harriet died in 1887, shortly after her mother, and is buried with both of her parents in Woodlawn Cemetery in Middlesex County, Massachusetts.[38]

MORRIS FAMILY

Robert Morris (1823–82) was born in Salem, Massachusetts. He was tutored in law by the white abolitionist Ellis Gray Loring and admitted to the Massachusetts bar in 1847.[39] In 1846 Morris married **Catherine Mason** (1827–95), who was born in Boston, Massachusetts, the daughter of a West Indian immigrant father and a Boston-born mother.[40] She converted to Roman Catholicism soon after

33. Martha Lockley entry, US Census, 1870.

34. Nell, "Colored Scholars."

35. Mary L. Lockley and St. John Appo entry, "Massachusetts, U.S., Marriage Records 1840–1915," database, Ancestry.com.

36. St. John Appo, household, Enumeration District 11, Hartford, CT, US Census, 1880, database, Ancestry.com; St. John Appo, household, Enumeration District 311, Brooklyn Ward 20, Kings, NY, US Census, 1900, database, Ancestry.com; St. John Appo, household, Enumeration District 728, Manhattan Ward 12, New York, NY, US Census, 1910, database, Ancestry.com; Mary L. L. Appo entry, "New York, New York, U.S. Index to Death Certificates, 1862–1948," database, Ancestry.com; Hobbs, *Chosen Exile*, 62–63.

37. Martha Ann Lockley entry, "District of Columbia, Select Deaths and Burials Index, 1769–1960," database, Ancestry.com.

38. Harriet E. Lockley, Woodlawn Cemetery, Everett, MA, Find a Grave, www.findagrave.com/memorial/206333226/harriet-e-lockley.

39. Davis and Bilder, "Library of Robert Morris," 471.

40. Catherine Morris entry, "Massachusetts, U.S., Death Records, 1841–1915," database, Ancestry.com.

their wedding.[41] The Morrises had three children, only one of whom survived to adulthood: Catherine (1846–56), Robert (1848–82), and Mason (1849–50).[42] Robert Morris filed and tried the first US civil rights challenge to segregated public schools in the 1848 case *Roberts vs. City of Boston*. The case was unsuccessful, and Boston public schools did not integrate until 1855, a few years after Morris and his wife moved to Chelsea to allow their children to take advantage of the integrated schools there.[43] Morris also helped establish the Boston Vigilance Committee to protect African Americans fleeing slavery and was active in the rescue of Shadrach Minkins, a fugitive from Virginia, in 1850.[44] In the 1860s the Morrises sent their son, Robert Jr., to France to enroll in a Catholic boarding school. He graduated in the fall of 1868; Rollin records in her diary Robert and Catherine's departure from New York to travel to France, presumably to attend his graduation exercises.[45] Like his father, Robert Jr. became a lawyer.[46] In 1870 the elder Robert Morris converted from Methodism to Catholicism. Robert Morris and Robert Jr. both died in 1882.[47] Catherine died in 1895 at the age of seventy.[48]

SIMONDS/MAHONE FAMILY

Ella Mahone (Brady) (1851–post 1920) was born in South Carolina, probably in Charleston. According to her 1886 marriage record, her father's name was Jones and her mother's first name was Ann.[49] In the 1860 census, Ella is listed as "Ellen Jones" and living with the carpenter Samuel Simonds (1835–92) and his wife **Anna (or Emma)** (1836–?), a seamstress, in Charleston.[50] In 1870 Ella had

---

41. Davis and Bilder, "Library of Robert Morris," 492.

42. Robert Morris, household, Chelsea, Suffolk, MA, US Census, 1850, database, Ancestry .com; Robert Morris, household, Chelsea, Suffolk, MA, US Census, 1860, database, Ancestry .com; Robert Morris, household, Chelsea, Suffolk, MA, US Census, 1870, database, Ancestry.com; Mason Morris entry, "Massachusetts, U.S., Death Records, 1841–1915," database , Ancestry.com; Robert Morris, household, Chelsea, Suffolk, MA, Massachusetts State Census, 1855, database, Ancestry.com.

43. Davis and Bilder, "Library of Robert Morris," 476–78.

44. Kendrick and Kendrick, *Sarah's Long Walk*, 189, 190–95.

45. Davis and Bilder, "Library of Robert Morris," 495; Rollin diary, 27 June 1868.

46. Davis and Bilder, "Library of Robert Morris," 495.

47. Davis and Bilder, "Library of Robert Morris," 496.

48. Catherine Morris entry, "Massachusetts, U.S., Death Records, 1841–1915," database, Ancestry.com.

49. Ella J. Mahone and Charles O. Brady entry, "Massachusetts, U.S., Marriage Records, 1840–1915," database, Ancestry.com.

50. Ellen Jones entry, Saml Simond household, Charleston Ward 8, Charleston, SC, US Census, 1860, database, Ancestry.com.

moved with the Simonds to Boston, where she worked as a copyist and was listed in the census as "Ella Mahone."[51] Although only nineteen years old at the time, she may have been briefly married. Ella was only eight years old when Rollin left Charleston to attend the Institute for Colored Youth, but because of Rollin's younger sisters, they might have known each other. Depending on when Ella and the Simonds moved to Boston, Rollin might also have been acquainted with them during her time in Charleston immediately after the war. In Boston Rollin seems to have been friendly with Ella and Anna Simonds, who board with the Lockley family on Garden Street.[52] In 1886 Ella married Charles Otis Brady, an African American machinist who, at the time of his death ten years later, was assistant engineer at the Boston State House.[53] The couple had two children, only one of whom, Charles Otis Brady Jr. (1895–?), lived to adulthood. After her husband's death, Ella worked as a dressmaker and operated a boardinghouse to support herself.[54]

Individuals

Ennals J. Adams (1823–94). Born in Maryland, Adams's first pastorate was at the Lombard Street Central Presbyterian Church in Philadelphia in 1855. A year earlier he had married Amelia W. Purnell (1832–92), the daughter of Benjamin Whipper's sister, making her William J. Whipper's first cousin.[55] Between 1855 and 1872, the couple had at least six children, only three of whom survived to adulthood.[56] Ennals also served in Hartford, Connecticut; Buffalo, New York; and Newark, New Jersey, before being sent to Sierra Leone by the American Missionary Association in 1863.[57] After the Civil War, he traveled south to minister to

51. Ella Mahone entry, Saml Simonds household, Boston Ward 6, Suffolk, MA, US Census, 1860, database, Ancestry.com.

52. Saml Simonds, household, US Census, 1870.

53. Ella J. Mahone and Charles O. Brady entry, "Massachusetts, U.S., Marriage Records, 1840–1915"; Charles O. Brady entry, "Massachusetts, U.S., Death Records, 1841–1915," database, Ancestry.com; "Death of Charles Otis Brady," *Boston Globe*, 6 Dec. 1896, 8.

54. Ella Brady entry, Enumeration District 1315, Boston Ward 11, Suffolk, MA, US Census, 1900, database, Ancestry.com; Ella J. Brady entry, Enumeration District 1425, Boston Ward 12, Suffolk, MA, US Census, 1910; database, Ancestry.com.

55. McCormick, "William Whipper," 44n82.

56. Ennels Adams, household, Buffalo Ward 5, Erie, NY, US Census, 1860, database, Ancestry.com; Amelia Adams, household, Enumeration District 99, Baltimore, Maryland, US Census, 1880, database, Ancestry.com.

57. Powers, *Black Charlestonians*, 210.

the recently enslaved at, among other places, the Shaw Presbyterian Church and the Glebe Street Presbyterian Church.[58] He served as an honorary member of the statewide Colored People's Convention held at the Zion Presbyterian Church in November 1865 and was appointed a Charleston city councilmember in 1868.[59] Rollin likely became acquainted with the Reverend Adams in Charleston after the war; she mentions receiving several letters from Adams while in Boston. It may have been through him that she met her future husband, as he married the couple in Charleston in September 1868.[60] Adams returned to Philadelphia in 1874 but died in Maryland in 1894.[61]

Martin Robison Delany (1812–85). Born in Charles Town, Virginia (now West Virgina), to an enslaved father and a free mother, Delany and his family moved to Pennsylvania in the early 1820s. In 1833 Delany apprenticed with a white physician. Admitted to Harvard Medical School in 1850, he was dismissed soon after beginning classes due to pressure from white students. Delany edited *The Mystery*, a Pittsburgh newspaper, and later joined with Frederick Douglass to produce the *North Star*. In 1852 he published *Condition, Elevation, Emigration, and Destiny of the Colored People of the United States*, in which he proposed that African Americans should emigrate to Central or South America or the Caribbean. A year later he organized and chaired a national Black emigration convention. In 1859 his sights turned to West Africa, and he toured the Niger Valley, publishing an account of this journey in *Official Report of the Niger Valley Exploring Party* in 1861. With the beginning of the Civil War and the announcement of the Emancipation Proclamation, Delany committed himself to the recruitment of Black troops and was commissioned as a major in the Union army. After the war he was assigned to the Freedmen's Bureau in Hilton Head, South Carolina, where he served for three years. It was at this point that he became acquainted with Frances Rollin, who went on to write his biography. Even as the book was being published, Delany became involved in South Carolina politics, where his pragmatic approach to partisanship put him at odds with most other Black politicians and activists in the state. In the mid-1870s, he worked to build Black support for the Democratic Party and opposed the election of African Americans to high office in state or federal government. After the election of Democrat Wade Hampton

58. Powers, *Black Charlestonians*, 210.

59. Powers, *Black Charlestonians*, 83, 96; Rebecca L. Schultz, "Path to the Council Chamber: African American Aldermen in Charleston, 1865–1868," Charleston, South Carolina, www .charleston-sc.gov/2533/Path-to-the-Council-Chamber-African-Amer, accessed 19 Feb. 2025.

60. Rollin diary, 17 Sept. 1868.

61. Smith-Gholston Family Tree, Ancestry.com.

in 1876, the new governor appointed Delany a trial justice. Delany married Catherine A. Richards (1822–94) in 1854, and the couple had six children together. During his time in South Carolina, Catherine seems to have lived in Xenia, Ohio, with their younger children. With the end of Reconstruction in 1877, Delany turned again to African American emigration, this time to Liberia, but did not receive the backing that he desired before his death in 1885 in Xenia.[62]

William Lloyd Garrison (1805–79). Garrison's newspaper *The Liberator* (1831–65) was central to abolitionist activity and politics in the United States. Born in Massachusetts to immigrants from New Brunswick, Garrison apprenticed as a compositor at age thirteen; when he was twenty-five, he joined the antislavery movement. In 1829 he worked with Benjamin Lundy on the *Genius of Universal Emancipation*, a newspaper published in Maryland. Influenced by his contact with African Americans, however, he broke with Lundy over his gradualist views on emancipation. Soon after the founding of *The Liberator*, Garrison helped organize the New England Anti-Slavery Society (later the American Anti-Slavery Society). He faced violence from advocates of slavery and resistance from those within the antislavery community who disagreed with his opinions on women's rights, pacifism, and the involvement of abolitionists in politics. With the end of the Civil War, Garrison announced the final issue of *The Liberator* and proposed that the society declare victory and be dissolved. In his later years, Garrison became a leader in the woman suffrage movement.[63]

Samuel Green (1847–?). Born in Beaufort County, South Carolina, Samuel was the son of Christopher "Kit" Green, the largest Black landowner in the county. Enslaved prior to the Union occupation of the Sea Islands, Kit Green began acquiring land in 1863, when he purchased a 400-acre plantation for one dollar per acre at the first US Direct Tax Commission Auction. He acquired additional land following the Civil War.[64] Samuel Green was emancipated with the arrival of Union troops and thereafter worked as a carpenter and a farmer. It is not clear how he and Rollin got to know one another, but he is the likeliest candidate for the correspondent she simply calls "Green." From 1870 to 1875, he represented Beaufort County in the South Carolina House of Representatives, and from 1875 to 1877, he served in the state senate. He was a US customs official in 1880.[65] In 1870 Green married Amelia Moultrie (1852–?).[66]

62. Information on Martin Robison Delany largely comes from "Delany, Martin R.," in Foner, *Reconstructions Lawmakers*, 59–61; and Levine, introduction to *Martin R. Delany*.

63. Information on William Lloyd Garrison largely comes from Mayer, *All on Fire*.

64. McGuire, "Getting Their Hands on the Land," 238, 239–40.

65. Foner, *Freedom's Lawmakers*, 91.

66. Samuel Green entry, Beaufort, Beaufort, SC, US Census, 1870, database, Ancestry.com.

Richard Theodore Greener (1844–1922). Greener and his mother moved from Philadelphia to Boston when he was nine years old. He studied at Oberlin Academy and Phillips Academy as a young man, then became the first African American student to graduate from Harvard University in 1870. He and Rollin became friends during his time as an undergraduate. From 1870 to 1872, Greener served as principal of the Male Department at the Institute for Colored Youth in Philadelphia before becoming the first African American faculty member at the University of South Carolina. In 1874 Greener married Genevieve Fleet (1849–91), with whom he had six children. In 1876 he earned his law degree but was forced to leave South Carolina the next year when Reconstruction ended and the university was closed, to open again for white students only in 1880. Greener moved to Howard Law School, where he eventually served as dean. From 1898 to 1905, Greener worked as a diplomat in India and Russia, where he began a new family with a Japanese woman.[67]

Charlotte Forten (Grimké) (1837–1914). Born into the prestigious Forten family of Philadelphia, Charlotte was the child of Mary Virginia Wood Forten (1815–40), who died when she was three years old, and Robert Bridges Forten (1813–64). After being educated in both private and public schools in the city, Forten moved to Salem, Massachusetts, and attended the all-white Salem Normal School. Upon graduation she obtained a teaching position in town. Forten became active in antislavery circles in the 1850s, publishing several poems in abolitionist periodicals. In 1861 she went to the Sea Islands of South Carolina to teach at the Penn School. Accounts of her experiences were published in *The Liberator* and the *Atlantic Monthly*, but she is now best known for her diaries, maintained between 1856 and 1864. From 1865 to 1871, Forten worked as a clerk for the New England Freedmens Aid Committee in Boston. In this role she served as a liaison between teachers in the South and benefactors in the North. Forten is mentioned in the 1868 diary several times, but she and Rollin likely met in 1867, when Rollin first moved to Boston. Forten married the Presbyterian minister Francis J. Grimké (1850–1937) in 1878. In 1880 the couple had a daughter named Theodora, but she died as an infant. The Grimkés lived in Florida and Washington, DC, where Francis was the minister of the prestigious Fifteenth Street Presbyterian Church. Forten Grimké remained active in the Black civil rights movement and the women's rights movement until her death.[68]

---

67. Information on Richard Greener largely comes from Chaddock, *Uncompromising Activist*.

68. Information on Charlotte Forten comes largely from Stevenson, introduction to *Journals of Charlotte Forten Grimké*; and Maillard, *Whispers of Cruel Wrongs*.

William Edward Johnston (1838–99). Representing Sumter County, Johnston was an AME minister and a delegate to the Constitutional Convention of South Carolina in January 1868.[69] He was later elected to the state senate. He was born in Charleston, South Carolina, and worked as a cabinetmaker until the Civil War, when he enlisted in the Twenty-Fourth US Colored Infantry at Camp William Penn in Philadelphia.[70] It is unclear whether he came to Philadelphia solely to enlist or had lived there prior to joining the Union army. Johnston may have courted Rollin in Philadelphia or in the two years she taught school in Charleston after the Civil War. He likely married late in 1868 or in 1869, as the 1870 census lists him as thirty-two years old; married to Cecilia S. Patterson Johnston (1848–?), twenty-one, who was also born in Charleston; and with a five-month-old daughter.[71] The couple went on to have at least five children together.[72] Johnston died in Charleston in 1899.

Charles William Lenox (1824–96). Born in Watertown, Massachusetts, Lenox worked with his father, John Lenox (1794–1886), as a barber or hairdresser. Charles was the grandson of Cornelius and Susannah Lenox, making the abolitionist lecturers Charles Lenox Remond (1810–73) and Sarah Parker Remond (1826–94) from Salem, Massachusetts, his first cousins.[73] Charles enlisted as a soldier in the Union army at the age of thirty-eight. For two and a half years, from February 1863 to August 1865, he served in the famed Fifty-Fourth Massachusetts Infantry, the second all-Black infantry unit to fight in the war; he was promoted to sergeant in 1864.[74] Lenox survived the 1863 assault against Fort

---

69. Foner, *Freedom's Lawmakers*, 120.

70. William E. Johnston entry, US Colored Troops Service Records, 1863–1865, database, Ancestry.com.

71. William E. Johnston entry, Sumter, Sumter, SC, US Census, 1870, database, Ancestry.com; Alcmena Cecile Lee entry, "South Carolina, U.S., Death Records, 1821–1971," database, Ancestry.com; Rowena S. Johnston entry, "South Carolina, U.S., Delayed Birth Records, 1766–1900," database, Ancestry.com.

72. William E. Johnson, household, Sumter, Sumter, SC, Enumeration District 127, US Census, 1880, database, Ancestry.com.

73. "Life of Charles Lenox, Black Man from Watertown Who Served in Civil War, Detailed by Historical Society," *Watertown (MA) News*, 14 Nov. 2020, www.watertownmanews.com/2020/11/14/life-of-charles-lenox-black-man-from-watertown-who-served-in-civil-war-detailed-by-historical-society/; Charles Lenox entry, Middlesex, Watertown, MA, Massachusetts State Census, 1855, database, Ancestry.com; Charles W. Lenox entry, Middlesex, Watertown, MA, Massachusetts State Census, 1865, database, Ancestry.com; Chals W. Lenox entry, Watertown, Middlesex, MA, US Census, 1860, database, Ancestry.com.

74. "Life of Charles Lenox"; Charles W. Lenox entry, "U.S. Colored Troops Military Service Records, 1863–1865," database, Ancestry.com.

Wagner on Morris Island in South Carolina, where approximately 40 percent of the regiment's soldiers were wounded, killed, or captured, and spent at least part of the rest of the war in and around Charleston. He may have crossed paths with Rollin when she returned to the city just after the war.[75] Shortly afterward, Lenox returned to Watertown and his father; he never married or had children.[76] The Lenox family business, which catered to a white clientele in the mostly white Watertown, operated continuously from 1815, when John opened it, to Charles's death in 1896.[77]

William E. Matthews (1843–94). Matthews was born in Baltimore, Maryland, the son of William and Maria Matthews. His father, who died in 1853, was a porter, and his mother was a washerwoman.[78] During the Civil War, he was pastor of a church in Baltimore and worked for the Galbraith Lyceum promoting African American education in Maryland. Beginning in 1867, Matthews was an agent for the AME Church, raising funds in Northern states for school and church building in Southern states.[79] His home base during this time seems to have been Boston. It is not clear how Matthews and Rollin met. On 27 October 1867, the two were staying in the same boarding house in New York City after Rollin's departure from Charleston.[80] They may have arrived there together, with Matthews, along with either the Revered Ennals J. Adams or Joseph H. Rainey, escorting her from South Carolina to New York. It is also possible that they met at the boardinghouse. Matthews received his law degree from Howard University in 1873 but seems to have worked as a clerk in the US Post Office Department in Washington, DC, throughout the 1870s and into the early 1880s.[81] In 1881 he

75. For a discussion of the Fifty-Fourth's months in Charleston immediately following the war, see Emilio, *History of the Fifty-Fourth Regiment*, 310–18.

76. Charles W. Lennox entry, Watertown, Middlesex, MA, US Census, 1870, database, Ancestry.com; Charles W. Lenox entry, Watertown, Middlesex, MA, Enumeration District 421, US Census, 1880, database, Ancestry.com.

77. "Life of Charles Lenox"; Charles W. Lenox entry, "Massachusetts, U.S., Death Records, 1841–1915," database, Ancestry.com.

78. William Matthews entry, Baltimore Ward 12, Baltimore, MD, US Census, 1850, database, Ancestry.com; William Mathews entry, Baltimore Ward 12, Baltimore, MD, US Census, 1860, database, Ancestry.com.

79. Thomas H. Clarke, "Wm. E. Matthews Is Dead," *Washington Bee*, 4 May 1894, 3; Simmons, *Men of Mark*, 246–47.

80. "Arrivals at Mrs. Hasikerson's [*sic*] Boarding House," *Christian Recorder*, 26 Oct. 1867, 171.

81. Simmons, *Men of Mark*, 247, 249; William E. Mathews entry, Baltimore Ward 13, Baltimore, MD, US Census, 1870, database, Ancestry.com; William E. Matthews entry,

opened an extremely successful real estate and brokerage firm in Washington and handled accounts for Frederick Douglass, Daniel A. Payne, and others active in the African American civil rights movement and the AME Church. While living in DC, he attended the Fifteenth Street Presbyterian Church, where Francis J. Grimké served as pastor.[82] Matthews married in 1883 and had a daughter, but he died in 1894 at the age of fifty-one.[83]

William Cooper Nell (1816–74). Nell's father, William Guion Nell (1795?–1843) was born free in Charleston, South Carolina. He left the South during the War of 1812 and afterward settled in Boston, where he married Louisa Marshall of Brookline and became a leader in the Black community. William Cooper Nell was educated at Boston's African School and became an apprentice to William Lloyd Garrison at *The Liberator* when he was a teenager. He later served as publisher for Frederick Douglass's *North Star*. In 1840 Nell coauthored a petition to the Massachusetts legislature demanding the desegregation of schools; his efforts contributed to the integration of Boston's public schools in 1855. He was also a cofounder of the Boston Vigilance Committee and an active participant in the Underground Railroad. Importantly for Rollin, Nell was an early scholar of African American military history, publishing *Services of Colored Americans in the Wars of 1776 and 1812* in 1851 and *The Colored Patriots of the American Revolution* in 1855. In 1861 he became the first African American to hold a federal position in the US Post Office Department. During the war, he worked to recruit African American men for military service. In 1868 he was central to Rollin's social circle, visiting her often at the Bailey's home, and helped her with her manuscript of the Martin Delany biography. Nell's sister, Louisa Nell Gray (1825–86), and her husband, Ira Smith Gray (1821–?), also boarded with the Baileys at this time. The following year Nell married and eventually had two children, stepping away from activism to focus on his family. He died of a stroke at the age of fifty-eight.[84]

Enumeration District 47, Washington, District of Columbia, US Census, 1880, database, Ancestry .com.

82. "A Scandal in Colored Society," *Evening Star* (Washington, DC), 1 Jan. 1883, 3.

83. Maillard, *Whispers of Cruel Wrongs*, 189n9; William E. Matthews and Euretta B. Bozeman, Marriage Record, Washington, District of Columbia, US Marriage Certificates 1870–1920, Marriage Licenses 1882–1886, database, Ancestry.com; Euretta B. Matthews, Enumeration District 53, Washington, District of Columbia, US Census, 1900, database, Ancestry.com.

84. Information on William Cooper Nell largely comes from Kantrowitz, *More Than Freedom*.

Wendell Phillips (1811–84). A white Harvard-educated lawyer, Phillips was converted to the abolitionist cause by the influence of two people: his wife, Ann Terry Greene (1813–86), whom he married in 1836, and the white abolitionist William Lloyd Garrison, editor of *The Liberator*. Phillips was a member of the American Anti-Slavery Society and the Boston Vigilance Committee and celebrated as one of the most effective orators of the antislavery movement. During the Civil War, he advocated for formation of African American regiments. After Garrison resigned as president of the society in 1865, Phillips led it until 1870, when the Fifteenth Amendment was passed and the organization disbanded. In 1870 he was the Labor Reform candidate for governor of Massachusetts. Phillips was also an active supporter of women's rights, working with Lucy Stone to conduct the first woman suffrage campaign in Massachusetts and to organize women's rights conventions in New England.[85]

Charlotte "Lottie" Rollin (1847–1928). Charlotte was the second eldest of William and Margaret Rollin's five daughters.[86] Like Frances, she was privately educated in Charleston, South Carolina, as a child; some accounts have her sent north for further studies during the Civil War.[87] After the war Charlotte and her sister Kate opened a Catholic day school for African American boys and girls in Charleston.[88] She became a formidable voice in the fight for woman suffrage during Reconstruction, giving a speech on the floor of the South Carolina legislature in 1869. She was secretary of the South Carolina Woman's Rights Association in 1870 and led a meeting at the state capital in 1871. She was also the organizer of the South Carolina chapter of the American Woman Suffrage Association and, in the fall of 1872, attended the association's national convention as the South Carolina representative.[89] The push for a state constitutional amendment for woman suffrage was defeated in 1872. When Reconstruction came to

---

85. Information on Wendell Phillips largely comes from Covert-Warnes, "Wendell Phillips," and Stewart, *Wendell Phillips*.

86. Charlotte Rollins entry, St. Michael and St. Phillip, Charleston, SC, US Census, 1850; Charlotte Rollins entry, Charleston Ward 5, Charleston, SC, US Census, 1860; Lotta Rollin entry, Columbia, Richland, SC, US Census, 1870; all database, Ancestry.com.

87. Rosalyn Terborg-Penn and Cappy Yarbrough, "Rollin Sisters," *South Carolina Encyclopedia*, 20 June 2016, www.scencyclopedia.org/sce/entries/rollin-sisters/.

88. "Day School for Colored Girls and Boys," reverse of letter from Charlotte and Catherine Rollin to Bishop Patrick Neeson Lynch, 29 Nov. 1867, Item 41S1, Pre-Diocesan and Episcopal Papers, Archives and Record Management Office, Roman Catholic Diocese of Charleston.

89. Terborg-Penn and Yarbrough, "Rollin Sisters."

an end, Rollin moved to Brooklyn with her mother and her sisters Florence and Louisa. There she seems to have passed as white and worked as a teacher.[90] She also cared for the two children of her sister Florence.[91] She died in 1928 of heart disease.[92]

Florence Rollin (1858–1934). Florence was the fifth daughter of William and Margaret Rollin.[93] Sometime before 1880, Florence moved with her mother and two sisters (Charlotte and Louisa) to Brooklyn, where she worked for a time as a music teacher. All three claimed their place of birth as South America and seem to have passed as white.[94] In 1884 Florence married a white man named James F. Kernan (1863–?), with whom she had two children: Manuela (1886–1961) and James Frank, usually called "Diego" (1888–1973).[95] She operated a boarding house near Bath Beach in Brooklyn in the 1890s and the early 1900s and died in 1934.[96]

Katherine "Katie" Rollin (1851–76). Katherine was the third of the five Rollin sisters, all of whom were privately educated in Charleston as children.[97] Along with her sister Charlotte, she opened a school for African American children

90. Charlotte Rollen entry, Enumeration District 129, Brooklyn, Kings, NY, US Census, 1880, database, Ancestry.com; Lottie Rollin entry, Enumeration District 559, Brooklyn Ward 30, Kings, NY, US Census, 1900, database, Ancestry.com; Carlota M. Rollin entry, Enumeration District 1052, Brooklyn Ward 30, Kings, NY, US Census, 1910, database, Ancestry.com.

91. Lottie Rollin entry, Enumeration District 4, Assembly District 18, Brooklyn, Kings, NY, New York Census, 1905, database, Ancestry.com; Lottie Rollin, US Census, 1900; Carlota M. Rollin, US Census, 1910.

92. Lottie M. Rollin entry, "New York, New York, U.S., Index to Death Certificates, 1862–1948," database, Ancestry.com; Lottie [Charlotte] M. Rollin, Holy Cross Cemetery, Brooklyn, NY, Find a Grave, www.findagrave.com/memorial/229790268/lottie_m-rollin.

93. Florence Rollins entry, Charleston Ward 5, Charleston, SC, US Census, 1860, database, Ancestry.com; Florence Rollin entry, Columbia, Richland, SC, US Census, 1870, database, Ancestry.com.

94. Florence Rollen entry, Enumeration District 129, Brooklyn, Kings, NY, US Census, 1880, database, Ancestry.com; Mary Rollin entry, Enumeration District 559, Brooklyn Ward 30, Kings, NY, US Census, 1900, database, Ancestry.com.

95. Florence Rollin and James F. Kernan entry, "New York, New York, Extracted Marriage Index, 1866–1937," database, Ancestry.com.

96. "Corn Parties at Bath Beach," *Brooklyn Daily Eagle*, 25 Aug. 1895, 10; "A General List of Hotels and Boarding Houses," *Summer Resort Guide and Directory of the Brooklyn Daily Eagle*, supplement, *Brooklyn Daily Eagle*, 17 June 1900, 3; "On a Landlady's Complaint," *Brooklyn Daily Eagle*, 5 July 1890, 6; Florence [Rollin] Kernan, Holy Cross Cemetery, Brooklyn, Kings County, NY, Find a Grave, www.findagrave.com/memorial/173344646/florence-kernan.

97. Kitty Rollins entry, Charleston Ward 5, Charleston, SC, US Census, 1860, database, Ancestry.com.

following the Civil War.[98] In 1868 she moved with her father and three of her sisters to Columbia, South Carolina.[99] Katherine worked alongside Charlotte in the cause of woman suffrage, serving as treasurer for the South Carolina Women's Rights Association in the capital.[100] In 1872 Katie purchased a house from the white state senator George McIntyre, with whom she seems to have been in a romantic relationship and planned to marry. In this house she and Charlotte hosted a salon attended by Black and white politicians and their advisors.[101] Katie died of consumption at the age of twenty-five.[102]

Louisa M. Rollin (1855–?). Louisa was the fourth daughter of William and Margaret Rollin, but not much is known about her.[103] Along with her sisters, she was privately educated in Charleston, South Carolina. She likely moved with her mother and sisters to Brooklyn in the early 1880s, but she is not mentioned on a New York census record until 1910, when she is living with Charlotte and Florence's son, Diego.[104]

Margaret Rollin (1825?–89). Frances Rollin's mother was likely born in South Carolina and was potentially, like her husband, the child of refugees from Saint Domingue. Her family may have come to the United States by way of South America after fleeing the violence of the Haitian Revolution. Margaret likely married William Rollin sometime in the early 1840s, and they had five daughters.[105] Sometime around 1880 and the time of her husband's death, she moved to Brooklyn with Charlotte, Louisa, and Florence. There they may have passed as white, claiming Spanish or South American descent. In the 1880 census, her place

---

98. "Day School for Colored Girls and Boys," reverse of letter from Charlotte and Catherine Rollin to Bishop Patrick Neeson Lynch, 29 Nov. 1867.

99. Kate Rollin entry, Columbia, Richland, SC, US Census, 1870, database, Ancestry.com.

100. Ione, *Pride of Family*, 175. All citations to *Pride of Family* refer to the 1991 edition unless otherwise indicated.

101. Ione, *Pride of Family*, 167–68, 173–75; "Southeast Corner of Sumter and Senate Streets," Historic Columbia, www.historiccolumbia.org/tour-locations/1020-sumter-street.

102. Katy E. Rollin entry, "South Carolina Death Records, 1875–1899," database, Ancestry .com.

103. Louisa Rollins entry, Charleston Ward 5, Charleston, SC, US Census, 1860, database, Ancestry.com; Lavinia Rollin entry, Columbia, Richland, SC, US Census, 1870, database, Ancestry.com.

104. Louisa M. Rollin entry, Enumeration District 1052, Brooklyn Ward 30, Kings, NY, US Census, 1910, database, Ancestry.com.

105. Margaret Rollins entry, Charleston Ward 5, Charleston, SC, US Census, 1860, database, Ancestry.com.

of birth is listed as Cuba.[106] On her death certificate, Margaret's place of birth is listed as Martinique and those of her father and mother as England and Spain, respectively.[107] Margaret died in Brooklyn in 1889. Her headstone documents her place of birth as Granada, Spain.[108]

William Rollin (1815–80). Frances Rollin's father was born in Charleston, South Carolina, likely the son of a free Black woman and a white man named Jean Baptiste de Caradeuc Jr.[109] Both were from Saint Domingue. Rollin was a fervent Roman Catholic, and he and his family attended St. John the Baptist in Charleston.[110] As a young man, he became a lumber merchant and owned a lumberyard and the boats necessary to transport wood and other products.[111] He married his wife, Margaret, in the early 1840s; the couple had five daughters.[112] Rollin and his family were a part of the free Black elite in Charleston, which enabled him to elude some of the restrictions placed on African Americans in antebellum South Carolina. He was, for example, able to travel to Northern cities and return home, which he did several times with Frances when she was a girl.[113] Around the time of the Civil War, Rollin's lumber business suffered, and he turned to farming.[114] His death in 1880 is marked in Frances's diary.[115]

William J. Whipper (1834–1907). Born in Glenville, Pennsylvania, Whipper was the son of Sophia King Whipper and her husband, Benjamin Whipper.[116]

106. Margaret Rollen entry, Enumeration District 129, Brooklyn, Kings, NY, US Census, 1880, database, Ancestry.com.

107. Margarita [Margaret] Rollin entry, "New York, New York, U.S., Index to Death Certificates, 1862–1948," database, Ancestry.com.

108. Margaret Irving Rollin, Holy Cross Cemetery, Brooklyn, NY, Find a Grave, www.findagrave.com/memorial/229790139/margaret-rollin.

109. Ione, *Pride of Family*, 134–35, 142–44.

110. Suzanne Krebsbach, pers. comm., 17 Apr.2023.

111. Ione, *Pride of Family*, 128; William Rollins entry, St. Michael and St. Phillip, Charleston, SC, US Census, 1850, database, Ancestry.com. 2023.

112. William Rollins entry, US Census, 1850.

113. Murray, "Sketch of Frances Rollin Whipper."

114. Ione, *Pride of Family*, 131.

115. William Rollin entry, "South Carolina, U.S., Death Records, 1821–1971," database, Ancestry.com.

116. Ione, *Pride of Family* (1991), 164; McCormick, "William Whipper," 24n5; Benjamin Whipper and Sophia Whipper entries, Canada West, Kent, 1861 Census of Canada, database, Ancestry.com; Benjamin Whipper, household, Ontario, Welland, Stamford, 1871 Census of Canada, database, Ancestry.com; Beng. Whipper, household, 1881 Census of Canada, database, Ancestry.com.

As a young man, he moved to Ohio, where he became involved in antislavery activism. Prior to the Civil War, he trained as a lawyer and married his first wife, Mary Elizabeth Byrd, with whom he had one child, Cyrenius (1866–?).[117] Whipper served for approximately nineteen months in the Thirty-First US Colored Infantry during the war.[118] After mustering out of the army in November 1865, he moved to Charleston and then Beaufort, South Carolina, where he began practicing law. His wife joined him there, and the couple informally adopted a fifteen-year-old boy named Demps Powell (1851–1953). Mary Elizabeth died soon after, likely in 1867.[119] In that same year, Whipper and Jonathan Jasper Wright became the first African American lawyers on record to practice before a legal tribunal in South Carolina; in 1868 Whipper and two partners opened the nation's first African American law firm in Charleston.[120] He also participated in the South Carolina Constitutional Convention and soon after was elected to the South Carolina House of Representatives from Beaufort. He married Frances Rollin in September 1868. The couple had five children, three of whom survived to adulthood. In 1874 Whipper was elected a circuit court judge, but Governor Daniel Chamberlain refused to sign the commission.[121] He practiced law in Beaufort until the early 1880s, when he joined his family in Washington, DC. Whipper returned to Beaufort in 1885 and was elected a county probate judge. In 1888, after a corrupt election in which he lost his judgeship, Whipper refused to turn over his probate records and was imprisoned for thirteen months.[122] In 1895 he was one of just six Black men at the constitutional convention called by Governor Ben Tillman.[123] Whipper died in Beaufort in 1907, having outlived his wife by six years.

117. Major, *Black Society*, 177.

118. William J. Whipper entry, "U.S. Compiled Service Military Records of Volunteer Union Soldiers Who Served With the United States Colored Troops: Infantry Organizations 31st through 35th, 1861–1865," database, fold3 by Ancestry; William J. Whipper entry, "Veterans Schedules of the U.S. Federal Census, 1890," database, Ancestry.com.

119. Demps Whipper Powell, "A Providential Revelation: Relationship with the Whipper Family," typescript, box 114-1, ser. B, Leigh R. Whipper Papers, Moorland-Spingarn Research Center, Howard University.

120. Smith, *Emancipation*, 244.

121. W. Lewis Burke, "William J. Whipper (1834–1907)," All for Civil Rights: African American Congressmen, Judges, and Lawmakers in South Carolina, University of South Carolina Law Library, last updated 24 Oct. 2024, https://guides.law.sc.edu/EqualRights/WhipperWilliamJ.

122. Ione, *Pride of Family*, 193–94.

123. Kantrowitz, *Ben Tillman*, 221.

The Diary

62   135

F. Rollin

    16 Blossom St.[1]

    Boston

    Mass.

.25   Shoes

~~2.25~~   Salmon

1.00   Lubin[2]

.25   Sundries

.25   Paper

.50   —

.50   Diary

.75   [Illegible]

3.75

.38   gloves

.12   stamps

.15

1.25

.90

.35

1.90[3]

1. While in Boston, Rollin boarded with the Bailey family at 16 Blossom Street in Boston. See Bailey Family in biographical notes.

2. Lubin's Extract was a perfume that sold for one dollar a bottle in 1868. It could be purchased at several different apothecary shops in Boston.

3. The sums on the inside front cover of the diary are followed by the front matter of the preprinted volume: two pages titled "Difference of Time"; one page titled "Rates of Postage"; five

Illuminated Diary for 1868

PUBLISHED BY TAGGARD & THOMPSON,
NO. 29 CORNHILL, BOSTON

Wednesday, January 1
Boston Mass.
A rainy gloomy day. Speakers tonight at the Tremont Temple[4] but so terribly rainy that there is no possibility of reaching there. I sent a letter to Mother[5] today which I wrote last night the latest hour nearly of the old year. The year renews its birth today with all of its hopes and sorrows. Uncertainty and doubt are in its wake. For me and mine I know not, but may God enable us whatever may be my lot. To murmur not, but patiently bear, and wait and labor.

Thursday, January 2
Clearing up today somewhat in the evening went to the fair at Horticultural Hall,[6] [truly] decorated I saw there an Ingine or Locomotive constructed by a

---

pages titled "A Complete Table of Stamp Duties As Approved July 15, 1866"; one with four short sections on "Eclipses in 1868," "Morning and Evening Stars," "Movable Fasts and Feasts," and "Chronological Cycles"; and twelve with information regarding the moon and tides for each month in the year. See the online images of the diary at the Smithsonian Institution, https://collections.si.edu/search/record/ark:/65665/fd5a9e1565e9c5d48e4b96f633bbf4852ff.

4. Tremont Temple was built in 1827 as a playhouse and was purchased in 1843 by the Free Church Baptists, who opposed the paying of rent for church pews. The Temple was made available for public events and hosted speakers like Ralph Waldo Emerson, Harriet Beecher Stowe, and Charles Dickens. The event that Rollin refers to here was in honor of the Emancipation Proclamation, which was issued preliminarily on 22 September 1862 and went into effect on 1 January 1863. The proclamation freed all individuals enslaved in Confederate-controlled territory and allowed African Americans to enlist in the military. According to one newspaper, Lewis Hayden presided at the event, which featured addresses by Wendell Phillips, William Wells Brown, and Charles Lenox Remond, among others ("New Year's Day. Celebration of the Abolition of Slavery," *Boston Journal*, 2 Jan. 1868, 4). For these individuals, see biographical notes.

5. Margaret Rollin. See biographical notes.

6. Boston's Horticultural Hall was often used for concerts and other events. The fair that Rollin attended was for the benefit of the AME Zion Church, better known as the North Russell Street Church ("Fair," *Boston Journal*, 1 Jan. 1868, 2).

Contraband with a jack knife. It is certainly ^a^ wonderful imitation and showed genius. Imogene Howard and I met we had been together to see "John Brown" at Child's Gallery.[7] I do not like the painters license. he is blessing instead of kissing the Negro Child. "The bold blue eyes grew tender and the stern harsh face grew mild, As he stooped amid the jeering ranks to kiss the Negro Child"[8] History notes the deed.

Friday, January 3
Writing as hard as ever. I know not ^with^ what success I shall meet but I feel there is a strength in the endeavor which will be of service to me hereafter.

Mr Richard Greener[9] has gone over some of it with me; but he is cynical and apt to discourage instead of acting otherwise. He lives in a grand intellectual sphere and is accustomed to [win] only perfection, and can ill judge the [cause].

Saturday, January 4
I am reading McCauley's History of England,[10] and Lamartine's History of the Girondists.[11]

7. Joan Imogene Howard. See Howard Family in biographical notes. *John Brown's Blessing* (1867) was one of a series of post–Civil War antislavery paintings done by Thomas Satterwhite Noble. On 2 January the painting was on exhibition at De Vries Gallery at 145 Tremont in Boston, not at A. A. Childs & Company, which was at 127 Tremont ("John Brown," *Boston Journal*, 1 Jan. 1868, 3). John Brown (1800–1859) was a white American abolitionist who led a raid against the US armory at Harpers Ferry, Virginia. He was captured, tried, and executed on 2 December 1859.

8. Rollin quotes from memory John Greenleaf Whittier's poem "Brown of Ossawatomie." The full stanza reads: "John Brown of Ossawatomie, they led him out to die; / And lo! a poor slave mother with her little child pressed nigh; / Then the bold blue eye grew tender, and the old harsh face grew mild, / As he stooped between the jeering ranks and kissed the negro's child!" Whittier published the poem in the *New York Independent* three weeks after Brown's execution (J.W.G. [John Greenleaf Whittier], "Brown of Ossawatomie," *The Independent* [New York City], 22 Dec. 1859, 1). As Rollin explains, Noble's painting represents the abolitionist placing his head on the child's head in a blessing rather than kissing them.

9. Richard Theodore Greener. See biographical notes.

10. Thomas Babington Macaulay's five-volume *History of England* was published in 1848 and covers the seventeen-year period between 1685 and 1702. Several publishers, including Harper & Brothers and Phillips, Sampson, and Company, published American editions in the 1850s.

11. Alphonse de Lamartine published *History of the Girondists; or, Personal Memoirs of the Patriots of the French Revolution* in eight volumes in 1847. It was translated into English by H. T. Ryde and published in the United States by Harper & Brothers in 1847–48.

Sunday, January 5

I attended on last Sunday the M. E. Church[12] and heard a fine sermon, this afternoon I got to Mr Grimes' Church[13] the sermon was humble, after Emily[14] and I went to Mrs Hayden;[15] we took tea there. Mr Chas Lennox[16] came there for me, and we went to <u>Church at the Boston Theatre</u>[17] Rev Ed Everett Hale[18] "The good that I would I do not but the evil that I would not that I do."[19] I was instructed, and thought of the grand intellectual development for generations through his family, and compared.[20]

12. Rollin may be referring here to the Revere Street Methodist Episcopal Church in Beacon Hill, one of the first Black Methodist churches in Boston. The other two Methodist churches in Boston attended by African Americans were specifically African Methodist Episcopal (AME) churches: the North Russell Street AME Zion Church and the First African Methodist Bethel Society, which would later become the Charles Street AME Church.

13. "Mr Grimes" is written over the words "The A.M.E." Reverend Leonard Grimes (1815–73) was the minister at the Twelfth Baptist Church on Phillips (formerly Southac) Street. Born free in Virginia, Grimes moved to Washington, DC, as an adult and used his work as a carriage driver as a cover for assisting the escape of enslaved people. In 1839 he was arrested and convicted for such activities, spending two years at hard labor in Richmond, Virginia. He experienced a religious awakening there and after his release returned to Washington, where he became a Baptist minister. Grimes and his wife moved to Boston in 1848 (Kantrowitz, *More Than Freedom*, 142).

14. Emily Bailey. See Bailey Family in biographical notes.

15. Harriet Bell Hayden. See Hayden Family in biographical notes.

16. Charles William Lenox. See biographical notes.

17. The Boston Theatre, located on Washington Street, opened in 1854. In the winters of 1867–68 and 1868–69, the Suffolk Conference of Unitarian and other Christian churches rented the theater for Sunday evening services (Tompkins and Kilby, *History of the Boston Theatre*, 146–47).

18. Edward Everett Hale (1822–1909) was pastor at the South Congregational Church in Boston. He was also a writer who published in the *Atlantic Monthly*.

19. From Romans 7:19 (King James Version). According to one newspaper, "The design of [Hale's] sermon was to show the way in which the good resolutions of the new year could be successfully carried out" ("Local Intelligence," *Boston Evening Transcript*, 6 Jan. 1868, 4).

20. Members of Hale's illustrious family include his great-uncle and American patriot Nathan Hale and his uncle, the politician and minister Edward Everett. His siblings were also well known: his sisters, Lucretia Peabody Hale and Susan Hale, were authors, and Charles Hale was a politician and diplomat. It is unclear what conclusions Rollin draws from comparing the "generations" of this white family with her own family.

Monday, January 6

Writing, but sick as possible letters from the Major.[21] Today Leedie[22] delivers the Eulogy on his friend Jordan.[23] He is ambitious and is appreciative of talents hence he possesses, but he does not exert himself to originate, or yet to search out for himself enough. He is malleable in an intellectual sense and in an atmosphere of the kind might expand. I think he will yet make his mark. His faults are those belonging to youth, and are only such.

Tuesday, January 7

I spent an impatient day waiting for Evening. I sat and listened to Dickens.[24] He acted as only Dickens can, he knows his characters so thoroughly that he and they are inseprable when acting "Mr Peggotty" was grand his genius never emitted a purer ray than when it covered the old rough sailor so simple and yet so honest. "I saw him as I have often see him sleep at School with his head resting on his arm.["][25] It was so naturally told that we all saw him. He is himself! Pickwick was memorable.

Wednesday, January 8

Writing and chewing the end of last evening's memory. I received a long loving letter from W. E. J.[26] I do not know how it will end with us. I think sometimes he

21. Martin Robison Delany. See biographical notes.

22. "Leedie" is William E. Matthews. See biographical notes.

23. Most of what is known about James Henry Jordan is found in this eulogy (see Matthews, *In Memorium*). Born in 1839 in Baltimore (*In Memorium*, 5), Jordan was an undertaker and cabinet maker (11) who served as secretary, vice president, and president of the Galbraith Lyceum (8); the editor of the *Lyceum Observer* (8); a trustee for the Saratoga Street AME Church (11); and during the Civil War, an active participant in the First Colored Sanitary Commission (10–11), among other roles. He seems to have been an intimate friend of Matthews, who was living in Boston at the time of Jordan's death in late 1867.

24. The British author Charles Dickens (1812–70) began his second tour of the United States in Boston at the Tremont Temple in November 1867. He returned to Boston in 1868 and gave a reading at the Tremont on Monday, 6 January. The reading that Rollin attended, to hear Dickens read from *David Copperfield* and *Pickwick Papers*, was on 7 January ("Mr. Charles Dickens," *Boston Evening Transcript*, 6 Jan. 1868, 4).

25. Rollin paraphrases here from *David Copperfield* (1850). Dickens's reading copy for his US tour, published by Ticknor and Fields, reads: "He was fast asleep, lying easily with his head upon his arm, as I had often seen him lie at school" (Dickens, *Readings*, 13). Dickens also read from *The Pickwick Papers* (1837).

26. William E. Johnston. See biographical notes.

might have done more for me when my means were out and thereby I would have been drawn more dearly to him, but he acted in many occasions so selfishly that the memory of it would mar our happiness if we were married.

Thursday, January 9
A letter today from L.[27] telling me all about his success and the holidays &c quite interesting which will give me a chance to ventilate Dickens that is if I can. Dickens is ^as^ extractless as the ocean the great genius of gives life and beauty to every period. No one could read his works as he can himself, so thoroughly does he understand them. The moral underlying them is perceptible. He is the forerunner of the age of better metal. Where the poor will not envy the rich nor the rich grind up faces at the poor.[28]

Friday, January 10
Wrote to Leedie giving him an account of Tom Downing's broken match[29] Poor Tom was heartsick over the disappoint I felt very sorry about it, but I am selfish enough to throw up my hat as it is not every day a woman can get a chance to get ahead of these selfish men. Pity it was not someone else however.

Saturday, January 11
Writing. A very long letter from Green[30] today. I do not understand it very well. I had my fortune told by an Irish woman today she described Green Delany and Mathews very accurately.

Sunday, January 12
At home reading the French Revolution[31] Miserable weather! No visitors to me.

---

27. Leedie (William E. Matthews).

28. Rollin refers here to Isaiah 3:15 (KJV): "What mean ye that ye beat my people to pieces, and grind the faces of the poor? saith the Lord God of hosts."

29. Thomas Downing (1845–1913) was the son of African American restauranteur and activist George T. Downing (1819–1903) and Serena DeGrasse Downing (1823–93), who relocated from Rhode Island to Boston in the 1860s to take advantage of the city's integrated schools (Baumgartner, *In Pursuit of Knowledge*, 168). Although the family had moved on to Washington, DC, by 1870, Thomas remained in Boston, where he married in 1872 (Thomas Downing entry, Boston Ward 3, Suffolk, MA, US Census, 1870, database, Ancestry.com). It is not clear who this "broken match" was with in 1868.

30. "Green" may be Samuel Green. See biographical notes.

31. Lamartine's *History of the Girondists*. See note 11.

Monday, January 13
Writing not feeling well quite cold.
Reading Lamartine's History of the Revolution
Mrs Hare's baby born[32]

Tuesday, January 14
Writing quietly today nothing of importance

Wednesday, January 15
Writing, very cold today. No letters from home.

Thursday, January 16–Friday, January 17
[No entries.]

Saturday, January 18
Writing under difficulties I expected L today but was disappointed

Sunday, January 19
At home all day, reading Emerson[33] which Mr Phillips[34] so kindly loaned me. In afternoon Misses Lockley[35] called also Mrs Howard.[36] Rich Greener[37] I read to him. Mr Lennox[38] came and went off. Richard G to tea with us. I like him yet I think him cynical.
　　Mr Lennox returned and we had quite an agreeable evening together

Monday, January 20
A letter today from L. who is now in Philadelphia. Writing as usual. In the afternoon went to Mr Phillips. How his grand prophet face lighted up when I advertently said I had succeeded! And how generously he offered to hear me read my MS though it would take up his time. He gave me ^an^ invitation for the Anti

32. "Mrs Hare" is Mary Bailey Hare, John and Ann Bailey's married daughter. The baby was William, named after his father. The Hares apparently lived with Mary's parents at this time, as they were two years later, when the 1870 census was taken. See Bailey Family in biographical notes.
　33. It is not clear what book by Transcendentalist and author Ralph Waldo Emerson (1803–82) Rollin means here.
　34. Wendell Phillips. See biographical notes.
　35. The "Misses Lockley" were Mary Louisa Lockley and Harriet Lockley. See Lockley Family in biographical notes.
　36. Joanna Louise Turpin Howard. See Howard Family in biographical notes.
　37. Richard Greener. See biographical notes.
　38. Charles Lenox. See biographical notes.

Slavery Festival, and gave me Emerson to read. How it cheers me to spend an hour with such a masterpiece of humanity, it reconciles me to Americans.

Tuesday, January 21

Writing with renewed zeal today. On yesterday I went to hear Mrs Ruffin[39] read I do not think time has made much improvement with her reading Sheridan's Ride[40] was given well. Miss Leslie sang very sweetly I did not care for the rest of the affair.

Wednesday, January 22

Writing in the morning in the afternoon dressed for the Anti Slavery festival[41] Mr Phillips came up and gave a generous grasp of the hand. Col. Higginson[42] spoke also a Mr Forthingham[43] The Redpaths[44] were there Minnie Brown[45] came

---

39. Josephine St. Pierre Ruffin (1842–1924) was born in Boston and married her husband, George Lewis Ruffin (1834–86), in 1858 when she was just sixteen years old. In 1868 George was attending Harvard Law School; a year later he became the first African American to graduate from that institution (Royster, *Making the World a Better Place*, 281–82). The Ruffins lived on the north side of Beacon Hill not far from the Haydens. In 1859 Josephine began doing dramatic readings like the one Rollin mentions here. The *Christian Recorder* called her "Madam Josephine Ruffin, the great Dramatic Reader" ("Personal," *Christian Recorder*, 23 Jan. 1864, 1).

40. "Sheridan's Ride" (1864), by poet Thomas Buchanan Read (1822–72), celebrates Union major general Phillip Sheridan's bravery at the Battle of Cedar Creek (Virginia) in 1864.

41. The Anti-Slavery Subscription Festival was held at Horticultural Hall. It was regularly scheduled for the day before the annual meeting of the Massachusetts Anti-Slavery Society ("The Anti-Slavery Subscription Anniversary," *Boston Daily Advertiser*, 23 Jan. 1868, 4).

42. Author and abolitionist Thomas Wentworth Higginson (1823–1911) served as colonel of the First South Carolina Volunteers (US), the first federally authorized African American regiment, from 1862 to 1864. The Volunteers were formerly enslaved men from the rice plantations of the Sea Islands. Reporting on the festival, the *Boston Daily Advertiser* quoted Higginson as "declar[ing] that abolitionists should continue in their work with the same cheerfulness" as soldiers entering battle during the Civil War ("Anti-Slavery Subscription Anniversary").

43. In 1855 Octavius Brooks Frothingham (1822–95) broke with the North Unitarian Church of Salem, Massachusetts, for which he served as minister, over the issue of slavery. By 1868, he had also moved away from Unitarianism and now worshipped with his congregation at New York's Lyric Hall as the Independent Liberal Church. Frothingham spoke at the festival on behalf of the *National Antislavery Standard*, asking for continued support of the newspaper and proposing that its name be changed to *The African* ("Anti-Slavery Subscription Anniversary").

44. James Redpath (1833–91) was a journalist and abolitionist from Malden, Massachusetts, who likely crossed paths with Rollin during his time as superintendent of public schools in Charleston, South Carolina, at the end of the Civil War. He and his wife, Mary Cotton Redpath (1823–1914), returned to Malden in 1866.

45. Rollin is likely referring to the Methodist minister Daniel Wise (1813–98), who published the children's novel *Minnie Brown; or, The Gentle Girl* under the pseudonym "Francis Forrester"

up and spoke ~~with me it~~ also I had a miscegenetic conversation with Mr Pierce editor of the Watchman and Reflector who introduced me to Mr Chas K. Whipple of the "Radical."[46] Mr Pierce gave me a history of a colored young lady and a young white gentleman who had loved and the prejudices kept[47] from marrying. They faced ostracism. America is not the world.

Thursday, January 23

Cloudy day. I went with Mrs Gray[48] to the meeting.[49] Col. Higginson spoke[50] so did ^Rev.^ Mr O. B. Frothingham. He is a fine impressive speaker I heard Stephen C. Foster[51] the great hearted anti Churchman of the Society. I agreed with his church views. O. B. Alcott[52] the almost infinitesimal metaphysical scholar. How spiritual his actual presence. Later Mr Phillips spoke with the usual effect.

---

in 1853. Wise was an abolitionist who, prior to the Civil War, advocated for the removal of all enslavers from the Methodist Church (Gardner, "'This Attempt of Their Sister,'" 231n18).

46. The identity of "Mr. Pierce" is unclear, as John W. Olmstead was the editor of the *Christian Watchman and Reflector* in 1868. Charles K. Whipple (1808–1900) was an abolitionist and assistant to William Lloyd Garrison at *The Liberator* prior to the Civil War; in 1868 he was a regular contributor to *The Radical*, a religious magazine published in Boston.

47. After this, the remainder of the entry is written along the left-hand margin of the page.

48. Likely Louisa Nell Gray (1825–86), sister of William Cooper Nell. See William Cooper Nell in biographical notes. Louisa and her husband, Ira Smith Gray (1821–?), also seem to have been boarding with the Baileys in 1868.

49. The thirty-fourth annual meeting of the Massachusetts Anti-Slavery Society was held in Mercantile Hall on 23 February 1868.

50. Higginson spoke against the society's opposition to Ulysses S. Grant's Republican candidacy for president ("Annual Meeting of the Massachusetts Anti-Slavery Society," *Boston Daily Advertiser*, 24 Jan. 1868, 4). He was supported in this by Frothingham.

51. Rollin no doubt means the abolitionist and minister Stephen S. Foster (1809–81). Foster was known for being a "come-outer" who would not participate in a church that condoned the institution of slavery. He often disrupted the church services of anti-abolitionist ministers. The *Boston Daily Advertiser* reported that Foster "spoke of prayer, and said that rather than look to heaven for help, we had better look into our hearts to see if we had there the love of our fellowmen in the shape of the negro. If we had that love there was no need of calling upon God to be present, for he would be already in our hearts. The church and clergy he denounced violently. … Some people, he said, thought it desirable to be at peace with their neighbors but he did not" ("Annual Meeting of the Massachusetts Anti-Slavery Society").

52. Rollin is almost certainly referring to Amos Bronson Alcott (1799–1888), a writer, philosopher, and reformer who was also the father of Louisa May Alcott, the first volume of whose *Little Women* was published in September 1868. Bronson Alcott, reported the *Boston Daily Advertiser*, "made an address on Mysticism" ("Annual Meeting of the Massachusetts Anti-Slavery Society").

His saying: The labor of years is entail on White men and their descendants for the bondage inflicted by them on the black man. Was a startling solution to the problem Truth

Friday, January 24

Happy day. Feasting on my yesterday's experience at the Anti Slavery meeting Mr Phillips remarks Mr Fosters and Rev Frothingham's still linger. A Mr Putnam[53] gave his vision of American religion as the fear of hell and that all little souls who are cowardly "cut for the church hence the poor progress of the Church in the cause of freedom.["] It was certainly a pleasure to me to be able to sit and listen to these old pioneers of the Anti Slavery warfare.

Saturday, January 25

Clear and cold as usual writing very briskly in the afternoon Mr Greener called and criticised for me In the eve Messrs Peter Williams of Brooklyn* called Ben Gregory[54] also. In the Mathews came today perfectly enthusiastic over his visit to Phil &c. He brought me messages from Cashins.[55] He is carried away with his lady friends.

*Williamsburgh, NY[56]

53. "Mr. Putnam" may be the poet and antislavery lecturer George W. Putnam (1812–96) of Lynn, Massachusetts.

54. Benjamin Gregory (1827–80) married Eliza Turpin (1827–?), Joanna Turpin Howard's sister, in 1852. In 1865 he worked as a porter and lived with his wife and their twelve-year-old son, Milton, in the South End of Boston. In 1870 he was working as a caterer, so he could have held either one of these positions in 1868. See Howard Family in biographical notes.

55. Rollin likely refers here to members of the Cashin family, who moved to Philadelphia from Georgia with their mother, Lucinda Bowdre (1820–?), in the middle to late 1850s (Lucinda Cashen, household, Precinct 10, Philadelphia Ward 1, Philadelphia, PA, US Census, 1860, database, Ancestry.com). Lucinda was likely of mixed race, while the father of her children was a white man named John Cashin Jr., who died in Georgia in 1859 or 1860. The couple had seven children together between approximately 1837 and 1856 (Cashin, *Agitator's Daughter*, 24). Evelina Cashin (1851–?) and Herschel Vivian Cashin (1854–1924) were in the Preparatory Department at the Institute for Colored Youth (ICY) in 1864, when Rollin left Philadelphia (*Objects of the Institute for Colored Youth*, 23). Older Cashin siblings, including Laura (1848–?), may also have been students at the ICY; their ages make them more likely to have been friends with Rollin during her time in the city. Frances mentions Laura in her entry for 30 July. She may have begun to write Laura's name here, as a capital *C* seems to have been written over a capital *L*.

56. This note appears at the bottom of the diary page. Rollin seems to be correcting Peter Williams's residence. It is not clear why she does it in this way rather than crossing out the word "Brooklyn" and replacing it with "Williamsburgh, NY."

Sunday, January 26
Home all day reading. Snowing, cold, and dreary L Mathews came and told of the grand meeting in his half of the A. M. E Church. Mr Lennox's brother the twin[57] came and played off as Chas Lennox to perfection. I was reading Emerson when he came in, and therefore could scarcely account for the singular change I supposed in Charles. It was a good joke on my expense and capitally done

Monday, January 27
Snowing heavily. Mr Chas Lennox called for a few minutes. In evening at Mr Phillips How ones heart opens and warms toward the great hearted humanitarian, his keen eyes though seeming to scan your inner most heart while you are in his presence beams so kindly withal that instantly you find yourself at home with him, as you say, he knows my strengths and my weaknesses yet his great mantle covers them all. He is the hero worthy of worship "the more man does for his fellow man the nearer he approaches to God." Esto perpetua.[58] He gave me his photograph and lots of encouragement and hope.

Tuesday, January 28
Today a letter from Major and [A. V.] for Dickens Reading. Immediately answered and gave him an account of my visit to the great Wendell. In the afternoon L. came I was angry with him for not going with me but he made an explanation

Wednesday, January 29
I went out today for the slippers for Green. Very cold [walk] went to Higginson for fried oysters and coffee. In afternoon begun it while Leed was here. He brought Mr John M. Brown[59] to see me I was ~~quite~~ favorably impressed with Mr B though prior to our meeting I was prejudiced against him It was L's fault from the first

Thursday, January 30
Writing in the morning. In afternoon L. came also Mr Greener and invited us to go to hear Ralph Waldo Emerson. We went and I considered it a rare intellectual

57. Charles Lenox's twin brother was John Minah Lenox (1824–1911). In 1870 John lived in Cambridge, Massachusetts, with his wife and five children and, like his father and brother, was employed as a barber.

58. Latin for "Let it be perpetual."

59. An AME deacon, John M. Brown (1817–93) worked with Matthews and others to create new AME churches and schools throughout the South. In May 1868 he was ordained an AME bishop, overseeing a district consisting of South Carolina, Florida, Georgia, and Alabama (Simmons, *Men of Mark*, 1117).

treat. We were not at the first of it. It was at Cambridge at the College Hall. Subject "The Immortality of the Soul." He argued with great force that there is no death and shared that as nature renews her form so does man but nature still. The next life is more perfect than this, to live here after is to live now.

Friday, January 31
Writing. How poor my efforts are to me now when I reflect on the great Emerson, yet I suppose he too had a beginning.

Saturday, February 1
Wrote today. Mr Greener came while reading L came in also Mr Mallory[60] It is a bitter cold day.

Sunday, February 2
At home all day reading in the afternoon

Monday, February 3
Write write write. In the afternoon company as usual

Tuesday, February 4
Received a note from Mr Nell[61] to meet Mr Garrison[62] at the Freedmen Rooms.[63] I went there to him. Mr Tomlinson[64] came in at the same time it was quite a surprise to me. Mr Garrisons voice is as familiar to my ears as possible, and yet I cant account for it. He was speaking of Charleston and of Sam Dickerson.[65] I did not read there to him but made an appointment for Thursday afternoon. His manners are as genial as his looks God preserve him

60. "Mr. Mallory" may be the hairdresser Charles Mallory who was boarding with the Lockleys at 31 Garden Street in 1868 (*Boston Directory*, 1868).

61. William Cooper Nell. See biographical notes.

62. William Lloyd Garrison. See biographical notes.

63. The New England Freedmen's Aid Society had their offices in the Studio Building on the corner of Bromfield and Tremont Streets. Founded in 1862, the society provided assistance to those until recently enslaved. One of their priorities was to match Northern teachers to the Southern schools that needed them.

64. Rollin is likely referring to Reuben Tomlinson (1832–1908), state superintendent of education in South Carolina from 1865 to October 1868.

65. Samuel Dickerson (1823–?) was an enslaved preacher from South Carolina. During a flag-raising ceremony at Fort Sumter immediately following the end of the war, Dickerson and his daughters awarded Garrison with a wreath to welcome him and show their gratitude (Mayer, *All on Fire*, 583.) According to the 1870 census, Dickerson, who was working as a whitewasher, lived with his two daughters, Mary Ellen, seventeen years old, and Mary Ann, sixteen years

Wednesday, February 5
Writing today quite briskly so as to be ready for tomorrow. L came in the afternoon brought me the a/c books[66]

Thursday, February 6
Writing all morning, but felt so badly I was compelled to go to bed could not go to Mr Garrison in consequence of it. L. came but could not see him. I never felt more like writing than today and just to think in the midst of it I was compelled to stop too bad!

Friday, February 7
Still miserable, in the afternoon L. came and brought me some letters to read. I recvd a long and beautiful letter from Georgie E. very complimentary to him in certain portions also recvd one from Green.[67] He is a singularly sensitive man, good hearted and full of good intention

Saturday, February 8
Writing and still sick. M. brought me his Report to the African Conference[68] there I saw the subscription list and the name among them that stirs a thousand memories.[69] Is as but a shadow or hope, or is a tangible reality for me?

Sunday, February 9
To Church a memorable day; with Ella Mahone[70] I was much pleased both with the service and the congregation.

---

old, as well as an infant named Sarah Ann (Samuel Dickerson, household, Charleston Ward 6, Charleston, SC, US Census, 1870, database, Ancestry.com). William C. Hine includes him in a list of Black men who were "important in Republican circles in Charleston" but did not hold "elective office" ("Black Politicians," 557).

66. Account books. Rollin may be helping Matthews prepare his "Report to the African Congress" that she writes about on 8 February.

67. Likely Samuel Green. See biographical notes.

68. Matthews's "Report to the African Conference" was likely a report to the Executive Board of the Missionary Society of the AME Church, accounting for the contributions gathered for the year of 1867. The one for 1868 was published in January 1869 in the *Missionary Reporter*. The report referred to here was probably published in the January 1868 *Reporter*, which unfortunately cannot be located. It is mentioned, however, in the *Christian Recorder* on January 25: "Mr. W. E. Matthew, who is one of the traveling agents of Wilberforce University, informs us that he has just made his report to the missionary board, to the amount of $1,075" ("Personal," *Christian Recorder*, 25 Jan. 1868, 2).

69. Rollin may be alluding to the man she refers to as "P." elsewhere in the diary. "P." seems to have lived in Philadelphia during the Civil War and may have been a minister.

70. See Simonds/Mahone Family in biographical notes.

Mr Lennox called and spent the evening very pleasantly.
Matthews out of the city today at Lowell.
At Boston Theatre to hear Mr Hepworth[71]

Monday, February 10
A note from Mr Garrison today he will call and see me. writing up very fast I do not know how good though!

Tuesday, February 11
Writing up stairs today very satisfactory as I do always when alone
I expected to go to Church this afternoon with Ella but was disappointed
Letter from M S Haynes[72]

Wednesday, February 12
Mr Wm Lloyd Garrison spent the morning with me. I think him a grand noble soul. A ^singularly^ perfect development of god highest humanity. A great intellect consecrated to one idea. I felt a reverence while in the presence of this great man, who came to the rescue of a dazed and helpless people. God marked him out from the number to proclaim his truths. But is he an humanitarian? How can his practiced pen and ready heart remain uninterested while the same wrong exists under another form.[73] God knoweth his purposes and the instruments best adapted

Thursday, February 13
Sent a letter to Mr Lennox today. Leed spent the afternoon with me but was so sick he was compelled to go home. Mr John M. Brown spent the evening with me. I enjoyed his society much. I spoke of my mission here quite freely to him.

71. George Hughes Hepworth (1833–1902) was a white Unitarian minister from Boston who served as a chaplain with the Seventy-Sixth US Colored Troops during the Civil War. Hepworth preached on Sunday evenings at the Boston Theatre in the late 1860s (Lewis, "Unitarian Churches of Boston," 25). The project was part of an attempt to open church service to the masses.

72. This note appears four lines below the previous line of the entry.

73. When the Civil War ended, Garrison ceased publishing *The Liberator* and argued for the dissolution of the American Anti-Slavery Society, as slavery had been abolished. The society remained intact and continued to fight for Black suffrage and civil rights.

He spoke of Mr Cain.[74] He told me of the intended visit of Mr Lowe[75] to me concerning Mr Cain's school.

Mr Brown promised to hear me read tomorrow if he does not go away.

Friday, February 14

Writing hard. Mr Brown did not come as expected. sent to find out how L was getting on. I do feel so much for one away from home.

Out with Leedie to tea at Nelly's Leedie does not know his own mind in regard to Miss Pet

Mr Nell called[76]

Saturday, February 15

Writing. I am worried sick about home matters and not hearing from them.

Sunday, February 16

Church of the Advent[77]

Mrs Simonds and Ella[78] called I was so nervous about home matters that I went

74. Richard H. Cain (1825–87) was an AME minister. Born in Virginia to a Black father and a Cherokee mother, Cain was educated at Wilberforce University. He moved to Charleston in 1865 to serve as superintendent of AME missions and minister of Emanuel Church, the oldest AME church in the South. He was a delegate to the state constitutional convention in 1868 and was elected to the South Carolina Senate in the same year (Foner, *Freedom's Lawmakers*, 35–36). As funding for educational efforts in the state dwindled in the late 1860s, Cain began to think about closing the school associated with Emanuel Church (Powers, *Black Charlestonians*, 146).

75. Charles Lowe (1828–74) was secretary of the American Unitarian Association. In early 1868 he reported to the Suffolk Conference of Unitarian and other Christian Churches on plans to cooperate with the AME Church in the Southern states. The AME requested assistance with "the distribution of books and tracts" and "the education of the ministry" ("Theological Miscegenation," *American Missionary*, Mar. 1868, 59).

76. This note appears toward the bottom of the page, with seven empty lines between it and the rest of the entry. Rollin may have been saving space to say more about Leedie's visit or whatever happened between that visit and William Cooper Nell's.

77. Boston's Episcopal Church of the Advent was begun in 1844 by members who opposed the renting of pews and the social divisions that such practices promoted. It also adhered more closely to Roman Catholic liturgical practices than did other Episcopal parishes. In 1868 the church was located on Bowdoin Street.

78. Anna/Emma Simonds and Ella Mahone. See Simonds/Mahone Family in biographical notes.

both to Mrs Barreu's[79] and Mrs Edwards[80] to hear something. Mathews came and brought me some flowers. In evening went with him to hear Rev Jas Freeman Clark[81] at Boston Theatre. ~~with Leedie~~

Monday, February 17

A letter today from Lizzie Kennedy[82] how much pleasure to be remembered by friends! In Eve went to the Sleigh Party. L took me. It was a very poor affair at best. A covered furniture wagon, packed with forty persons. I knew but few. The ride was miserable. I met John Oliver[83] there. Reached home about four o'clock ^next morning^ from Stoneham,[84] out of breath and spirits. I shall never attempt to go under such auspices again. Snowed.

Tuesday, February 18

Good day. Two letters from home; one from Lottie[85] and the other from Barquet[86] The first crushed me to earth with its sad contents of fathers failures, and his

79. "Mrs. Barreu" may be Elizabeth Barreau (sometimes spelled "Barrow" in census records), who was born Elizabeth Davis in South Carolina in approximately 1829. She married John Barreau (1829–?), a carpenter, and they seem to have moved to Boston sometime between 1860 and 1865 along with her mother, Eliza Davis (1800–?) (John E. Barrow, household, Boston Ward 5, Suffolk, MA, Massachusetts State Census, 1865, database, Ancestry.com).

80. "Mrs. Edwards" is likely Sarah E. Plummet Edwards (1828–81), a native of Charleston who moved with her husband, James L. Edwards, a carpenter, to Boston sometime between 1860 and 1865 (James Edwards, household, Charleston Ward 7, Charleston, SC, US Census, 1860, database, Ancestry.com; James L. Edwards, household, Boston Ward 5, Suffolk, MA, Massachusetts State Census, 1865, database, Ancestry.com).

81. Along with Edward Everett Hale, the white theologian and writer James Freeman Clarke (1810–88) officiated at the Boston Theatre in the winter of 1867–68 (Tompkins and Kilby, *History of the Boston Theatre*, 147).

82. Elizabeth B. Kennedy. See Kennedy Family in biographical notes.

83. This may be a reference to John Oliver (1821–99), a carpenter and abolitionist who was born free in Virginia and moved to Boston by 1850. In 1862 he went to eastern Virginia to work in contraband camps under the auspices of the American Missionary Association (Foner, *Freedom's Lawmakers*, 164). Oliver lived in Philadelphia, where he may have met Rollin, from mid-1863 to 1865 and directed an employment office for freedmen. He returned to Virginia, living in Richmond for the rest of his life, but may have been in Boston in 1868 (Ripley and Finkenbine, *Black Abolitionist Papers*, 5:136–37n4).

84. Stoneham, Massachusetts, is about ten miles north of Boston.

85. Charlotte "Lottie" Rollin, Frances's sister. See biographical notes.

86. Possibly Joseph Humphries Barquet (1823–80). Barquet was, like Rollin, the child of a free person of color from Saint Domingue (Bellows, *Two Charlestonians*, 13, 17–18). Born in 1823 to

general pecuniary losses. How hard this is the accumulations of years should in his most needed time be swept away! "Ruin" is written in every homestead of South Carolina. But why should the unoffending suffer?

The other cheered me on to my work. L. called Mr Greener also

Wednesday, February 19
Almost a Spring day Before I left my room Ella Mahone called to invite me to tea, and to go to see the "White Fawn"[87] I went vidi but not vici.[88] The scenery was gorgeous resembling enchantment almost but there was no plot to the play. The dress presented a most indecorous appearance tout en decollete.[89]

L was there he certainly had no idea of seeing me there, nor I of seeing him. It was rather amusing to me to be even with him.

Thursday, February 20
Writing in morning in afternoon L. came sort of made up in evening wrote and read Macauley England.[90] I have been reading Carlisle's Heroes, The Northmen and also Mahomet and had nearly ~~begun~~ completed the Hero as Poet—Dante and Shakespeare.[91]

Friday, February 21
Writing in afternoon went out to Mrs. Edwards Still reading English History

---

John Pierre (1785–1838) and Barbara Barquet (1795–1846), Joseph grew up among the free African American elite in Charleston (*Two Charlestonians*, 11). He left the city in 1846, the year after Rollin's birth, to fight in the Mexican-American War (1846–48). After time spent in New York, Ohio, Wisconsin, and finally Illinois, where he lived for ten years, Joseph enlisted in the Fifty-Fourth Massachusetts Infantry. He likely met Rollin in Charleston after the fall of the city.

87. The fairy pantomime *The White Fawn* was produced for the first time in January 1868 at Niblo's Garden, a theater on Broadway and Crosby Street. Rollin went to see "the grand spectacular drama" at the Boston Theatre, which boasted of spending $100,000 on its production ("Amusements," *Boston Evening Transcript*, 10 Feb. 1868, 3).

88. Borrowing from the Latin phrase "Vini, vidi, vici" ("I came, I saw, I conquered"), Rollin implies that she saw the play but either it or she did not conquer.

89. French for "all in low neckline." The production of *The White Fawn* included ballet dancers, some of whom might have worn what Rollin considered "indecorous" dress.

90. Thomas Macaulay's *History of England*. See note 10.

91. Rollin refers here to *On Heroes, Hero-Worship, and the Heroic in History* (1841), a collection of lectures given by Thomas Carlyle (1795–1881) in 1840. She mentions specifically "The Hero as Divinity," "The Hero as Prophet," and "The Hero as Poet."

Saturday, February 22

Washington's Birth Day.

But if things continue as they are there will be but little Country left to celebrate it. For myself I am no enthusiast over Patriotic Celebrations as I am counted out of the body Politic I wrote very satisfactory today Mathews brought me the Commonwealth[92] and other papers. There was a grand description of Rev Dr Bartol Charles Eliot Norton and Bronson Alcott[93]—a seer of finest spiritual essence. I heard him at the Anti Slavery meeting also O B Frothingham![94]

Sunday, February 23

I went today to Rev Bartols Church[95] the Sexton was about giving me a pew in the Gallery. I declined and left. He said the lower were rented.[96] We are compelled to be sensitive ^and tenacious of our rights^ or else we will be sunken by this Americause. I went to the Advent,[97] but was too much engrossed with the Bartol Church incident to enjoy my religious duties except the Litany.

In afternoon Mathews came I am not sure he understand the highest female character.

Monday, February 24

Here all day; hard at work finishing up my writing I was introduced to a colored lady at one of the Medical Colleges here.[98] She is certainly well balanced. In

92. The abolitionist *Commonwealth* was a weekly newspaper that ran from 1862 to 1896.

93. The "grand description" that Rollin refers to was in an article titled "The New Religious Movement" and published in the *Commonwealth* on Sunday, 22 February. Cyrus Augustus Bartol (1813–1900) was a Unitarian minister and Transcendentalist who in 1867 met with other Unitarians to form the Free Religious Association. The association was opposed to organized religion and privileged reason and the individual conscience over any sort of spiritualism. The author of the article, editor and social critic Charles Eliot Norton (1827–1908), was said not to be "an attendant upon the club meetings" of the Free Religious Association but "otherwise lends a helping hand to the cause, in every way within his power." For Bronson Alcott, see note 52.

94. Octavius Brooks Frothingham. See note 44. While the author of "The New Religious Movement" mentioned Frothingham's participation in the Free Religious Association, he was not profiled in the way Bartol, Alcott, and Norton were.

95. Bartol was pastor of the West Unitarian Church in Boston.

96. Prior to the twentieth century, most churches collected funds from congregants by renting out pews. The closer a pew was to the altar or pulpit, the more they paid for rental. Rollin seems to be angered by the fact that, while Bartol is a radical religious thinker, his church still charges rent for pews. She may also be upset about the attempt to seat her in the gallery, as galleries were often used to seat Black churchgoers.

97. Church of the Advent. See note 77.

98. This is almost certainly Rebecca Lee Crumpler (1831–95), who in 1864 became the first African American woman to graduate with a medical degree. She attended the New England

afternoon received a letter and check for $50.[99] I am afraid that I can not afford to pursue the course marked out. To write one must be above want I should think. Mathews came in and spent the afternoon.

Tuesday, February 25
Went to the Post Office today. State St. excited over the Washington news.[100] Andrew Johnson sends an explanatory message to Congress.
In eve went to Church at Rev Dr Kirks[101] heard three fine discourses relative to the formation of a commission to form City missions over the country

Wednesday, February 26
Writing unsatisfactorily In afternoon went out South End to Mrs Purcell and Mrs Gregory.[102] In evening Leedie came read to me his brothers letter in return I gave Katie's[103] which I rcvd today. All quiet on the Potomac tonight[104]

Thursday, February 27
Wrote all the morning, in the afternoon went out and a terrible snow storm came up In the eve went with Mr Baily[105] to Dickens He delighted me more than ever, there was the genial and grand face of Longfellow,[106] the kingly Publisher Fields[107]

Female Medical College in Boston after working as a nurse for eight years. After the Civil War, she worked for several years with the Freedmen's Bureau in Virginia ("Dr. Rebecca Lee Crumpler," Changing the Face of Medicine, online exhibit, NIH: US National Library of Medicine, https://cfmedicine.nlm.nih.gov/physicians/biography_73.html).

99. The note and the check were from Delany.

100. On 24 February 1868, the US House of Representatives voted to impeach President Andrew Johnson (1808–75), who had repeatedly defied congressional efforts to reconstruct the Southern states after the Civil War. The president was charged with high crimes and misdemeanors, the primary charge being his removal and replacement of Edwin Stanton as secretary of war.

101. Edward Norris Kirk (1802–74) was pastor at Mount Vernon Congregational Church in Boston from 1842 to 1871.

102. Eliza Turpin Gregory, the sister of Joanna Turpin Howard. The Gregorys lived on Shawmut Avenue in the South End neighborhood of Boston. See note 54.

103. Katherine Rollin. See biographical notes.

104. "All Quiet along the Potomac," a poem by Ethel Lynn Beers, was originally published as "The Picket Guard" in *Harper's Weekly* on 30 November 1861. The poem was reprinted widely and then set to music in 1863.

105. John B. Bailey. See biographical notes.

106. Henry Wadsworth Longfellow (1807–82) was one of the best-known and loved poets in nineteenth-century America. He was also one of the best-paid writers of his day.

107. James T. Fields (1817–81) was the senior partner in the publishing firm Ticknor and Fields.

in the same line with us, brilliant authors and handsome women Upper Tendom was there in full blast Christmas Carol and Boots at the Holly Tree Inn. How he touched every heart with Tiny Tim, and convulsed us with Boots "most curiousest" thing he ever saw, as well as Mr Scrooge's conversion.[108]

Friday, February 28
Writing still. Mr B. received three tickets from Mr Ticknor.[109] Leedie came and wanted to impress me with the belief that he loves me. He might see that it would be advantageous to have me near to direct him but further than that I do not know.
I read after he left. I wrote several letters.

Saturday, February 29
Working still, and quite satisfactory. M. came in and spent the afternoon received a letter from Miss Georgie.
I have not experienced a much colder day than this. Mr Smith clipping hair for me.
I read the Christian Register[110] which L. brought to me.

Sunday, March 1
Worked on my book the first time since I begun it. In afternoon I read Macaulay. Later Leedie Mathews came and there was a sitting for spiritual purposes.[111] The table was clearly lifted and twisted about and the spirit answered to C.L.

---

108. Charles Dickens gave a reading at the Tremont Temple on the evening of 27 February 1868. As Rollin notes, he read from *A Christmas Carol* (1843) and "Boots at the Holly Tree Inn" (1855). "Boots" was originally part three of a portmanteau story—a work with parts written by different authors—called "The Holly-Tree Inn" and published in *Household Words*. The other authors were Wilkie Collins and Adelaide Proctor. Dickens's contribution opens with the narrator recounting a conversation with Boots, a gardener: "Where had he been in his time? He repeated when I asked him the question. Lord, he had been everywhere!" The narrator continues, "What was the curiousest thing he had seen?" (Charles Dickens, "The Boots," pt. 3 of "The Holly-Tree Inn," *Household Words*, vol. 12, 15 Dec. 1855, 18). The main character of *A Christmas Carol*, Ebenezer Scrooge, is transformed into a better man by the ghostly visitation of his former business partner and the spirits of Christmas Past, Present, and Yet to Come.

109. Benjamin Holt Ticknor (1842–1914) continued to work in the firm that his father co-founded after William Ticknor's death in 1864. His partner was James T. Fields; see note 109. These tickets were for another public reading by Charles Dickens.

110. *The Christian Register* was a weekly newspaper published by the American Unitarian Association in Boston.

111. Spiritualism was extremely popular in the United States after the Civil War, as Americans struggled to cope with the deaths of loved ones. In addition to meetings, Spiritualists published books and hosted lectures attended by Americans of all religious faiths. Having lived with Isaac

I felt as though it meant Grandma. I left the room. I am no skeptic "I thank God" as Goethe said that I do not doubt the possibility of any thing. I also sketched our Josephus.

Monday, March 2
Writing hard to get the work finished. The deepest snow storm I have seen yet. M.[112] came in the ~~afternoon~~ evening and interrupted me. I wrote in the evening also. Mr Nell came in and I read some portions to him. I am finishing up very rapidly.

Tuesday, March 3
Book completed[113]
At work writing. Mr Nell came in and I read my Finis to him. Late in the afternoon I completed it. It has been no easy task to me writing under so many difficulties and uncertain of my prospects while it is in the hands of the publishers. I am not feeling very well about my scant pay while writing. I think I have not been dealt with according to the letter of the contract. I would gladly have written otherwise if circumstances were different, but as it is, it is more con amore than for cash.[114]

Wednesday, March 4
This morning I took the MS. Mr Fields[115] told me he would present Mr Garrison's letter[116] to the firm which is to have a meeting and would let me know. I tremble for my success somehow. I suppose it is natural for a novice to feel so. Home and sewed for Miss Emily.[117] In afternoon L. came of course we quarreled to begin with. I read after he left. I wrote to Major.[118] I feel so much better now that I am through with the Ms. Yet I know that I can better it.

---

and Amy Post in Rochester in the late 1850s, William Cooper Nell had become a firm believer in Spiritualism. While his interest had waned by 1868, he may have introduced the Baileys and other Boston African Americans to such beliefs (Wesley and Uzelac, *William Cooper Nell*, 22–23).

112. Rollin likely refers here to William E. "Leedie" Matthews.

113. This is written at the top of the page, between the date and the first line of the page.

114. "Con amore" is Italian for "with love or devotion." Rollin means that she has written her book out of love for the project, rather than for the compensation promised by Delany.

115. James T. Fields. See note 107.

116. William Lloyd Garrison wrote a letter of introduction for Rollin to Fields. See appendix A.

117. Rollin may be assisting Emily Bailey with her work as a dressmaker. See Bailey Family in biographical notes.

118. Martin Robison Delany. See biographical notes.

Thursday, March 5

A beautiful clear day. Went to Chelsea to see Mrs Richards[119] had a most friendly reception from her. She seemed really glad to see me. Mr Richards came over to Boston with me. I went to see old Mrs Mann and Mrs Needman. I anticipate going to Portland with Mrs N. They are all most comfortably situated. I also saw Mr Morris.[120] I attended in the evening the Attuck celebration.[121] Several speeches were made. Leedie spoke favorably and truthfully the rest were at random and partisan speeches

Friday, March 6

Fine morning. I went with L. to see Rev Henry Ware[122] about the schools.[123] I did not meet him, saw Miss Lottie Forten[124] at the Freedmens Rooms.[125] I went home sick. In eve heard of Fannie Clark's death. Poor child not married four months yet. She was married on the 19th of Nov my birthday scarce had the bridal wreath

---

119. Elizabeth Richards (1832–?) and her husband, David W. Richards (1821–?), a blacksmith who worked in shipyards, were born in South Carolina and lived in Chelsea with their three children and a seventeen-year-old relation named Sophia Richards (1853–?), also born in South Carolina (David W. Richards, household, Chelsea, Suffolk, MA, US Census, 1870, database, Ancestry .com). The Richards were in Massachusetts prior to the birth of their first son in 1858 (David W. Richards, household, Chelsea, Suffolk, MA, US Census, 1860, database, Ancestry.com).

120. Robert Morris (1823–82). See biographical notes.

121. In 1858 William Cooper Nell organized the first Attucks Celebration on 5 March, the anniversary of the Boston Massacre and traditionally observed as the beginning of the American Revolution. Crispus Attucks (1723–70), a stevedore of African and Native American descent, is widely regarded as the first person killed in the Revolution. Official Attucks Celebrations ended in 1870 (Wesley and Uzelac, *William Cooper Nell*, 36–37).

122. Rollin is likely referring here to John Fothergill Waterhouse Ware (1818–80). Ware was a Unitarian minister who was born and worked most of his life in Massachusetts. In 1864, however, he moved to Baltimore and helped found the Baltimore Association for the Moral and Intellectual Improvement of the Colored People, which established schools for African American students (Matthews, *John F. W. Ware*, 442–44). Ware was in Boston around this time: on March 12 one newspaper printed a notice of a lecture titled "Practical Thoughts for Young Men and Women" to be delivered the following evening at the Channing Church ("Newton Corner," *Boston Evening Transcript*, 12 Mar. 1868, 2). William E. Matthews, according to the address he delivered upon Ware's death in 1881, became acquainted with him in 1867 (Matthews, *John F. W. Ware and His Work for the Freedmen*). Leedie likely told Rollin about the teaching opportunity in Maryland.

123. On 4 March 1868, the New England Freedmen's Aid Society noted that a committee from the John A. Andrew Society in Maryland was seeking another teacher (Daily Record, 1868–69, vol. 3, folder 1, box 2, New England Freedmen's Aid Society Record Books, 1862–78, Digitized Collections, Massachusetts Historical Society, https://www.masshist.org/collection -guides/digitized/fa0423/b2-f01#19). The record books were maintained by Charlotte Forten.

124. Charlotte Forten (Grimké). See biographical notes.

125. The New England Freedmen's Aid Society. See note 63.

faded when the bride passed away. Requiescat in pace. They are distressed to death about her at the house. I have been there tonight. It is appalling![126]

Saturday, March 7
Clear over head but terrible under feet. Mr Fields told me the firm had refused to entertain the proposition of receiving my Book. I was scarcely disappointed.[127] I met Mr Haynes in the street quite unexpectedly. I went to Mrs Clark.[128] Mrs Williams spoke very plainly about the death. All kinds of rumors are afloat in regard to it suspicion of foul play rife.[129] I visited Mrs Carey who had just returned from Charleston also Lockleys[130]

Sunday, March 8
Not feeling well today. In afternoon went to Church at the Advent found it closed after went to Mrs Clarke's found they had poor Fannie packed away in ice.[131] It is horrible to be put up in that manner. I think humanity too sacred to be so roughly handled, yet in some cases death renders the nearest and dearest so repulsive to the senses that science gently interposes to reconcile the defects.
In the evening I went to hear Mrs Dall[132] she is an able woman and gave us a nice treat.

126. On 19 November 1867, Fanny L. Clark (1843–68) married Charles Johnson (1843–78), a waiter. Fanny's parents were Anthony F. Clark (1812–?), a barber, and Fanny Lenox Clark (1818–1905), daughter of Sibel (1798–1843) and John Lenox (1794–1886) of Watertown. Fanny Lenox Clark's brother was Charles Lenox (see biographical notes). Anthony and Fanny lived at 82 Phillips Street, just a block away from the Haydens (*Boston Directory*, 1867). According to her death record, Fanny Johnson died of puerperal fever, a uterine infection that follows childbirth; she was ill for two weeks prior to her death, meaning that she gave birth around mid-February (Fanny L. Johnson entry, "Massachusetts, U.S., Town and Vital Records, 1620–1988," database, Ancestry.com). Puerperal fever is caused by a bacterial infection of the reproductive tract and results in intense abdominal pain, fever, and debility.

127. Rollin may not have been very disappointed because she may have already contacted Lee & Shepard about publishing the book. See entry for 10 March.

128. Fanny Lenox Clark, the mother of Fanny Clark Johnson. See note 126.

129. It is not clear why there would have been "suspicion of foul play" in Fanny's death. It is possible that the family suspected she had not been given proper medical care during or after the birth of her child.

130. See Lockley Family in biographical notes.

131. Rather than being taken to a mortuary, Fanny's body was laid out at home, where it was placed on ice to delay the decomposition process until her funeral could take place.

132. Caroline Healey Dall (1822–1912) was a white author and reformer whose writing in the 1860s primarily addressed women's rights. While Rollin could not have known it, Dall was also a diligent diarist whose approximately seventy-five-year, multivolume diary is now held by the Massachusetts Historical Society in Boston.

Monday, March 9

Beautiful day, went out to Roxbury[133] to Mr Garrison his house is built on a high rocky hill a wild rocky scenery. His parlor is adorned with sculptured busts of himself and the kingly orator Phillips[134] and portraits of Thompson[135] and Phillips and himself Lincoln[136] Washington.[137] In tintype are Liberty and a Swiss scenery. There were several albums among them portraits of Mazzini[138] to him. In the afternoon the funeral took place. Dr Lathrops[139] spoke most touchingly of the solemn occasion.

Tuesday, March 10

This morning at Lee & Sheppard[140] about the Book. All right there. In the afternoon at Mrs Howard's Addie gave me Edmonia Lewis'[141] picture. After dinner went to Cambridge to Wm Wells Brown's[142] had quite a pleasant visit there they always treat me so hospitably that I cant help liking them. He seems so honest

133. The city of Roxbury was annexed by Boston in January 1868. Garrison moved there in 1864.

134. Wendell Phillips. See biographical notes.

135. British abolitionist George Thompson (1804–78).

136. Abraham Lincoln (1809–65), the sixteenth president of the United States.

137. George Washington (1732–1799), the first president of the United States.

138. Giuseppe Mazzini (1805–72) was an Italian nationalist whose thinking on republicanism and political freedom was influential in the Unites States.

139. This is likely Samuel Kirkland Lothrop (1804–86), a white Unitarian minister who also had married Fanny and Charles in November 1867 (Fannie L. Clark and Charles Johnson entry, "Massachusetts, U.S., Marriage Records, 1840–1915," database, Ancestry.com). Lothrop served at the Brattle Street Church from 1834 to 1876.

140. William Lee (1826–1906) and Charles Augustus Billings Shepard (1829–89) established the publishing firm Lee & Shepard in 1861. Their office was located at 149 Washington Street (*Boston Directory*, 1867).

141. The sculptor Mary Edmonia Lewis (c. 1844–1907) was the daughter of an African American father who had escaped enslavement and a mother who was of mixed African American and Ojibwe heritage. Lewis lived and worked in Boston from 1864 to 1866, when she went to Rome, where she spent most of the rest of her life. While in Boston, she boarded with the family of Alfred G. Howard, who shared a home with his brother, Edwin F. Howard; his wife; and their two daughters (Edwin F. Howard, household, Boston Ward 5, Suffolk, MA, Massachusetts State Census, 1865, database, Ancestry.com). In July 1865 Lewis and Adeline Howard traveled together to Richmond, Virginia, to find positions teaching freedpeople. They returned to Boston soon after, perhaps because their trunks were stolen, and Lewis sailed for Italy in August (unititled, *The Liberator*, 25 Aug. 1865, 135). See Howard Family in biographical notes.

142. William Wells Brown and his second wife, Anna Elizabeth Gray Brown. See biographical notes.

in his kindly interest in me. I reach home at nine oclock. A letter from Leedie at Providence.

Wednesday, March 11
I received a letter from L today went to the Freedmans Rooms to see Mr Ware.[143] Miss Lottie Forten conversed very freely with me and showed me a letter of Mrs Child's[144] to her concerning her criticism of "Waiting for the Verdict."[145] Says Mrs Child "Every quadroon and Mulatto bears upon his face the refutation of the instinctive shrinking of the white race from the black."
I am much pleased with Mr Ware. I answered L.'s letter and sent the one at the Browns from "Milton Mass" to him.[146] Sewed and retired early. Sent a letter to Major D.

Thursday, March 12
Clear day. A letter from Lizzie Kennedy[147] and the Anti Miscg. book from Charleston. Mr Nell brought me a book on Color.

143. The records of the New England Freedmen's Aid Society indicate that Rollin was offered and had accepted a teaching position in Maryland: "At Mr Ware's request, the Soc will take Miss Frances Rollins, who is going to Maryland—will offer her to the John Andrew Soc" (entry, 11 Mar. 1868, Daily Record, 1868–69, vol. 3, folder 1, box 2, New England Freedmen's Aid Society Record Books, 1862–78, Digitized Collections, Massachusetts Historical Society, www.masshist.org/collection-guides/digitized/fa0423/b2-f01#20).

144. Lydia Maria Child (1802–80) was a white abolitionist, women's rights activist, and author whose novel, *A Romance of the Republic*, was published by Ticknor and Fields in 1867.

145. *Waiting for the Verdict*, a novel by Rebecca Harding Davis (1831–1910), was published in New York by Sheldon and Company in 1868. Forten had written a letter to the *National Anti-Slavery Standard* in response to Caroline Healey Dall's review of the novel that claimed, "A very delicate comprehension of the colored race is shown in these pages" (Dall, review of *Waiting for the Verdict*, by Rebecca Harding Davis, *National Anti-Slavery Standard*, 25 Jan. 1868, 3). Published on 22 February, Forten's letter disagrees with this sentiment, asserting, "I had read but a few pages when I said to myself, 'How plain it is to see that she who wrote this book . . . has not outgrown the prejudice against the outcast race.'" She goes on to argue against Davis's sense "that the prejudice against color is instinctive and natural to the whites" and insists instead that prejudice is "the result of false education." Forten concludes by comparing "the spirit of caste" in *Waiting for the Verdict* with "the broad, loving humanity breathing from" Child's *Romance of the Republic* (Forten, "*Waiting for the Verdict*," letter to editors, *National Anti-Slavery Standard*, 22 Feb. 1868, 3).

146. Rollin twice sent letters to Matthews that were delivered to the residence of William Wells Brown and his wife. See also entry for 14 Mar. 1868. It is possible that Matthews boarded with the Browns in Boston between his travels for the AME Church.

147. Elizabeth B. Kennedy. See Kennedy Family in biographical notes.

Friday, March 13
Writing received a letter from Leedie today he is delighted with Providence.
Made a pleasant visit to Lockley's.
For, of the soul, the body form doth take,
For soul is form, and doth the body make—Spenser[148]

Saturday, March 14
Finished my writing today I trust satisfactorily.
No letters from home, but answered the one which Leedie sent me also sent those
from Brown's for him.

Sunday, March 15
To Church at the Advent after to Chelsea to dinner with Mrs Richards had quite
a pleasant time In the afternoon left with Mr R for the Theatre to hear Mr Ware
and the crowded house showed the popularity of the orator.[149] It was a grand
treat well delivered seemingly without effort, appealing to the heart as well as the
reason. He denied that man was weak. Be then strong is written in every page of
Holy Writ. In conclusion he allowed the audience to join in repeating the Lord's
Prayer. A stillness fell upon us it was impressive.

Monday, March 16
Took my book to Mr Lee's[150] today and was very kindly received by him I pray
for success.
In afternoon Leedie came seeming quite happy and on the best terms with himself. He took me to the Entertainment for Phil Smith's Benefit.[151] I did not think
much of any portion of it. Mr Greener[152] read Dicken's Christmas Carol. I saw
Mr Trotter[153] there and Dr Miller[154] for the first time. It rained very hard as we
came out. L tried to make believe Pet & I were one.

---

148. This couplet is taken from Edmund Spenser's "A Hymn in Honor of Beauty" (1596).

149. According to the *Boston Evening Transcript*, the Reverend Ware was the fifteenth in a
series of sermons in the Boston Theatre sponsored by the Suffolk Conference of Unitarian and
other Christian Churches. Ware's text was Matthew 13:27 (KJV): "From whence then hath it
tares?" ("Preaching in the Boston Theatre," *Boston Evening Transcript*, 16 Mar. 1868, 4).

150. William Lee of Lee & Shepard. See note 140.

151. A benefit performance was one in which a theater awarded the artist some or all of the
proceeds from the event. It is not clear if Phil Smith was an actor or someone else in need of
funds.

152. Richard Greener. See biographical notes.

153. Likely James Monroe Trotter (1842–92), who served in the Fifty-Fifth Massachusetts
Infantry Regiment and probably knew Rollin in Charleston.

154. Charles N. Miller (1834–78) was a Black physician born in Rochester, New York.

Tuesday, March 17

Took a walk today and went to Studio Building[155] to meet the ~~Walcott~~ ladies of the Society by whom I will be employed. I found them young and rather hesitating in their manners I liked them very much as they meant to be kind. Today being St Pat's day the Irishman was in his glory and made his parade an all day nuisance. Leedie came and spent the afternoon and evening. I went with Mr Wells Brown to the Templars Entertainment.[156] The tableaux and declamation were excellent.

Wednesday, March 18

Home reading Macauley's today. Nothing of interest intervening. Leedie came and spent the afternoon. In evening I read until bedtime and finished the volume. I am feeling very nervous about going on the boat tomorrow.

Thursday, March 19

Went to Church to see Dr Miller and Miss Cooley married[157] but ~~they~~ as I was too early I could not wait so went over Chelsea to Mrs Needmans. Got home and heard about the wedding being very cold. In afternoon Leedie came to say good bye he to go to New Bedford I to go to Providence he was drefful confectionate.[158] Went to Lawyer Morris' and he sent his office boy to take my bundles.[159] ~~I met~~ Mrs Bowling[160] Mrs Needman and I started for Portland at 5 oclock.[161] Miss Sibly the stewardess is very fine looking and has traveled much. She is a catholic.

155. The offices of the New England Freedmen's Aid Society were in the Studio Building. See note 64.

156. The Boston Knights Templar, or Freemasons, hosted an entertainment at Tremont Temple in honor of their sixty-second anniversary on the evening of 17 March 1868.

157. Charles Miller married Ariana Cooley (1842–?), originally from Williamsburg, Virginia. They were likely married at the Church of the Advent, as the Reverend James A. Bolles (1810–94) performed the ceremony (Ariana Cooley and Charles Miller entry, "Massachusetts, U.S., Marriage Records, 1840–1915," database, Ancestry.com). Bolles was the rector at Church of the Advent from 1859 to 1870.

158. Rollin seems to be using dialect here to say Leedie was "dreadfully affectionate."

159. The lawyer referred to here might be Robert Morris, who had an office in Scollay's Building in Scollay Square. See Morris Family in biographical notes.

160. Possibly Margaret A. Bowling (1840–?), wife of John W. Bowling (1840–?), steward on a steamboat. This couple lived with the Howards in 1870 and may have lived there in 1868 as well (Edwin F. Howard, household, Chelsea, Suffolk, MA, US Census, 1870, database, Ancestry.com).

161. Rollin may have taken a steamer like one advertised in a Boston newspaper in March 1868. Here Agent William Weeks announced. "Steamers leave Boston, foot of India Wharf daily . . . at 5 o'clock P.M." Fare from Boston to Portland was $1.50 ("For Portland, Montreal and Quebec," *Boston Evening Transcript*, 18 Mar. 1868, 1).

Friday, March 20

Arrived this morning in Portland and found Elbridge[162] waiting for me, went up to Talbots[163] and was warmly received by them all. They are all married now, and I am left alone.[164] Maddie has a large house nearly built and is in very prosperous circumstances.[165] Angie is newly married and is as a matter of course very happy. I am much pleased with Mr Ayres her husband I hope they will continue happy.[166] The City is being rapidly built up, but so many wooden buildings. I am astonished at the fact.[167] The line gale[168] set in tonight.

162. Likely Elbridge P. Talbot Jr. (1844–1919), a painter and the only surviving son in the African American Talbot family. His father was also named Elbridge P. Talbot, of course, but it seems unlikely that Rollin would have referred to this forty-eight-year-old man by his first name.

163. It is unclear how Rollin knew the Talbot family of Portland, Maine. It is possible that she met them while traveling with her father between 1857 and 1859 (Daniel Murray, "Sketch of Frances Rollin Whipper," n.d., Daniel Murray Papers, Micro 577, Wisconsin Historical Society, reel 8). Elbridge P. Talbot Sr. (1821–80), a wealthy African American sea captain, and his wife, Mary Wilson Stevenson (1815–86), were both from Maine and seem to have lived most of their lives there. They had six children, four of whom survived to adulthood: Ellen Angelina (1838–93), Madeline A. "Maddie" (1840–89), Maria Louisa (1842–75), and Elbridge P. Jr. (Elbridge P. Talbot, household, Portland Ward 1, Cumberland, ME, US Census, 1850, database, Ancestry.com; Benjamin A. Talbot entry, 1857, Cumberland, ME, US, Death Records, 1761–1922, database, Ancestry.com.

164. By "all," Rollin apparently means all the Talbot daughters. Elbridge Jr. never married.

165. In 1859 Madeline married William Wilberforce Ruby (1834–1906), the son of Reuben Ruby, an antislavery activist, conductor on the Underground Railroad, and founder of the Abyssinian Meeting House, Portland's first Black congregation (Madeline A. Talbot and William W. Ruby entry, "Maine, U.S., Marriage Records, 1713–1922," database, Ancestry .com; *Portland Freedom Trail*, map, https://www.mainehistory.org/documents/41/Portland _Freedom_Trail.pdf). On 4 July 1866, a massive fire destroyed approximately 1,800 buildings in Portland, or one-third of the city. William Ruby saved the Meeting House from burning by draping the building in wet blankets (Kelly Bouchard, "The Man Who Shouted 'Fire!,'" The Great Fire, online exhibit, *Portland Press Herald*, 2016, https://specialprojects.pressherald.com /portlands-great-fire/man-who-shouted.html).

166. Ellen Angelina "Angie" Talbot married James F. Ayers (1838–82), a brickmaker, in November 1867 (Ellen A. Talbot and James F. Ayers entry, "Maine, U.S., Marriage Records, 1713–1922," database, Ancestry.com). They lived in Westbrook, Maine, about seven miles from Portland.

167. Portland residents worked quickly to rebuild the city after the fire of 1866. Despite Rollin's concern here about "wooden buildings," which were clearly vulnerable to another conflagration, the city was largely reconstructed in brick and stone (Randy Billings, "City Rises from the Ashes," The Great Fire, online exhibit, *Portland Press Herald*, 2016, https://specialprojects .pressherald.com/portlands-great-fire/from-the-ashes.html).

168. A "line gale" is an equinoctial storm, one believed to accompany either a vernal or autumnal equinox.

Saturday, March 21
Portland
A heavy snowstorm is on us. I left the Boat to go to Talbots and it was almost im-
passable, not a soul in the streets but us and the snow blinding us as we walked. I
was soon at home. How they laughed at me for going off last night! I sent a letter
off home today. I had a good sociable time in the house as it was snowing too
much to go out. This is certainly the most sudden and the deepest fall of snow
I have yet seen. Mrs Needman came in we had music and singing. Angie played
^and sang^ some old songs of other days for me. My wreath is still kept!

Sunday, March 22
Portland
Clearing off today. I took leave of my old friends after my very pleasant sojourn and
left at 12 oclock for Boston. I was terribly sea sick. They sang a Hymn O tell me no
more[169] which stirred so very many memories of home that my old longing came
strongly upon me to get back. We reached home about 8:30. I was thankful that
we had encountered no disasters. When cunning the lines, thou mad'st death, and
lo his foot is on the skull thou hast made.[170] We know not why but thou art just.

Monday, March 23
Feeling miserably today haven't got over my seasickness yet Cold and sloppy. Received a letter from Leedie this morning. I am feeling very happy over my Hilton
Head letters I received a very long one from the Major today reiterating his promises and seeming to bear the disappointment very philosophically.[171] Went after
my dyed dress today.

Tuesday, March 24
Clear but terribly muddy. Went to Publisher's after to Studio Building to Miss
Forten about the School.[172] I afterwards went to Mr Ware's house or at Dr

169. "O tell me no more" is a hymn by the Moravian clergyman John Gambold (1711–71).
The first stanza is: "O tell me no more of this world's vain store, / The time for such trifles with
me is now o'er; / A country I've found where true joys abound, / To dwell I'm determined on
that happy ground."

170. From the prelude to "In Memoriam," by the British poet Alfred, Lord Tennyson
(1809–92).

171. Rollin is likely referring here to Fields's rejection of her manuscript.

172. According to the records of the New England Freedmen's Aid Society, Rollin told Forten
that she would not go to Maryland and recommended "Miss Lyons, of Providence" in her place
(entry, 24 Mar. 1868, Daily Record, 1868–69, vol. 3, folder 1, box 2, New England Freedmen's
Aid Society Record Books, 1862–78, Digitized Collections, Massachusetts Historical Society,
www.masshist.org/collection-guides/digitized/fa0423/b2-f01#23).

Bowditches[173] was shown into a handsome Library. No visitors called. I wrote to Leedie today in answer to his very thoughtful one occasioned by the storm in which he supposed I was.

Answered Mr Lennox's[174] letter and little Ann Ezekial.[175]

Wednesday, March 25

Clear and beautiful overhead went to Chelsea, on my way saw Mr Phillips he rode on the platform of the same car wherein I sat. In afternoon I went to his house, he greeted me so kindly, we conversed a long while about my prospects in the literary world and on leaving he gave me a copy of his Speeches[176] which is as precious to me as the apple of my eyes God bless the great hearted kingly Phillips give him length of days and strength to continue steadfast to the end. Peace within thy palaces, plenty within thy walls.[177]

Mrs Robt Morris[178] called during my absence.

Thursday, March 26

Home & sick reading all day "Whitefriars"[179] I have a severe cold taken in Portland. Today my dream of P.[180] is stronger than ever upon me, my every effort has the same source like Burns.

"E'en then a wish, I own its power
A wish that to my latest hour
Shall strongly heave my soul
That I for poor auld Scotland's sake
Some usefu' plan or beuk can I make
Or sing a song at least."[181]

---

173. John Ware is likely staying at the home of Dr. Henry Ingersoll Bowditch (1808–92) at 113 Boylston Street while in Boston.

174. Charles Lennox. See biographical notes.

175. Ann Ezekial. See Ezekial Family in biographical notes.

176. This was likely *Speeches, Lectures, and Letters by Wendell Phillips*, published in 1863 in Boston by James Redpath.

177. The quote from Psalms 122:7 (KJV) reads, "Peace be within thy walls, and prosperity within thy palaces."

178. Catherine Mason Morris. See Morris Family in biographical notes.

179. Likely *Whitefriars; or, The Days of Charles the Second* (1844), a historical novel by the British writer Emma Robinson (1814–90).

180. The identity of "P." is unclear. See note 69.

181. Rollin quotes here from "Epistle to Mrs. Scott," by the Scottish poet Robert Burns (1759–96). The poem was written in response to one by Elizabeth Scott (1729–89) and was published posthumously in 1801 in *Alonzo and Cora with other Original Poems*.

Perhaps it will all come right some day. "The Gods are to each other not unknown"[182] and hearts gravitate to each other by the same divine necessity.

Friday, March 27
Clear overhead today, walked out in the morning went to Mrs Hayden.[183] Met Mr
Wells Brown on the street. In afternoon sewed and read retired early.
Invited by the Dancing School but did not go

Saturday, March 28
Clear overhead went out stop'd at Sheppard and Lee saw Mr Lee he had not heard
anything of the MS. I hope it augured well for me. Mrs Wentworth[184] called to
invite me to go spend tomorrow with her I accepted
In afternoon went to Mrs Prindell's she told me of Pete Johnson's sister how she
killed herself for mere public opinion God preserve me and guide my footsteps

Sunday, March 29
Beautiful day went to the Tremont Temple with Miss Ellen Brown[185] and heard
a splendid sermon from a mere youth. Went to Lockleys after to Brown's dined
and went to Grimes Church.[186] Spent a most delightful evening at Brown's with
Mr Lennox with whom I talked Dickens Mr Nell with whom I talked Phillips.
Mrs Alf Howard[187] was there she is a cripple but a most active woman Mr Lennox
escorted me home

182. The full quote from Ralph Waldo Emerson's essay "Character" (1844) reads: "If we are
related, we shall meet. It was a tradition of the ancient world, that no metamorphosis could
hide a god from a god; and there is a Greek verse which runs, 'The Gods are to each other not
unknown.' Friends also follow the law of divine necessity; they gravitate to each other and cannot otherwise."

183. Harriet Hayden. See Hayden Family in biographical notes.

184. "Mrs. Wentworth" is likely Caroline A. Brown Wentworth (1841–1901), wife of a barber
named George Wentworth (1836–?). Along with Caroline's mother, Fanny Brown (1813–86),
the Wentworths lived with William Cooper Nell at 13 Phillips Street (*Boston Directory*, 1867).
They were clearly intimate with many of Rollin's Boston friends, as they were living with the
Haydens when the 1860 census was taken (Fanny Brown, household, Boston Ward 6, Suffolk,
MA, US Census, 1860, database, Ancestry.com).

185. Ellen Brown (1836–?) was the sister of Carolina Brown Wentworth. She was a dressmaker
(Ellen F. Brown entry, Boston Ward 6, Suffolk, MA, US Census, 1860, database, Ancestry.com).

186. Twelfth Baptist Church. See note 13.

187. Martha A. Howard (1818–?) was the wife of Alfred G. Howard (1818–?), Edwin F. Howard's brother. See Howard family in biographical notes.

Monday, March 30

To church in the morning in the afternoon Leedie came and spent the after and took me to the Exhibition at the Temple. Shylock was well rendered by Mr Francis. Mr Smith is a good actor I was agreeably disappointed with the whole performance. Addie Howard and Hattie Lockley sat beside me and together we enjoyed ourselves. After we went to Wiley's[188] for oysters. At home a party of Ladies and Gentlemen came and prolonged the enjoyment until the wee hours of morning.

Tuesday, March 31

Went to Publishers and after promenaded in Washington St. Met Leedie showed me a letter which he had written. Approved. In afternoon walked over Cambridge to Brown's and spent a pleasant time there as usual. L came out for me. Home at 10 p.m. Nothing of importance save having the pleasure of reading Grace Greenwood's "Records of Five Years."[189] I was a little disappointed in it. Having seen the collection in her Scrap Book years ago and heard The Lights of the War Clouds delivered by her.[190] Letters from Mrs Ezekial[191] and Green.[192]

Wednesday, April 1

Peter[193] brought me out of bed early this morning telling me of a package downstairs for me (April fool of course) I sewed all the morning in afternoon as Leedie was To take leave I waited for him all the morning and went to Mrs Howard's[194] where I should have gone instead of waiting for him. He came and went off angry I enjoyed my visit to Mrs H and Addie very much. Went to Mrs Prindells for old Mrs Murray and reached home about ten oclock

---

188. Rollin is likely referring to Wiley & Stubbs, fish and oyster dealers located on Commercial Street, about a fifteen-minute walk from Tremont Temple (*Boston Directory*, 1867).

189. Grace Greenwood was the pseudonym of writer Sara Jane Lippincott (1823–1904). *Records of Five Years*, published by Ticknor & Fields in 1867, was made up of two sections: one of pieces written "In Peace" and the other of pieces written "In War."

190. "The Lights of the War Clouds" appears in the "In War" section of *Records of Five Years*. In this piece Greenwood says that had the war ended earlier, slavery would likely not have been abolished. "The experiences of the last three years," she writes, "should have taught us a lesson of patience, when great national undertakings are at hand. We should not forget no war was ever fought over so stupendous an area, or had such mighty questions and interests at stake" (133). Prior to publishing *Records*, Greenwood delivered "Lights of the War Clouds" as a lecture.

191. Georgianna Ezekial. See Ezekial Family in biographical notes.

192. Likely Samuel Green. See biographical notes.

193. Peter Bailey. See Bailey Family in biographical notes.

194. Joanna Turpin Howard. See Howard Family in biographical notes.

Thursday, April 2
Clear and beautiful the Fast Day appointed by the Gov of Mass.[195] Of course it is Church in the morning and feasting in the aft! I went with Mrs Wentworth to the Temple to hear Mr Fulton[196] preach. A minister from Africa was present and spoke also Mr Grimes.[197] Mr Fulton prayed for and spoke most earnestly ably of the Sec. of War,[198] of his prayerful spirit of AJ's[199] usurpation not as a man under authority but of authority.

Friday, April 3
Went to Church, after to Mrs Haydens read to Mr H. Garrison's letter against Mr Phillips[200] I am sorry for it. In afternoon read and evening went to the Dancing

195. Alexander Bullock (1816–82) was in the final year of his three consecutive one-year terms as Governor of Massachusetts. He set aside Thursday, 2 April as "Fast Day," a day of reflection and prayer. All business in the state was suspended and much of the population, like Rollin, attended "able discourses . . . in regard to the great national subject which now occupies so prominent a place in the public mind" ("Fast Day," *Boston Evening Transcript*, 3 Apr. 1868, 2). The annual Fast Day tradition began in the late seventeenth century but ended in 1894, replaced with Patriot's Day. Fast Day sermons in 1868 focused largely on the impeachment of Andrew Johnson. The House of Representatives had impeached the president on 2–3 March.

196. Justin Dewey Fulton (1828–1901) was a Baptist minister who preached at the Tremont Temple for nine years beginning in 1863.

197. Leonard Grimes, minister of the Twelfth Baptist Church. See note 13.

198. Edwin M. Stanton (1814–69) served as secretary of war under Abraham Lincoln and continued in this position under Andrew Johnson. He opposed Johnson's lenient policies toward the former Confederate States. When the president removed Stanton from office, the House of Representatives issued eleven articles of impeachment against Johnson, including the violation of the Tenure of Office Act, passed in 1867 over Johnson's veto.

199. Andrew Johnson (1808–75), seventeenth president of the United States.

200. On 14 March 1868, William Lloyd Garrison published a letter in the *National Anti-Slavery Standard* regarding his role in the controversy over the will of white abolitionist Frances Jackson (1789–1861). Jackson bequeathed $10,000 to his trustees (including Garrison and Phillips) "not for their own use, but in trust, . . . for the preparation and circulation of books, newspapers, the delivery of speeches, lectures, and other such means as in their judgment will create a public sentiment, that will put an end to Negro Slavery in this Country" (Francis Jackson entry, "Massachusetts, U.S. Wills and Probate Records, 1635–1991," database, Ancestry. com). Because slavery had been abolished, Phillips wanted the money to go to the *Standard*, the official publication of the American Anti-Slavery Society, of which he was president after Garrison resigned in 1865. While Garrison and two other trustees initially advised the court to split the money between the *Standard* and the New England Freedmen's Union Commission to aid in the education of the freedmen, he changed his mind after the passage of the Reconstruction Acts, which gave African American men the right to vote on new state constitutions. The court took this advice, to which Phillips objected publicly, claiming that Garrison had acted as

School and <u>mirabile dictu</u>[201] I actually danced even waltzed with Mr Robt Howard! He escorted me home and played the gallant to perfection. If I intended waltzing through <u>life</u> I might fancy him for a partner.

Saturday, April 4

Started for church this morning but stopping at Mr J B Smith to ask him about the Memorial Biography of Col Shaw I was detained in conversation until after the hour.[202] I recvd a letter today from Miss Lyons of Providence R.I[203] and one for the Association. Miss Forten informed me that the Association will not send

---

if he was the only trustee and had worked with the law, which had always been the enemy of the antislavery cause ("Mr. Garrison and the Jackson Bequest," *National Anti-Slavery Standard*, 24 Aug. 1867, 2). Garrison's "letter against Mr. Phillips" presented what he saw as "the simple facts in the case" in his defense, as Phillips's "accusations against me and my associates . . . affect[ed] our honor and integrity as Trustees, and our Character as Abolitionists" (Garrison, "Will of the Late Francis Jackson," *National Anti-Slavery Standard*, 14 Mar. 1868, 2).

201. Latin for "strange to say" or "wonderful to relate."

202. Joshua Bowen Smith (1813–79) was a caterer and abolitionist of mixed English, African, and Native American descent. Likely born enslaved, as an adult Smith moved to Boston, where he may have worked as a waiter for the parents of Robert Gould Shaw (1837–63) before becoming one of the best-known caterers in the city ("Joshua B. Smith," National Parks Service, https://www.nps.gov/people/joshua-b-smith.htm, accessed 21 Apr. 2025). Shaw would go on to command the nation's first African American regiment, the Fifty-Fourth Massachusetts. He was killed at the Second Battle of Fort Wagner in July 1863, and his body was buried in a mass grave with those of the Black soldiers. Rather than attempting to retrieve his body, Shaw's parents insisted it was an honor for him to be buried with his men. While working for the Shaws, Smith befriended Charles Sumner, then an attorney but later US senator from Massachusetts from 1851 until his death in 1874. When he heard about Shaw's death, Smith told Sumner that a monument should be erected in the officer's honor and began to raise money ("Expanding the Story of the Shaw/54th Memorial," Saint-Gaudens National Historical Park, National Parks Service, last updated 2 Feb. 2022, https://www.nps.gov/saga/learn/historyculture/expanding -the-story.htm). He did not live to see the monument unveiled in 1897. Rollin's reference to a "Memorial Biography" implies that there was a simultaneous effort to publish a biography of Shaw; it is not clear whether she is putting herself forward as a prospective author of this book.

203. Therese Lyons (1846–1924) was the daughter of Albro and Mary Lyons, New Yorkers who had moved to Providence, Rhode Island, after the violent Draft Riots of 1863. Prior to the Civil War, the family ran a boarding house for Black sailors and sheltered enslaved people fleeing slavery on the Underground Railroad ("Lyons Family," Museum of the City of New York, www.mcny.org/sites/default/files/2021-06/LyonsFamily.pdf, accessed 21 Apr. 2025). It is not clear how Rollin knew Therese.

any teacher as I cannot go.[204] Went to Haydens they are both very kind to me. Received a very disheartening letter from home Ma has the dropsy[205] God have mercy on me

Sunday, April 5
Palm Sunday[206]
Feeling miserable over that [strikethrough] letter from home Snowing hard when I got up
Read all day. No visitors and I am glad of it. I tried to read the "History of the Girondists" par Lamartine but my poor head wandered to my mother ill at home and perhaps without any comfort whatever. How long O God how long! triflingly written[207]

Monday, April 6
Who is it who comes from Edam with dyed garments from Bozra.[208] heard P.[209] read that lesson the Monday night after the Surrender of Lee.[210] Memory cherished as fondly as ever. At Church in the morning after to Lee's He thinks Major

204. On 4 April the New England Freedmen's Aid Society noted: "Miss Rollin brought an application from Thérèse Lyons, Providence, who had been requested to apply by Mr. Ware. Told her that it was not probable the Soc. would send any new teachers to Md. this spring—they preferred adopting one of those already employed there" (entry, 4 Apr. 1868, Daily Record, 1868–69, vol. 3, folder 1, box 2, New England Freedmen's Aid Society Record Books, 1862–78, Digitized Collections, Massachusetts Historical Society, www.masshist.org/collection-guides /digitized/fa0423/b2-f01#26).

205. "Dropsy" is a nineteenth-century term for edema, an accumulation of excess fluid in the body's tissues. It can be caused by several conditions, including congestive heart disease or liver disease.

206. This is written at the top of the page, between the date and the first line.

207. This note is written on the left-hand side of the page, even though there are several lines left at the bottom. These words seem intended to replace the crossed-out words at the beginning of the entry.

208. Rollin quotes here from Isaiah 63:1 (KJV): "Who *is* this that cometh from Edom, with dyed garments from Bozrah? this *that is* glorious in his apparel, travelling in the greatness of his strength?"

209. The identity of "P." is unknown. See note 69.

210. General Robert E. Lee (1807–70) surrendered the Army of Northern Virginia to Union Lieutenant General Ulysses S. Grant (1822–85) at Appomattox Court House, Virginia, on 9 April 1865. While other Confederate forces had yet to surrender, this was and remains widely perceived as the end of the Civil War.

Delany a Conservative. I fear he is set against him in consequence of his refusal of the Senatorship of So Ca.[211] In afternoon at "Wiley's" with Emily[212] Tom her cousin. In Eve at Church heard a most instructive sermon. At Hayden's

Tuesday, April 7

Sick in bed. Snowing furiously! A letter from Toadie.[213] Watching the weather. I am so disappointed as I was to hear Dickens read The Story of Little Dombey and the trial from Pickwick.[214] Mr Bailey gave me a ticket.

I finished the History of the Girondists I am charmed with it I hated respect pity regret Robespierre[215] Truly he is undefined and shadowy. He had more of weakness than cruelty in his nature.[216] & counterpart of the time in which he lived.

Wednesday, April 8

Home clear day to church morning and evening heard a good sermon. Christ Temptation in the Garden of Olives.

Mrs Bailey went to Dickens with Mrs Hare.[217] They said he had a profusion of flowers about him it was his last in Boston. How I regret not being there.

I read The Hour and the Man[218] am much pleased with it I wonder why the Haytian Government allow the remains of great Toussaint to remain so long away from his beloved St Domingue

---

211. In early 1868 the Colored Members of the State Nominating Convention asked Delany to run for Congress; he refused, implying that African Americans should not seek to hold public office yet (Delany, "Delany to Douglass").

212. Likely Emily Bailey. See Bailey Family in biographical notes.

213. Toadie seems to be a female friend living in Charleston. See entries for 29 August, 14 September, and 15 September.

214. Dickens returned to Boston for his "Final Farewell Readings" on 1, 3, 6, 7, and 8 April ("Tremont Temple," *Boston Evening Transcript*, 1 Apr. 1868, 3). "The Story of Little Domby" was adapted from *Dombey and Son* (1846–48). "The Trial from Pickwick," or "Bardell and Pickwick," was condensed from Dickens's first novel, *The Pickwick Papers* (1836).

215. Maximilien Robespierre (1758–1794) was a key figure in the French Revolution and the architect of the Reign of Terror, during which somewhere between 18,000 and 40,000 people were executed.

216. The rest of this entry is written along the left-hand margin of the page.

217. Ann E. Bailey and her daughter Mary Hare. See Bailey Family in biographical notes.

218. *The Hour and the Man: An Historical Romance* (1841), by Harriet Martineau, is a novelized account of Toussaint-Louverture's rise from enslaved man to leader of the Haitian Revolution.

Thursday, April 9
Clear day went with Mrs Bailey to Lynn. Shoes! Shoes! on every side[219] It is a bright manufacturing City The air sharp and piercing in Winter but bracing and delightful in Summer; hence the resort at Lynn Beach[220] in the sultry days of August. We reached home late after spending a pleasant day at Mrs Lewis and the evening at Mr Wests.[221]
No letter but a note from Amelia Howard for the Leap Year party.[222]

Friday, April 10
Good Friday[223]
Snowing furiously making the forty-second snow storm this season. Cordelia Downing[224] called.
Nothing of importance transpired. I could not go to church in consequence of the snow.
Mrs Simons[225] very kindly sent me some Rice and cowpeas[226] today I ate though it was Good Friday
Mr Mabury sent us some Lobster and we had salad Mr Lennox called

Saturday, April 11
Clear day went to Addie Howard's and spent a real pleasant time Mrs H explained to me the imprudence of some of the girls out here. I am sorry for the state of affairs Felt so sick I was obliged to leave, found a letter from Leedie on

219. Lynn, Massachusetts, was a center of leather and shoe making. While shoes were made in small workshops prior to the mid-nineteenth century, by 1860, employers began building large factories that employed thousands of workers.

220. In the mid-nineteenth century, Lynn's coastline was a popular beach resort.

221. Mr. West is likely Ottoway West (1821–1901), an African American barber from Virginia who had resided in Lynn for approximately a decade by the late 1860s. In 1870, he lived with his five children, ages five to twenty-four, two of whom were also barbers (Ottoway West, household, Lynn Ward 5, Essex, MA, US Census, 1870, database, Ancestry.com).

222. Since 1868 was a leap year, it had 366 days instead of the usual 365. It is not clear why Leap Year is being celebrated in April.

223. This is written at the top of the page, between the date and the first line.

224. Cordelia Downing (1848–post 1917) was the daughter of George T. and Serena De-Grasse Downing and the sister of Thomas Downing, whose "broken match" Rollin mentions on 10 January.

225. Likely Anna (or Emma) Simonds. See Simonds/Mahone Family in biographical notes.

226. Rice and cowpeas is a traditional Caribbean dish and remains popular in South Carolina, where it is known as "Hoppin' John."

my return. I have a miserable cold L informed me of Mrs Keckley's debut as a literary lady[227] I am fast losing confidence in her mainly I fear there is too much sham every where

Sunday, April 12
Easter[228]
Foggy looking day sick in bed. Musing on evry thing. Time [never] [lost] his glass and the bitterness of past injustice arises up to me when I should leave vengeance to him who today breaks the bondage of the tomb and tramples sin under his feet and arise and go to him who said Come unto me all you that labor and are heavy laden and I will give you rest.[229]
[best] not leave any room.

Monday, April 13
Feeling very badly weak sent my answer to Amelia Howard and Mr Lennox In evening went with Addie to Cambridge to the Party Mr Greener[230] Ch. Mitchel[231] Mr Robt Howard Mr de Mortie[232] Mr Nell and lots of my gentlemen friends I

---

227. In 1868 Elizabeth Hobbs Keckley (1818–1907), a formerly enslaved woman and Mary Todd Lincoln's personal modiste, published *Behind the Scenes; or, Thirty Years a Slave and Four Years in the White House* with G. W. Carleton & Company in New York. Keckley was criticized for having made personal details and correspondence public and her relationship with the Lincoln family was irreparably damaged. It is unclear how well Rollin knew Keckley. They may have met when both worked with freedmen after the Civil War. They had at least been in the same company less than six months prior to this entry: in October 1867 the *Christian Recorder* noted that both Keckley and Rollin had arrived at Mrs. Hankerson's boardinghouse on Green Street in New York City ("Arrivals at Mrs. Hasikerson's Boarding House," *Christian Recorder*, 26 Oct. 1867, 171).

228. This is written at the top of the page, between the date and the first line.

229. Rollin quotes here from Matthew 11:28 (KJV): "Come unto me, all ye that labor and are heavy laden, and I will give you rest."

230. Richard Greener. See biographical notes.

231. Likely Charles Lewis Mitchell (1829–1912), a Hartford, Connecticut, native who worked as a printer for Garrison at the *Liberator* prior to enlisting with the Fifty-Fifth Massachusetts. At the Battle of Honey Hill (South Carolina, 30 November 1864), he was injured and part of his right leg and foot had to be amputated. After the war, he returned to Boston and began working at the Boston Custom House ("Expanding the Story of the Shaw/54th Memorial").

232. Mark Réné De Mortie (1829–1914) was likely of mixed French and African descent like Rollin and may have been enslaved as a child in Norfolk, Virginia. After working to move fugitives from slavery from Virginia to Massachusetts, he relocated to Boston in the early 1850s. De Mortie served the Fifty-Fourth Massachusetts as a sutler, then in 1870 married Cordelia Downing, the daughter of the wealthy businessman George T. Downing (Brent Tarter, "Mark R. DeMortie (1829–1914)," *Dictionary of Virginia Biography*, Library of Virginia, 2019, https://www.lva.virginia.gov/public/dvb/bio.asp?b=DeMortie_Mark_R).

met them escorted by ladies We escorted the gentlemen to table helped them and played several games sang & danced and had a good time generally then returned home about two oclock next morning. Letters from Mr. Green and Lottie.[233]

Tuesday, April 14

To church at ten oclock after went to DeGrasses to see the Downings,[234] met Addie there went with her to see Mrs Clark[235] she had a large photograph hanging of poor Fannie. Home and in the afternoon to Lee & Sheppard, nothing heard yet of my book.

Wrote letters in the evening to Mrs Ezekial[236] Lizzie and Miss Lyons.

Wednesday, April 15

Went to Chelsea to Mrs Richards finding fault as usual with poor Sophie[237] she has not an abundance of charity Went also to Mrs Simmons also to Mrs Morris.[238] She is being very handsome minded but so intensely Catholic she is that she does not seem to open her hospitality to Protestants I met a Mrs Otis there belonging to the Fraternity[239] she is very much interested in the Freedmen, and the Schools she asked particularly of Jennie Weston[240]

Thursday, April 16

Cloudy and rained in the morning went to Mr Redpaths[241] he greeted me very kindly. Suggested to me write a story on misceg. I will finish that which I have. Mr Lee loaned me Mrs Keckley's book I finished reading it before five oclock. It is well written but not by Mrs K that's clear. Read all the evening

233. Charlotte "Lottie" Rollin. See biographical notes.

234. Rollin presumably goes to visit the Downing family at the home of Serena Degrasse Downing's brother, John V. DeGrasse (1825–68). John DeGrasse was a physician who lived at 42 Grove Street in what was considered then to be part of the West End (*Boston Directory*, 1868). He died of tuberculosis in November of 1868 (John V. DeGrasse entry, "Massachusetts, U.S., Town and Vital Records, 1620–1988," database, Ancestry.com).

235. Fanny Lenox Clark. See note 128.

236. Georgianna Ezekial. See Ezekial Family in biographical notes.

237. Sophia Richards. See note 119.

238. Catherine Mason Morris. See Morris Family in biographical notes.

239. Rollin likely means that Mrs. Otis was Roman Catholic.

240. This may be a reference to Jane Weston. According to Ronald E. Butchart's dataset, no "Jennie Weston" taught in the freedmen's schools. Jane, however, taught in Charleston for three years under the auspices of the New England Freedmen's Aid Society. Several other Weston family members, including Joanna, Maria, and Mary F. (who taught with Rollin), taught in that city after the war (Butchart et al., "Freedmen's Teacher Project").

241. James Redpath. See note 44.

Friday, April 17
Returned the book Mr Lee went shopping. Warm day. Went to the Brown's. In afternoon went to Mrs Howard and Mrs Gregory
In eve went to Dancing School Mr Howard presented me with a nice pair of opera glasses. Mary Lockly Hattie and others were there

Saturday, April 18
Home all day sewing about twelve Leedie returned and called to see me He told me Mrs Keckley is studying for a Reader[242] I am more than astonished. He came in the afternoon also.
In evening there came a letter from the Major with $40 I am provoked when I think of it

Sunday, April 19
Beautiful clear day went to the Advent in the morning. In afternoon Leedie came and remained till tea, went off and returned, went off and returned again. Mr Lennox ditto

Monday, April 20
Heard this morning from Mr Adams[243] and W W.[244] news of the murder of Ben Capers by Arthur Chisolm.[245] God pity us all who cannot govern our passions.

Tuesday, April 21
Went to Malden today to the Redpaths

Wednesday, April 22
Beautiful clear day walked out to Mrs Gregory's to spend the day. She was out in the afternoon at Child's Gallery with Mrs Redpath[246] to see some paintings.

---

242. Rollin means that Keckley is planning to do public readings of her own work and that of other writers. See also entry for 25 June.

243. Ennals J. Adams. See biographical notes.

244. Possibly William J. Whipper. See biographical notes.

245. On 9 April 1868, twenty-one-year-old Arthur Spearing, who went by the name of Arthur Chisolm, murdered Benjamin LeGrand Capers, a twenty-seven-year-old sailor, at a dance in Charleston, South Carolina. Both men were African Americans. Capers had asked Chisolm's girlfriend to dance, and when she refused, he insulted her. A fight ensued in which Chisolm stabbed Capers. Although charged with murder, Chisolm was convicted by the jury of manslaughter and sentenced to ten years in the state penitentiary ("Court of General Sessions and Common Pleas," *Charleston Daily News*, 9 May 1868, 3; see also Benjamin L. Capers entry, "Return of Deaths Within the City of Charleston," database, Ancestry.com).

246. Mary Cotton Redpath. See note 44.

Thursday, April 23
Shopping and to Lockleys[247] Out in the morning in the afternoon to Watertown alone.[248] L. did not care for it at best so he was but too glad

Friday, April 24
To Brown[249] this morning about my dress at 10 Leedie not up.
In afternoon at Howards made a pleasant visit as usual Mrs Chapman came down with me. Leedie came about nine oclock. We quarreled about Dickens. He is so thoroughly selfish that it makes him rude in every thing.

Saturday, April 25
Home reading in after Leedie came told me of my computed faults pedantic and soulless. Recvd a letter from Florence[250] today, answered it immediately.

Sunday, April 26
To church at the Advent

Monday, April 27
Home all morning reading Whitefriars.
Leedie came and brought me a lot of books &c. Addie Howard called Leedie left for New York this afternoon

Tuesday, April 28
At Dr Birmingham's[251] this morning. He wishes me to revise a Ms. for him. He

247. This is written between the date and the first line, even though there is room left at the bottom of the page.

248. Frances was likely going to Watertown to visit Charles Lennox and his father.

249. Possibly Ellen Brown. See note 185.

250. Likely Florence Rollin, Frances's sister. See biographical notes.

251. Dr. Samuel Till Birmingham (1800–96) was an African American physician with an office on Cambridge Street in the West End of Boston. Despite having been formally trained, he began advertising himself as a "Botanical Doctor" or a "Native Indian Physician" in the 1850s (Joe Orfant, "The Sad, Curious Death of Mary Ann Birmingham," *Curious Mysteries* (blog), 1 Mar. 2023, https://curiousmysteries.wordpress.com/2023/03/01/the-sad-curious-death-of-mary-ann -birmingham/). Rollin seems to have been hired to do some editing of a manuscript for Birmingham. She was likely introduced to him by the Haydens; his friendship with the couple is evidenced by both a photo album inscribed from Birmingham to Harriet Hayden (Harriet Hayden Albums, vol. 2, Boston Athenaeum Digital Collections, https://cdm.bostonathenaeum .org/digital/collection/p16057coll52/id/439/rec/1) and the naming of one of Birmingham's sons after Lewis Hayden (Lewis Hayden Birmingham entry, "New Hampshire, U.S Births and Christenings Index," database, Ancestry.com).

seemed to be liberal minded. A letter from Katie[252] and her Photograph also a pamphlet from G.[253]

In afternoon walked out in Beacon St.

For the evening to Mrs Barrows[254] to get Mr B to take my valise to Charleston. Wrote to Westons[255] and Katie

Wednesday, April 29[256]

A letter from Green

I wrote to Willie at Mr Hayden's after wrote for him until nine oclock. Home and sewed until bed time. Theophilus Shiong[257] called and gave me an account of Ben Capers' murder

Thursday, April 30

Home all morning in afternoon to State House[258] was introduced to the Sec. of State Mr Oliver Warner[259] we conversed very freely on public affairs

Friday, May 1

Cloudy it snowed in some places I am told went to Lowell at ten oclock a most delightful ride it was. Had a pleasant visit to Dr Birmingham[260]

---

252. Katherine Rollin. See biographical notes.

253. Possibly Samuel Green. See biographical notes.

254. Likely Elizabeth Barreau. See note 79.

255. The Weston family was among the wealthiest of the mixed-race elite in Charleston. In the will of white enslaver Plowden Weston, Anthony Weston (1791–1876) was granted the control of his time after 1833 in gratitude for faithful service. While Anthony was never officially emancipated, he effectively lived as a free man, paying the capitation taxes required of free Black residents, running a successful business as a millwright, and in his wife Maria's name, enslaving at least twenty people himself (Powers, *Black Charlestonians*, 50).

256. The top six lines of the space allotted for this day are left blank. It is possible that Rollin was saving space to write about something that occurred on the morning of April 29.

257. Theophilus E. Chion (1841–69) was born in Charleston, South Carolina, in 1841. In 1869, just before his death of consumption, he was a student at Wesleyan Academy in Wilbraham, Massachusetts, a Methodist school for young men intending to enter the ministry (Theophilus Chion entry, "South Carolina, U.S., Death Records, 1821–1971," database, Ancestry. com; *Annual Catalogue of Wesleyan Academy, Wilbraham, Mass., 1869, and Circular for 1870* [Boston: Rand, Avery, & Frye, 1869], 17). Chion may have lived in Boston prior to enrolling at the school or may have been visiting the city from Wilbraham when he called on Rollin.

258. The Massachusetts State House is on Beacon Street in Beacon Hill.

259. Oliver Warner (1818–85) served as Massachusetts secretary of state from 1858 to 1876. Lewis Hayden worked for him as a messenger for thirty years beginning in 1858. Hayden seems to have helped Rollin obtain a position as a copyist at the state house.

260. Samuel T. Birmingham lived in Lowell, Massachusetts, with his family.

Saturday, May 2
Rainy day Sewed very diligently on my dress in the afternoon went out shopping later helped Emily with hers. Nothing of importance took place.

Sunday, May 3
At home all day, in the afternoon Mr Lennox came and we spent the time very pleasantly together His cold gray eyes are fathomless as they are piercing Nothing escapes his attention. He is a hypochondriac apparently but I have my doubts sometimes that his repining are ~~not~~ diplomacy. A noble self sacrifice he has made through life for his father's sake. God will reward him someday

Monday, May 4
In bed sick. Mrs Redpath called did not see her Mr Lennox came for me to go out with him but was too indisposed. He went out and brought me some fruit I received a letter from Leedie today telling me of the wedding of Miss Bishop and Mr Rich Mason Fannie[261] and Mrs Hare went to the Hop.[262] Emily and Hen[263] were in a terrible fracas in consequence of E. going with T.M.[264] I am truly sorry for her The human heart like a millstone forever on the round. If there is nothing for them[265] to grind, they must themselves be ground.[266]

261. Likely Fannie Bailey. See Bailey Family in biographical notes.

262. The "Hop" was likely a dancing party.

263. "Hen" may be Henry Bailey, Emily's younger brother. See Bailey Family in biographical notes.

264. "T.M." may be Theodore M. C. Mundrucu (1839–98), whom Emily would marry in 1887. In 1868, however, he was operating the family's secondhand-clothing store on 32 Brattle Street near Harvard University. It is not clear why his escorting Emily to the Hop would have caused a "terrible fracas." It is possible that he is married or divorced: in the 1880 census, Mundrucu is noted as being either widowed or divorced (Theodore M. C. Mundrucu entry, Enumeration District 795, Chelsea, Suffolk, MA, US Census, 1880, database, Ancestry.com). Despite this fact, when he later marries Emily, it is said to be the first marriage for both bride and groom (Emily C. Bailey and Theodore Mundrucu entry, "Massachusetts, U.S., Marriage Records, 1840–1915," database, Ancestry.com).

265. The rest of this entry is written along the right-hand margin of the page.

266. Rollin paraphrases Martin Luther here: "The human heart is like a millstone in a mill; when you put wheat under it, it turns and grinds and bruises the wheat to flour; if you put no wheat, it still grinds on, but then 'tis itself it grinds and wears away. So the human heart, unless it be occupied with some employment, leaves space for the devil, who wriggles himself in, and brings with him a whole host of evil thoughts, temptations, and tribulations, which grind out the heart" (Hazlitt, *Table Talk of Martin Luther*, 275).

Tuesday, May 5
Sick all morning went to Dr Birmingham's also to Lockley's
Returned home and sewed. Nothing of importance occurred. No letters save from Theophilus Shiong offering to take the package home for me.

Wednesday, May 6
Cold sewed all morning In afternoon went to State House say Mr Warner went to Wiley's[267] with Mr Hayden had oysters and coffee.
To Lee & Sheppard to get a ticket for Mrs Frances Kemble's Reading[268] on Friday night. I am resolved to take some step forward to promote my success in Literature.

Thursday, May 7
Rainy day not feeling well. Wrote to Leedie

Friday, May 8
Sewing on my dress and writing for Mr Hayden

Saturday, May 9
At home sewing until 12 oclock then to the State House and wrote until four oclock, then to Mr Phillips could not see him as he was attending Mrs Rockwell in her sick chamber where she has been for three weeks.
Went to Addie Howard's spent the afternoon with her did not get home until 8 oclock Addie received today two Photographs of Edmonia Lewis[269] from Rome taken in her Studio dress.
Home and sewed like a Trojan until 12 oclock

267. Wiley & Stubbs. See note 188.

268. Frances "Fanny" Kemble (1809–93) was a British actress who in 1834 married a wealthy Philadelphian, Pierce Mease Butler (1810–67), who owned cotton, rice, and tobacco plantations on Butler Island off the coast of Georgia as well as the hundreds of enslaved people who lived there and worked the land. During a visit to the island in 1838 and 1839, Kemble kept a diary, which she later revised and published as *Journal of a Residence on a Georgian Plantation in 1838–1839* in 1863, long after her marriage had ended in a bitter divorce. To support herself, Kemble began a career as a reader of Shakespeare. An advertisement in the *Boston Evening Transcript* on 6 May 1868 announced three readings at the Tremont Temple: *Macbeth* on the sixth, *Henry the Fifth* on the eighth, and *Twelfth Night* on the ninth ("Morning and Evening Readings"). Rollin was apparently planning on attending the reading of *Henry the Fifth* on 8 May. It is not clear whether she attended, as she does not write about it in her diary.

269. The sculptor Edmonia Lewis. See note 141.

Sunday, May 10

Hattie Lockly brought my bonnet here[270]

Went out with my new suit to Chelsea, after to Hayden's there I met Mr Boling[271] Mr Lennox went there for me to go to Mr Wells Brown's lecture at Tremont Temple on the origin of the African Race.[272] I ^don't^ think he proved anything particularly but generally it was a good instructive historical lecture. Mr Phillips introductory was graceful logical and grandly eloquent as usual. He seemed warm and fatigued he left early as he had to prepare for New York. Mr Seargent[273] took his place

Monday, May 11

At home feeling allright went to Dr Birmingham will not go out until Friday to his house. Next to the State House to the Secretary of State had a pleasant chat with concerning affairs generally He gave me a poem from Punch on Lincoln to read.[274] He read the Lock Haven article concerning Katie or the Rollin family School.[275] Wrote in the Library. Wells Brown spent the morning with me.

Tuesday, May 12

Writing at the State House still. ~~Was at Birminghams to know about the Lowell matter Friday af~~ Feeling very low spirit about the Book Matter recvd a letter this morning from Major sent the money to Lee & Shepherd[276]

Letter from Mr Adams[277]

270. This note is written between the date and the first line of the page.

271. Possibly John W. Bowling. See note 160.

272. The *Boston Evening Transcript* notified readers of this upcoming event, saying that Brown's lecture, "The Origin and Early History of the African Race," "has been well received wherever it has been delivered" ("William Wells Brown's Lecture," *Boston Evening Transcript*, 9 May 1868, 2). This material was eventually published in 1874 by A. G. Brown & Company as *The Rising Son; or, The Antecedents and Advancement of the Colored Race.*

273. Likely the Unitarian minister John Turner Sargent (1807–77).

274. The poem may be Tom Taylor's "Abraham Lincoln, Foully Assassinated," published in the British magazine *Punch* on 6 May 1865. Taylor (1817–80) was also the author of *Our American Cousin*, the play that Lincoln was attending when he was assassinated.

275. Katherine and Charlotte Rollin operated a Roman Catholic day school for African American children on Line Street in Charleston from early 1867 to the summer of 1868. It is not clear what the "Lock Haven" article is ("Day School for Colored Girls and Boys," reverse of letter from Charlotte and Catherine Rollin to Bishop Patrick Neeson Lynch, 29 Nov. 1867, Item 41S1, Pre-Diocesan and Episcopal Papers, Archives and Record Management Office, Roman Catholic Diocese of Charleston).

276. Martin Delany appears to be subsidizing the publication of *Life and Public Services*.

277. Ennals J. Adams. See biographical notes.

Wednesday, May 13

At the State House writing in after ~~have~~ to Mrs Hayden home and found letters from Mr & Mrs Ezekial[278]

Thursday, May 14

At the State House writing the Secretary introduced me to the Treasurer[279] concerning the Bank Affair They are doing all they can to secure the place for me. He gave me a lot of paper and envelopes again and borrowed the Lock Haven matter[280] from me to show the Treasurer He took me to Mr Loud's department

Friday, May 15

At home watching the weather was to go to Lowell today but could not on account of the rain went to Lee & Shep. was told of the Major sending the money to them. Mr Lee being sick nothing could be done as yet. At the State House writing. Rain poured when coming home

Saturday, May 16

At the State House Library writing until one oclock got Randolph of Roanoke[281] from there. Read the biography of Josiah Quincy par Edmund Q[282] Present of a leather bag from Mr Hayden, sewed on Mrs Hare's dress until 12 p.m. Read for Mr Hayden at his House. Mr Greener spent the afternoon very pleasantly with me. The vote on Andrew Johnson impeachment taken Ross Trumbull and Fessenden of the Rep. side voted for acquittal[283] Shame!

Sunday, May 17

To church at the Advent this morning in afternoon read in evening Mr Lennox came and spent with me until 10 p.m. Read Randolph of Roanoke ^by Garland^ until late

278. Phillip and Georgianna Ezekial. See Ezekial Family in biographical notes.

279. The treasurer and receiver-general of Massachusetts from 1866 to 1871 was Jacob H. Loud (1802–80).

280. See entry for 11 May.

281. *The Life of John Randolph of Roanoke*, by Hugh A. Garland (1805–54), was published in 1850 by D. Appleton and Company. Randolph (1773–1833) was a planter and politician from Virginia. He was one of the founders of the American Colonization Society in 1816. He enslaved hundreds of people to work his tobacco plantation, manumitting them in his will.

282. *Life of Josiah Quincy of Massachusetts* (1867) was written by Quincy's son, Edmund Quincy (1808–77), and published by Ticknor and Fields. Josiah Quincy (1772–1864) served as mayor of Boston from 1823 to 1828 and president of Harvard University from 1829 to 1845.

283. Republican senators Edmund G. Ross (1826–1907) from Kansas, Lyman Trumbull (1813–96) from Illinois, and William P. Fessenden (1806–69) from Maine voted against the impeachment of President Andrew Johnson. The Senate vote was 35–19, with a clear majority

Monday, May 18
Rain. Went to Dr Birmingham's he is put out with me because I did not follow his prescription closely. home feeling miserably, wrote some letters. In afternoon Mr Hayden came Went to Msrs Lee & ^S^ about the Book saw Mr L. very satisfactory wrote to Major

Tuesday, May 19
Sick as I need be from my Medicine, nothing of importance today Went to bed sick

Wednesday, May 20
Sick in bed today so weak that I could not get dressed. In afternoon walked out with Mrs Hare to Lee & S home and read the remainder of the eve

Thursday, May 21
Raining Feeling badly still. Went to the State House in the afternoon the Secretary[284] came in to see me. Went home with Mr Hayden. Raining very hard Miss Howard came in[285]

Friday, May 22
Sick. raining still went to the State House—wrote some left about one oclock went to Lee & Shepard he gave me Andrew ^J's^ trial[286] Home and out again to Haydens. Wrote and Read all the evening. No visitors Sewed for Mrs Hare Letter from Katie this morning telling me of the children taking part in Mr Adams' Exhibition

Saturday, May 23
At the State House writing until one oclock. Took Muller's Literature of Greece[287] home. Raining. Went on Tremont Row caught in the rain. No letters today. Sewed and read Mr Phillip's speeches in New York. Read until late. I am interested in the Prince of Orange[288] as delineated by McCauley.

---

voting to impeach. But the Constitution requires a two-thirds majority to convict and remove from office, and the tally fell one vote short, which is presumably why Rollin and others were so upset with Ross, Trumbull, and Fessenden, who had been expected to vote guilty. Four other Republican senators also voted to acquit.

284. Oliver Warner. See note 259.

285. It seems likely that this visitor is Imogene Howard, as Rollin refers to Addie Howard by her first name multiple times throughout the diary. See Howard Family in biographical notes.

286. The *Trial of Andrew Johnson, President of the United States, Before the Senate of the United States, on Impeachment by the House of Representatives for High Crimes and Misdemeanors* was published in three volumes by the US Government Printing Office immediately following the trial.

287. Karl Otfried Müller's *History of the Literature of Ancient Greece* was translated and published in English in London in 1840.

288. William III of England (1650–1702) was also known as the Prince of Orange.

Sunday, May 24
At home all day reading McCaulay's. Rainy day. In afternoon Lts Dupree and Trotter[289] called to see me for the first time since I have been here they made the amende honorable[290] After read until about ten then wrote to Katie

Monday, May 25
Went to Lee & Sheppard saw a sample sheet.[291]
Went to the State House and read all the morning in the Library. Whittiers Prose Writings[292] and a portion of de Quincey's letters &c.[293] Saw the Sec. Mr Hayden gave me Albert G Brown's Sketch of the Life of John A. Andrew.[294] Wrote until near six for him. Home a letter from Leedie telling me of having met Wm Johnson[295] it is singular that they should meet. Wrote a letter to Willie Read McCauley's England until quite late when I fell asleep. Mr Wells Brown and wife called to see me.

Tuesday, May 26
At the State House today writing was introduced to Dr J G Palfrey[296] former Sec. of State Senator and more recently Post Master. In eve went to Mr Phillips who gave me a note to admit me into the Tremont Temple to the Freedmen Meeting[297] went and was charmed with Dr Tompkins of London[298] he says he has devoted

289. Like James Monroe Trotter (see note 153), William H. Dupree (1839–1934) was from Ohio and served in the Fifty-Fifth Massachusetts Infantry Regiment. Both were among the few African American soldiers promoted to second lieutenant during the Civil War. After the war the men married sisters, moved to Boston, and got jobs in the post office.

290. French for a formal apology to a person whose honor has been offended.

291. This note is written between the date and the first printed line of the page and may have been added after the rest of the entry was written. She is referring here to a sample sheet of her Delany biography.

292. The *Prose Works of John Greenleaf Whittier* was published in two volumes in 1866 by Ticknor and Fields.

293. Rollin may be referring to *Letters to a Young Man and Other Papers*, by the British writer Thomas DeQuincey (1785–1859), published by Ticknor and Fields in 1854. This was part of a twenty-two-volume series published by the American firm between 1851 and 1859.

294. *Sketch of the Official Life of John A. Andrew as Governor of Massachusetts*, by Albert Gallatin Browne Jr. (1835–91), was published by Hurd and Houghton in 1868.

295. Possibly William E. Johnston. See biographical notes.

296. John G. Palfrey (1796–1881) served as secretary of state for Massachusetts from 1844 to 1848, then began a six year term as postmaster of Boston in 1861.

297. The New England Branch of the Freedmen's Union Commission held a meeting at Tremont Temple that evening ("The New England Branch Freedmen's Union Commission," *Boston Evening Transcript*, 26 May 1868, 3).

298. Dr. Frederick Tomkins (1814?–?) was secretary of the British and Foreign Freedman's Aid Society and the author of *Jewels in Ebony*, published in 1865.

the remainder of his life to the service of these worthy but oppressed people he spoke of the unchristian prejudice against us and spoke of Chester as a "jewel in ebony" Hugh L Bond of Maryland[299] Judge Russel[300] and Mr Ware[301] followed

Wednesday, May 27
Went early to the Anti Slavery meeting Mr Phillips surpassed himself on both occasions morning and evening. Mr Chas Burleigh[302] pleased me much

Thursday, May 28
[No entry.]

Friday, May 29
This morning went to the meeting of the Free Religion Association[303] heard Mssrs O B Frothingham[304] John Weiss[305] Revs Olimpia Brown[306] Robt Collier[307] and Freeman Clark[308] Mr Collier facetiously told them he gave hearty welcome to

299. Hugh Lennox Bond (1828–93) was a judge of the Baltimore City Criminal Court from 1860 to 1867. He was also an abolitionist. During the Civil War, his letter to Secretary of War Edwin Stanton advocating the enlistment of enslaved men in Maryland (who had not been freed by the Emancipation Proclamation) was widely published.

300. Likely Judge Thomas Russell (1825–87), who in 1868 was collector of customs for the Port of Boston.

301. John Fothergill Waterhouse Ware. See note 122.

302. Charles Calistus Burleigh (1810–78) was an antislavery editor and activist from Connecticut.

303. The Free Religious Association was formed in 1867 in opposition to organized religion and dogma. Its members believed instead in rationality, the perfectibility of humanity, natural rights, and the individual. The association sought to create a more inclusive faith that would welcome all freethinkers. On 30 May 1867, it held a large meeting at Horticultural Hall to discuss "the conditions, wants, and prospects of Free Religion in America" (*Free Religion*, 3). One year later, in 1868, the association hosted a series of meetings throughout the day on Friday, 29 May; Rollin attended the 10:00 a.m. meeting "for Religious discussion at Tremont Temple" ("Meetings This Day and Tomorrow," *Boston Evening Transcript*, 28 May 1868, 4).

304. Octavius Brooks Frothingham. See note 43. Frothingham was the president of the Free Religious Association.

305. John Weiss (1818–79) was a Unitarian minister and supporter of abolition and women's rights.

306. Olympia Brown (1835–1926) was the first woman to graduate from an established theological school and, when she became a minister of the Universalist Church, the first to be ordained with official approval from a national denomination.

307. Robert Collyer (1823–1912), originally from England, was a Unitarian minister known for his oratorical skills.

308. James Freeman Clarke was a Unitarian minister, author, and editor. His church was the Church of the Disciples, founded in 1841 in Boston. See also note 81.

this new child born into the world and hoped after going through the whooping cough &c and getting over the spankings which is being lavished upon it, it would grow to worthy manhood[309] and that its freedom may not be like that of the solitary ass of the dessert. R Greener spent eve very pleasantly

Saturday, May 30
At the State House writing all day in the afternoon rainy but went out met Mrs Needman who told me Mrs Richards had a baby on Monday last weighing thirteen and ¾ lbs![310]
Home sewing Miss Emily Bailey made my blue silk bonnet went out with Mrs Bailey in evening to buy a calico ~~Letters from William J Leedie Lottie~~. Secretary read Tennyson[311] for me. Was introduced to Gov Bullock[312] in his room where I went to see the procession on the way to decorate the graves of the dead soldiers.[313]

Sunday, May 31
Went to Chelsea. Mrs Richards indeed has a fine boy dined there and after came home about six oclock went to the Lockly's and Simons'[314]
Mr Lennox came and staid a short while then Mr Hayden feeling tired I retired early, to sleep perchance to dream[315]

---

309. Robert Collier welcomed "this new child of God, as I hope and trust it is, that is now born into the world, that does not seem to know much about itself as yet, and is getting very thoroughly spanked by one and another. I gladly believe that by and by, when it has got through the whooping cough and the measles and the scarlet fever, if it gets it, and all the various ailments of little children, it may grow up a strong, grand, noble embodiment of the truth of God, and a blessing to humanity" (*Proceedings of the First Annual Meeting of the Free Religious Association*, 30).

310. Elizabeth and David Richards's large baby boy was named Abraham.

311. Alfred, Lord Tennyson (1809–92) was an English poet whose work was immensely popular in the United States. It is not clear what work the secretary read to Rollin.

312. Alexander Hamilton Bullock (1816–82) was the twenty-seventh governor of Massachusetts and served from 1866 to 1869.

313. The first nationally observed Memorial Day was on 30 May 1868. The holiday was proclaimed by the commander in chief of the Grand Army of the Republic, a fraternity of veterans of the Union army, who instructed, "all over the land the graves of loyal soldiers and every monument reared to their honor will be visited and decorated" ("The Memorial Celebration," *Boston Evening Transcript*, 29 May 1868, 2).

314. In 1868 the Lockleys and the Simons lived at 31 Garden Street in the West End. See Lockley Family and Simonds/Mahone Family in biographical notes.

315. From Shakespeare's *Hamlet*, 3.1.63–64: "To die, to sleep; / To sleep: perchance to dream: ay, there's the rub."

Monday, June 1

Went to the State House to see the parade of the Ancient and Honorable Artillery this their 230th Anniversary.[316] In their Continental uniform they made a fine appearance supported by representatives of the other Companies of the State. They were commanded by Maj Gen Banks[317] as Capt. They came for ~~the~~ Gov Bullock with much ceremony and escorted him to Hollis St. Church where the "Election Sermon" was preached by Dr Storrs[318] of Brooklyn ^N.Y.^. Hawthorne described this in the Scarlet Letter.[319] In the after at 5 oclock arrived the Artillery salute "the Gov took his seat" in the Common, and I took sick

Tuesday, June 2

Feeling quite badly but writing for Mr Hayden as hard as possible sewed a little on my plaid dress. In the afternoon Mr Hayden came to see me. A letter from Mr Ezekial.

Wednesday, June 3

Felt better this morning sewing on my dress ~~went~~ Mr Hayden came could not go with him to the State House. In the afternoon feeling miserable again went however Mr Harris[320] gave me an invitation to visit his family at Jamaica Plains I like him very much he always seems so fatherly to me.
Mr Hayden introduced me to Judge Russell[321] Came home sick and went to bed.

Thursday, June 4

Still sick nothing of importance only I am kept in a fever about the book. Not a line from Major Delany Letters from Leedie William EJ.[322] Lottie

316. Chartered in 1638, the Ancient and Honorable Artillery Company of Massachusetts is the oldest military organization in the United States. On the first Monday of June, or June Day, the company elects its officers and sergeants for one-year terms and parades through Boston.

317. Nathaniel P. Banks (1816–94) was a state legislator, senator, former governor of Massachusetts, and Union major general.

318. Richard Salter Storrs (1821–1900) was a Congregationalist minister.

319. The election sermon preached by the Reverend Dimmesdale in Nathaniel Hawthorne's *The Scarlet Letter* (1850) marks the election of a governor rather than officers of the Ancient and Honorable Artillery Company, but Rollin presumably means that the sermon is of the same genre as the one preached in the novel.

320. William Harris was a clerk in the Secretary of State's Office. Nothing more is known of him other than the fact that he and his family lived in Jamaica Plains, a town south of Boston.

321. Judge Thomas Russell. See note 300.

322. William E. Johnston. See biographical notes.

Friday, June 5
Went to Lee & Shepherd in the morning after to the State House sat with the Secretary who introduced me to a Mr[323] The Sec spoke of his Mother very feelingly
she is to be buried tomorrow.[324] We conversed for a long while but taken with a
chill I was obliged to leave and come home to bed sick all day long

Saturday, June 6
Feeling a mite better sat up in bed sewing A letter from Major Delany. I am tried
beyond endurance. Today is Lulie's[325] birthday and I have nothing to give her To
think Major Delany should prove so recreant to his many promises

Sunday, June 7
Very sick all day long Miss Emily attended me very kindly as did Mrs Gray.[326]
O how I miss Nenain![327]

Monday, June 8
Quite sick still a letter from Mrs Ezekial

Tuesday, June 9
Sick in bed still fever and chill.

Wednesday, June 10
Sick in bed still. Very homesick. What would I give to be able to have Nennain
with me?

Thursday, June 11
Sick still feverish and low spirited

323. A blank space is left after "Mr." Rollin presumably forgot the man's name and intended
to fill it in later.
324. Secretary of State Oliver Warner's mother, Rhoda Bridgman Warner (1784–1868), died
on 3 June 1868 (Rhoda Warner entry, "Massachusetts, U.S., Death Records, 1841–1915," database, Ancestry.com).
325. "Lulie" may be a nickname for Louisa Nell Gray. See note 48.
326. Louisa Nell Gray. See note 48.
327. The identity of "Nenain" is unknown, but she is clearly a woman who cared for Rollin in times of illness and distress. On 10 June she writes again of longing for this woman
after expressing her homesickness, so it is possible that "Nenain" was from Charleston, South
Carolina.

Friday, June 12
Feeling miserable but compelled to get up so as to take the Proofs[328] to Mr Lee.
Went to the State House to see Mr Hayden saw Mr Harris also Came near faint-
ing at Mr Lee's
Home and in bed again sick.

Saturday, June 13
Sick in bed all day no letters

Sunday, June 14
Felt much better got up in the after received Mr Lennox ~~and~~ Mrs Simons and
Mrs Lockley[329] in the afternoon I got ill again and felt more homesick than ever.

Monday, June 15
Felt a little comfortable ~~went down stairs~~ kept in bed until four oclock thinking
Mr Baker[330] would bring the proofs to let me see. Ella Mahone kindly brought
me some chicken soup and rice I enjoyed it very much as it is a long time since I
have been able to eat anything

Tuesday, June 16
Feeling miserable went for Quinine pills[331] also to Mrs Hayden's Home with
chills and fever for the remainder of the day and night
Mrs Anne Brown and Carrie Butler Grey[332] called and brought me a bouquet.
Fever did not leave until about 11 oclock.

328. Proofs are the preliminary version of a printed piece intended to show what the final
version will look like. They allow an author, a publisher, or both to check for printing errors.

329. Martha Ann Lockley (1815–86). See biographical notes.

330. Likely George Melville Baker (1832–90), who worked for Lee & Shepard.

331. Rollin's desire for quinine indicates that she had malaria. The symptoms of malaria include chills, fever, and aches, all of which she experiences. The disease was very common in
South Carolina, particularly the low country, because of the "semitropical climate and marshy
topography" as well as its "plantation economy," which provided a breeding ground for the
mosquitoes that transmit malaria (McCandless, "Malaria").

332. Caroline E. Butler Gray (1844–?) was the sister-in-law of Anna Gray Brown, William
Wells Brown's wife. See Brown Family in biographical notes. Carrie Butler married Anna's
brother, Horace J. Gray, in 1866 (Caroline E. Butler and Horace Gray entry, "Massachusetts,
U.S., Town and Vital Records" database, Ancestry.com).

Wednesday, June 17
Went to walk today feeling much better Washington St deserted everybody at Charlestown to the celebration of the battle of Bunker Hill.[333] Mr Lee gave me great encouragement concerning the book being out in July. Mr Lennox took me on the Common in the afternoon and to Copeland's[334] for cream Mary Lockley came and brought a letter from de Randamie[335] to me. Mr John Richmond came and spent the evening with us told of [Jerry] Miller's marriage[336] Mrs Buchanan called also to see me

Thursday, June 18
Did not feel any disagreeable effects from my walk yesterday. Went to the State House and saw the Secretary and my friend Mr Harris.

Friday, June 19
Feeling all right again I trust these chills will not return.

Saturday, June 20
Preparing to go out when Matthews came in. He spoke of having met Mr Wm Johnson[337] and also spoke of Miss Fryer he brought in her photograph this time. I was charmed with her. A letter from home today.

Sunday, June 21
Rained all day long Read &c Ben Glover[338] the only visitor
Reading the Restoration par Lamartine

333. Boston celebrated the ninety-third anniversary of the Battle of Bunker Hill in 1868 with parades, dinners, concerts, and a regatta on the Mystic River ("Seventeenth of June in Charlestown," *Boston Evening Transcript*, 15 June 1868, 4).

334. In 1868 confectioner Charles Copeland's business was located at 4 Tremont Row (*Boston Directory*, 1868).

335. Constantine De Randamie (1825–1910) was born in Surinam and educated in Holland. He served as agent for the American Colonization Society and lived in Liberia for approximately ten years in the 1850s and early 1860s. Rollin likely met him in October 1867, when the two stayed at Nancy Hankerson's boardinghouse in New York City ("Arrivals at Mrs. Hasikerson's Boarding House," *Christian Recorder*, 26 Oct. 1867, 171).

336. The remainder of the entry is written along the right-hand margin of the page.

337. Possibly William E. Johnston. See biographical notes. See also entry for 25 May.

338. Likely Benjamin H. Glover (1833–76), a hairdresser who was born in Charleston, South Carolina, in 1833. He moved to Boston sometime before 1862, when he married Satira C. Remick. The couple were married by J. Sella Martin (1832–76), pastor at the African Meeting House on Joy Street in Boston from 1859 to 1863 (Satira C. Remick and Benjamin Glover entry, "Massachusetts, U.S., Marriage Records, 1840–1915," database, Ancestry.com).

Monday, June 22

At Mr Phillip's but did not see him after at Addie's. Home and helped Mrs Gray[339] sew all day long.

In the afternoon went out again but did not accomplish my business.

Tuesday, June 23

At the State House all the morning reading In the afternoon went to Chelsea to see Mrs Morris before her departure[340] had a very pleasant visit with Miss Wall there I was charmed with her sweetness and intelligence Mrs Morris and I got a little exercised at one time about Church matters,[341] but upon the whole it was a charming visit I did not get home till late. Mr Harris[342] of N.C. had called.

Wednesday, June 24

Mr Baker brought me some proof sheets We had a long conversation about literati Oliver Optic[343] Julia Ward Howe[344] Mrs Dall[345] Speaker Phelps who has out a life of Gen Grant[346] &c.

Matthews came in the evening &c

Mr Lennox has sent me a beautiful bouquet.

339. Louisa Nell Gray. See note 48.

340. Catherine Mason Morris. See biographical notes. The Morrises were preparing to go to France to retrieve their son after his graduation from a Roman Catholic boarding school.

341. Presumably, matters having to do with the Catholic Church, which Rollin seems to have left by this time.

342. James Henry Harris (1832–91) was a delegate to the North Carolina Constitutional Convention in 1868 and soon after was elected a member of the North Carolina House of Representatives. Born free, he apprenticed as an upholsterer in Raleigh before opening his own business (Foner, *Freedom's Lawmakers*, 96–97). After two years Harris moved to Chatham, Ontario. As an agent of the National Emigration Convention, he visited Sierra Leone and Liberia and supported Delany's exploration of the Niger Valley (Ripley and Finkenbine, *Black Abolitionist Papers*, 2:398n13).

343. Oliver Optic was the pseudonym of William Taylor Adams (1822–97), a popular author of books for children. Lee & Shepard published his children's magazine, *Oliver Optic's Magazine: Our Boys and Girls*, from 1867 to 1875.

344. Julia Ward Howe (1819–1910) was a poet and a reformer, likely best known in 1868 for "The Battle Hymn of the Republic," a song that was written to the tune of a soldier's song called "John Brown's Body" and first published in 1862. It became incredibly popular during the Civil War. Howe published *From the Oak to the Olive: A Plain Record of a Pleasant Journey* with Lee & Shepard in 1868.

345. Caroline Healey Dall. See note 132. In 1867 Dall published a series of lectures titled *The College, the Market, and the Court; or, Women's Relation to Education, Labor, and Law* with Lee & Shepard.

346. In 1868 Lee & Shepard published *Life and Public Services of Ulysses S. Grant*, by Charles A. Phelps (1820–1902), who was Speaker of the Massachusetts House of Representatives from 1856 to 1857.

Thursday, June 25

At Lee & Sheppards today also at Mr Phillips the latter I did not see at all. Mr Baker brought me tickets for Mrs Keckley's Reading. Mr & Mrs Bailey went with me I felt nervous all the while It was poor to say the least of it.[347] We went up and spoke to her at the conclusion of it. It is too late in the day for her to attempt it especially without a first class teacher.

This afternoon went to see Mr Morris[348] before leaving

Friday, June 26

Went to Mr Phillip's[349] saw him for a moment he gave me a photograph Called at the Adams House[350] to see Mrs Keckley but she had left for Salem Went to Addie's met Cornelius Lennox[351] heard from him of Mr Watson's first wife coming in to claim a portion of the property. It seems so romantic that her existence was never heard of and now her Child's right will certainly be respected equally with Anna Watson's.[352]

Saturday, June 27

Matthews called this morning while I was reading spoke of Pet K.

347. A newspaper advertisement announced the "Extraordinary Novelty" of Keckley's appearance at the Tremont Temple. Identified as "The Colored Authoress" and "A Natural Genius," Keckley is said to have planned to read "The Assassination of President Lincoln" (from her recent work, "Behind the Scenes,") and "The Wooing of Hiawatha," from "Longfellow's celebrated Poem" ("Extraordinary Novelty. Mrs. Elizabeth Keckley," *Boston Evening Transcript*, 23 June 1868, 3.).

348. Robert Morris. See biographical notes.

349. The first words of this entry are written at the top of the page between the date and the first printed line.

350. The Adams House was a hotel on Washington Street in Boston.

351. Cornelius Lenox (1827–1905) was Charles Lenox's younger brother. He was a barber who lived in Boston (Cornelius Lenox entry, Boston Ward 6, Suffolk, MA, US Census, 1870, database, Ancestry.com).

352. New York caterer Robert Watson died in early 1868 at the age of seventy-one. He left more than $100,000 in property and considerable real estate to his wife, Eunice, and daughter, Anna. But the will was soon contested by a woman named Polly Watson and her son, Albert. Polly claimed to have been married to Robert when both were enslaved in Virginia. She testified that she had not seen him in thirty years, after he "was sold to a Georgia planter, and was then taken further south" ("A Fight for a Fortune of $100,000," *New York Tribune*, 19 Feb. 1868, 5). Robert's body was disinterred and identified by Polly Watson as that of her husband ("An Extraordinary Will Case," *New York Tribune*, 2 June 1868, 2). The case was taken to court and, in April 1869, was decided in favor of Anna Watson (then Brooks, having married in the interim) and her mother ("The Watson Will Case," *The Elevator* [San Francisco], 8 Apr. 1869, 2).

In afternoon went to the State House to Mr Hayden. Home and sewed until late.
Mr Chas. Johnson sent me some ice cream
Mr & Mrs Morris left for France today from New York

Sunday, June 28
Sunday up early and went in the Public Garden with Miss Fannie[353] about six
oclock returned about eight. In afternoon got dressed found it a little cool. Mrs
Wentworth brought her husband here[354] I was provoked with her. It was barefaced impudence!

Monday, June 29
At the State House to Mr Hayden Sent a book to Mr Ezekial then read in the
Library a long while. In the afternoon went up South and to Mrs Howard's and
spent a very happy time until ten oclock. Had letters from Mrs Ezekial Mr Green
and Mr Lennox nothing of importance seemed to make a note cut. Mr W W
Brown called when I was away.

Tuesday, June 30
Went to the State House this morning Mr Warner got me to blot for him while
he signed After went to Addie's and spent a long while then home In afternoon
felt strong symptoms of chills and fever Matthews came and told me of the narrow escape he and the Ruby family had from being burnt, the house having been
set on fire to[355] He wished me to go to a Concert with him which I refused Mrs
Hatten came and persuaded me to go to Mde Desque to do some sewing for her.

Wednesday, July 1
Went out to sew today I thought when I begun literature that ended but I find it
otherwise It is at a French lady's I like her much and it is quite private Her [hem-
ming] shows that genius is not confined to paintings &c In the afternoon I returned home Matthews had called to take me to see Mrs Lancaster and returned

353. Likely Fannie Bailey. See Bailey Family in biographical notes.
354. Caroline A. Brown Wentworth, wife of barber named George Wentworth. See note 184.
It is unclear why her bringing her husband to the Bailey's house was "barefaced impudence."
355. Matthews was apparently in Portland, Maine, visiting the Ruby family when a fire was
set in William Wilberforce Ruby's shed. While the flames did not reach the house to which the
shed was attached, considerable damage was done by smoke ("Fire," *Portland [ME] Daily Press*,
29 June 1868, 2). Approximately two weeks later, on 18 July, Ruby's house and store were "almost
entirely destroyed" by another deliberately set fire. A newspaper report stated, "this is the third
time within a few months that this same building has been set on fire" ("Fire," *Portland [ME]
Daily Press*, 18 July 1868, 2).

in the evening to find out where I had been I suppose. I was much tried by him
this evening. Geo Johnson and Mr Richardson of Washington called

Thursday, July 2

Sewing at Mde Desque took sick there She very kindly attended me. I had chills
and fever in its strongest form She kindly sent for a carriage and sent me home in
it. Went to bed as soon as I reached home. I feel miserably despondent about my
poverty No letters

Friday, July 3

At Mde Desque sewing today I remained there until seven oclock as I went late
this morning. I never met a pleasanter woman charmingly French in everything
Went to Dr Treadwell[356] this morning He seemed pleased to see me. Spoke of
Dr Briggs[357] and his sentimentality &c Charleston and Mrs King[358] and lots of
gossip.
In evening Matthews brought a letter from Major Delany given to him by Mr
Nell I sat down and answered it immediately not a dollar sent to me again I was
provoked. Went to bed at 2 A.M.

Saturday, July 4

Up at four as I had no sleep whatever. Took the quinine which unfitted me for
the day. It grew hotter every hour there was not a pleasant room in the house so
I kept in mine all day had a slight chill but much fever. In afternoon dressed and
went downstairs did not eat dinner Saw the Secretary[359] as he stopped to converse
a while with me at the window. Mr Smith brought me some Ice Cream In eve Mr
Bailey took Peter and me on the Commons to the Fireworks a dense crowd there
felt sick while there

---

356. Joshua B. Treadwell (1840–85) was a white physician who served for four months in 1865
as a first lieutenant and surgeon for the Fifty-Fourth Massachusetts Infantry Regiment.

357. Charles E. Briggs (1833–94) was a white major and a surgeon with the Fifty-Fourth Massachusetts from November 1863 until the end of the war.

358. In Charleston in June 1865, Charles Briggs was introduced to the notorious socialite
and novelist Susan Petigru King (1824–75). During the Civil War, King was rumored to have
flirted outrageously with Confederate officers in Columbia; after the war she associated indis-
criminately with Union soldiers, seemingly including Major Briggs. On 25 June 1865, Briggs
wrote to his sister: "Last Wednesday I was presented to Mrs. King the daughter of Mr the late
Mr. Petigru, a Queen of Society. . . . I was very much charmed by Mrs. King and found her
conversation very piquant." At the end of the letter, he noted Joshua B. Treadwell's presence in
Charleston (Charles E. Briggs to Emma Briggs Allen, 25 June 1865, Charles E. Briggs Letters,
Massachusetts Historical Society).

359. Massachusetts secretary of state Oliver Warner. See note 259.

Sunday, July 5

A baking hot day long to be remembered. Trying to keep cool all day in afternoon a thunder storm seemed imminent but it only sprinkled a little. In after went to Howard's and spent a real pleasant time until nine oclock. Matthews had called during my absence. Retired about eleven oclock to dreams of P.

Monday, July 6

Went to the Doctor's[360] this morning as it was quite pleasant. Enjoyed my walk. I imagine P. left today for his vacation. Seeing a Chelsea car looking cool and inviting I entered and went there without a moments thoughts. Mrs Spenser was moving out. I heard her history today. I am being fast convinced that our men prefer that class of women to respectable virtuous ones. I reached home about six after went to Mr Hayden's and sat a little while there.

Tuesday, July 7

Letter from Mr Ezekial today[361]

Mr Baker brought me the proofs in the afternoon went there and we had a time about the Dedication I never did approve of it but Major D insisted I suppose we will have a fuss about it anyhow[362] Mr Lee gave me Queen Victoria's book.[363] Went to Addie Howard's and staid a while with her. In eve went home went to walk with Jim[364] and Anna Maria on the Bridge. Matthews was at [window] when we returned. We differed as usual. Whipper[365] was not chosen speaker as I expected.

Wednesday, July 8

The So Ca legislature convened today[366]

Drizzled a little this morning went to the State House with Anna Maria Hennessy went up into the Cupola and viewed Boston and its surroundings. After on

360. Likely Doctor Samuel Till Birmingham. See note 251.

361. This line is written at the top of the page, between the date and the first line.

362. It is not clear exactly what Rollin means when she refers to the "dedication," but it is possible that she is talking about the epigraph, "et niger arma Memnonis," an alteration of the line "et nigri Memnonis arma" from Virgil's *Aeneid*, which translates as "the arms of black Memnon."

363. In 1868 Queen Victoria of Great Britain (1819–1901) published *Leaves from the Journal of Our Life in the Highlands, From 1848 to 1861* with the London publisher Smith, Elder, and Company.

364. Possibly James Bailey. See Bailey Family in biographical notes.

365. William J. Whipper. See biographical notes.

366. This line was written at the top of the page, between the date and the first line. The South Carolina legislature, elected in 1868, was the first state legislature in the United States with a Black majority.

Common thence home. In afternoon went to State House to Mr Hayden God bless his kind heart for all he has done for me and others. After to the Doctor's[367] promenaded on Washington St. met W Wells Brown Home and continued reading the Restoration par Lamartine. Feeling very depressed no money.

Thursday, July 9

Cloudy day dreamed of seeing Phil[368] last night. I wonder if he is here! Read all day. Toothache and tongue cancered In afternoon went down stairs to see Mr Greener.[369] After went out with Anna Maria. In eve Emily Fanny[370] Mr Johnson and I went to Franklin Square to hear the event by Dodworth's Band.[371] Home sweet home translated me as performed by them. Returned home about half past ten and retired. No letters nor a sign of P.'s being here.

Friday, July 10

Weather still gloomy. The news of the nomination of Seymour and Blair produces no enthusiasm among Democrats, but their unpopularity cheers the Republicans.[372] Went to the State House in afternoon Later on Washington St thence to the Public Garden with Anna Maria remained until after seven oclock. Home sang and played for some time after supper Still dreaming in my day musings of P. retired early Matthews came after I retired.

Saturday, July 11

Sultry inclined day. No letters. At one prepared to go to Mr Hayden's.

Sunday, July 12

Weather still gloomy

Monday, July 13–Sunday, July 26

[No entries.]

Monday, July 27

Up early and went out

---

367. Likely Dr. Samuel Till Birmingham. See note 251.

368. "Phil" is likely the same person as "P."

369. Richard Greener. See biographical notes.

370. Likely Fanny (or Fannie) Bailey. See Bailey Family in biographical notes.

371. The concert by Dodworth's Band, led by Harvey B. Dodworth (1822–91), was held in Franklin Square in front of the elaborate St. James Hotel ("Concert by Dodworth's Band in Front of the St. James," *Boston Evening Transcript*, 10 July 1868, 4).

372. The Democratic nominees for president and vice president in 1868 were New York Governor Horatio Seymour (1818–86) and Representative Francis Preston Blair Jr. (1821–75) of Missouri. The party's platform was anti-Reconstruction and African American suffrage and pro-reconciliation and states' rights.

Tuesday, July 28
Boston Vale[373]
Up very early my last day in Boston dear dear Boston went to Lee & Shepherd Mr L gave me "Planchette"[374] Also a Yankee in Canada[375] The Memoirs of Mme Recamier[376] went to see Addie for the last Clarence[377] Mr Hayden and Wells Brown Anthony Clarke[378] and his mother[379] called went to see Mrs Barreau,[380] later Mrs & Imogene Howard and Ella Mahone called Left at five for Newport with Mr Richmond Mr Haynes and Vanhorn[381] met us at the boat

Wednesday, July 29
New York[382]
Arrived in New York at 7 A.M. The view was somewhat obscured by the fog yet I saw the Prisons better.[383] Left at ten for Philadelphia the joy of meeting old

373. This line is written at the top of the page, between the date and the first line. "Vale" is Latin for "farewell" or "goodbye."

374. The quotes around "Planchette" indicate that Rollin is not referring to a book; as the next sentence demonstrates, she does not put quotes around titles. A planchette is a small piece of wood, usually heart shaped, and fitted with casters and a pencil pointed down. The device is used in seances to produce automatic writing, or writing produced by spirits. Newspaper advertisements and stories indicate that the planchette was usually referred to simply as "Planchette," with the name often capitalized and placed in quotation marks.

375. *A Yankee in Canada, with Anti-Slavery and Reform Papers*, by Henry David Thoreau (1817–62), was published by Ticknor and Fields in 1866.

376. *Memoirs and Correspondence of Madame Récamier*, translated and edited by Isophene M. Luyster (1832–?), was published in Boston by Roberts Brothers in 1867. Jeanne Françoise Julie Adélaïde Récamier (1777–1849), known as Juliette, was a French socialite and *salonnière*.

377. Possibly Edwin Clarence Howard (1846–1912), the brother of Adeline Howard. See Howard Family in biographical notes.

378. Anthony F. Clarke Jr., the brother of Fanny Clarke Johnson, whose death is mentioned in the diary on 6 March.

379. Fanny Lenox Clarke. See note 126.

380. Elizabeth Barreau. See note 79.

381. Mahlon Van Horne (1840–1910) was principal of the Zion School for Colored Children in Charleston, South Carolina, when Rollin taught there. In 1869 he accepted a pastorate in Newport, Rhode Island, at the Union Congregational church. He served there for twenty-eight years ("Reverend Mahlon Van Horne," Rhode Island Heritage Hall of Fame, https://riheritage halloffame.com/Reverend-Mahlon-Van-Horne/, accessed 21 Apr. 2025).

382. This is written between the date and the first line of the page.

383. Governor's Island in New York harbor was the location of two Civil War prisons, Fort Columbus and Castle Williams.

friends the affectionate greeting and interest manifested I can never forget Dora has grown so much Lizzie looked thin. Mama Sidney[384] as of old Hattie Johnson[385] as ever Raymond Burr[386] and Tom Boling[387] called. Eliza Jane Gordon[388] was overjoyed seeing me again called to see Mrs Douglass[389] but could not see her

384. "Dora" is Isadora Kennedy, the sister of Rollin's Philadelphia friend, Lizzie Kennedy. "Mama Sidney" is her mother, Sidney Kennedy. See Kennedy Family in biographical notes.

385. Harriet C. Johnson (1845–1907) was an 1864 graduate of the Institute for Colored Youth (ICY). In 1868 she was appointed principal of the ladies and preparatory divisions at Avery College in Pittsburgh but had apparently not moved there yet ("Harriet C. Johnson," A Great Thing for Our People: Institute for Colored Youth in the Civil War Era, online exhibit, Falvey Library, Villanova University, https://exhibits.library.villanova.edu/institute-colored-youth/graduates/harriet-c-johnson, accessed 12 Oct. 2023).

386. Raymond Johnson Burr (1842–1924) was born in Philadelphia and attended the ICY. He was the son of John Emory Burr (1819–95) and Elizabeth Curtis (1822–1901), making him the great-grandson of Aaron Burr (1756–1836), third vice president of the United States, and a domestic servant from India named Mary Eugénie Beauharnais Emmons (c.1760–c.1832) ("Raymond J. Burr," A Great Thing for Our People, https://exhibits.library.villanova.edu/institute-colored-youth/graduates/raymond-j-burr, accessed 12 Oct. 2023).

387. Thomas H. Boling (1846–96) graduated from the ICY in 1864. He married another ICY classmate, Margaret Masten (1846–?), and became a flour dealer and a grocery-store owner. ("Thomas H. Boling," A Great Thing for Our People, https://exhibits.library.villanova.edu/institute-colored-youth/graduates/thomas-h-boling, accessed 12 Oct. 2023).

388. Eliza Jane Gordon (1851–?) was six years old when Rollin moved to Philadelphia. It is not clear how Rollin knew their family, but David Gordon (1820–89), Eliza's father, was born in South Carolina. He married Mary Letitia Burr (1820–1913), the sister of John Emory Burr. (Eliza is, therefore, the cousin of Raymond Johnson Burr.) The Gordon family was in Philadelphia by 1839, when David was named vice president of the Demosthenian Institute, a self-improvement society for young African American men (Willson, Elite of Our People, 115). In the 1850 and 1860 censuses, the Gordon family is listed as living in Norwich, Connecticut, and their youngest four children were born in Connecticut (David Gordon, household, Norwich, New London, CT, US Census, 1850, database, Ancestry.com; David Gordon, household, Norwich, New London, CT, US Census, 1860, database, Ancestry.com). (The older two were born in Pennsylvania.) They must have moved back to Philadelphia after 1863, when their youngest child was born, which means that they were there during Rollin's last two years at the ICY. In 1868 Eliza would have been seventeen years old; in the 1870 census, she is listed as a dressmaker (Eliza Gordon entry, District 44, Philadelphia Ward 15, Philadelphia, PA, US Census, 1870, database, Ancestry.com).

389. Sarah Mapps Douglass (1806–82) was a teacher at the ICY from 1853 to 1866. She was a well-known educator and activist. After becoming the first African American woman to attend the Female Medical College of Pennsylvania, she lectured publicly on female anatomy, hygiene, and health.

Thursday, July 30
Philadelphia[390]
We talked almost all night so we kept breakfast waiting went out for my ticket
directly after O V Catto[391] called during my absence I called on Mrs Douglass I
drew years of comfort from seeing her once more I did not see Phillips nor Grace
Mapps[392] my idols Carrie Lecount[393] dined with us, in afternoon we enjoyed our-
self L. Mama Sidney & I inquiring over the past Sarah Iredell[394] Laura Cashin[395]
Carrie and Miss Ketchum accompanied me[396] to the depot left at 11 p.m.[397]

Friday, July 31
On the line Annemessic[398]

390. This is written at the top of the page, between the date and the first line.

391. Octavius V. Catto (1839–71) was a teacher of English and mathematics at the ICY, his
alma mater, beginning in 1859, the year Rollin moved to Philadelphia. He became principal of
the Male Department in 1869.

392. Grace A. Mapps (1835–97) attended McGrawville College, graduating in 1852. She became the principal teacher of the Female Department at the ICY in 1852 and remained in that
position until 1865.

393. Carrie LeCount (1846–1923) graduated from the ICY in 1863. She began teaching at the
Ohio Street School in Philadelphia in 1865 and was named principal in 1867. She was engaged
to marry fellow ICY graduate Octavius V. Catto prior to his murder in 1871 ("Carrie Le Count,"
A Great Thing for Our People, https://exhibits.library.villanova.edu/institute-colored-youth
/graduates/caroline-lecount-bio, accessed 12 Oct. 2023).

394. Sarah Iredell (1849–1908) attended Oberlin in the late 1850s and became a teacher in
the Philadelphia Public School System. During the Civil War, she was a founding member of
the Ladies Union Association, which provided support for sick or wounded African American
soldiers. After the war, she taught in Philadelphia, Maryland, and Washington, DC (Maillard,
Whispers of Cruel Wrongs, 42–44).

395. Rollin may be referring here to Laura F. Cashin, who may have attended the ICY with
her brother, Herschel V. Cashin. She may instead be referring to Sarah Iredell's sister, Laura
Iredell, who graduated from the ICY in 1869 ("Laura") and Herschel Cashin ("Cashin"). Without any punctuation here, it is difficult to tell.

396. The rest of this entry is written along the left-hand margin of the page.

397. Rollin likely took a train of the Philadelphia, Wilmington, and Baltimore Railroad,
which left the depot at the corner of Broad Street and Washington Avenue at 11:00 p.m. daily.
Its final stop was at Crisfield, Maryland, where passengers could transfer to a "boat for Fortress
Monroe, Norfolk, Portsmouth, and the South" ("Philadelphia, Baltimore, and Wilmington
Railroad," *Philadelphia Inquirer*, 31 July 1868, 6.).

398. This is written at the top of the page, between the date and the first line. The "Annamessic Line" was advertised as a "great short route" for passengers traveling from Norfolk and Portsmouth, Virginia, to Northern cities—presumably, the other way around as well ("Annamessic
Line!," *Norfolk Virginian*, 31 July 1868, 4).

Rode until about 10 A.M. and took the boat for Portsmouth.[399] The sail up the Chesapeake Bay was delightful and cheerful the RipRaps[400] could be seen plainly we stopped for a while at Fortress Monroe[401] reached Portsmouth about four oclock p.m. and took the train for Weldon[402] reached Weldon at 7 P.M. and took the train for Raleigh[403] travelled all night long in a close dirty car alone until near daybreak when some few passengers entered

Saturday, August 1
Raleigh[404]
Arrived here about nine oclock this morn Went to Mr J H Harris's residence where I was most cordially received by him and his very amiable wife[405] I soon felt myself at ease having refreshed myself I enjoyed my visit very much I left at five oclock for Charlotte, N.C. On the cars I was much annoyed by the stares of the poor whites. Secesh[406] women abounded therein. reach Charlotte about 11 p.m.

Sunday, August 2
Columbia, S.C.[407]
Reached Columbia about six oclock Mr Whipper[408] met me at the depot with his buggie, and took me to my boarding place where an elegant and spacious room awaited me; breakfast was tempting. My dear friend Mr Adams[409] was in to see me very soon after my arrival. Charlotte came to see me in the morning but

399. Portsmouth, Virginia.

400. The Rip Raps are an artificial island at the mouth of the Hampton Roads harbor. It was the site of Fort Wool (formerly known as Fort Calhoun), which, along with Fortress Monroe, protected the harbor during the Civil War.

401. Fortress Monroe, at Hampton, Virginia, remained in Union hands throughout the Civil War and served as a logistical hub and launch point for US forces. More importantly for Rollin, the fort became a destination for freedom seekers, or "contrabands," who appealed to the army for protection (Mary Koik, "The Civil War in Hampton Roads: Fort Monroe," American Battlefield Trust, https://www.battlefields.org/learn/articles/civil-war-hampton-roads-fort-monroe, accessed 21 Oct. 2024). For two years, from May 1865 to May 1867, Jefferson Davis, the former president of the Confederacy, was imprisoned at Fort Monroe.

402. Weldon, North Carolina.

403. Raleigh, North Carolina.

404. This is written at the top of the page, between the date and the first line.

405. James Henry Harris. See note 342. Harris's wife was Isabella Hinton Harris (1831–76).

406. "Secesh" was a colloquialism used to describe a secessionist, or someone who was or remained supportive of the Southern states seceding from the Union.

407. This is written at the top of the page, between the date and the first line.

408. William J. Whipper. See biographical notes.

409. Ennals J. Adams. See biographical notes.

Kate did not.[410] Went to Church in the morning with Harry Maxwell[411] and Mr Adams. The Gov[412] and all the members were there. Quite an excitement created on account of the disappearance of Joe Howard after the riot of the Ku Klux Klan at night.[413]

Monday, August 3
Went to the Committee Room this morning copied a few bills and left early Joe Howard heard from at Kingsmill the youngest man Dallas Smith who was shot died and Joe's disappearance was made capital of by the rebels. This afternoon on his arrival he was arrested but Mr Whipper got out a writ of Habes Corpus and got him out.[414] Joe seemed terribly frightened about it.
Kate came up to see me this morning she looks delicate Spent the afternoon with them.

410. Rollin's sisters Charlotte and Kate. See biographical notes.

411. Henry J. Maxwell (1837–1906) was born free on Edisto Island, South Carolina, and served in the Second US Colored Artillery during the Civil War. After the war he was a teacher under the auspices of the Freedmen's Bureau in Bennettsville, South Carolina. In 1868 he was elected to the South Carolina Senate and would soon be appointed postmaster of Bennettsville (Foner, *Freedom's Lawmakers*, 143).

412. The first Republican governor of South Carolina was Robert Kingston Scott (1826–1900), a former Union army officer and assistant commissioner of the South Carolina Bureau of Refugees, Freedmen, and Abandoned Lands from 1865 to 1868. He served as governor until 1872.

413. Newspaper coverage of this incident did not represent it as a Ku Klux Klan "riot." Instead, one paper claimed that several young white men were "in search of several brothels . . . , and by mistake, entered a colored boarding house" in which African American members of the South Carolina legislature resided ("Fatal Affray—A White Citizen Murdered," *Daily Pheonix* [Columbia, SC], 4 Aug. 1868, 1). The innocence and respectability of the white men and disreputable neighborhood in which the boardinghouse was located were asserted in most of the mainstream coverage of the incident. Black residents of the boardinghouse were said to have shot at the white men, with Joseph Howard (1840–1915), the son of African American merchant and alderman Robert Howard (1808–183), fatally wounding a white post-office clerk named Dallas Smith (1845–68).

414. One Charleston newspaper reported that witness testimony had established that Smith was "shot by a black man." This item was followed by the note that "Joseph Howard, who was reported missing, turns up at Kingsville, and was arrested by a telegraph from the Chief of Police, at this place, but afterwards released" ("The Legislature—The Victim in the Late Fracas—The Missing Boy Found," *Charleston [SC] Daily Courier*, 4 Aug. 1868, 1). While not directly stating it, this article, and others like it, implied that Howard had killed Smith but was not being held accountable. Whipper was able to have Howard released by producing a writ of habeas corpus, alleging his unlawful detention.

Tuesday, August 4

At the Committee room Joe Howard came in and spoke appeared much frightened I advised him to get Mr Whipper to go with him to the examination before the Coroner[415]

In the afternoon went back wrote several letters for Mr Whipper he accompanied me home.

Henry Maxwell called to see me

Wednesday, August 5

At the Committee room Mr William Johnston[416] called there to see me on business walked home with me When there he raved about Mr Whipper sending for me to clerk for him. He told me he felt like cutting his throat when he heard I was to come here under Mr Whipper's auspices.

Thursday, August 6

Went to Committee Room had a chill had to come home Mr W. called Also Mr A. O. Jones[417] and Mr Wright.[418]

Friday, August 7

[No entry.]

Saturday, August 8

Went to Committee room in after went out to drive with Mr Whipper to the races but did not go in for the reason no ladies were there

415. Howard likely testified before William B. Johnston, the African American coroner of Richland County in 1868. A white man, Thomas P. Walker, had also insisted that he had been elected coroner but was forced to stand down by the attorney general of South Carolina ("History of Coroners," Richland County [SC] Coroner's Office, https://rccosc.com/history-of-coroners). Both Johnston and Walker held inquests into the incident at the boardinghouse that led to the death of Dallas Smith. Walker's inquest, with a jury made up entirely of white men, rendered a verdict of murder, implicating a Black Colleton County legislator, Thomas Richardson (1840–?). Johnston's inquest, with seven white men and five African American men, was split along racial lines, with the Black citizens refusing to call Smith's death a murder ("Coroner Walker's Inquest," *Daily Phoenix* (San Francisco), 18 Aug. 1868, 2).

416. William E. Johnston. See biographical notes.

417. Originally from North Carolina, Albert O. Jones (1843–?) was clerk of the South Carolina House of Representatives from 1868 to 1876.

418. Likely Jonathan Jasper Wright (1840–85), who was elected a state senator, representing Beaufort County, in 1868. Born and raised in Pennsylvania, Wright came south to teach formerly enslaved people in the Sea Islands (Foner, *Freedom's Lawmakers*, 236).

Sunday, August 9
Sunday sick in bed with chills Mr Whipper sent a note inviting me to go to Church with him
In afternoon Mr Jones of Washington Clifton Hurston and Mr Ezekial also Mr Whipper came and spent afternoon with me Henry Maxwell also

Monday, August 10
[No entry.]

Tuesday, August 11
Went out riding with Mr Whipper today Had quite a pleasant drive.[419]

Wednesday, August 12
[No entry.]

Thursday, August 13
This morning at the Committee Room quite a time about the Civil Rights Bill introduced by Dr Boseman[420]

Friday, August 14
Dr Boseman called I wrote an answer to Mr Whipper's letter asking a delay of the decision (matrimonial)[421] Dr B walked as far as Sue's with me. Mr W was at the office when I got there also McIntyre[422] one of the Committee I watched my chances and placed it between the leaves of a book, which he was reading. I saw him take it out.

419. This entry is written in the middle of the page, as if Rollin had intended to go back and write about something that happened prior to her ride with Whipper.

420. Dr. Benjamin A. Boseman Jr. (1840–81) was elected in 1868 to the South Carolina House of Representatives, where he introduced the first civil rights bill in South Carolina history (Newmark, *Without Concealment*, 164, 165). A native of New York, Boseman earned a medical degree in Maine and served as a contract surgeon with Union soldiers on Hilton Head Island during the Civil War (161, 163).

421. It is not clear when Whipper asked Rollin to marry him. It may have been during the "pleasant drive" on Tuesday, 11 August.

422. George Francis McIntyre (1843–?) was a white man from Charleston who represented Colleton County in the South Carolina Senate from 1870 to 1872. He was engaged to marry Kate Rollin when she died in 1876. See Katherine Rollin in biographical notes.

Saturday, August 15
Went to the Room with Henry Maxwell He showed me a letter of Miss Cooper[423] Did not see W.

Sunday, August 16
To Church with Mr Adams. Did not see W.

Monday, August 17
Went out with Mr Adams in afternoon made some visits with him met Mr W. did not call in evening

Tuesday, August 18
To be or not to be[424]
Wrote all day on the the Justice of the Peace bill in the afternoon Mr W called and asked me to go riding with him Mr Adams has been talking with him in regard to the letter without any solicitation of mine felt awfully put out over it. In evening W. came and spoke over the affair rather business at one time, non committal throughout but I felt he did not want a No. I said yes. He kissed me good night.

Wednesday, August 19
Feeling the most curious this morning. Wondering how W. felt. Received a letter from him by Bennie. I wonder how he will meet me this evening. Went shopping. W. came while at Supper He froze me up completely. Spent a most curious time which baffles all of my philosophy. What was it? Was the manes[425] of his departed wife present unseen unwilling to give up her claims or what? Both of us were unlike our real selves

423. On 20 October 1868, Henry Maxwell married Rebecca Sass Cooper (1835–69) in Philadelphia (Rebecca Sass Cooper and Henry Johnson Maxwell entry, "Pennsylvania, U.S., Episcopal Diocese of Pennsylvania Church Records, 1759–1972," database, Ancestry.com). She died less than a year after their wedding, a month after giving birth to their first child (Rebecca Sass Cooper Maxwell entry, "Philadelphia, Pennsylvania, U.S., Death Certificates Index, 1803–1915," database, Ancestry.com; Paris Cooper Maxwell entry, "Pennsylvania and New Jersey, U.S., Church and Town Records, 1669–2013," database, Ancestry.com).

424. This is written at the top of the page, between the date and the first line. Rollin quotes here from Shakespeare's *Hamlet*, 3.1.55.

425. This is a Latin word for the spirit or shade of a dead person.

Thursday, August 20
Woke early. Wondering whether to throw up the sponge or accept a loveless life or not. Felt as though W. could not love anyone. A letter came from him today which restored and reinvigorated me. A real love letter.

Friday, August 21
[No entry.]

Saturday, August 22
Promised Will

Sunday, August 23
Raining hard. Feeling between middling and prime. W. came to see me feeling quite ugly about yesterday. Boseman called also.

Monday, August 24–Thursday, August 27
[No entries.]

Friday, August 28
Home early.
Between going to Charleston tomorrow and staying until time to be married. Mr Adams urging and Mr. Whipper saying to stay. About nine oclock made up my mind to go sent after W. he came and brought me money.
Jillson, Johnson, Swails, Green and others at house during the afternoon.[426] Mr Johnson bowing Mr Whipper out. Oh my!

426. Justus K. Jillson (1839–81) was a white man born in Massachusetts who taught in Camden, South Carolina, for the Freedmen's Bureau from 1866 to 1868 (Butchart et al., "Freedmen's Teacher Project"). He was state superintendent of education from 1868 to 1876 ("Justus K. Jillson," South Carolina Department of Education, https://ed.sc.gov/newsroom/former-state-superintendents-of-education/justus-k-jillson/, accessed 21 Apr. 2025). Stephen A. Swails (1832–1900) was a free Black man from Pennsylvania and New York who worked as a boatman and a waiter prior to joining the Fifty-Fourth Massachusetts Regiment (Egerton, *Thunder at the Gates*, 20, 28). He remained in Charleston after the Civil War, marrying Susan Aspinall (324). He was elected to the state senate in 1868 (Foner, *Freedom's Lawmakers*, 207). See Samuel Green and William E. Johnston in biographical notes.

Saturday, August 29
Columbia
Left this morning for Charleston Though home disheartened me. Ma looked much the same. Carried my Book home for Pa.[427] Saw Weston's[428] Aspinalls[429] and others. Told Toady[430] about my intended marriage. She made no comments but promised her hearty cooperation. ~~Gave her the nightgown~~

Sunday, August 30
Home all day long with the family Nothing special broached about the engagement Pa was not exactly in for it I could see plainly

Monday, August 31
Sent letter to W today. Went shopping for myself and the children. Toady took the night gown chemises and promises to make the dress. Miss Sophia[431] will make the drawers and the reception dress.

Tuesday, September 1
[No entry.]

Wednesday, September 2
Started for Columbia to my darling.

Thursday, September 3–Saturday, September 12
[No entries.]

427. Rollin likely carried home unbound proof pages to give to her father, as her book does not seem to have been published until after she wrote the introduction dated 19 October 1868 in Charleston.

428. It is unclear which branch of the large Weston family Rollin visits with. As a teacher for the American Missionary Association in Charleston immediately following the Civil War, she had taught with Mary Weston (1843–1905), the daughter of Furman Weston and Louisa Bonneau Weston, so she may have spent time with her.

429. Albert Aspinall Sr. (1810–?) was a tailor. He and his wife, Mary (1812–?), had a daughter, Susan (1844–1903), who was close to Rollin's age. Susan married Stephen A. Swails in 1866 (Egerton, *Thunder at the Gates*, 324).

430. Rollin notes the receipt of a letter from "Toadie" while in Boston. See note 213.

431. Sophia Morris (1833–91?) was an African American dressmaker who lived in Charleston with her sister and brother-in-law's family (Sophia Morris entry, Charleston Ward 6, Charleston, SC, US Census, 1870, database, Ancestry.com; Sophia Morris entry, Enumeration District 64, Charleson, Charleston, SC, US Census, 1880, database, Ancestry.com).

Sunday, September 13

This is my last unmarried Sabbath. Felt sad at intervals not knowing how they were at home about the intended marriage and a sort of dread to enter that state wonder whether it will be

Monday, September 14

Left Columbia for Charleston at 5-30 arrived at three oclock Went to Toady's. Met Pa on returning home. From dusk till nearly midnight the contest lasted between Pa, C,[432] & I. C. begun preparing for Columbia Pa consented at last not to interfere and allow the marriage to come off on Thursday morning. He thought it was too soon &c. Wanted time to prepare house &c. Scylla[433] baked the cakes &c.

Tuesday, September 15

~~W. arrived this~~ ^Went out this^ morning Pa expected to win Will over to his side and postpone the wedding but W could not be persuaded. I was out ~~when~~ shopping with Toady bought two dresses in for the marriage and to travel in the other for the reception. Met Mrs Knight and hinted to her about coming up Thursday morning. Theo Smith & Mr Ezekial came. Their innuendos about W nearly put me crazy. What they meant at first I could not tell.

Wednesday, September 16

Busy as a bee. Could not stop to think how I felt.[434]

W came from Columbia with Mr Adams. I was at Miss Sophie Morris ^to^ try on the dress. Met Will at home when I got there. Pa could not move him one inch. Mr Adams I have not felt yet as though I am to be married tomorrow. W came in the afternoon to bring the ring to try. Miss Ellen Humphries[435] met him there. Came back again nearly went to ride with him. [Virrells] Mr Adams Amelia Ann[436] & Miss Amanda W. former slept at home

432. Probably Charlotte "Lottie" Rollin. See biographical notes.

433. While it is impossible to identify Scylla, her name suggests that she may have been enslaved prior to the Civil War. Many African Americans were given classical names as an ironic gesture meant to mock the dignity of the enslaved.

434. This is written at the top of the page, between the date and the first line.

435. Ellen Humphries (1842–86) was a dressmaker and the daughter of Joseph P. Humphries (1814–71) and Margaret Campbell Barquet Humphries (1815–93), making her the niece of Joseph Humphries Barquet. The Humphries family lived in Philadelphia in 1850 but had moved back to Charleston by the late 1860s (Joseph Humphries, household, Philadelphia Pine Ward, Philadelphia, PA, US Census, 1850, database, Ancestry.com); Ellen Humphries entry, Charleston Ward 4, Charleston, SC, US Census, 1870, database, Ancestry.com). See note 86.

436. Likely Amelia Ann Shrewsbury (1845–?), who taught alongside Rollin and Mary Weston in the American Missionary Association–sponsored school for recently enslaved children.

Thursday, September 17

Up by times this morning getting ready.[437] Married by Mr Adams. Very nervous. Left for Columbia. Found it very annoying at Branchville impudent conductor[438] reached C. Elliott[439] & Lee at the depot A. O. Jones Capt Lottie & Kate Ella Tolland[440] at the house. Quite an ovation. In the evening a grand reception all the State Officers nearly ditto for the members of both Houses a few outsiders. Peter Miller[441] improvised a most amusing wedding song retired about 11 p.m.

Friday, September 18

Today I am beginning to realize the affairs of the past few days but am happy enough to leave them behind me. W seems happy too may God enable us to continue it.

Amelia Ann worked as a teacher in Charleston until she married Henry Ellison (1817–83), a wealthy African American man from Sumter, South Carolina (Johnson and Roark, *Black Masters*, 333–34).

437. Rollin begins this entry just under the date, as if anticipating that it will be a long one and will exceed the lines provided.

438. For another version of this story, see appendix F, "Sketch of Frances Rollin Whipper," by Daniel E. Murray.

439. Robert B. Elliott (1842–84) was born in England to West Indian parents. He studied law and served in the Royal Navy, arriving in the United States in 1867. By March, he was appointed associate editor of the *South Carolina Leader*, a Black-owned Republican newspaper in Charleston. He opened a law practice in the city late that year. After serving as a delegate at the state constitutional convention, he was elected to the South Carolina House of Representatives along with Whipper (Foner, *Freedom's Lawmakers*, 69–70). Later he and Macon Allen joined Whipper in forming the nation's first African American law firm (Smith, *Emancipation*, 244).

440. An Ella Tolland listed in the 1870 census as twenty-two years old might be this friend (Ella Tolland entry, Columbia, Richland, SC, US Census, 1870, database, Ancestry.com). This Ella is white but is reported living in what appears to be a boardinghouse with others identified as Black or "Mulatto," so she might simply have light-colored skin. This Ella (1848–89) married John Augustus Barre (1845–?), a barber, between 1870 and 1872, as they have an eight-year-old daughter in the 1880 census (John A. Barr, household, Enumeration District 163, Columbia, Richland, SC, US Census, 1880, database, Ancestry.com). All the members of the family are listed as mulatto. In 1900, however, after Ella's death, he is described as "Black" (Jno Bane entry, Charleston Ward 4, Charleston, SC, US Census, 1860, database, Ancestry.com; John A. Barr entry, Enumeration District 86, Columbia Ward 2, Richland, SC, US Census, 1900, database, Ancestry.com). His death certificate also describes him as "negro" (John Barr entry, database, "South Carolina, U.S., Death Records, 1821–1972," Ancestry.com).

441. This is likely the same Peter Miller who served as assistant sergeant at arms at the constitutional convention in January 1868 (*Proceedings of the Constitutional Convention of South Carolina*, 12, 21). Nothing more is known about him.

Visitors. In the afternoon Mr & Mrs. Cardoza[442] and Mrs Henry Cardoza.[443] Mr & Mrs Rancier,[444] Bob DeLarge[445] Bob & W were not speaking. W. E. Johnston came up and congratulated Willie. Green came also.

Saturday, September 19
Looking over W's things today.
Jillson & Swails[446] came and spent the evening

442. Francis Lewis Cardoza (1836–1902) was the son of Lydia Williams Weston (1805–64), a free Black woman, and Isaac Nunez Cardozo (1793–1855), a white Jewish man (Kinghan, *Brief Moment in the Sun*, 7. Francis was educated at the University of Glasgow and worked as a minister in Connecticut before returning to South Carolina in 1865 as a teacher for the American Missionary Association. He was the superintendent of the Saxon School, at which Rollin taught (Foner, *Freedom's Lawmakers*, 39). His wife, Catherine Romena Howell Cardozo (1843–1912), was from New Haven, Connecticut, and was the daughter of a white English woman and a West Indian man (Kinghan, *Brief Moment in the Sun*, 24).

443. Catherine F. McKinney Cardozo (1830–?) was born free, a member of the elite McKinney family of Charleston. She married Francis Cardozo's brother, Henry (1830–86), a tailor, in Charleston around 1855. They left the South just prior to the Civil War, living in Cleveland, Ohio, until 1865 (Henry Cardozo, household, Cleveland Ward 4, Cuyahoga, OH, US Census, 1860, database, Ancestry.com). Henry served as auditor of Charleston County and served in the state senate from 1870 to 1874 (Foner, *Freedom's Lawmakers*, 40).

444. Louisa Ann Carroll (1838–75) was born free in Charleston and married Alonzo Jacob Ransier (1834–82) in 1856. Like Rollin, Ransier was of mixed French and African descent and was born in Charleston. He worked as a clerk in a shipping firm prior to the Civil War. Along with Elliott, he served as associate editor of the *South Carolina Leader*. In 1868 he served as a delegate to the constitutional convention and was elected to the South Carolina House of Representatives from Charleston. Ransier joined Whipper in the legislature in advocating for women's suffrage. In 1870 he was elected lieutenant governor of South Carolina (William C. Hine, "Ransier, Alonzo Jacob," *South Carolina Encyclopedia*, 20 June 2016, https://www .scencyclopedia.org/sce/entries/ransier-alonzo-jacob/).

445. Robert Carlos DeLarge (1842–74) was the son of a woman born in Saint Domingue, like Frances Rollin's father. During the Civil War, DeLarge was employed by the Confederate navy. In 1868 he served as a delegate to the constitutional convention and was elected a member of the South Carolina House of Representatives alongside Whipper (Caryn E. Neumann, "DeLarge, Robert Carlos," *South Carolina Encyclopedia*, 17 May 2016, www.scencyclopedia .org/sce/entries/delarge-robert-carlos/).

446. Stephen A. Swails. See note 426.

Sunday, September 20

Did not go out to Church. Read Enoch Arden[447] for W. & Smalls.[448] In afternoon lots of company. Eve John Langston[449] H. J. Maxwell Purvis[450] & Randolph[451] spent ~~every~~ took tea with us. Nothing of importance. Mr Cardoza came to invite W. and I to dine with him on Monday.

Monday, September 21

Clear and bright Felt put out just a little because W did not come home in time to dress to go to the dinner. Had a pleasant time at Mr Cardoza's Randolph Haynes[452] and John Langs Mr & Mrs Adams.[453] John Langston spoke that

447. Published in 1864, Alfred Tennyson's *Enoch Arden* is a narrative poem about a fisherman who returns after a long absence to find that his wife has married another man.

448. Robert Smalls (1839–1915) was enslaved in Beaufort, South Carolina, prior to the Civil War. A maritime pilot, he seized control of the Confederate steamship *Planter* in May 1862 and freed himself, his crew, and his family, turning the vessel over to Union forces. He was elected to the South Carolina House of Representatives in 1868 ("Robert Smalls," Fort Sumter and Fort Moultrie National Historic Park, Reconstruction Era National Historic Park, National Parks Service, last updated 20 Feb. 2025, www.nps.gov/people/robert-smalls.htm).

449. John Mercer Langston (1829–97) was inspector general for the Freedmen's Bureau. Born free in Virginia, Langston became the first African American to pass the bar in Ohio in 1854. During the Civil War, he acted as a recruiter for the Fifty-Fourth and Fifty-Fifth Massachusetts. In 1864 he was one of the founding members and the first president of the National Equal Rights League, which advocated for full citizenship for Black men in compensation for military service (Joshua Johnson, "John Mercer Langston: A Civil Rights Activist," White House Historical Association, 5 May 2022, www.whitehousehistory.org/john-mercer-langston).

450. Henry W. Purvis (1843–1907) was the son of Harriet Forten Purvis (1810–75) and Robert Purvis (1810–98). After graduating from Oberlin, Purvis came to Columbia, South Carolina, as vice president of the Union League. In 1868 he was elected to the South Carolina House of Representatives representing Lexington County (Bacon, *But One Race*, 168).

451. Born in Kentucky and the child of free African Americans, Benjamin Franklin Randolph (1820–68) graduated from Oberlin College in 1862 and was ordained as a minister. He volunteered to serve as chaplain to the Twenty-Sixth US Colored Troops during the Civil War. Randolph was appointed assistant superintendent of Charleston schools by the Freedman's Bureau. He represented Orangeburg County in the 1868 constitutional convention and was elected a state senator and chair of the Republican state central committee (Foner, *Freedom's Lawmakers*, 175-76).

452. Possibly Henry E. Hayne (1840–?), who was born to an enslaved mother and a white father in Charleston and served in the First South Carolina Volunteers during the Civil War. He was a delegate to the South Carolina Constitutional Convention in early 1868 and was elected to the South Carolina Senate in 1870 (Michael Robert Mounter, "Hayne, Henry E.," *South Carolina Encyclopedia*, 15 Apr. 2016, www.scencyclopedia.org/sce/entries/hayne-henry-e/).

453. Ennals J. and Amelia Adams. See Ennals J. Adams in biographical notes.

evening and paid quite a tribute to Willie. Took the girls home. Saw Moses[454] and Emory spoke to them. ~~W. and Ell~~

Tuesday, September 22–Thursday, September 24
[No entries.]

Friday, September 25–Monday, September 28[455]

Tuesday, September 29
serve
thing burnt[456]

Wednesday, September 30–Thursday, 15 October
[No entries.]

Friday, October 16
Miller of Georgetown[457] S.C. by invitation to speak

Saturday, October 17
[No entry.]

Sunday, October 18
At Church today heard of the brutal murder of poor Randolph at Cokesbury on Friday last.[458]

Monday, October 19
Randolph buried this afternoon at Columbia.

Tuesday, October 20–Sunday, November 8[459]

454. This is likely Robert J. Moses (1838–1906), a white lawyer and editor who was Speaker of the South Carolina House from 1868 to 1872, when he became governor.

455. These pages are torn out of the diary.

456. It is not clear who has written these words.

457. Franklin F. Miller (1835–?) was a white member of the South Carolina House of Representatives representing Georgetown.

458. On 16 October 1868, Benjamin Franklin Randolph (see note 451) was assassinated by the Ku Klux Klan (Brook, *Accident of Color*, 120). Randolph was murdered while on a tour promoting the national Republican ticket. While changing trains in Hodges, South Carolina, he was gunned down by three white men in the presence of multiple witnesses ("Murder of B. F. Randolph, Negro Senator from Orangeburg," *Orangeburg [SC] News*, 24 Oct. 1868, 3). While two of the suspected attackers were identified and arrested, no one was ever brought to trial for the murder.

459. There are no entries written by Frances Rollin Whipper in the diary between 20 October and 8 November. Sometime in the middle to late 1870s, her daughter Winifred Whipper (1870–1907) has scribbled on the pages provided for 22 October and 23 October as well as several pages that follow.

Monday, November 9
W Whipper

Tuesday, November 10
Winnifred Whipper

Wednesday, November 11–Monday, November 16
[No entries.]

Tuesday, November 17
Spiced Beef[460]
Boil a shin of ten or twelve pounds of beef until the meat readily falls from the bone. Pick the meat to pieces and mash the gristle very fine rejecting all parts that are too hard to mash. Set the liquor in till cool; then take off all the fat. Boil the liquor down to a pint and a half, then return the meat to the liquor and while hot add any salt and pepper that may be needed, a half teaspoonful of cloves the same of cinnamon a little

Wednesday, November 18
nutmeg, a half teaspoon of parsely chopped fine a very little sage ~~and summer savory~~ Let it boil up once and put it into a deep dish to cool. Cut in thin slices for breakfast or tea.
Macaroni Pie
Boil the macaroni in water until quite tender, drain the water off, put into the baking pan, add a tablespoon of butter & 2 lb of grated cheese a pt milk salt pepper and mustard to taste

Thursday, November 19–Wednesday, December 30
[No entries.]

Thursday, December 31
Clean & salt for one hour.
Then put one qt of water to one string then cut two onions in slices ^& some parsley^ and put in, then put one teaspoon of ground ginger pepper and salt to taste. When done stir in to a bowl yolk of 6 eggs and juice of 4 lemons, stir this in to the fish and give one boil up.

460. This is written at the top of the page, between the date and the first line. It is unclear when these recipes were written in the diary.

Friday, January 1, 1869[461]

Saturday, January 2, 1869
William Rollin died morning of the 24th ^Feb. 80.^ about 2 oclock ~~Feb.~~ In the
65 years of his age.[462]

Memoranda[463]
Dec. Received from D. 50.00—
    for Board from 2 Nov

to 1st Dec		32.00
Dress		9.00
Bonnet	3.75	
Cloak &c		3.75
Stolen		3.00
Total		50.00

Cash Account. January[464]

Date.	Received.	Paid.
	5.00	

Cash Account. January

Date.	Received.	Paid.
Dickens		2.00
Paper		1.00
Slippers		1.37
Sacque a/c		2.00
Oil		.50
Oysters		.50

461. The last dated pages in the preprinted diary were for 1 January and 2 January 1869. These
pages may have allowed a diarist time to acquire a new diary for 1869 if they had not already
done so.

462. This is written sideways across the page.

463. Preprinted diaries often had pages at the back headed "Memoranda." This page follows
the page for 2 January 1869 and is followed by the "Cash Accounts" pages for January.

464. Rollin's diary contained two pages per month for cash accounts in the back of the diary.
On each of these pages, "Cash Account." is preprinted at the center top, followed by the month,
while "Date." (to the left) and "Received." and "Paid." (to the right) are preprinted as column
headers.

Cash Account. February.

Date.		Received.	Paid.
24	From Major D.	50.00	
25	For Board to 22nd		36.00
	Oil & [glues]		1.75
	[Skirt] & Oysters		1.80
	"		.50
	Dickens		2.00
	Paper		.25
	Diary		.55
	Lubin[465]		1.00
	Soap and paper		.30
	Shoes		.25[466]

June 28th. /69[467]

Memoranda

Sheets 2

PillowC 3

Bolster 1

Towels 2

Table C

Doilys 3

Shirts 2

Chemises 3

Drawers 1

H Skirts

Dresses

Night gown 1

Sacques 3

Nt Shirt 1

Bud[468] 8

465. Lubin's Extract. See note 2.

466. At this point Rollin stops using the preprinted cash accounts pages.

467. The date is handwritten at the top of the page. "Memoranda" is preprinted. The page is apparently intended for additional notes as it contains three column headers: one (to the left of the page) titled "Date," and two (to the right) titled "Dolls." and "Cts."

468. "Bud" may be a reference to Cyrenius Whipper (1866–?), William J. Whipper's son from his first marriage. He would have been three or four years old in June 1869.

Collars 4
Cuffs 2
Handk 2
Stock 3

"Oh North! give him beauty for ^rags^[469]
And honor O South! for his shame
Nevada coin thy golden crags
With Freedom's image and name.

Up and the dusky race
That sat in darkness long—
Be swift their feet as antelopes
And as behemoth strong.
　　　　　R Waldo Emerson

```
        14
         4
  ───   ───
  16     56
   3     50
  ───   ───
  48      6
  16     16
  ───   ───
  64     22
  50     12
  ───   ───
  14     34
         12
  ───   ───
        $35
```

469. This poem is copied on a blank page at the back of the diary, after the final "Memoranda"
page. Ralph Waldo Emerson's "Boston Hymn" was written to be read at Boston's Music Hall at
a concert given to celebrate the issuing of the Emancipation Proclamation on 1 January 1863. The
poem was first published in *Dwight's Journal of Music* on 24 January 1863 and was then collected
in Emerson's *May-Day and Other Pieces* (Ticknor and Fields, 1867). These two stanzas are the
nineteenth and twentieth of its twenty-two rhyming quatrains.

1.00 [illegible]
3.00 [Red]
3.00 Mr Bailey
1.75 Cotton Cloth
1.00 A. Howard
 .07 Braiding
 .50 Car fare
 .52

———

10.84

Letter from William Lloyd Garrison
to James T. Fields, 11 February 1868

Frances Rollin's introduction to William Lloyd Garrison was arranged by William Cooper Nell. On 4 February 1868 she went to the offices of the New England Freedmen's Aid Society in Boston and was thrilled to meet the famed abolitionist and editor of *The Liberator*. She arranged to come to his home in Roxbury, Massachusetts, on the following Thursday to read part of her manuscript to him. While illness prevented her venturing out on the appointed day, Garrison came to her at the Baileys' house less than a week later; it was probably during that visit that he gave Rollin this letter for the publisher James T. Fields. "Mr Wm Lloyd Garrison spent the morning with me," she writes excitedly in her 12 February entry. "I think him a grand noble soul." Her next mention of Garrison in the diary is on 4 March, when she writes: "This morning I took the MS. Mr Fields told me he would present Mr Garrison's letter to the firm . . . and would let me know."

Source: James Thomas Fields Papers, mssFI, box 23, The Huntington Library, San Marino, California. I am grateful to Ira Dworkin for telling me about this letter and sharing a scan with me.

Roxbury, Feb. 11, 1868.

Dear Mr. Fields:

The bearer of this, Miss Frances A. Rollin of Charleston, S.C., a young lady who has been well educated, desires to confer with you in regard to publishing a biography of Major M. Delany, which she has written con amore,[1] and very creditably to herself. Maj. Delany was the first colored citizen who received the

---

1. "Con amore" is Italian for "with love or devotion." This is how Rollin describes her work on the book a few days later in a diary entry on 3 March.

appointment of Major by President Lincoln, through the hands of Secretary Stanton,[2] and he is still retained in the service at Hilton Head.[3] He has long been well and favorably known to many who were engaged in the Anti-Slavery movement, but still better by those who are identified with him by complexion. He has had a somewhat eventful life, and has distinguished himself in various ways. He possesses uncommon versatility of talent; and whether as a writer for the press or a student in the field of science, whether as a platform orator or a military officer has "made his mark."

It was Major Delany who, when in England in 1860, (having just returned from a visit to Africa,) while attending an International Scientific and Statistical Congress, was received with immense éclat by that learned body when introduced by Lord Brougham; his Lordship calling the particular attention of Mr. Dallas, (then our Minister to the Court of St. James,) who was present, to the fact that no distinction of race or color was made in that assembly; a reference and a fact which so disgusted and enraged all the delegates from our Southern States that they forthwith withdrew from the sittings! The occurrence made a great sensation on both sides of the Atlantic at that time.[4]

The chief interest pertaining to this biography of Major Delany lies in the fact that his career will help to stifle the foolish cry of "inferiority of race," and furnishes additional incentives to labor for the elevation of a race ^people^ so long subjected to chains and slavery. Of course, it is for you to decide whether you will entertain the proposition for its publication.

Very truly yours,
Wm. Lloyd Garrison
James T. Fields, Esq.

2. In February 1865 Delany visited President Lincoln to propose a corps of African American soldiers led by African American officers. Lincoln asked Delany to take command and gave him a card introducing him to Secretary of War Edwin Stanton (1814–69). Less than a week later, Delany received his commission as major.

3. After the end of the Civil War, Delany remained on detached duty with the Freedmen's Bureau and was stationed in Hilton Head, South Carolina.

4. In 1860 Delany attended the International Statistical Congress in London. The meeting "drew together over 500 statisticians, civil servants, social reformers, and politicians for lengthy discussions on the collection, compilation, standardization, and comparability of social statistics" (Goldman, *Victorians and Numbers*, xliiv). Delany was invited to speak to the congress about the treatment of cholera (lv). One of its leaders, Lord Brougham, used the opportunity to embarrass the American ambassador, US vice president George M. Dallas, by facetiously pointing out "there [was] a negro present, a member of the Congress" (lv). Augustus Baldwin Longstreet, the official US delegate and an enslaver, walked out of the congress in protest (lvi).

Frank A. Rollin, Introduction to
Life and Public Services of Martin R. Delany

Rollin's *Life and Public Services of Martin R. Delany* was published in the
fall of 1868. She almost certainly wrote this introduction to the biography
after returning home to Charleston. She knew personally many of the African
American soldiers she discusses here. Indeed, as a teacher in post–Civil
War Charleston and an activist in her own right, Rollin was part of the
same "Emancipation Circuit" that these soldiers traveled.[1]

*Source: Life and Public Services of Martin R. Delany, Sub-Assistant Commissioner Bu-
reau Relief of Refugees, Freedmen, and of Abandoned Lands, and Late Major 104th U.S.
Colored Troops* (Boston: Lee & Shepard, 1868).

At the close of every revolution in a country, there is observed an effort for the
gradual and general expulsion of all that is effete, or tends to retard progress; and
as the nation comes forth from its purification with its existence renewed and
invigorated, a better and higher civilization is promised.

Before entering upon such an effort, it is usual to compute the aid rendered
in the past struggle for national existence, and the present state of the auxiliaries
in connection with it. In this manner, as the sullen roar of battle ceases, as the
war cloud fades out from our sky, we are enabled to look more soberly upon the
stupendous revolution, its causes and teachings, and to consider the men and new
measures developed through the agency, the material with which the country is
to be reconstructed.

In reviewing the history of the late civil war, it will be found, as in former
revolutions, that those who were able to master its magnitude were men who,

1. See Davis, *Emancipation Circuit.*

prior to the occasion, were almost wholly unknown, or claimed but a local reputation. Measures which before were deemed impracticable and inexpedient, in the progress of the war, were considered best adapted to meet the exigencies of the time. A race before persecuted, slandered, and brutalized, ostracized, socially and politically, have scattered the false theories of their enemies, and proved in every way their claim and identity to American citizenship in its every particular. While the war between sections has erased slavery from the statutes of the country, it has in no wise obliterated the inconsistent prejudice against color. Among the white Americans, since the rebellion, from the highest officer to the lowest subaltern, there is a recognized precedence for them, in view of their patriotism and valor in the hour of peril and treachery. They recognized their duty when Southerners had ignored it: for this we honor them; and none would gainsay an atom of the praise bestowed: the country had always honored and protected them at home and abroad, and in enhancing her prestige, they have added to their own as American citizens. But in the same dark hour of strife and treachery, there went forth from the despised and dusky sons of the republic a host, who, though faring differently, contributed no meagre offering to the cause of the Union. In the foremost rank of battle they stood, stimulated alone by their sublime faith in the future of their country, instead of being deterred by the disheartening experiences of the past. From their first hour in the rebellion to the last, theirs was a fierce, unequal contest; they were found enlisting, fighting, and even dying under circumstances from which the bravest Saxon would have been justified in shrinking. For them there was "death in the front and destruction in the rear"[2]—torture and death as prisoners in the rebel lines, and the perils of the mob in many of the loyal cities awaiting them when seen in the United States uniform. Despite all opposition, they have traced their history in characters as indestructible as they are brilliant, to the confusion of their enemies. On every field, negro heroism and valor have been proved by them in a manner which has established for their race a grandeur of character in American annals, that, when read by the unprejudiced eyes of futurity, will gleam with increased splendor amid their unfavorable surroundings; while in song and story their deeds of prowess will live forever,

2. Rollin quotes here from Lord Byron's *Childe Harold's Pilgrimage*, canto II, line 849: "Death in the front, Destruction in the rear!"

reflecting the glories of Port Hudson,[3] the crimson field of Olustee,[4] and the holy memories which cluster about Fort Wagner.[5]

Of an army of more than a quarter of a million men, less than a decade received promotion for their services. Lieutenant Stephen A. Swails, of Elmira, New York, a member of the Fifty-fourth Massachusetts Volunteers, had the honor of being first, for having signally distinguished himself both at Wagner and Olustee.[6] Later followed the promotion of Lieutenants Dufree,[7] Shorter,[8] James T. Trotter,[9] and Charles Mitchell,[10] from the Fifty-fifth Massachusetts Volunteers;

3. Port Hudson, Louisiana, was one of the last Confederate strongholds on the Mississippi River when it fell to the Union army on 9 July 1863. Early in the Union siege, which lasted forty-eight days, hundreds of African American soldiers from the First and Third Louisiana Native Guard Infantry participated in an unsuccessful assault that left many dead and wounded.

4. On 20 February 1864, Union forces engaged Confederate forces in Olustee, Florida. When Union forces recognized their defeat and began retreating toward Jacksonville, the Fifty-Fourth Massachusetts Infantry Regiment and the Thirty-Fifth US Colored Troops prevented an attack on their rear. In retaliation, the Confederates killed all wounded and captured Black soldiers.

5. The Second Battle of Fort Wagner, on Morris Island in Charleston harbor, was led by the Fifty-Fourth Massachusetts on 18 July 1863. While the soldiers managed to scale the walls of the fort, they were forced to retreat after suffering heavy casualties. Of the approximately 600 enlisted soldiers from the Fifty-Fourth engaged in the battle, more than 250 were killed, wounded, or missing (Emilio, *History of the Fifty-Fourth Regiment*, 91).

6. Stephen A. Swails (1832–1900) was the first African American commissioned as a combat officer. He was promoted to second lieutenant in the Fifty-Fourth Massachusetts Infantry in March 1864 and first lieutenant in April 1865. Swails later visited William and Frances Rollin Whipper after their marriage: see the 19 September entry in Rollin's diary.

7. William H. Dupree (1839–1934) was promoted to second lieutenant in the Fifty-Fifth Massachusetts Infantry. The spelling "Dufree" was, no doubt, a printer's error, as Rollin knew Dupree well enough to visit with him in Boston. See the 24 May entry in Rollin's diary.

8. John Freeman Shorter (1842–65) was one of the leaders in the fight for equal pay for Black soldiers. He was promoted to second lieutenant in the Fifty-Fifth Massachusetts Infantry. After being wounded at the Battle of Honey Hill in November 1864, he was honorably discharged but died in 1865.

9. James Monroe Trotter (1842–92) was promoted to second lieutenant in the Fifty-Fifth Massachusetts Infantry. Rollin writes about her visit with Trotter and his friend William H. Dupree in a diary entry for 24 May.

10. Charles Lewis Mitchel (1829–1912) was promoted to second lieutenant after being wounded at the Battle of Honey Hill in November 1864. He was later one of several "gentleman friends" at a party that Rollin attended on 13 April.

Lieutenants Peter Vogelsang (Quartermaster),[11] and Frank Welch,[12] from the Fifty-fourth Massachusetts Volunteers. Dr. Alexander Augusta, of Canada, had been previously appointed surgeon, with the rank of major.[13] Besides these, several complimentary promotions were given prior to the muster out of these two regiments. None of the officers above named have been retained in the service; one alone remains, who, during the rebellion, had attained the highest commission bestowed on any of the race by the government—that of Major of Infantry.[14] Him whom the government had chosen for this position we have made the subject of our work. His great grasp of mind and fine executive ability eminently befitted him for the sphere, and the success which attends his measures renders him a distinct and conspicuous character at his post. His career throughout life has been very remarkable. Prior to his present appointment his name was familiar with every advance movement relative to the colored people: once it fell upon the ear of the terror-stricken Virginians, in connection with John Brown, of Ossowatomie;[15] and scarcely had it been forgotten when it was borne back to us from the

11. At forty-six, Peter Vogelsang (1817–87) was the oldest member of the Fifty-Fourth Massachusetts Infantry. He was promoted to first lieutenant and regimental quartermaster in 1865.

12. Frank M. Welch (1841–1907) was promoted to first lieutenant in the Fifty-Fourth Massachusetts Infantry.

13. Alexander Thomas Augusta (1825–90) was born in Norfolk, Virginia, and trained as a physician in Toronto, Canada. He returned to the United States in 1863 to offer his services to the Union. He received a major's commission as surgeon with the Seventh US Colored Infantry and was later appointed head of a hospital for African Americans in Washington, DC ("Dr. Alexander Augusta," Ford's Theater, National Parks Service, www.nps.gov/foth/learn/historyculture/alexander-augusta.htm).

14. On 27 February 1865 Delany was commissioned a major in the US Colored Troops.

15. According to Rollin, John Brown sought Delany out in Chatham, Ontario, where Delany was practicing medicine and planning his African expedition. Brown informed Delany that he wanted "to make Kansas, instead of Canada, the terminus of the Underground Railroad; instead of passing the slave off to Canada, to send him to Kansas, and there test, on the soil of the United States territory, whether or not the right to freedom would be maintained where no municipal power had authorized" (Rollin, *Life and Public Services*, 87). Delany helped Brown organize a convention to meet with supporters, at which he later told Rollin "the idea of Harper's Ferry was never mentioned, or even hinted" (88). But as Robert Levine concludes, "Delany offered Rollin his account of the convention at a time when he would have been loathe to reveal his past insurrectionist activities. The evidence suggests that Brown had called the Chatham convention with the intention of gaining the support of black leaders for a plan to organize and lead a rebellion of the slaves of the United States" (Levine, *Martin Delany, Frederick Douglass*, 287n10).

Statistical Congress at London, encircled with the genius of Lord Brougham.[16] To no more advantageous surroundings than were enjoyed by the masses he owes his successes; hence his achievements may be safely argued as indicative of the capability and progress of the race whose proud representative he is. The isolated and degraded position assigned the colored people precluding the possibility of gaining distinction, whenever one of their number lifts himself by the strength of his own character beyond the prescribed limits, ethnologists apologize for this violation of their established rules, charging it to some few drops of Saxon blood commingling with the African. But in the case of the individual of whom we write, he stands proudly before the country the blackest of the black, presenting in himself a giant's powers warped in chains, and evidencing in his splendid career the fallacy of the old partisan theory of negro inferiority and degradation.[17]

In this history will be noticed certain strong characteristics peculiarly his own, which are traceable more to the circumstances of his birth than his race. Aiming to render a faithful biography of this remarkable man, we narrate minutely his singularly active and eventful life, which, in view of the narrow limits apportioned to him, will bear favorable comparison with the great Americans of our time.

Charleston, S. C., October 19th, 1868

16. See appendix A for Garrison's letter to Fields, in which he discusses this event, and note 4 there for more details of the congress.

17. Delany took pride in the blackness of his skin and his unmixed heritage. Later in *Life and Public Services*, Rollin quotes Frederick Douglass as saying, "I thank God for making me a man simply; but Delany always thanks him for making him a *black man*" (19). As Robert Levine points out, it is not clear whether Douglass actually said those words (introduction to *Martin R. Delany*, 3)

Editorial Review of "Life of Maj. Delaney," 31 October 1868

This brief editorial notice of Rollin's *Life and Public Services of Martin R. Delany* was the first of three reviews of the book to appear in the *Christian Recorder*. This piece is almost certainly by Benjamin Tucker Tanner (1835–1923), African Methodist Episcopal minister, who began his long tenure as editor of the *Recorder* in June 1868.

Source: Christian Recorder, 31 October 1868, 122.

LIFE OF MAJ. DELANEY

We have perused this work. It would doubtless have read a great deal better had we not been so well known to the subject and for years too. Why in 1844 we carried his paper "The Mystery," from its office, No. 44 Hand street. As a writer, Miss Rollin gives evidence of possessing a germ, which if cultivated will eventually bloom into something more beautiful and vigorous. She seems to be enamoured with her hero. Does he let his hat fall, he lets it fall in a manner altogether princely. None could have done it with the same dignity. Indeed herein lies the weakness of the book. In her eyes every mole hill over which the Major passed was as the Alps. Take for a sample chapter xviii, entitled "Private Council at Washington." Had the strangely adventurous life of the Major and successful as well, have been told with no attempt at magnifying every incidental event, it would have been a greater success. There is enough of the really great about the Major, without the use of a microscope; for no American Negro has attained to as many substantial points of honor as he. Withal the work should be on the shelf of all who desire to keep posted.

Review of *Life and Public Services,*
7 November 1868

The identity of the author of this review, who goes only by "Sometimes," is unclear. The only other piece published under this name in the *Christian Recorder* is a glowing review of *What Answer?*, a novel by the white activist and orator Anna Dickinson (1842–1932). Dickinson was known as a powerful speaker in the service of antislavery and women's rights and, after the Civil War, threw herself into the cause of Black civil rights. Her novel, published by Fields, Osgood, and Company (the successors to Ticknor and Fields) in 1869, was set during the Civil War and featured an interracial marriage. "Sometimes" asserts that *What Answer?* "should be in the hands of every man in the land. It is a book as noble, as enthusiastic and as brave against America's greatest weakness and crime—Caste—as was 'Uncle Tom's Cabin' against slavery."[1] The same reviewer does not comment on Dickinson's private life or criticize her writing style, as he does in this review of Rollin's book.

Source: "Sometimes," "Miss Rollin's Book of Major Delaney," *Christian Recorder,* 7 Nov. 1868, 1.

For the Christian Recorder.
MISS ROLLIN'S BOOK OF MAJOR DELANEY.
BY SOMETIMES.
Mr. Editor: The long expected book, "Life and Services of Martin R. Delaney," by Frank A. Rollins, has at last put in an appearance. The book has been eagerly looked for, not only on account of the man whose career it was to present, but we were all anxious to know with what amount of strength and grace the authoress would wield the pen; for the book is the work of a woman, notwithstanding the

---

1. "Sometimes," "Anna E. Dickinson's Book," *Christian Recorder* 8, no. 35 (21 Nov. 1868):1.

rather masculine Frank, which the writer seems to have preferred to the more gentle and certainly more feminine Frances.

Miss Rollin is a native of Charleston, S.C. She received her education at the High School, Philadelphia; has had some experience in school teaching in her native city. Since turning her attention to book-making, she has performed another very sensible act, in taking to herself a husband. So that she now rejoices in the name of Mrs. Whipper, her husband being the Hon. Gentleman who bears that name, member of the South Carolina Legislature. But what of the book? We are free to express that it is not without faults, and not a few at that. Certainly a simpler and less strained style would have been, by far, more acceptable. The writer, too, has spread her material over too large a space, and thereby greatly weakened her effort. Yet there is much to commend; probably as much as there is to find fault with. Judged by the average of books, the work is a success; but when compared with the life of "Josiah Quincey,"[2] or "Parton's Jackson,"[3] it dwindles into insignificance. We were, therefore, hopeful, that Miss Rollin would give us a book in which we could glory—but with sorrow we say that we are disappointed. True, her subject might not have been the most fruitful one—but then she might have given us what she has, in a much more acceptable and less labored manner. The book, with a few exceptions, is written in very good English; something by the bye, one does not always meet with, even in books—and then she has brought to her work an enthusiasm which at times fairly make her pages gleam with intellectual life. On the whole, we doubt not that she has made as much of the subject as the material would allow, and the Major may congratulate himself on having the services of so earnest and felicitous a writer. As a book *for colored people*, it will serve a useful end, as it has presented the history of a man who, at best, has been but poorly understood and too little appreciated. For Major Delaney, with all his eccentricities of character and intense egotism, has performed noble service for the race.

Miss Rollin is a *little* pedantic. She seems to have a contempt for simple language. She glories in adjectives. Plain "Mr" will not do for her, and even "Hon." and "Rev." must be prefaced by some higher sounding title. Thus she parades the "distinguished" Douglass[4]—the "great and generous hearted gentleman" Lord

---

2. Edmund Quincy's *Life of Josiah Quincy of Massachusetts* was published by Ticknor and Fields in 1867. Rollin notes reading this book on 16 May 1868.

3. James Parton's *Life of Andrew Jackson* was published by Mason Brothers in three volumes in 1859–60.

4. African American author and activist Frederick Douglass (1818–95).

Brougham[5]—"the learned" J. W. C. Pennington[6]—the "zealous" Mr. Dawes[7]—the "accomplished scholar" Geo. B. Vashon[8]—the "chivalric Governor" Joseph Ritner[9]—the "eminent Judge" Wm. B. McClure[10]—the "eloquent" Charles L. Remond[11]—the "able and accomplished" Henry Ward Beecher[12]—the "time honored" Joshua Leavitt[13]—the "dauntless and inspire apostle of Liberty"—Wm. Lloyd

5. This description of Henry Brougham, First Baron Brougham and Vaux (1778–1868) is taken from Delany's own account of the International Statistical Congress in London in 1868 (qtd. in Rollin, *Life and Public Services*, 117).

6. It is Delany who is quoted in *Life and Public Services* calling the African American minister James W. C. Penningon (1808–70) "learned." Writing about the limited opportunities for education for African Americans in the antebellum period, Rollin writes:

> Then, no college or academy of note in the United States received within its walls a black student, no matter how deserving, save under obligations hereafter to be mentioned, not excepting Dartmouth, ostensibly established for Indians, nor the great, independent Harvard, of ancient pride. "At this time," said Martin Delany, "or shortly after, the *now* learned J. W. C. Pennington, D. D., who received the degree of Doctor of Divinity at the University of Heidelberg, under Prince Leopold, president, was standing ether behind the door of Yale College, or perhaps on its threshold, listening to instructions given in the various branches by the professors, and considering it a privilege, as it was the closest proximity allowed him towards entering its *sacred* precincts as a student" (*Life and Public Services*, 41).

7. William Dawes, a white abolitionist and Oberlin College trustee.

8. George Boyer Vashon (1824–78) was the first African American graduate of Oberlin University. He read law and passed the New York bar in 1848. He was an abolitionist, a teacher, and a practicing lawyer prior to the Civil War. At the time Rollin was writing *Life and Public Services*, Vashon was teaching at Howard University, one of the first Black professors to do so.

9. Joseph Ritner (1780–1869) was the governor of Pennsylvania from 1835 to 1839. Rollin calls Ritner "chivalric" for his anti-slavery views (*Life and Public Services*, 52). According to her, while Delany was editing *The Mystery* in Pittsburgh, he "charged a certain colored man with treachery to his race by assisting the slave-catchers, who, at that time, frequented Pennsylvania and other free states" (51). When Delany was found guilty of libel and fined $250, Governor Ritner remitted the fine (51–52).

10. William B. McClure (1807–61) was the judge in a second case brought against Delany after the success of the first resulted in a $250 fine. According to Rollin, this follow-on case "resulted in a verdict of acquittal without the jury leaving the box" (*Life and Public Services*, 53).

11. Charles Lenox Remond (1810–73) was a Black abolitionist and lecturer who was widely known as an accomplished orator.

12. Henry Ward Beecher (1813–87) was the most famous minister in the United States from approximately 1850 to 1880.

13. The white minister Joshua Leavitt (1794–1873) was well known as a writer, editor, and publisher of abolitionist literature.

Garrison,[14] &c. While she very gravely informs us that of an army of more than a quarter of a million men less than a *decade* received promotion. And thus we might continue to pick out objections all through the book, but we forbear. Miss Rollin has made a fair beginning; she will do better in the future; she exhibits the elements of a writer of no mean order.

Messrs. Lee & Sheppard, the publishers, deserve the thanks of the book-reading public for the handsome manner in which they have presented it. The book contains 367 pages, is richly bound in cloth, and sells for $1.50. The last 70 pages of the book are devoted to the writings and speeches of the Major—terse, prosy and tremendously metaphysical.

New York, Oct. 19, 1868

14. William Lloyd Garrison. See biographical notes.

Review of *Life and Public Services,* 20 March 1869

Perhaps because the review by "Sometimes" was so negative, the *Christian Recorder* published another review of Rollin's book four months later. This one is signed "Rufus" and may be by African American Baptist minister and editor Rufus L. Perry (1834–95). In 1869 Perry lived in Brooklyn and edited *Freedmen's Torchlight*, a publication of the African Civilization Society (ACS). The ACS was an emigrationist organization founded by Martin Delany and Henry Highland Garnet in 1858. With the beginning of the Civil War, however, the ACS shifted its focus to education and in 1866 began publishing *Freedom's Torchlight*, "devoted to the temporal and spiritual interests of the Freedmen; and adapted to their present need of instruction in regard to simple truths and principles relating to their life, liberty, and pursuit of happiness."[1] He also edited the *People's Journal* at around the same time.

Source: "Life and Services of Martin R. Delaney," *Christian Recorder*, 20 March 1869, 1.

LIFE AND SERVICES OF MAJOR MARTIN R. DELANEY
BY FRANK A. ROLLIN

This book is at once a chronicle of the leading events connected with the colored race for the last 30 years in America, and a *lively, strongly* written, *truthful* biographical sketch of one of the most remarkable men of this age. The book shows a capacity and knowledge of details in authorship, that will win laurels for Frank A. Rollin in future.

1. Quoted in Wellman, *Brooklyn's Promised Land*, 126.

It is decidedly the best book of its kind that has yet emanated from a colored author in this country, and opens up a vast field of labor and research to coming biographers and historians of the colored race.

The services of Maj. Delaney to his country and race are detailed in a straight-forward manner devoid of romance or attempt at fiction, and present a record to history that will do much toward dispelling the delusion entertained in relation to the capacity of his race.

Maj. Delaney as editor, physician, traveller, explorer, lecturer, or political econ-omist, seems to have seized the work with giant grasp, and hold on with almost superhuman tenacity till attaining to a position hitherto seemingly impossible to men of his race. He has received even-handed justice, however, from the author of this work, for which posterity should be thankful.

There are some minor errors, historical and statistical, in the book—these are excusable in consideration of the author's inexperience in this line.

Maj. Delaney's life is a vivid illustration of what may be accomplished by a man of indomitable will and perseverance, when actuated by the grand emotion of patriotism and a pure self-sacrificing love of *equal* and *exact* justice.

From verifying facts which have come to our knowledge we are compelled to accord to Maj. Delaney a place in the front ranks of American Statesmen and philanthropists. Commencing in his early manhood, he has, for a quarter of a century, battled against the terrible cast—prejudice—which has kept his people under the iron heel of oppression for two hundred and fifty years; and though battling under the trying disadvantages of extreme poverty, sometimes wanting even the necessaries of life. Yet has he succeeded in accomplishing more *pract-ical* good for his people than any man of his race now living in this country. The highest need of praise that can be according to him is, that Martin R. Delaney is now a *poor man*. He has ever been in the pioneer ranks of the most radical of the friends of liberty, and always prepared to make such sacrifices as were necessary to bring about the grand consummation, the benefits of which are now *partially* accorded to his people. The martyred Lincoln was the first of the men in power to recognize his merits and fully appreciate his labors for the cause of humanity; and, as a poor reward, for a life-time of self-sacrifice and privation, placed him in a position which thus seemed the stepping-stone to the highest honors attainable by any man. The war closed, however, but Delaney's usefulness did not end with its close, and he was retained in the service of his country as a Sub. Asst. Com. of the Bureau, R. F. and A. L.,[2] when many of the volunteer officers of the veteran

2. The official name of the agency usually known as the Freedmen's Bureau was the Bureau of Refugees, Freeman, and Abandoned Lands.

army of the Republic were mustered out of the service. His retention, we believe, was at the request of Generals Sickles[3] and Scott,[4] which request was nobly responded to by Secretary Stanton.[5]

His services in this position have been invaluable, and his plans—always original—uniformly successful.

It affords pleasure to extend to Frank A. Rollin the highest credit for thus adding the brightest pages to our history as a race; and we predict alike for the subject of the "historical" biography and its author, a future that will be a proud record of reference for our people for all time to come.

We venture to predict that the end of Martin R. Delaney's usefulness is not yet, and that, in these happy and peaceful times, he will receive a proper recognition of his merits from a grateful and happy people.

It is a proud moment to him to find the labor of his life crowned with success, and it is not asking much of the American people to request that he be permitted to pass the last days of his useful life in some high position of honor and trust in the Republic.

RUFUS

3. When the Civil War ended, Major General Daniel Sickles (1819–1914) became military governor of South Carolina until 1867.

4. Brigadier General Robert Kingston Scott was assistant commissioner of the South Carolina Bureau of Refugees, Freedmen and Abandoned Lands from 1865 to 1868.

5. Secretary of State Edwin Stanton (1814–69). See appendix A, note 2.

Daniel E. Murray,
"Sketch of Frances Rollin Whipper"

Daniel E. Murray (1851–1925) was an African American bibliographer and historian who worked as an assistant librarian at the Library of Congress from 1871 to 1922. Murray's correspondence with Frances Rollin Whipper in 1901 came out of his lifelong interest in African American history and authorship. The sketch below, which is based on and includes portions of Rollin Whipper's two letters to Murray, was likely intended to be part of Murray's "Historical and Biographical Encyclopedia of the Colored Race throughout the World," which he died without publishing.[1]

The letters included here are no longer extant; they exist only in the typescript that Murray left upon his death. I have made small corrections for readability when words have clearly been mistranscribed, which are explained in footnotes. I have added words and punctuation in brackets when their absence seems clearly to be a mistake on the part of whomever did the typescript. I have silently removed quotation marks when they do not seem necessary. When it is not obvious, I have also done my best to indicate in footnotes when the narrative shifts from Rollin Whipper's voice to Murray's.

Source: Typescript, Daniel Murray Papers, Micro 577, Wisconsin Historical Society, Madison.

---

1. Taylor, *Original Black Elite*, 327, 376.

FRANCES ANN ROLLIN WHIPPER
(Distinguished Literateur and Critic)

In 1868 there was published from the house of Lee and Shepard, Boston, Mass., a well written and in some respects ambitious book entitled: "Life and Public Services of Major Martin R. Delany, etc[.]," by Frank Rollin. Following the general principle then believed as to authorship it was accepted as settled that Frank Rollin was a white man who had seen some profit, prospectively in exploiting the career of the colored Major, and few if any independent of inside information, thought otherwise.

The prevailing opinion among the white people naturally fixed upon that view, few believing any colored writer could produce a book with well turned rhetorical sentences, with orderly digested matter and each event in the narrative following in its proper sequence[2] and relation to the whole. Another feature of the book which strengthened the idea that the author was a white man, was found in the fact that, all proper dates were present, an uncommon occurrence in books by Afro-American authors. It is true, though it is a pity it is true, that nearly every book written or compiled by an Afro-American author is built on the fiction plan, to be read and then thrown aside wholly wanting in a reference quality, which every book secures through being filled with accurate dates in regards to the matters[3] treated. The Afro-American author is great on books of the essay order, but few, through lack of accurate dates have any permanent value.

A writer speaking on the subject affirmed that if every book written by them was thrown into the sea, the loss would not be appreciable, since they have written so little of a permanent character.[4]

For years I had seen and handled the book referred to but never a suspicion came into my head that the writer was other than a white man and the fact that the book was written by the lady whose name is at the head of this sketch was learned in an accidental manner. I was seeking matter and dates for my sketch of Major Delany and consulted Col. Hinton's "Life of John Brown"[5] who had some relation with Major Delany in Canada. I there found it stated that "Frank

---

2. "Sequence" was typed as "srquence," with no correction made.

3. "Matters" was typed as "natters," with no correction made.

4. This paragraph is not indented in the original.

5. Murray refers here to *John Brown and His Men* (Funk and Wagnalls, 1894), by white journalist and author Richard J. Hinton (1830–1901).

Rollin," was Mrs. Whipper of South Carolina,[6] not being disposed to accept un-questioned statements that can be verified on inquiry I wrote to Mrs. Whipper at Beaufort, S. C., and got the desired information. Further she gave me some particulars of reconstruction days that I believe sufficiently interesting to incor-porate in this sketch.

Mrs. Whipper during her residence in Washington enjoyed the reputation of being a very fine conversationalist. She and Miss Lucy E. Moten, Principal of the Normal School of Washington City[7] being very highly rated. Mrs. Whipper was very quick at repartee, as the following incident will show: It was the practice of some Southern women of low origin to embrace every opportunity possible to covertly insult nicely dressed colored ladies riding in the street cars. One of them tried her game on Mrs. Whipper, who was then a clerk in the Land Office. Said she to Mrs. W., "I would like to get a nice cook, one like you, can you read?" Mrs. W. quickly replied, "I should scarcely venture to tell you yes, yet I am a clerk in the Land Office."

Miss Kate Moten was the first colored clerk appointed in the Agricultural Dept. under Commissioner Le Duc,[8] recalls a similar experience.[9] The day of her advent she heard one of the white clerks say to a group, "I suppose you know we got in some new dye stuff this morning."

---

6. In *John Brown and His Men*, Hinton writes of Martin Delany's "biographer Frank Rollins (Mrs. Whipper, of South Carolina)" (32). Murray may have known Frances Rollin Whipper personally, as both seem to have attended St. Luke's Episcopal Church in Washington, DC. Murray lived in DC from about 1869 until his death in 1925. Rollin Whipper lived there from 1882 to approximately 1899.

7. The words "of Washington City" are written by hand in what seems to have been a space left blank when the sketch was typed. Lucy Ella Moten (1854–1933) was principal of the Miner Normal School in Washington, DC, from 1883 to 1920. The Miner School trained African American teachers. Out of a desire to better care for her students, Moten enrolled in med-ical school at Howard University, receiving her MD in 1897 (Stephen Preskill, "Moten, Lucy Ellen," *American National Biography*, 1999, published online Feb. 2000, https://doi.org/10.1093/anb/9780198606697.article.0900523).

8. Kate E. Moten (1857–1914) was Lucy Moten's sister. She worked as a copyist in the Depart-ment of Agriculture and then in the Recorder of Deeds office (*Hearings before Subcommittee of House Committee on Appropriations*, 58). She worked there at the same time as Rollin Whipper (Womack, *Official Register of the United States*, 1034). William Gates Le Duc (1823–1917) was commissioner of agriculture from 1877 to 1881.

9. The words "recalls a similar experience" are handwritten above the typewritten line.

The novelty of colored clerks in every branch of the public service has long since passed and no insidious comments are now heard on that head. The unchristian, nay more, inhuman color prejudice is dying a slow death; but dying all the same.

FRANCES ANN ROLLIN WHIPPER

Was born in the city of Charleston, South Carolina, November 19th, 1844.[10] Says she in her letter conveying the information,

I could not have chosen a more auspicious time had the choice devolved upon me, for it was in the days when the free colored people were at the zenith of their prosperity. They possessed the trades with few exceptions and colored workmen were generally preferred. My father was of French extraction, a descendant of one of the proudest and most honored families of St. Domingo. At a very early age I was sent to the parish school in Charleston taught by an old French family. I was too young to go unattended. French was taught and I was lisping French long before I could clearly speak English. We had a number of excellent private schools for the education of the free colored people, in fact neighboring cities like Savannah and Augusta sent their well to do pupils to Charleston for instruction. Two of the schools were taught by white men, known as the Wilbour and Wood schools. They were of a very high grade, very exclusive and quite expensive. Wilbour was the son of a slave broker, and very devoted to his pupils. His folks[11] had means and why he taught a school kept for colored children was a mystery never made clear to us as children. He kept his school open each day including Saturdays apparently anxious to avoid the loss of a day. Suddenly he gave up teaching and shortly after his mind was impaired, which necessitated his incarceration in an asylum of which he [is] an inmate to-day. My father designing to have me go abroad to enter a French boarding school at Paris[12] employed private teachers to prepare me. Not aware of the benefits in store for me I showed an unwillingness to go so far from home and it was finally settled I should attend school in Philadelphia, particularly since I had made many friends in that city while visiting in 1857 in company with

10. Rollin Whipper was born on 19 November 1845, not 1844. See the introduction for a contextualization of Rollin Whipper's account of her life in these letters.
11. "Folks" was typed as "floks," but someone has added a curved line to indicate that the *o* and the *l* should be reversed.
12. "Paris" was typed as "Parus." An "is" was written on top of the typewritten *u*.

my father who annually went North to buy goods. I was regularly installed in 1859 with the family of Mr. Morris Brown, formerly a Charlestonian,[13] and took the course at the Institute for Colored Youths,[14] The Hon. E. D. Bassett our first Minister to Haiti[15] was then principal. Here I came in contact with and formed a lasting friendship with two of the noblest, purest and best women that ever graced the earth, Mrs. Sarah M. Douglass[16] and Miss Grace A. Mapps.[17] The beautiful lives of these pioneers of higher culture for women are a benediction and inspiration for the women of our time. The breaking out of the War of the Rebellion in 1861 cut off my supplies from home and interrupted my studies. This within a few short months of graduation. Among my class mates of the class of '64 were Jno. W. Cromwell of Wash. D. C.,[18] Jas. Baxter of Newark, N. J.,[19] and Mrs. F. D. Loudin of Ravenna, Ohio.[20] Soon after the fall of Charleston I returned home

13. Morris Brown Jr. (1812–1890), a shoe and bootmaker, was the son of Morris Brown Sr., American Methodist Episcopal (AME) bishop and one of the founders of the AME church in Charleston.

14. I have removed a closed quotation mark that appeared here in the typescript.

15. Ebenezer Don Carlos Bassett (1833–1908) was principal of the Institute for Colored Youth (ICY) from 1856 to 1869.

16. Sarah Mapps Douglass (1806–82) was a teacher at the ICY from 1853 to 1866.

17. Grace A. Mapps (1835–97) was principal teacher of the Female Department at the ICY from 1852 to 1865.

18. John Wesley Cromwell (1846–1927) was born to enslaved parents in Virginia, but by 1851, his father had purchased his family's freedom. They moved to Philadelphia, where Cromwell graduated from the ICY in 1864. He went on to become a teacher, a lawyer, and a clerk in the US Treasury Department ("John Wesley Cromwell [1846–1927]," A Great Thing for Our People: Institute for Colored Youth in the Civil War Era, online exhibit, Falvey Library, Villanova University, https://exhibits.library.villanova.edu/institute-colored-youth/graduates /john-wesley-cromwell, accessed 12 Oct. 2023).

19. James M. Baxter Jr. (1845–1909) was born in Philadelphia and graduated from the ICY in 1864. He became principal of the State Street Public School in Newark, New Jersey, at the age of nineteen and worked there for the rest of his career ("James M. Baxter, Jr. [1845–1909]," Great Thing for Our People, https://exhibits.library.villanova.edu/institute-colored-youth /graduates/james-m-baxter-jr-bio, accessed 12 Oct. 2023).

20. Harriet C. Johnson Loudin (1845–1907) graduated from the ICY in 1864 and became a teacher ("Harriet C. Johnson [1845–1907]," Great Thing for Our People, https://exhibits.library .villanova.edu/institute-colored-youth/graduates/harriet-c-johnson, accessed 12 Oct. 2023). She married musician Frederick Loudin in 1870. Loudin was part of the second company of the Fisk Jubilee Singers (1874–78) and, after the American Missionary Association ceased its support of the troupe, the Loudins reorganized it "as a black-owned joint stock company." Harriet Loudin was the company's manager (Cook, "Finding Otira," 92). The Loudins lived in Ravenna, Ohio, near where Frederick was born.

and for a while taught under the auspices of the Freedmen's[21] Bureau. Later I taught for an increased salary under the American Missionary Association of New York, our Consul at St. Thomas, W. I., Mr. Mahlon Van Horn, being principal.[22] I mention this since it was while teaching under these auspices that I undertook the preparation of the Life of Major Delany. This was in 1866, the next year, 1867, and part of 1868, I spent in Boston superintending the publication of the book. After completing my book in Boston I hied back again to South Carolina, and on the 17th of September, 1868, I was married to William J. Whipper, a man of Northern birth and education, a lawyer by profession and at the time of our marriage one of the most conspicuous figures of the Reconstruction era in the Southland.[23] It is proper here to say Mr. Whipper possessed the necessary ability and courage to command any honor in the gift of his party, while his wife had all the ambition, zeal, and bravery to urge him to the front. She was his trusted aid in his political battles and like the Duchess of Marlborough the last to acknowledge defeat, at times he chafed under her guardianship, to which she would reply, "You may be a wiser and better politician, but I fancy my womanly intuition can read more accurately the signs of the coming storm than all your weather-wise experience." Always alert to her husband's interest she was often able to assist him in thwarting and over-turning many of the well laid schemes of his political opponents. Speaking of this Mrs. Whipper says: "When the 'Whippers' were spoken of it did not always mean his immediate followers, consequently when the 'Sceptre departed from Judah' following the election of 1876[24] I reaped no little share of the bitterness displayed by our vindictive and victorious enemies. Previous to my marriage in '68 I served as clerk to the Judiciary Committee of the South Carolina House of Representatives of which Mr. Whipper was chairman[.] I continued to serve as such sometime after my marriage and daily came into contact with the

21. "Freedmen's" was typed as "Freedmens'," with no correction.

22. Mahlon Van Horne was appointed US consul to St. Thomas in the Danish West Indies in 1896. He was impeached and removed from office in 1903.

23. The next three sentences seem to be Murray's interruption of Rollin's narrative in her letter.

24. Genesis 49:10 (King James Version) reads, "The sceptre shall not depart from Judah, nor a lawgiver from between his feet, until Shiloh come; and unto him shall the gathering of the people be." Here Rollin is noting the end of Reconstruction with the election of Rutherford B. Hayes in 1876. In order to secure the presidency in a contested election, Hayes agreed to cede the state governments of the South to Democratic control.

most prominent men of the State black and white of both political parties and I can honestly say at this distance from those stirring times, that with all the errors growing out of the lack of experience in Legislative matters, the colored leaders are worthy of the highest praise and the impartial historians of the future will fittingly accord them their just dues somedays when Truth shall get a hearing. It was customary among the prominent South Carolina politicians to get their views before the people through the medium of a personal organ. My husband had his and as editor I acquired some little experience in newspaper work both as editor and contributor. I write now occasionally an article for the press under a nom de plume, sometimes for others. From 1868 to 1876 I was prosperous and happy in the latter year the treachery of Rutherford B. Hayes to the Republican governments of the South caused their overthrow and with it my personal and political aspirations in the Southland vanished as completely as the flimsy realities of a dream.

My husband left the State in 1882 and during the Arthur administration[25] sought to begin life anew by practicing law in Washington, D. C. and in March of that year I was appointed to a clerical position in the Land Office. In 1885 my husband returned to South Carolina to take an important case and unfortunately for his family reentered politics. On the accession to power of the Democrats under Pres. Cleveland[26] I was June 30th, 1885, dismissed from my position. "Offensive partisanship"[27] was the cause assigned, but in further explanation I was told, that my husband's holding an office (having been elected County Judge) made me ineligible.

Immediately my venerable friend, Hon. Frederick Douglass, then Recorder of Deeds for the District of Columbia,[28] gave me a place in his office which I held[29] until C. H. J. Taylor's incumbency of the office in 1893 closed my connection

25. Republican Chester Alan Arthur (1829–86) was president of the United States from 1881 to 1885.

26. In 1885 Stephen Grover Cleveland (1837–1908) was the first Democratic candidate to be elected to the presidency after the Civil War.

27. Murray used double quotation marks here, but I have changed them to single quotation marks as this is still Rollin Whipper speaking.

28. The activist and author Frederick Douglass (1818–95) was recorder of deeds in Washington, DC, from 1881 to 1886.

29. "Held" was typed as "helf," with no correction made.

with official life in Washington.[30] In the election of 1888 Mr. Whipper was again elected County Judge on the Harrison ticket,[31] but with the rest of the ticket counted out by the County Canvassers. He refused to surrender his office, the contestant appealed to the County Court and obtained a favorable decision[.] Mr. Whipper appealed to the Supreme Court of the State, but was thrown into jail on contempt proceedings before the County Court. The Supreme Court held the case for 13 months in the hope that the Republicans remaining in jail, awaiting the decision, would surrender their rights and party to obtain their liberty, which they did one at a time. Mr. Whipper alone fought the matter to a finish, his indomitable spirit sustaining him in refusing to surrender. Though broken in health and fortune he continued the struggle until the final decision of the Supreme Court divested him of his rights. In the meantime I supported the family in Washington. (Like Horatius she held the bridge.) We had five children, two of whom died in infancy while three survive to honorable manhood and womanhood. My three children, Winifred,[32] Ionia Rollin, and Leigh Rollin, are products of Washington Public Schools and Howard University. The girls are now engaged in teaching at Washington, D. C., one of whom is also pursuing a medical course at Howard University. Ill health caused me to leave Washington and seek my old home a veritable[33] "Sleepy Hollow"[34] notwithstanding the terrible blight Tillmanism[35] like a pall, cast over this fair land.

Being so pleased with the above I further solicited Mrs. Whipper to give me additional information touching the reconstruction period and some additional dates, to which she kindly responded.

---

30. Charles Henry James Taylor (1857–99) was recorder of deeds from 1894 to 1896. Rollin Whipper likely worked in the Recorder of Deeds Office until a bit later than she indicates here, as she is listed in the 1895 record of civil employees (Womack, *Official Register of the United States*, 1034).

31. Republican Benjamin Harrison (1833–1901) was elected president in 1888 and served from 1889 to 1893.

32. "Winifred" was typed as "Winfred," with no correction.

33. "Veritable" was typed as "vertiable," with no correction made.

34. "Sleepy Hollow" is a reference to Washington Irving's short story "The Legend of Sleepy Hollow," first published in 1820.

35. "Tillmanism" was a movement led by white South Carolina governor Benjamin "Pitchfork" Tillman (1847–1918). Its hallmarks were violence against African Americans, white supremacy, hostility to Northern business interests, and a restoration of aristocratic Southern white leadership.

In her second letter she writes:

Beaufort, South Carolina,
August 24th, 1901.
Daniel Murray, Esq.,
Assistant Librarian of Congress,
Wash. D. C.

Dear Mr. Murray:

In compliance with your request I have jotted down a few items as I thought of them, making up in accuracy what they lack in finish. I thank you sincerely that you deem me worthy to be inscribed among those who have contributed to the progress and uplifting of the race. I have always classed myself with those who never reached the mark they had in sight, though perhaps in some other sphere, "the soul must win the goal that erst were possible."[36]

First I wish to modify my previous statement as to my visit to Boston. I felt it was longer than the fact. It was from Nov. 1867 to Aug. 1868. Those months contained such a wealth of literary enjoyment that the memory of them remains with me still.

The lectures that Winter[37] I think had never been surpassed in the eminence of the persons appearing, if ever equalled? I heard Dickens on his first Boston night and being the only one of my race in the Hall, because of the fabulous prices demanded by speculators for tickets, I divided in some measure with him the attention of the audience. During my stay in Boston I met frequently the golden tongued orator, Wendell Phillips, and was the recipient of many personal courtesies at his hands the remembrance of which will ever remain among my most cherished memories. He frequently urged me to publish my Life of Major Delany having frequently listened to my reading of the manuscript. To me the North was not new, since between 1857 and 59 I visited in company with my father all the principal cities, Boston, Philadelphia, Providence, Newport, Portland and New York.

I may here recall the fact that it was unlawful for a free colored person to leave South Carolina and go North and return, but my father's business interest was so interwoven with that of the most influential element of both races no[38] account

36. The quote is from lines 5–6 of "Has Been" (1891), by the poet Ella Wheeler Wilcox (1850–1919).
37. The words "that Winter" are written by hand above the typewritten line.
38. The word "no" is written by hand above the typewritten line.

was taken of the law in his case. Indeed there was a much friendlier feeling then[39]
than exist[s] to-day among the races in Charleston, South Carolina.

From my earliest childhood I have lived in an atmosphere charged with exciting politics. My father was by birth, tradition and choice a staunch adherent of
the church of Rome, and having a wood and lumber yard, and[40] City contracts
for material, with Sloops plying between the outlying plantations and the city, he
gave employment to his church friends, all Irish, and had in consequence a large
Irish following whom he was able to influence during election days. And though
denied the right to vote himself he was much sought after by the candidates who
wanted that Irish vote and in return for my father's influence towards securing it,
looked carefully after his interest. I left Philadelphia for home the very day Pres.
Lincoln's remains passed through that city, April, 1865.

Referring again to the decision of the Supreme Court, it was in January 1888
that Mr. Whipper and his associates were sent to jail for contempt of the order of
the lower court and not until Feb. 1890 was the decision of the Supreme Court
rendered affirming the lower court decision.

An episode in connection with this case may be of interest. The books of the
Probate Judge's office (Mr. Whipper's) had been diligently sought for by the Democratic incumbent of the office and on several occasions the town was aroused by
false rumors that they had been[41] recovered.[42] When every legal means had been
exhausted by Mr. Whipper to secure his rights he decided of his own volition to
surrender the books. He arranged to have them delivered to him at the jail between midnight and daybreak, and as the wagon containing them neared the jail
a confederate of his extinguished the street lamps in the immediate vicinity. The
trunk was deposited at the jail door and in the darkness the vehicle drove away.
Mr. Whipper then rung up the jailer to open the outer door. Simultaneously the
town bell began tolling and everybody was aroused. The sentimentalist and su-
perstitious declared[43] it the last act in the drama of the passing forever of Republican power in South Carolina. An old woman an intense partisan speaking to
me of the affair, said in all earnestness, "Some of dem old publican ghostes toll
dat bell for sure dat nite, to sho dere sorrow wid we." The tolling of the bell was
an accident[44] and arose through the incarceration of a degenerate son of a former

---

39. The word "then" is written by hand above the typewritten line.
40. The word "and" is written by hand above the typewritten line.
41. The word "been" is written by hand above the typewritten line.
42. "Recovered" is typed as "recoved," with no correction made.
43. "Declared" is typed as "delcared," with no correction made.
44. "Accident" is typed as "accidnet," with no correction made.

prominent Republican in the guard house and in his drunken humor tolled the bell to amuse himself.

It may be of interest to recall an incident of the[45] Reconstruction period, particularly in contrast with these days of bitter hostility and proscription upon which we have fallen, when colored passengers, no matter how cultured, refined, or able to pay, whether on land or sea in the Southland, are subjected to the most humiliating and degrading treatment. I refer to what I believe was the first case in the contest for equal rights following[46] the close of the War in 1865.

I was refused first class passage on the steamer Pilot Boy, Capt. W. T. McNelty plying between Beaufort and Charleston. This refusal was in direct conflict and a violation of Military Order "74 Par. 8," issued by Major Genl. Daniel E. Sickles,[47] then in command of the Carolinas. The Captain was arrested and brought before a Military Court convened for the purpose. He was pronounced guilty and sentenced to pay a fine of $250.00. The event was so startling that for years it rankled in the bosoms of many of the railroad conductors and steamboat captains.

On the 17th of November,[48] 1868, I had a never-to-be-forgotten and almost tragical experience; a few days before my marriage. I was leaving Columbia for Charleston to attend as clerk to the Judiciary Committee of which Mr. Whipper my intended husband was chairman. He accompanied me to the cars though[49] I was going alone. I attempted to enter the ladies car, the conductor holding the knob of the door abruptly said, "You can't go in there this is my private car." Mr. Whipper ordered the car open, the conductor sullenly obeying, but in turn took the white ladies who had been seated there, into another car. I entered and rode the entire distance having the whole car to myself, the conductor not even venturing to collect my ticket. But he had his revenge a few days later. We were married in Charleston and started for our home in Columbia accompanied by the officiating clergyman, we had a fine car from Charleston to Branchville, 58 miles distant where three railroads met, and where a change was necessary to reach Columbia. As our party boarded a first-class car and were about to enter we were confronted by our antagonist, pistol in hand, who had changed with the regular conductor for the purpose, backed by an armed scowling mob, he shouted to us,

45. The word "the" is written by hand above the typewritten line.

46. "Following" is typed as "folowing," with no correction made.

47. Major General Daniel E. Sickles (1819–1914) was military governor of South Carolina after the Civil War until 1867.

48. This is likely a mistake on Murray's part, as Rollin Whipper was married in September 1868. See the 17 September 1868 entry in the diary.

49. The first "h" in "though" is written by hand above the typewritten line.

"I am Master here and you go into that car you do it at the peril of your lives." See-ing remonstrance would have been futile, resistance death, since we were wholly unprepared for such a scene we were obliged to submit. I did not, however, faint or show how terror stricken I was, but the nervous chill came on when we were several miles away from the platform at Branchville.

To-day when the mob is supreme in this section, and barbarism that would have shamed the Indians one hundred years ago is accorded public approval, that bridal party would have been swinging to cypress branches, riddled with bullets and later their bodies been food for vultures.

In the hey day of Negro ascendancy[50] that very Railroad Company issued or-ders for its trains to stop at any time opposite to Mr. Whipper's plantation for him to get on or alight.

The news of the indignity to us at Branchville was the reason for putting in the code a stringent civil rights clause which prevented such an outrage being practiced up to the enactment of the "Jim Crow law."

(THE COLORED MAN DURING THE RECONSTRUCTION PERIOD.)[51]

The able skillful[52] and[53] statesman-like course pursued by our leaders considering how meagre and lacking in public experience they were is something wonderful. If they were ignorant as their opponents would have the public believe they were, they could not have held the power they[54] undoubtedly did, and for so long a time.

The charge of venality and corruption is a stock one for political opponents, and is bandied about between the ins and outs in both Nation and State. Hence the hue and cry against the colored men of that period gathers no additional el-ement of truth on that account. Since had they been as chaste as ice they could have not escaped calumny.

To-day the press of the Democratic party is filled with accounts exposing a state of corruption in public officers exceeding anything ever charged against the Radicals by their bitterest opponents. The present Dispensary law is prolific in

---

50. "Ascendancy" is typed as "ascendany," without any correction.

51. Subtitles in parentheses are almost certainly written by Murray.

52. "Skillful" is typed as "skilful," without any correction.

53. The word "and" is typed above the line, with a caret indicating where it should be read.

54. The word "they" is typed above the line, with a caret indicating where it should be read.

furnishing choice morsels of corrupt practice, unequalled anywhere in the United States.[55]

(Social life in South Carolina—1866–1877)

The social life of the Reconstruction period when the black man enjoyed unrestrained freedom of action and mingled on equal terms with the controlling white element is something to be remembered, and in Charleston, S. C. and Columbia, together with Mobile and New Orleans, it was during the period 1867–1877 seen at its best. The State functions of formal character and unofficial dinners and receptions were ordered and conducted in a manner that suffers nothing by comparison with similar functions in Washington official life, now, or at any period in the past.

The white official in power knowing their lease depended upon the favor of the colored voter did not attempt the freezing process practiced to-day toward the "Brother."

One of the manliest specimens of the white officials, the product of Republicanism was our first Governor, General Robert Kingston Scott, formerly of Napoleon, Ohio.[56] He and his equally whole-souled wife[57] gave public receptions to which the members of the legislature and any distinguished strangers who might at the time be in the City, were invited. On these occasions, there were generally about as many white as colored present. The executive and his family were as thoroughly free of colorphobia as it were possible to find anywhere. They recognized culture and refinement without regard to color. I have frequently been their guest both at private and public functions, and through his two terms in

55. The South Carolina Dispensary Law operated from 1893 to 1907 and gave the state a monopoly on liquor sales. It was instituted by Governor Tillman, who was pressured by the temperance movement to enact change. The law allowed the governor to reward those loyal to him with appointments as constables, dispensers, and members of county and state boards of control. Stephen Kantrowitz writes, "Many opponents feared that the dispensary would ultimately amount to an 800-man patronage machine" for Tillman and his party (*Ben Tillman*, 184).

56. Brigadier General Robert Kingston Scott (1826–1900) was assistant commissioner of the Freedmen's Bureau in South Carolina from 1865 to 1868, when he resigned from the military and became the first governor of the reconstructed state. He served two terms as governor, ending in 1872.

57. Governor Scott's wife was Rebecca J. Lowery Scott (1831–1907).

the executive office was the recipient of distinguished consideration always at the Executive Mansion. An incident well remembered by the Cardozas,[58] Wilders,[59] Bozemans,[60] and others who frequently attended the Governor's receptions will point a moral, perhaps adorn a tale. On a very swell occasion at the Executive Mansion, an old negro couple dressed in the cast of finery of employers, probably their former owners, he particularly grotesque in his claw-hammer coat,[61] with its over pluss of a material for such a sized man quite enough for a boy's suit and some to spare, and its cut and brass buttons indicating the colonial period or earlier. While his dame conspicuous as she was in her red bandana head-dress and white cotton gloves and broad expanse of self, presented themselves in the Executive drawing room, amid the sheen of laces silks and diamonds, lavishly displayed by the invited guest. A more grotesque minstrel picture could scarcely be imagined. Both the Governor and his wife quickly took in the situation, suspecting that they were sent by their Democratic employers to throw ridicule on the occasion and if they were ordered out the press of the city would make great reading matter for its next issue. So they were treated kindly and feeling uncomfortable they left soon after being fed. (Which by the way has a dispersing effect on parties even among the most refined.) The act was never repeated at any subsequent function.

I am able at this time to recall another incident in regard to which the press of the city were mute. On a certain evening we were about leaving home to spend the evening as callers at the Executive Mansion, when the Governor entered and said he had come to spend the evening with us and talk over some matters with Mr. Whipper, on learning of our previous intention he insisted that we accompany him to his house that his wife might share our company, since he felt certain it would be agreeable to her. He further suggested that, as he had some matters to talk over with my husband, he would ride with him. They started off and I

58. There were three Cardozo (not Cardoza) brothers. Rollin Whipper refers here either to Francis Lewis Cardozo and his wife, Catherine Howell Cardozo, or to Henry Cardozo and his wife, Catherine F. McKinney Cardozo. During Scott's tenure as governor, Francis was principal of the Avery Normal Institute and in 1868 was elected secretary of state of South Carolina. Henry served as Charleston County auditor in 1868 and was elected to the state senate from 1870 to 1874.

59. Charles McDuffie Wilder (1837–1902) participated in the state constitutional convention of 1868 and was elected to the South Carolina House of Representatives in the same year (Foner, *Freedom's Lawmakers*, 229). His wife was Maria Coleman Wilder (1836–?).

60. Dr. Benjamin A. Boseman Jr.'s wife was Virginia Boseman (1848–?).

61. A claw-hammer coat, or dress coat, has two knee-length tails in the back. Its front and sides are waist length. The claw-hammer coat would have been out of fashion after the Civil War.

entered the Governor's couple and followed closely behind them. As we reached the Public Park which lay in our way the report of a pistol rang out on the night air bringing the horses to a sudden stand-still. In a minute the occupants of the leading vehicle were out and beside me, and the very poorly lighted park searched in the hope of finding the assailant or explaining the shot. Whoever it was had made good his escape, nor was the matter ever solved. The more reasonable view of the matter, however, is that, someone was lying in wait to assassinate the Governor and supposed he was in the rear carriage, the one occupied by me.

Such attempts were not uncommon and in those perilous times every official as a matter of safety, went armed to the teeth. It is possible to give in a sketch only a few incidents of that stormy period, which can be thoroughly understood only by those who were a part of that wonderful drama.

THIS VERY GRAPHIC DESCRIPTION of the reconstruction period by Mrs. Whipper is intensely interesting and it is a pleasure to assist in its preservation. Mrs. Whipper died after a short illness, October 17th, 1901, at Beaufort, S. C., and was buried there on the 20th.

*The above description was received by Mrs. Whipper on the 27th of Aug. 1901 less than two months before her death and is probably the last she wrote. D.M.

Primary Sources

Archives and Manuscript Collections

Avery Research Center for African American History and Culture, Charleston, SC
    Edmund Lee Drago Collection, Series, photocopied material from American Missionary
        Association Archives, Amistad Research Center
Charleston County Public Library, Charleston, SC
    List of the Tax Payers of the City of Charleston for 1860
    Tax Book: Charleston Free Persons of Color, 1861, 1862, 1863
Library of Congress, Washington, DC
    Early Copyright Records Collection
Louisiana State University Libraries, Special Collections, Baton Rouge
    Free People of Color in Louisiana and the Lower Mississippi Valley: Revealing an
        Unknown Past, https://lib.lsu.edu/sites/all/files/sc/fpoc/index.html
Massachusetts Historical Society, Boston
    Charles E. Briggs Letters, 1862–1869
    New England Freedmen's Aid Society Records, 1862–1878
Moorland-Spingarn Research Center, Howard University, Washington, DC
    Francis James Grimké Papers
    Freeman Henry Morris Murray Papers
    Leigh Whipper Papers
National Archives and Record Division, Washington, DC
    Records of the Office of the Judge Advocate General
        Court-Martial Case Files, 1894–1917
National Museum of African American History and Culture, Washington, DC
    Frances Anne Rollin Diary, 1868
New York State Library, Albany
    Emma Waite Diary, 1870
Roman Catholic Diocese of Charleston, Archives and Record Management Office,
        Charleston, SC
    Pre-Diocesan and Episcopal Papers
University of Oregon Libraries, Special Collections and University Archives, Eugene
    Dorothy Sterling Papers
Wisconsin Historical Society, Madison
    Daniel Murray Papers, 1881–1955, 1966

Census Databases

Census of Canada, 1861, 1871, 1881, Ancestry.com
US Census, 1850, 1860, 1870, 1880, 1900, 1910, 1920, 1930, Ancestry.com
Massachusetts Census, 1855, 1865, Ancestry.com
New York Census, 1892, 1905, Ancestry.com

Directories

BOSTON

The Boston Directory, Embracing the City Record, a General Directory of the Citizens, and a Business Directory. Boston: Samson, Davenport, 1867.
The Boston Directory, Embracing the City Record, a General Directory of the Citizens, and a Business Directory. Boston: Samson, Davenport, 1868.
The Boston Directory, Embracing the City Record, a General Directory of the Citizens, and a Business Directory. Boston: Samson, Davenport, 1869.

DISTRICT OF COLUMBIA

Boyd's Directory of the District of Columbia. Washington, DC: Wm. H. Boyd, 1885.
Boyd's Directory of the District of Columbia. Washington, DC: Wm. H. Boyd, 1886.
Boyd's Directory of the District of Columbia. Washington, DC: Wm. H. Boyd, 1887.
Boyd's Directory of the District of Columbia. Washington, DC: Wm. H. Boyd, 1888.
Boyd's Directory of the District of Columbia. Washington, DC: Wm. H. Boyd, 1898.

NEW YORK CITY

Trow's New York City Directory. 1867. New York Public Library Digital Collections. https://digitalcollections.nypl.org/items/46e14e50–536e-0134-b015–00505686a51c.
Trow's New York City Directory. 1869. New York Public Library Digital Collections. https://digitalcollections.nypl.org/items/050245b0–5374–0134-ac00–00505686a51c.

PHILADELPHIA

McElroy's Philadelphia City Directory for 1867. Philadelphia: A. McElroy, 1867.
Boyd's Co-Partnership and Residence Business Directory of Philadelphia City. Philadelphia: C. E. Howe, 1904.
Gopsill's Philadelphia City Directory for 1899. Philadelphia: James Gopsill's Sons, 1899.

SAVANNAH, GEORGIA

Sholes Directory of the City of Savannah. Morning News Print, 1890, 1891, 1892, 1896, 1898, 1900.

Online Source

Black Abolitionist Papers, 1830–1865. ProQuest. https://about.proquest.com/en/products-services/blk_abol_pap/.

Newspapers

American Missionary	*The Freedmen's Record*
Anderson (SC) Intelligencer	*The Freeman* (Indianapolis)
Boston Daily Advertiser	*The Independent* (New York City)
Boston Evening Transcript	*National Anti-Slavery Standard*
Boston Globe	*The National Freedmen* (New York City)
Boston Journal	*The New York Times*
Brooklyn Daily Eagle	*New York Tribune*
Charleston (SC) Daily Courier	*The Norfolk Virginian*
Charleston (SC) Daily News	*Portland (ME) Daily Press*
Charleston (SC) Mercury	*The Sumter (SC) Watchman*
Chicago Defender	*The Sun* (New York City)
Christian Recorder	*The Vincennes (IN) Weekly Western*
The Daily Pheonix (Columbia, SC)	*Washington (DC) Bee*
Douglass's Monthly	*Watertown (MA) News*
The Elevator (San Francisco, CA)	*Woman's Journal* (Boston)
Evening Star (Washington, DC)	

Published Primary and Secondary Sources

Adeleke, Tunde. *Without Regard to Race: The Other Martin Robison Delany*. University Press of Mississippi, 2003.

Andrews, Sidney. *The South since the War: As Shown by Fourteen Weeks of Travel and Observation in Georgia and the Carolinas*. Boston: Ticknor and Fields, 1866.

Annual Catalogue of Wesleyan Academy, Wilbraham, Mass., 1869, and Circular for 1870. Boston: Rand, Avery & Frye, 1869.

Bacon, Margaret Hope. *But One Race: The Life of Robert Purvis*. State University of New York Press, 2012.

Baumgartner, Kabria. *In Pursuit of Knowledge: Black Women and Educational Activism in Antebellum America*. New York University Press, 2019.

Bellows, Barbara. *Two Charlestonians at War: The Civil War Odysseys of a Lowcountry Aristocrat and a Black Abolitionist*. Louisiana State University Press, 2018.

Biddle, Daniel R., and Murray Dubin. *Tasting Freedom: Octavius Catto and the Battle for Equality in Civil War America*. Temple University Press, 2010.

Billington, Ray Allen, ed. *The Journal of Charlotte L. Forten: A Free Negro in the Slave Era*. 1953. Reprint, New York: Norton, 1981.

Billington, Ray Allen, ed. Introduction to *The Journal of Charlotte L. Forten: A Free Negro in the Slave Era*, edited by Ray Allen Billington, 7–41. Norton, 1953.

Birnie, C. W. "Education of the Negro in Charleston, South Carolina, Prior to the Civil War." *Journal of Negro History* 12, no. 1 (January 1927): 13–21.

Bovoso, Carole. "Discovering My Foremothers." *Ms.*, September 1977, 56–59.

Bragg, George Freeman. *Men of Maryland*. Church Advocate Press, 1925.

Brook, Daniel. *The Accident of Color: A Story of Race in Reconstruction*. W. W. Norton, 2019.

Brown, Lois. Introduction to *The Memoir of James Jackson, the Attentive and Obedient*

Scholar, Who Died in Boston, October 31, 1833, Aged Six Years and Eleven Months by His Teacher Miss Susan Paul, edited by Lois Brown. Harvard University Press, 2000.

Brown, Lois. "Reclaiming Black Biography." *Legacy: A Journal of American Women Writers*, 22 September 2020. https://legacywomenwriters.reclaim.hosting/salon/reclaiming -black-biography/.

Butchart, Ronald E. *Schooling the Freed People: Teaching, Learning, and the Struggle for Black Freedom, 1861–1876.* University of North Carolina Press, 2010.

Butchart, Ronald E., Melanie Pavich, Mary Ella Engel, Christina Davis, and Amy F. Rolleri. "The Freedmen's Teacher Project: Teachers among the Freed People in the U.S. South, 1861–1877." 2022. Harvard Dataverse, V1. https://doi.org/10.7910/DVN/oHBDZD.

Bynum, Tara. *Reading Pleasures: Everyday Black Living in Early America.* University of Illinois Press, 2023.

Cashin, Sheryll. *The Agitator's Daughter: A Memoir of Four Generations of One Extraordinary African American Family.* Public Affairs, 2008.

Catalogue of the Officers and Students of Howard University, from March, 1887, to March, 1888. Washington, DC: R. Beresford, Printer, 1888.

Chaddock, Katherine Reynolds. *Uncompromising Activist: Richard Greener, First Black Graduate of Harvard College.* Johns Hopkins University Press, 2017.

Chapin, E. N. *American Court Gossip; or, Life at the National Capitol.* Marshalltown, IA: Chapin & Hartwell Bros. 1887.

Cheek, William, and Aimee Lee Cheek. *John Mercer Langston and the Fight for Black Freedom, 1829–1865.* 1989. Reprint, Illini Books Edition. University of Illinois Press, 1996.

Cook, James W. "Finding Otira: On the Geopolitics of Black Celebrity." *Raritan* 34, no. 2 (Fall 2014): 84–111.

Coppin, Fanny Jackson. *Reminiscences of School Life, and Hints on Teaching.* A.M.E. Book Concern, 1913.

Covert-Warnes, Kathy. "Wendell Phillips." In *Encyclopedia of African American History, 1619–1895: From the Colonial Period to the Age of Frederick Douglass,* edited by Paul Finkelman. Oxford University Press, 2009. www-oxfordreference-com.proxy.wm.edu/display /10.1093/acref/9780.

Cromwell, John Wesley. *History of the Bethel Literary and Historical Association, and Programme for the Year 1895–6.* Washington, DC: R. L. Pendleton, 1896. Digital Howard @ Howard University, Moorland Spingarn Research Center. https://dh.howard.edu /bethelliterary/1/. Accessed 3 May 2025.

Dakers, Beryl, dir. *SC Suffragists: The Rollin Sisters through 1895.* SCETV, 18 March 2021. www.scetv.org/stories/2021/sc-suffragists-rollin-sisters-through-1895.

Davis, Laurel, and Mary Sarah Bilder. "The Library of Robert Morris, Antebellum Civil Rights Lawyer and Activist." *Law Library Journal* 111, no. 4 (2019): 461–508.

Davis, Thulani. *The Emancipation Circuit: Black Activism Forging a Culture of Freedom.* Duke University Press, 2022.

Delany, Martin R. "Call for a National Emigration Convention of Colored Men to Be Held in Cleveland, Ohio, on the 24th, 25th and 26th of August, 1854." In *Martin R. Delany: A Documentary Reader,* edited by Robert S. Levine, 240–42. University of North Carolina Press, 2003.

Delany, Martin R. *The Condition, Elevation, Emigration, and Destiny of the Colored People of the United States*. Published by the author, 1852. Project Gutenberg, www.gutenberg.org /files/17154/17154-h/17154-h.htm. Accessed 19 February 2025.

Delaney, Martin R. "Delany to Douglass: Trial and Conviction." In *Martin R. Delany's Civil War and Reconstruction: A Primary Source Reader*, edited by Tunde Adeleke, 183–213. University Press of Mississippi, 2019.

Dickens, Charles. *The Readings of Mr. Charles Dickens, as Condensed by Himself:* David Copperfield *and* Boots at the Holly-Tree Inn. Boston: Ticknor and Fields, 1868.

Drago, Edmund. *Initiative, Paternalism, and Race Relations: Charleston's Avery Normal Institute*. University of Georgia Press, 1990.

Egerton, Douglas R. *Thunder at the Gates: The Black Civil War Regiments That Redeemed America*. Basic Books, 2016.

Emerson, Ralph Waldo. "Character." *Ralph Waldo Emerson*. Edited by Richard Poirier. Oxford University Press, 1990.

Emilio, Luis F. *History of the Fifty-Fourth Regiment of Massachusetts Volunteer Infantry, 1863–1865*. 2nd ed. Boston: Boston Book, 1894.

Ernest, John. "Life Beyond Biography: Black Lives and Biographical Research." *Commonplace: The Journal of Early American Life* 17, no. 1 (Fall 2016). https://commonplace.online /article/life-beyond-biography/.

Fagan, Benjamin. *The Black Newspapers and the Chosen Nation*. University of Georgia Press, 2016.

Fleischner, Jennifer. *Mrs. Lincoln and Mrs. Keckly: The Remarkable Story of the Friendship between a First Lady and a Former Slave*. Broadway Books, 2003.

Foner, Eric. *Freedom's Lawmakers: A Directory of Black Officeholders during Reconstruction*. Rev. ed. Louisiana State University Press, 1996.

Fortieth Anniversary Report of the Secretary of the Class of 1881 of Harvard College. The University Press [Harvard], 1921.

Foster, Frances Smith. "A Narrative of the Interesting Origins and (Somewhat) Surprising Developments of African-American Print Culture." *American Literary History* 17, no. 4 (Winter 2005): 714–40.

Foster, Frances Smith, and Larose Davis. "Early African American Women's Literature." In *The Cambridge Companion to African American Women's Literature*, edited by Angelyn Mitchell and Danielle K. Taylor, 15–31. Cambridge University Press, 2009.

Foster, Frances Smith, and Chanta Haywood. "Christian Recordings: Afro-American Protestantism, Its Press, and the Production of African American Literature." *Religion & Literature* 27, no. 1 (Spring 1995): 15–33.

Free Religion: Report of Addresses at a Meeting Held in Boston, May 30, 1867, to Consider the Conditions, Wants, and Prospects of Free Religion in America; Together with the Constitution of the Free Religious Association There Organized. Boston: Adams & Co., 1867.

Fuentes, Marisa J. *Dispossessed Lives: Enslaved Women, Violence, and the Archive*. University of Pennsylvania Press, 2016.

Gardner, Eric. "African American Literary Reconstructions and the 'Propaganda of History.'" *American Literary History* 30, no. 3 (Fall 2018): 429–49.

Gardner, Eric. *Black Print Unbound: The* Christian Recorder, *African American Literature, and Periodical Culture*. Oxford University Press, 2015.

Gardner, Eric. "Elizabeth Taylor Greenfield." In *African American National Biography*. Oxford African American Studies Center. Article published online 31 May 2013. https://doi.org/10.1093/acref/9780195301731.013.34419.

Gardner, Eric. "'This Attempt of Their Sister': Harriet Wilson's *Our Nig* from Printer to Readers." *New England Quarterly* 66, no. 2 (June 1993): 226–46.

Gardner, Eric. *Unexpected Places: Relocating Nineteenth-Century African American Literature*. University Press of Mississippi, 2009.

Garrigus, John D. *Before Haiti: Race and Citizenship in French Saint-Domingue*. Palgrave Macmillan, 2006.

Gatewood, Willard B. "The Rollin Sisters: Black Women in Reconstruction South Carolina." In *South Carolina Women: Their Lives and Times*, vol. 2, edited by Marjorie Julian Spruill, Valinda W. Littlefield, and Joan Marie Johnson, 50–67. University of Georgia Press, 2010.

Geggus, David P. "The Caradeux and Colonial Memory." In *The Impact of the Haitian Revolution in the Atlantic World*, edited by David P. Geggus, 231–52. University of South Carolina Press, 2001.

Gillikin, Margaret Wilson. "Saint Dominguan Refugees in Charleston, South Carolina, 1791–1822: Assimilation and Accommodation in a Slave Society." PhD diss., University of South Carolina, 2014. https://scholarcommons.sc.edu/cgi/viewcontent.cgi?article=4049&context=etd.

Goldman, Lawrence. *Victorians and Numbers: Statistics and Society in Nineteenth Century Britain*. Oxford University Press, 2022.

Gould, Virginia Meacham, ed. *Chained to the Rock of Adversity: To Be Free, Black, & Female in the Old South*. University of Georgia Press, 1998.

Greenspan, Ezra. *William Wells Brown: An African American Life*. Norton, 2014.

Grimké, Charlotte Forten. *The Journals of Charlotte Forten Grimké*. Edited by Brenda Stevenson. Oxford University Press, 1988.

Harris, Robert L., Jr. "Charleston's Free Afro-American Elite: The Brown Fellowship Society and the Humane Brotherhood." *South Carolina Historical Magazine* 82, no. 4 (October 1981): 289–310.

Hartman, Saidiya. "Venus in Two Acts." *Small Axe*, no. 26 (vol. 12, no. 2) (June 2008): 1–14.

Hartman, Saidiya. *Wayward Lives, Beautiful Experiments: Intimate Histories of Riotous Black Girls, Troublesome Women, and Queer Radicals*. Norton, 2019.

Hawks, Esther Hill. *A Woman Doctor's Civil War: Esther Hill Hawks' Diary*. Edited by Gerald Schwartz. University of South Carolina Press, 1984.

Hazlitt, William, ed. *The Table Talk of Martin Luther*. London: H. G. Bohn, 1857.

Hearings before Subcommittee of House Committee on Appropriations. US Government Printing Office, 1906.

Henderson, Desirée. *How to Read a Diary: Critical Contexts and Interpretive Strategies for 21st-Century Readers*. Routledge, 2019.

Hine, William C. "Black Politicians in Reconstruction South Carolina: A Collective Study." *Journal of Southern History* 49, no. 4 (November 1983): 555–84.

Hinton, Richard J. *John Brown and His Men*. Rev. ed. Funk & Wagnalls, 1894.

Hobbs, Allyson. *A Chosen Exile: A History of Racial Passing in American Life*. Harvard University Press, 2014.

Hodges, Graham Russell Gao. "Nell, William Cooper." In *Encyclopedia of African American History, 1619–1895: From the Colonial Period to the Age of Frederick Douglass*, edited by Paul Finkelman. Oxford University Press, 2009. www-oxfordreference-com.proxy.wm.edu /display/10.1093/acref/9780195167771.001.0001/acref-9780195167771-e-0408?rskey =1a3rDv&result=408.

Holt, Thomas. *Black over White: Negro Political Leadership in South Carolina during Reconstruction.* University of Illinois Press, 1977.

Institute for Colored Youth By-Laws of the Board of Managers, and Rules for the Government of the Schools, and for the Regulation of the Library and Reading Room. Philadelphia: Ringwalt and Brown, 1865. A Great Thing for Our People: Institute for Colored Youth in the Civil War Era, online exhibit, Falvey Library, Villanova University. https://exhibits .library.villanova.edu/institute-colored-youth/their-own-words/institute-colored-youth -laws-and-rules.

Ione, Carole. *Pride of Family: Four Generations of American Women of Color.* Summit Books, 1991.

Ione, Carole. *Pride of Family: Four Generations of American Women of Color.* 2nd ed. Harlem Moon, 2004.

Johnson, Michael P., and James L. Roark. *Black Masters: A Free Family of Color in the Old South.* Norton, 1984.

Johnson, Michael P., and James L. Roark, eds. *No Chariot Let Down: Charleston's Free People on the Eve of the Civil War.* University of North Carolina Press, 2001.

Johnson, Rashauna. "From Saint-Domingue to Dumaine Street: One Family's Journey from the Haitian Revolution to the Great Migration." *Journal of African American History* 102, no. 4 (2017): 427–43.

Journal of the Constitutional Convention of the State of South Carolina. Columbia, SC: Charles A. Calvo Jr., State Printer, 1895.

Joyce, Dee Dee. "The Charleston Landscape on the Eve of the Civil War: Race, Class, and Ethnic Relations in Ward Five." *Carolina's Historical Landscapes: Archaeological Perspectives* (1997): 175–85.

Kantrowitz, Stephen. *Ben Tillman & the Reconstruction of White Supremacy.* University of North Carolina Press, 2000.

Kantrowitz, Stephen. *More Than Freedom: Fighting for Black Citizenship in a White Republic, 1829–1889.* Penguin, 2012.

Keckley, Elizabeth. *Behind the Scenes: Formerly a Slave, but More Recently Modiste and Friend to Mrs. Lincoln; or, Thirty Years a Slave, and Four Years in the White House.* Edited by Frances Smith Foster. University of Illinois Press, 2001.

Kendrick, Stephen, and Paul Kendrick. *Sarah's Long Walk: The Free Blacks of Boston and How Their Struggle for Equality Changed America.* Beacon, 2006.

Kinghan, Neil. *A Brief Moment in the Sun: Francis Cardozo and Reconstruction in South Carolina.* Louisiana State University Press, 2024.

Koger, Larry. *Black Slaveowners: Free Black Slave Masters in South Carolina, 1790–1860.* McFarland, 1985.

Krebsbach, Suzanne. "Black Catholics in Antebellum Charleston." *South Carolina Historical Magazine* 108, no. 2 (April 2007): 143–59.

Lamson, Peggy. *The Glorious Failure: Black Congressman Robert Brown Elliott and the Reconstruction in South Carolina*. Norton, 1973.

Lejeune, Phillippe. "The Continuous and Discontinuous." In *On Diary*, edited by Jeremy D. Popkin and Julie Rak, 175–86. University of Hawaii Press, 2009.

Lejeune, Phillippe. "Counting and Managing." In Popkin and Rak, *On Diary*, edited by Jeremy D. Popkin and Julie Rak, 51–60. University of Hawaii Press, 2009.

Lejeune, Phillippe. "Diary on Trial." In *On Diary*, edited by Jeremy D. Popkin and Julie Rak, 147–67. University of Hawaii Press, 2009.

Leonard, Fred Eugene. *A Guide to the History of Physical Education*. Lee & Febiger, 1923.

Levine, Robert S. Introduction to *Martin R. Delany: A Documentary Reader*, edited by Robert S. Levine. University of North Carolina Press, 2003.

Levine, Robert S. *Martin Delany, Frederick Douglass, and the Politics of Representative Identity*. University of North Carolina Press, 1997.

Lewis, Edwin J., Jr. "The Unitarian Churches of Boston in 1860." *Proceedings of the Unitarian Historical Society*, vol. 1, pt. 2. Beacon, 1928.

Locke, Mamie E. "William Whipper." In *African American National Biography*. Oxford African American Studies Center. Article published online 1 December 2006. https://doi.org/10.1093/acref/9780195301731.013.16817.

Maillard, Mary, ed. *Whispers of Cruel Wrongs: The Correspondence of Louisa Jacobs and Her Circle, 1879–1911*. University of Wisconsin Press, 2017.

Major, Gerri. *Black Society*. Johnson Publishing, 1976.

Matthews, William E. *In Memorium: Eulogy, Delivered on the Life and Services of the Late James Henry Jordan, before the Members of the Monumental Club of Baltimore, Delivered by William E. Matthews, January 6, 1868*. Baltimore: Daugherty, Maguire, and Wright, 1868.

Matthews, William E. *John F. W. Ware and His Work for the Freedmen*. Boston: Geo. H. Ellis, 1881.

Mayer, Henry. *All on Fire: William Lloyd Garrison and the Abolition of Slavery*. St. Martin's, 1998.

McCandless, Peter. "Malaria." In *South Carolina Encyclopedia*. 2 August 2016. Last modified 11 August 2022. www.scencyclopedia.org/sce/entries/malaria/.

McCarthy, Molly. *The Accidental Diarist: A History of the Daily Planner in America*. University of Chicago Press, 2013.

McCormick, Richard P. "William Whipper: Moral Reformer." *Pennsylvania History* 43, no. 1 (January 1976): 23–46.

McGill, Meredith. "Frances Ellen Watkins Harper and the Circuits of Abolitionist Poetry." In *Early African American Print Culture in Theory and Practice*, edited by Lara Langer Cohen and Jordan Stein, 53–74. University of Pennsylvania Press, 2012.

McGuire, Mary Jennie. "Getting Their Hands on the Land: The Revolution in St. Helena Parish, 1861–1900." PhD diss., University of South Carolina, 1985. ProQuest.com (8518039).

McKivigan, John. *Forgotten Firebrand: James Redpath and the Making of Nineteenth-Century America*. Cornell University Press, 2008.

Megginson, W. J. *African American Life in South Carolina's Upper Piedmont, 1780–1900*. University of South Carolina Press, 2006.

Miles, Tiya. *All That She Carried: The Journey of Ashley's Sack, a Black Family Keepsake*. Penguin Random House, 2021.

Miller, Edward A. *Gullah Statesman: Robert Smalls from Slavery to Congress, 1839–1915*. University of South Carolina Press, 1995.

Moody, Joycelyn K. "Crafting a Credible Black Self in African American Life Writing." In *A History of African American Autobiography*, edited by Joycelyn K. Moody, 1–20. Cambridge University Press, 2021.

Moody-Turner, Shirley, ed. *The Portable Anna Julia Cooper*. Penguin, 2022.

Moore, Louis. "The African American Athlete." In *A Companion to American Sport History*, edited by Steven A. Riess. 434–53. Wiley Blackwell, 2014.

Moore, Louis. "Fit for Citizenship: Black Sparring Masters, Gymnasium Owners, and the White Body, 1825–1886." *Journal of African American History* 96, no. 4 (Fall 2011): 448–73.

Moses, Wilson Jeremiah. *Alexander Crummell: A Study of Civilization and Discontent*. Oxford University Press, 1989.

Nell, William Cooper. "Colored Scholars in the Public Schools." *The Liberator*, 3 August 1860. In *William Cooper Nell: Nineteenth-Century African American Abolitionist, Historian, Integrationist*, edited by Dorothy Porter Wesley and Constance Porter Uzelac, 591. Black Classic, 2002.

Nelson, Anna. "Behind the Seams: The 'Colored Historian' of the White House and Her Parodists." *PMLA* 133, no. 3 (May 2018): 542–58.

Newmark, Jill L. *Without Concealment, Without Compromise: The Courageous Lives of Black Civil War Surgeons*. Southern Illinois University Press, 2023.

Nussbaum, Felicity. "Toward Conceptualizing Diary." In *Studies in Autobiography*, edited by James Olney, 128–40. Oxford University Press, 1988.

Objects of the Institute for Colored Youth, with a List of the Officers and Students, and the Annual Report of the Board of Managers, for the Year 1864. Philadelphia: Sherman, 1864.

Peel, Mark. "On the Margins: Lodgers and Boarders in Boston, 1860–1900." *Journal of American History* 72 (1986): 813–34.

Powers, Bernard. *Black Charlestonians: A Social History, 1822–1885*. University of Arkansas Press, 1994.

Proceedings of the Constitutional Convention of South Carolina, Held at Charleston, S.C., beginning January 14th and ending March 17th, 1868, including the Debates and Proceedings, vol. 1. Reported by J. Woodruff, Phonographic Reporter. Published by Order of the Convention. Printed by Denny and Perry, 1868.

Proceedings of the First Annual Meeting of the Free Religious Association. Boston: Adams, 1868.

Ralph, Julian. *Dixie; or, Southern Scenes and Sketches*. New York: Harper and Brothers, 1896.

Reid, Whitelaw. *After the War: A Southern Tour, May 1, 1865, to May 1, 1866*. London: Sampson Low, Son, & Marston, 1866.

Ripley, C. Peter, and Roy E. Finkenbine, eds. *The Black Abolitionist Papers*. Vols. 2 and 5, *Canada, 1830–1865*. University of North Carolina Press, 1986.

Ripley, C. Peter, and Roy E. Finkenbine, eds. *The Black Abolitionist Papers*. Vol. 5, *The United States, 1859–1865*. University of North Carolina Press, 2000.

Robertson, Mary D. Prologue to *A Confederate Lady Comes of Age: The Journal of Pauline DeCaradeuc Hayward, 1863–1888*. University of South Carolina Press, 1997.

Rollin, Frank [Frances] A. *Life and Public Services of Martin R. Delany, Sub-Assistant Commissioner Bureau Relief of Refugees, Freedmen, and of Abandoned Lands, and Late Major 104th U.S. Colored Troops*. Boston: Lee & Shepard, 1868.

Royster, Jacqueline Jones. *Making the World a Better Place: African American Women Advocates, Activists, and Leaders, 1773–1900*. University of Pittsburgh Press, 2023.

Ryan, Barbara. "Behind the Scenes: A Case of Cross-Purpose Editing?" *American Studies in Scandinavia* 35, no. 1 (2003): 38–50.

Scruggs, Lawson Andrew. *Women of Distinction: Remarkable in Works and Invincible in Character*. Raleigh, NC: L. A. Scruggs, 1893.

Sherman, Stuart. *Telling Time: Clocks, Diaries, and English Diurnal Form, 1660–1875*. University of Chicago Press, 1997.

Simmons, William J. *Men of Mark: Eminent, Progressive, and Rising*. Cleveland, OH: Geo. M. Rewell, 1887.

Sinor, Jennifer. *The Extraordinary Work of Ordinary Writing: Annie Ray's Diary*. University of Iowa Press, 2002.

Smith, John Clay. *Emancipation: The Making of the Black Lawyer, 1844–1944*. University of Pennsylvania Press, 1993.

Solnit, Rebecca. *River of Shadows: Eadweard Muybridge and the Technological Wild West*. Penguin, 2004.

Sterling, Dorothy. *The Making of an Afro-American: Martin Robison Delay, 1812–1885*. Doubleday, 1971.

Sterling, Dorothy, ed. *We Are Your Sisters: Black Women in the Nineteenth Century*. Norton, 1984.

Stevenson, Brenda, ed. *The Journals of Charlotte Forten Grimké*. Oxford University Press, 1988.

Stewart, James. *Wendell Phillips: Liberty's Hero*. Louisiana State University Press, 1986.

Taylor, Elizabeth Dowling. *The Original Black Elite: Daniel Murray and the Story of a Forgotten Era*. HarperCollins, 2017.

Tompkins, Eugene, and Quincy Kilby. *The History of the Boston Theatre, 1854–1901*. Houghton Mifflin,1908.

Ullman, Victor. *Martin R. Delany: The Beginnings of Black Nationalism*. Beacon, 1971.

Wellman, Judith. *Brooklyn's Promised Land: The Free Black Community of Weeksville, New York*. New York University Press, 2019.

Wesley, Dorothy Porter, and Constance Porter Uzelac, eds. *William Cooper Nell: Selected Writings, 1832–1874*. Black Classic, 2002.

Whitehead, Karsonya Wise. Introduction to *Notes from a Colored Girl: The Civil War Pocket Diaries of Emilie Frances Davis*, edited by Karsonya Wise Whitehead. University of South Carolina Press, 2014.

Wikramanayake, Marina. *A World in Shadow: The Free Black in Antebellum South Carolina*. University of South Carolina Press, 1973.

Wilcox, Ella Wheeler. "Has Been." *Lippincott's Monthly Magazine* 47 (February 1891): 247.

Williams, Heather Andrea. *Self-Taught: African American Education in Slavery and Freedom*. University of North Carolina Press, 2005.

Williams-Forson, Psyche. "Where Did They Eat? Where Did They Stay?: Interpreting the Material Culture of Black Women's Domesticity in the Context of the Colored Conventions." In *The Colored Conventions Movement: Black Organizing in the Nineteenth Century*, edited by P. Gabrielle Foreman, Jim Casey, and Sarah Lynn Patterson, 86–104. University of North Carolina Press, 2021.

Williamson, Joel. *After Slavery: The Negro in South Carolina during Reconstruction, 1861–1877*. University of North Carolina Press, 1965.

Willson, Joseph. *The Elite of Our People: Joseph Willson's Sketches of Black Upper-Class Life in Antebellum Philadelphia*, edited by Julie Winch. Pennsylvania State University Press, 2000.

Wise, Stephen R., and Lawrence S. Rowland, with Gerhard Spieler. *Rebellion, Reconstruction, and Redemption, 1861–1893*. Vol. 2, *The History of Beaufort County, South Carolina*. University of South Carolina Press, 2015.

Womack, Emmett, comp. *Official Register of the United States, Containing a List of the Officers and Employees in the Civil, Military, and Naval Service on the First of July, 1895; Together with a List of Vessels Belonging to the United States*. Vol. 1, *Legislative, Executive, and Judicial*. Washington, DC: Government Printing Office, 1895.

Young, Elizabeth. *Disarming the Nation: Women's Writing and the American Civil War*. University of Chicago Press, 1999.

Zuczek, Richard. *State of Rebellion: Reconstruction in South Carolina*. University of South Carolina, 1996.

INDEX

Page numbers in italics refer to illustrations.

Abbott, Anderson Ruffin, 55

Adams, Amelia W. Purnell, 86, 121, 177, 206

Adams, Ennals J., 56; biographical note for, 121–22; marriage to William J. Whipper's cousin, 86; marries FR and William J. Whipper, 92–93, 206

—in FR's diary, 179, 107; accompanies FR to church, 197, 200; and FR's wedding, 201, 203–4; letter from 172; visit from, 196; and William J. Whipper's marriage proposal, 200

Adams, William Taylor (pseud. Oliver Optic), 187

African American education, 225n6; and teachers, 33, 35–36, 41–48, 70, 124; in post–Civil War Charleston, 41–48, 147n74; in pre–Civil War Baltimore, 56, 126; in pre–Civil War Boston, 65, 68, 114, 120, 127; in pre–Civil War Charleston, xiv, 23–26, 40–41. *See also* Institute for Colored Youth

African American soldiers: recruitment of, 33, 53, 68, 115, 116, 123, 127, 206n449; service of, 215–18; treatment of, 89. *See also* Fifty-Fifth Massachusetts Infantry; Fifty-Fourth Massachusetts Infantry

African Meeting House, Boston, 71

African Methodist Episcopal (AME) Church, 127, 136, 143n59, 147; in Charleston (Mother Emanuel), 23, 28, 57, 147; establishing new AME churches in the South, 57, 126, 145; First African Methodist Bethel Society (later Charles Street AME Church), 136n12; fundraising for, 145; North Russell Street AME Zion Church, 136n12; in Philadelphia (Mother Bethel), 28, 71

Alcott, Amos Bronson, 141, 150

Allen, Macon B., xvi, 90

Allen, Richard, 28

"All Quiet along the Potomac" (Beers), 151

Alston, William J., 43

American Anti-Slavery Society, 67, 116, 123, 128, 146n73, 165n200

American Missionary Association (AMA), 41–42, 43, 44–45, 56, 121, 148n83, 203n436, 235n20, 235

Andrew, John A., 116, 180

Anti-Slavery Subscription Festival, 140–41

Aspinall family, 40, 202

Augusta, Alexander Thomas, 3n3, 218

Ayres, Ellen Angelina (Angie) Talbot, 160, 161

Bagby, Lucy, 88

Bailey, Ann (Annie) Eliza, 6, 65–67; attends reading by Elizabeth Keckley, 77; as aunt of Frances Harper, 66, 113; biographical note for, 113–14; in FR's diary, 168, 169, 182, 188, 192

Bailey, Emily C., 65–67, 114; in FR's diary, 136, 153, 168, 175, 182, 184; marriage to Theodore Mundrucu, 66n194, 175n264

Bailey, Frances (Fannie) Ann, 114, 175, 189, 192

Bailey, Henry A., 65, 114, 175

Bailey, James L., 65, 114, 191

Bailey, John Baptiste, 6, 65–67, *66*; attends reading by Elizabeth Keckley, 77; biographical note for, 113–14; in FR's diary, 151, 152, 168, 188, 190

Bailey, Peter, 67, 114, 165, 190

www.ingramcontent.com/pod-product-compliance
Lightning Source LLC
Chambersburg PA
CBHW031337020726
47499CB00005B/1302